An Undividable Glow

The first ever book on the formation and first season of FC United of Manchester

First published in Manchester in 2006 by
Rubberybubberyboy Parchment
308 Ducie House
37 Ducie Street
Manchester
M1 2JW

ISBN 0-9553620-0-8

A catalogue record for this book is available from the British Library. It will cost you a few bob to get down to London to read it there. Also, unless you can read really quick, you might have to stay in an hotel overnight, so that you can go back to the library in the morning to finish it. Save money and just buy one you tight get.

Printed and bound in Ancoats, east central Manchester by Pelican Press.

Programme notes...

This book was only completed because of the love I have for my Mam and Dad. I never gave them the grand child their love so deserved. I didn't mean not to, it just sort of went past. This book took me nine bumpy months to write. It is no coincidence. I have written a love story because my life has been immersed with nothing but love from them both from the very day I dripped severed umbilical blood onto the newspaper put down on the bedroom oilcloth of 119 Nelson Street, Beswick. I was gathered into their giving arms, wrapped in unconditional kindness, embraced in glistening adoration and I never left.

Club honours list...

I had a pair of green trunks when I was about six or seven. I was never that enamoured with swimming. I'm not a bad swimmer but I wouldn't queue up to do it. I get fed up. As soon as I had taken my clothes off, put my green trunks on and got near water I was cooled down enough and wanted to take them off again, put my clothes back on and go and sit down. Consequently my green trunks became known within our family as 'The trunks that never got wet'. That could possibly be entered for 'The annual longest nickname for an item of clothing competition' if such a competition exists. I'm wearing 'The trunks that never got wet' on the front cover of this book. You'll notice the absence of water nearby. There's a caravan though. The maelstrom that became FC United of Manchester in the season of 2005/2006, saw all our trunks get a proper sopping as we all plunged into the six foot end without using the big stone steps to get in.

In the richly imbued history of Manchester United, never have its fans' suffered so much from the Mancunian circumstance known as Anarcolepsy. This is the condition where Reds want an irreversible shift in the forces of production, are willing to grapple against a fucker of a foe for it, but also want to go and have a little nap'ette on the settee at the same time. It's Sacho and Venzetti with bits of DFS lobbed in. All so many wanted to do was have a football club that they could truly love. And that would love them back. I've unashamedly written a love story that has made me cry. It could be no other way. From 1878 the Red thread has wrapped Mancunians in warmth. This book is a very personal attempt to intertwine the precious love for Red family, Red friends, a Red city and for the football club that takes our bloodline back, on the unpaid for train, to those east central Manchester, Newton Heath railway workers. It would be my honour if you came for a walk with me. Fetch your pac-a-mac Jack and your stickle back Joe. I promise to help you home before it gets dark. We've all done some circuitous walking this last season, sometimes in circumstances where we got on our own nerves, but, as we all are aware, all walks should be worthwhile.

This time the love of our life has been aggravated burgle bummed by an American occupying force. The book tries to bring you back to hatred and anger, recognising the sullen and the shoulders down, but also the churning to resistance and organisation, and the inspiration that is pulling out a piece of three-by-two and twatting them back, and getting up and living. There is soul and there is northern soul. There is Manchester United Football Club, that we fell in love with as a child, and there is FC United of Manchester. After May the 12th 2005 there was a number of ways to write that same love story. All of equal worth, all of equal value. The only decision that could ever be wrong was in not fighting Glazer in however way you thought appropriate. The swirling majority of Reds are open and can see and respect all decisions that were made.

Mine was by doing 22 chapters documenting the nativity of FC United of Manchester. A chapter is used on our FA Cup final against Arsenal in 2005 and the weeks around it. When we took our good hiding. When the barricades were strewn down Warwick Road, but the message was still clearly sent to those that would seek to take away our love. The message was fuck you and fuck your family. Two chapters document the inception of FC United of Manchester in that same summer. One chapter on the first ever home game and 18 on each of the league away games in the North West Counties League division two. A league where it is considered a good day if a dog doesn't turn out a mix in the centre circle. Where most away fans look as if they thought they could get into Grammar School by taking their 11 plus twice. Getting five and a half each time.

Twenty two chapters. One for each player of the two teams with one soul. Two lungs breathing, one heart beating. It is a unity offensive book mixed with a hooterama of the happenings that have befallen the section of the resistance that chose to drop down ten divisions. We entered a world containing puckery necked sweatshirts, owners of Parker Pen box sets still in their original box, Postal Chess Society members and blokes who have Bel Air laquered, well cladded wives who they say : "Fart and give us a clue" to. We've sang: "Coz Darwen are a massive club. Foot" and "You're once, twice, an eleven fingered lady" at Nelson fans. And all in weather that you wouldn't send Neil Webb out in. There was an MDF knocking together of a football club with curdled grease from the underside of our frying pans, with oxidised lost head nails that we retrieved from the skips that were sent to some takeover friendly businesses and a couple of pippy gonglers that we forgot to give David Gill. In the same tradition I am publishing the book myself. I wanted no toffee nosed get in their late 20s, who was at a diddy publishing company they didn't want to be at, telling me what to write about my loss. I'm drinking water and eating ice cubes to pay for it. It is a love story though. That should never have a price. I've mugged myself that if the book doesn't flow elegantly or if it is biz wax wet or kippery knickered uncouth, it is because it represents the level of football FC United of Manchester fans have been watching.

There are others to blame for this book as it wouldn't be here without them. Blame Daz Roper, my lad, for his settery-outery knowledge of what a book should be set out like. Blame Scott 'comma chameleon' Taylor and his punctuationary pokery. There is nothing that lad doesn't know about colons. Fill in Martin Morris, as if he hadn't borrowed so much money off me, I could have afforded to go out and gotten paralytic and therefore not been tippy-tappying away on the typewriter. There's a culpability attached to Doctor Adam Brown as his insights of how to trap off with vulnerable women always brought me round when I was feeling fedster and fucking it off. There are in existence, Reds who actually contributed to this by doing writing or taking photographs when I asked them to. Just because I asked doesn't mean to say you should listen. There's been a lack of responsibility from Pound Empire in Piccadilly as that is where I first discovered pound glasses and they let me buy them. Station Chippy, also in Piccadilly, that closed on Sunday the 19th of June 2005, has had its moments. Its role in providing Manchester's finest gravy, poured over a variety of ingredients, to late night Reds returning from aways has been invaluable. Sustaining us over so many seasons, to enable us to have the strength to resist and organise. Blame every single Red who won't be beat. It's a big book for a big season. You can always use it to stand on to get your used-only-once-Breville down from the top of the kitchen cupboard or use it as an overlarge Millwall brick to keep one of your eyes open if you're tired.

No one has gone away, no one ever could. The Manchester United Football Club, Mancunian embrace with the temperate, giving smile that says here it is, it's yours. You came and found it and now it can no longer leave you. You were brought near by others love, but for your own love you had to go on your own shaping walk. Those who love you knew that. They knew it because they had done it before. You didn't have to come back with anything. No one has ever asked you to. You saw. You didn't have to see. Nothing would be ill of you if you hadn't seen. But you did. There is an unshiftable, footballing belief that beauty will always remain to see its hopes cleared. This book might be shite but hopefully it can be considered as our shite. We won't melt. We'll do alright.

Spilled Contents...

The first ever book on the formation, and first season, of FC United of Manchester is a big bulbous one. Take your time. It's not going anywhere. Bin it if you get bored.

CHAPTER ONE

FOR ALL MY LIFE A CONTINENT CAME...

Arsenal, Cup Final day, May 21st 2005.

You went away and my heart went with you...

A 17-seater van pulls up on Oldham Street in Manchester town centre. It's five to six on a watery sunned, F.A Cup Final, Saturday morning. I'd moved to Manchester town centre almost five years before, in the August of 2000, leaving decades of living in east central Manchester behind me. I'd reasoned that watching Manchester United was costing me too much in Joes home, as getting back at all hours from away games and drinking late after home games necessitated the use of a variety of taxis both legitimate and snide. Town centre living was worth the extra money in rent to take away the vagaries of not knowing what vehicle was going to take you home in your pixelated state and how much the vehicle driver was going to nail your hat on for. You can charge a pissed up May Queen taxi passenger anything and they'll still say: "Aww, thanks mate, cheers, ta, thanks, aww, you're great you" because they are desperate for their feather and will pay anything to get in its high tog surroundings.

Town centre living also means that you are central and therefore handy for early morning trips like this one going to see Manchester United and Arsenal at Wembley. Except we were going to Cardiff. That's why I don't drive. I wouldn't have meant to but I would have taken us to Wembley. Many years ago when I was an apprentice bricklayer in a two-and-one gang with my Dad and Tommy the hod carrier, our Christine had said that I should learn to drive. She reasoned that, as neither my Dad nor Tommy the carrier could drive, it would be useful to get around from building site to building site. Bricklaying is not a 'job for life' factory job. You pack a packet of peas in a pea-packing factory and another packet of peas will be coming right behind it, pea'ily pleading with you to pack it. The pea mad society that we are means that there is a constant clamour for peas. Prove me wrong by telling me you know an out of work pea packer. Pea packers have no concept of what a P45 is as they have never been given one. Is there some significance in P45 having a 'P' in front of it? Almost certainly.

With bricklaying you set your first brick down in the footings and you are that one brick closer to putting yourself out of collar. You might earn a wedge whilst you are putting yourself out of work but putting one on top of two will eventually add up to P45. So you can see that my sister, Christine, had a point when she said that I should learn to drive, as your place of work as a bricklayer is forever relocating itself. I had never learned to drive as I had always lived on a bus route to town. I was from that last generation of blokes who didn't deem it life-affirming to own a mustard coloured Datsun with walnut trims at 17. You gave the bus driver a few bob and he took you to work or to town for a pint. There was no need to have lessons or to pass a test or to buy a car and talk about your big end going. Transport came via a shared experience with 71 other people, with standing only downstairs and a cunning periscope mirror that enabled the bus driver to see upstairs from his driving seat downstairs, so that he could cop you writing 'Docherty walks with god' on the dralon or leatherette bus seats in magic marker.

Our Christine was now shaking these firmly held values. The proposition was that I should learn to drive. I could see my Dad on the settee putting his Morning Star down into his lap and contemplating winters being ferried about. The 'click, slide, cachung, click ' as his brain moved from picture to picture in his mind of him on a car seat with a heater on in February, was now out-noising the rustle of his Morning Star's headline about a go-slow at Longbridge. In his daydreaming head it's lashing down and it's two coats cold but he is oblivious as he has taken his cement burnt, whiteboots off and is warming his holey-socked, bottom ends by the hot blower of the car I am newly driving him around in. Tommy the carrier is in the backseat with a Hawaiian shirt on to signify his bus stop free delight but also being careful not to spill his kalooha or catch his garland on the window winder upper.

My simple life of buses at this juncture is severely under threat. I can feel the ten bob notes slipping out of my brown paper, sticky-top sealed, wage packet and into the hands of a galloot driving instructor from the 'They shall not pass' driving company. At this low ebb my Mam comes into the living room from the kitchen and sticks her sheep's head into the conversation, over riding any dialogue our Christine and my daydreaming Dad are having. She firmly and with scientific authority states: "Our Robert shouldn't learn to drive as his mind wanders." She then goes back into the kitchen feeling no need to empirically back up her accusation or justify its intent with any further well-delivered arguments.

Our Christine sees my Mam disappearing back into the kitchen and says: "Yeah, you're right" and goes back to choking us all by spraying Batisse in her hair to avoid washing it as apparently Batisse stopped it getting greasy. No it didn't, chip pan. My Dad quietly says goodbye to a life of being a chauffeured U.C.A.T.T. Lady Penelope and goes back to reading about Derek 'Red Robbo' Robinson. And I go back to a Life Of On The Buses. Which probably wasn't one of the 'On The Buses' film titles. But might have been.

So on the 21st of May 2005 I am not driving the 17-seater van to Wembley for two reasons. One being as just explained - my mind wanders so I cannot drive, and two - reiterating the previously made point and not wishing to labour it but I need to say it twice before I forget it - because my mind wanders - I would take us to Wembley when we really need to get to Cardiff. As, technicality or not, that is where Manchester United are playing this day in the F.A. Cup Final against Arsenal.

In my defence I've done much worse...

I might not be too clever at driving but I'm good at throwing wrinkly, pass their sell by date, tomatoes out of fourth floor windows. I'm looking out of my fourth floor flat window at the 17-seater van below me and the 16 dark-clothed Reds who are about to get in it. I spot a weak wildebeest. It's five to six on an F.A. Cup Saturday morning and it is not too hard to shout out and be heard. I pick on Kennybobblesbombom. I know I shouldn't as Kennybobblesbombom is a lovely lad but as well as being lovely he is just far too trustworthy. He's from a proper peg selling, lucky heather toting, 'that tarmac is far too thinly coated on my drive the grass will grow through' family from Whalley Range but now living in Hattersley, so he should have more of an inner city suss about him. But he hasn't. Shame on me for exploiting it. Kennybobblesbombom hears my fourth floor shout and comes across with a perplexed 'What?' face on. He crosses Oldham Street and into my range.

Kennybobblesbombom has tomatoes for breakfast. I legitimise it with myself by arguing that I have provided him with one of his five necessary portions of fresh fruit or vegetables for the day. Actually, don't feel too sorry for the recently redecorated Ken as he once put me in a fountain at Lille away the first time we met them in the Champions League, so his tomatoe'ing was a revenge dish best served sun ripened. Anybody from that van that says they thought they were watching the paraplegic Olympics and that I missed him by fckn miles and hit the old Woolworth's building behind him are big fat fibbers whose grubbies will eventually set on fire.

We wear black on the outside because slack is how we feel on the inside...

Coming downstairs and getting into the 17-seater van I thought I'd entered the canteen at Leeches Funeral Parlour. The Independent Manchester United Supporters Association and Shareholders United, the two main fan-based independent organisations, had called for Reds to dress in black for F.A. Cup Final day in protest at Malcolm Glazer's aggressive take over of our football club. Not strictly Molotov but symbolic and well meaning, and hardly a hardship to adhere to as the majority of these gets in the van wore black anyway. Their wearing of black at the match on most other occasions was not an attempt to look moody but more that most of them agreed that black was very slimming and could be offset with a whole number of matching fashion accessories in a variety of colours.

May the 12th 2005, when Glazer had succeeded in taking majority control of the football club we all adored, was a deeply, deeply black day. We dressed accordingly.

The called for demonstration outside Old Trafford on the early evening of the 12th of May against this take-over was more of a depressing wake than a vitalised fight back against overwhelming adversity. The faces of good Reds that day on the forecourt were crushed faces. I saw Reds' faces that day that I had seen in Barcelona only six years before. Faces that couldn't contain the amount of glee inside them, it was a physical impossibility to suppress the joy inside on the 26th of May 1999. If a Catalan doctor had approached me that night on The Ramblas and told me that every window, every corridor, every ward in Barcelona General Hospital was covered in internal organs due to Mancunians bursting, I wouldn't have worried or even have taken the preventative measure of going into a shop and buying a girdle to keep me safe from explosion as I would have willingly joined the burst. I might even have unbuttoned my powder blue Armani shirt to gladly welcome a warriors end. If you are going to go you might as well be going to a go-go and go.

Happiness and chaos theory bathed together on that sultry, Solskjaer solstice when the longest day came early. Simplicity and wonder. They passed each other thick, luxurious Egyptian cotton towels to dry themselves with. They giggled and hugged and looked up at the expanse above them and then got back in and bathed together some more. There was nothing they could do besides join Manchester; there was nothing they wanted more to do than join Manchester. And so they did. The world turned because we made it turn - 80,000 Timberland's, Adidas Samba's, Patrick Cox's and Gucci loafers became like the feet of the Anthill Mob from Whacky Races, where they would put their feet through the floor of their car and run and make the car go that little bit faster. We joined with the loved ones left behind in Manchester and ran our little feet so hard that we became one across the many miles that separated us and we spun the world. The world had to go to Argos the next day and buy a new axis, as we broke the original. Gravity politely requested permission from us to keep grafting but could we please stop showing it up, as we were patently ignoring the strict rules it has always laid down, about us not just willy nilly lilly'ly floating off somewhere. We banged, we bounced, we chanted, we hymned, we hummed. We just knew.

Change of direction, change of bond...

If there was an extreme polemic to the May the 26th 1999 bliss then the 12th of May 2005 was a polemic with a big fuck off pole stretching the polemic further. We had been beaten. We all knew we had been beaten. Not just beaten in a way where we have taken a dig, but have not gone down, and everything is to fight for if we just regain our breath and our composure, but beaten in a way where we have been struck down, overpowered, taken advantage of and forcefully ravaged afterwards. We had been taken to a quiet place and left to die in the cold and wetness. Welts weeping, insides curdled, hearts unmendable. No Red felt clean that day. No amount of showering would wash off the soiling we had been exposed to. No matter how hot the water, no matter how hard we scrubbed, the fuckers cancerous crust that was festering over our bodies was hardening. Nothing could cleanse the outrage, nothing would open the lid that would ease the hurting, no amount of lint would wrap across and absorb the pain. Nothing, and all that was or has ever been called nothing, could disguise the defeat. This was our March 1985.

Insider dealings…

And here we all were trundling to the F.A. Cup Final in a humperty, bumperty army truck. Obviously not the original humperty bumperty army truck as that was from Camblewick Green. Or Trumpton. Someone in the van asked if Camblewick Green was just a green like Ardwick Green within the town of Trumpton or was it its own separate conurbation? No one knew. Regardless, no one, be that Mrs Honeyman or any other associated 'Watch With Mother' character, would have believed that the 17 occupants of that van were living through their last day of following Manchester United Football Club together as a 17-seater unit.

Rubbing it Red…

We did the usual things that you do on Cup Final day in Cardiff: We found that large, chain café near the ground that always puts up its full breakfast prices by half a brick when we're visiting. This gross exploitation of football fans was again negated by our actions of 17 breakfasts ordered, eaten and then runnered from. It's only a few spots saved, I know, but it is the principle. It's better in our paw than theirs. It is more annoyingly petty than gross exploitation. They think that football fans, who will be providing them with their biggest pay, can just be taxed that little bit more. We're football fans: We're thick, we'll never notice, we eat with our mouths open anyway and mix brown sauce and red sauce so, therefore lash 50 pence onto the breakfast price. We see the mixing of brown and red sauce on the plate as culinary adventurousness, a willingness to open our palates to a variety of experiences. They see it as scruffiness.

You cannot feel welcome in a place that is laughing at you and setting you out as an exploitable dick before you have even sat down. Duns might have left roadworks in the toilet bowl to add to our principled, if miniscule, rail against localised, corporate cheekiness. At least he flushed it though, as we're not that rough. He even went and got a coathanger from the woman behind the till to break his deposit up as it was an oversized fella and wasn't abiding by any one flush law. Not sure if Duns gave her the coat hanger back after using it though, but somewhere in that, despite our non payment, we were still being polite to the staff.

We bought cans from an offy. But this was no ordinary offy. It was an offy in a speciall pllace. 'Speciall pllace' having two 'l's as they like that down here. The speciallness of the speciall pllace had started before the breakfast. So, I'll jump you back an hour or so in our day. We had rolled into Cardiff exhausted but glad that no one had opened cold egg sandwiches on the journey. You then, as always on Cup Final day, face the mither of finding a parking spot. It was still only nine o'clock as we'd done the journey in three hours, as Forrest the driver pays no real attention to roads. I know a lot of other drivers seem to but Forrest considers that pernickety on their part. He is also cavalier to the health and safety aspect of rolling a joint with one hand whilst driving. Rolling a joint with one hand is an admirable skill to have, you'll agree, but not when the dial finger on the speedometer has got a stitch. You also wish that the pills he is taking are medicinal but you know they are not. It's always nice to arrive and live if Forrest is driving. You arrive there quick but also very appreciative of life. His driving technique perhaps might explain Duns large shit in the café.

Cardiff gets on everyones nerves as a Cup Final/Community Shield destination. Always rammed, miles away, different country. The same as London really, including the different country bit, but there was something about it that got on your tits even more than being surrounded in London by people who insist on saying: "Big shout out for." And: "Do what?" It was probably because we had been ordered to go here by the expense claimers from the Football Authorities. Wembley might be shite but at least there was some vestige of tradition, even if it was only shaking your leg to get the piss from the passageway off your shoes when you got to a dry bit of concrete walkway. And Christ knows we've lost some traditions since football became the new preserve of middle management.

But here we all were looking for a parking spot right at the side of the ground. We had no real faith in the voices from the back of the van insisting we'd be right. Then we did something we had not done before on our visits.

We crossed the river.

The Irk, Irwell and Medlock treble - Now only our rivers run three...

Now what you must bear in mind is that some of us in that van only found out that there was a river running at the side of the ground after our Cup Final visit against Millwall the year before. We'd always got to the ground from the other direction. It's a knocking bet that there'll be some Reds reading this who have only just found out there's a river at the side of the stadium at Cardiff because they've just read it. Thickies. And we're really thick so that makes you really, really thicker. There would be some fierce competition to be hailed as the thickest Red but if you had to start drawing up a thickie finalists list to get down to finding a thickie winner, then you would be on it. Put down this book and only ever use it again as a step to get your deep fat fryer down from the top shelf of the kitchen wall cupboard.

We'd arranged to leave the Millwall Cup Final game of the previous year at 80 minutes, as we had to get back to Manchester early. We were going to the Manchester Evening News Arena to see Morrissey's first visit to our home in 11 years. We decided at the 79th minute that the 2-0 scoreline was not going to change so we'd leave that minute early before the arranged 80th minute off time. As we got to the back of the stand Ruud made it three. We moaned like bleeding hell that we should have stayed that extra minute as planned and we would have seen the goal. This spiral of moaning, directed at one of our party who had been at the behest of the request to leave that minute early as "Fuck all is happening here, come on let's get on the toe train," was broken when the shock of seeing a river at the side of the ground usurped it from its position as number one point of interest. Who put that river there? Is it real? Put your finger in and check. Had it always been there? How deep is it? What's it called? Do you think you'd dissolve before you drowned if you fell in it? Would you go on it in a canoe because you'd be in bricking distance from kids on the bank? And you couldn't canoe fast enough to the bank to give them a chase. In fact canoe'ing nearer the bank would just give them a better shot to dobber you with. Can you see any prams? It's not a proper river if it hasn't got a Silver Cross pram in it.

As the questions whipped in we were walking above the river on a timber-slatted boardwalk. On, not under.

Water palaver ...

So here we were, veterans of crossing the river at the side of the stadium in Cardiff but still no nearer parking. Then we noticed that on this side of the river there was parking if you got a yellow display badge. You got them from a Post Office. That's daft, where are we going to find a Post Office to get a yellow display badge from so that we can park? Oh look, there's a Post Office. The speciall pllace was beginning to show us its speciallness without us knowing. I was delegated to go into the Post Office. I wasn't pleased. The Post Office near work by the Apollo in Ardwick always has enormous queues and was full of people who smell of pre-war terrace kitchen cupboard under the sink. And shin pads. Mixed in with off mop bucket. Not in the speciall pllace. There was no one in. No one. Not one single person in a large Post Office besides the cute, white haired granny behind the counter.

Now I'm wary of cute, white-haired grannies since we went to Aston Villa a few seasons ago. Thirty-odd of us had got on the seven o'clock morning train to Birmingham New Street. We were going to The Kerryman pub in the town centre as it was open early McSquirly doors, ie half eight. Thirty-odd of us traipsed across a deserted Birmingham town centre on a Sunday morning in search of this breakfast beer. Outside of a dedicated paraffin, no one should want a beer at that time of day. The yardarm is still in the yard. We found The Kerryman pub and sure enough, with the experience of the peeping Toms within our party, we could see through the crack in the curtains that it was full. I was delegated to knock on the side door to arouse the Landlord's attention. There's a theme of me being delegated here that I've never noticed before but never mind. I must have a trustworthy face.

I banged on the door and it eventually opened with a creaky, creakster befitting of a castle gate that Scooby Do and Raggy are about to investigate. As the door opened I could see and hear the raucous beeryness going on inside the packed pub. Bad blaring music and Benson smoke - the perfect accompaniment to a petit dejeuner. My jealousy and my thirst whizzed skywards. Stood right in front of me having opened this big double door was the sweetest, littlest, white hair pinned back in a bun, pinny'd up, luscious soft wool cardigan'd, diddiest, dinkiest little Irish granny that you could ever imagine. I thought she had fallen off the picture on an Irish Tourist Board approved, souvenir Irish fudge box she was that edible. I knew she was human but she was so soothing that all you could sense was the comfort of a piece of luxury, home made fudge with a nice cup of tea on a saucer to go with it.

You wondered how her dainty little arms had managed to open such a bank vault door sized, thick wooden, side entrance. She stood there, painting by numbers cute and I managed to politely stammer out: "Hiya love, is it alright if we come in for a pint?" She frailly looked up at me and I could see her gentle Irish green eyes with the love of tens upon tens of her grand children and the thick, delicious gravy of a million roast meat dinners in it. She opened the door enabling her to slowly, sagely gaze at the 30-odd Reds waiting behind me outside her pub door. She unhurriedly opened her mouth and said clearly and unreservedly: "You can fuck off", and banged the bleeding door shut in a blistering blur. Devode. The old get was quietly wished nothing but furred up arteries caused by the butter she has ploughed on too thick on her doorstop sandwiches. So we did.

So that was my previous experience of cute, white haired grannies. I was expecting the same from this Post Office woman in Cardiff. We were still learning of the speciallness of the llovelly speciall pllace. The white haired granny told us that you could park for periods of up to four hours. We obviously needed to have two sets of four hour yellow badges to get us past the time the match ended. She apologised profusely, stating that she was sorry that because it was more than four hours it would cost us more. Then without a smidge of sarcasm she sincerely said: "It will cost you a pound for the first four hours but because you are staying for a further four hours it will cost you a further one pound. So I'm afraid that's two pounds altogether." She was genuinely upset that we'd had to fork out a pound more. I thought she was going to go: "Arhh mugged ya, flange off it will cost you a 50 spot" or something as they do in London where they go right through you like the drug squad. But not in the speciall pllace. As it was, we spent 11.76 pence each to park right at the side of the stadium. And I mean right at the side. It was no more than ten Terry Gibson's laid end-to-end away. Possibly 11. As we parked and got out of the back of the van there was a railway bridge a few yards away and then the United end of the stadium across the water. Prince handy.

The day was full of great instances like that. The offy was just up from the van down a side street. It was empty all afternoon of course. The canned beers were cold and priced like a normal supermarket. We didn't bother getting six at a time as they just went warm on the pavement so we treated it like a bar in a pub and went up for one as we needed it. There was a ginnel going nowhere just near where we were standing that ended in a load of over grown bushes. It was ideal for a lag. You didn't have to spoil anyone's back garden because it was at the side of a railway arch with no houses near it. You wasn't in view of anyone because it can't be that pleasant seeing blokes piss on the streets. The bushes and waste ground absorbed the urine so it didn't come flooding out. Ideal outdoor toilet facilities. Admittedly, the females with us had to go a bit further and into the back entry between some of the houses to get their bums out but that's only because they were being shy. We all volunteered to watch over them whilst they got their tweebies out and sploshed but surprisingly they refused our generous offers.

We stood at the side of the river right opposite the ground, with our turnstile that we were going to go through in a few hours time, fully in view. The weather was warm but getting muggy and clouding over but it was still a pleasant enough temperature to all sit or stand around gabbing. We could all sit down if we wanted to on the river wall or on the steps that banked away from it. There were a few, queueless vans selling hot bacon or roasted pork muffins and all was well. We all took it in turn to give IMUSA and Shareholders United leaflets out about the take over situation at United and what we were proposing to do. The amount of people wearing black was a credit to our fight and our club.

Six dicks…

We had friends, we had beers, we had bogs, we had nosebag, we had seats, we had temperate weather, we had our Cup final tickets in our pockets and we had a flowing river at the side of us. No one could not love being at the side of water. It's the amoeba in us that came from the oceans all those countless millions of years ago. That sea salt amoeba is still in us somewhere. I really hope I manage to move to the side of some water be that the sea or a river. A stream would do. Actually it will probably have to be besides the sea as to move to the side of another river that wasn't the Irwell, the Irk or the Medlock would be heartless sedition. Walking at the side of the sea has the coal fire effect. Time just passes without you knowing. A fire never makes the same movements and neither does the sea. It's an ever-changing art installation that never re-invents itself because it has never been fully invented yet as it is always changing, therefore never complete, therefore if it's not complete you can't re-invent it. Or something like that. Unfortunately, not being that well wedged I think I might have to settle for an unfixed gutter to get the sound of running water in the morning as you wake.

We tasted of cherryade…

And all this while just yards across the river there were thousands and thousands of Reds buffeting each other about in a pongy throngy. They must have been able to see across the water and see our spaced and spaced out happiness. It was as if they were frightened of finding the river and dying of 'Seeing a river' shock. Or if they had found the river then it must be a magic one as it was never there before.

So, if they crossed the magic river its evil would turn them into David Sadler's potting shed or make sure that they were never able to order hot chocolate fudge cake again without accidentally ordering hot chocolate fishcake. Or their complete box set of back catalogue editions of 'Bless This House' would levitate and set on fire for no apparent reason, or they'd wait ages for a bus and then three would never, ever come along at once and they'd slump and expire at the bus stop because they were so desperate to moan about three buses coming along at once that they'd rather kick it than think that three had come along at once just as they'd given up and gone home. Or that they'd grow really tall so that they could see into upturned lamp standards and the light would shine on their faces and make them look like Draclia so they'd lose all their mates or they'd become the person who shouts out on the coach when seeing the second driver going to the back: "Woe, woe, woe, who's driving the coach?" Or they'd get in the papers for being the first person to be electrocuted and found unconscious by the paramedics due to the fact they had spunky, wet fingers as they turned their '60, sagging and gagging' porno off. Which was still playing when the Ambulance Service came around. And they had to put surgical gloves on to turn it off because your spermatazoa that had caused the electrocuting accident was still on the 'off' button.

Whatever the reasons, the thousands upon thousands of Reds were scared and stayed to their side of the river all crowded and cramped and we stayed on ours. We weren't purposely being splitters, we'd just found a better place for us. We're equal but different, it's obvious. Sometimes you yearn for togetherness but sometimes you need a divide. S Club 7 exemplifies this. If S Club 7 didn't have a divide between the names then they would just be called Sclub 7, and I'm sure that wouldn't have been so successful both commercially and artistically. We weren't in the mood for Sclubbing so we kept our divide and continued S Clubbing. Follow your hearts desire, reach.

A section of us did cross the divide though on their way to the arranged spot by that beer house, that I've forgotten the name of, by the ground. A mass demonstration against the American occupying force had been arranged. Despite valiant individual protests it never really happened and that was the only low of the day. If we don't count the low of the eventual defeat to Arsenal on extra time penalties. Which we will, so it was one of only two things on the day that was Mark Robins.

Listen to the music of the falling rain, telling me just what a kagoul I've been...

A third low of the day could have been the rain that poured and poured on us before the game. It came around half one'ish. We ignored it for a bit taking it in turns to dive into the phone boxes but that was only ever going to be limited in its practicality. We were surprised that the speciall pllace had allowed the rain to fall on us but there was a reason for everything. At first we thought the speciall pllace had just been kind to us when we first noticed that we didn't need to be getting wet by the river anymore - we could go into the arch under the railway bridge just where we had parked the 17-seater van.

It became more than just an arch under a railway bridge where we could take shelter from the rain.

Don't get us wrong; the railway bridge was consummate in its functional ability to stop us getting piss wet through. It was raining as heavy as the day they crucified Jesus in that scene from Ben Hur where he finds his Mam and sister and their leprosy goes but we were dry as a bugger in our axis of anti-evil. What happened next just developed naturally. As naturally as things can develop when beer is involved.

Stature is a language can't you read...

Driven to us by the driving rain, the other Reds that we wanted to meet on the day bravely crossed the river of death and misfortune, and came to our outdoor beer house under the railway bridge. A big blob of black Redness blocked the pavement entrance under the railway arch. An ugly human cork stopper stopping the flow of fans trying to use the railway bridge as a way of getting to the ground. The railway bridge was like all railway bridges in that the walls were damp and not for leaning on and its lights were that dark yellow lamp light that is use nor ornament. Our increasingly boisterous, clumped together, dark-clothed, heaving mob must have looked a bit daunting in that semi-darkness for any football fans who came around the corner and walked straight into us.

Arsenal fans were very quiet on approach, with nothing on our persons to designate who we supported. They stayed even quieter when they realised who we were as they excused their way through us. Many giving that unmeant friendly smile that really translates as 'Don't hit me', as their shoulders went lower to tell you that this was their sign of passivity that they had learnt from Rex their dog. Reds, on realising that we were Reds, could then relax and become aware that it was only the semi-darkness that made us look as if we were up for a read and write.

I wouldn't like a belt off any of the company I was with as all of them are not behind the door. They're just confident enough to know that laughing is better. If you want it, you can have it, but if you don't, and you're not a div, then get the beer in. That's not a too bad a way to run your footballing life and this company I was with had naturally evolved from that hee-hee-ffoss. A harmonious, egalitarian hegemony where beer is sacrosanct and your club is the hemp rope that knots and binds you all. I felt very honoured to have met them. I wouldn't ever tell them of course. I was also very honoured and forever thankful to Manchester United Football Club for bringing us all together. Without the soul of this football club, the soul of our friendships could never have embraced. And not in a fey way. Although Peanut probably would the big Gary Bear. He stayed on at school and did drama at 'A' level and we all blame that. Although his impression of a free roaming Afghan hound is unbettered so it wasn't all a 'Make like a tree or today you're a chair' waste.

On noseying closer, those meek Arsenal fans, who cowered when they passed us, would have discovered that only a galloot could be scared of a company of blokeys and lady blokeys who were risking rib ache through laughing and were doing things like singing non-football songs and putting a cardboard box on the Ginger Princess' head and telling her we had never seen her looking so fit, or were discussing that it is a sad, comedic loss that no one seems to stand on rakes anymore, or that if we play a Greek side in the Champions League next year then we should find a scruffy Greek Red and call him 'Paraffinaikos.' No one should be afraid of that. If some 'trenchcoat with a belt' southerner is afraid, then that is their mock-Jacobean garage owning fault.

If I can go back a sentence or two there - when I say semi-darkness I mean it was a half-light situation not that any of us had a semi on in the dark as, as previously stated, the girls in our company went around the corner to piss so there were no good blimps to effect our trousers. Can I also go back a few lines to the sentence, 'Blokes who were risking rib ache and singing none football songs'?

Forget Everysin And Remember...

Rightly or wrongly our group of lads had a reputation for singing poor songs when under the influence. This arrestable repertoire included traditional old ones and complete bollocks new ones. I'm running the risk of guilt by association here but some of them might go like this:

> Shine your buttons with Brasso, it's only three h'appence a tin, you can buy it or nick it from Woolworths but I doubt if they'll have any in.

Or:

> In my Special Brew world, in my Special Brew world, it tastes like an old grid or a cheesy dog's dick, it gets you a charge sheet at Bootle Street nick, find me a parker hood coz I want to be sick, in my Special Brew world, in my Special Brew world. Get totally mango'd, spend a fortnight in bed, it's glory and honour the great man he said, there is nothing on earth quite like being a Red, in my Special Brew world.

That last song was inspired by the New Years resolution I once made to drink Special Brew for a year. I got to March. Or:

> Eyes, nose, cheeky, cheeky chin, cheeky, cheeky chin, cheeky, cheeky chin
> Eyes, nose, cheeky, cheeky chin, cheeky, cheeky chin, nose, eyes.

Or:

> A finger of fudge is just enough to give your kids a treat; a finger of fudge is just enough until it's time to eat. It's full of Cadbury's goodness but very small and neat. A finger of fudge is just enough to give your kids a treat.

Or:

> There's a tavern in the town, in the town, and they keep their prices down, prices down. They even hang wallpaper in the lavatory for all you nice people to see, while you're having a wee, it's the Old Monkey.

The Old Monkey being a Holt's pub in town.

Or:

> Francis Lee he went to Greggsy's bakery, Francis Lee he went to Greggsy's bakery, Francis Lee he went to Greggsy's bakery and this is what they said: Lose some weight you big fat bastard, lose some weight you big fat bastard, lose some weight you big fat bastard and your haircut's fckn daft.

Or:

> If there's somebody with a lob on ... Dwight's the one.

Or, even the once legendary but now over batteredly tiresome, 'city are a massive club' song can be subject to a cheerying with:

> They've got tile on a roll in the Oasis suite,
> We love Gary Owen wearing polo necks,
> It took the nit nurse 12 months to check Joe Royle's head,
> They feed their football players on prem sliced thin,
> Debenham's was called Paulden's when they last won a cup,
> They've got under soil heating on Economy Seven,
> With Ferrero Roche they were spoiling us,
> Because city are a massive club.

Or:

> Chesty, Chesty Morgan, Chesty Morgan on the wing.

Or to the same watch your ging gang goo'ly tune:

Yvonne Goolley, Goolley, Goolley, Goolley, Goolley, Goolagong, Goolagong,
Yvonne Goolley, Goolley, Goolley, Goolley, Goolley, Goolagong, Goolagong.

Or:

And number one was Monty Don
And number two was Danny La Rue
And number three was Shooey McPhee - the Scottish chef from Crossroads
And number four was Diana Dors - would you?
And number five was Ernie Wise
And number six was wiffy knicks - always welcome here
And number seven was Aneurin Bevan
And number eight was Terry Waite - and wait and wait and wait
And number nine was Patsy Cline - doing a line
And number ten was Mr Benn - he never bought anything
And number 11 was Patrick Nevin
And number dozen was me cousin - you try rhyming 12
We all live in a populated world, a populated world, a populated world.

Or:

Hark now hear the bandwagon role and Keegan wears the crown,
But we want to know where the city fans were, when they played Mansfield Town.

Or:

Take a trip down Ancoats, Little Italy is so grand,
Take a trip down Rochdale Road and you're in Ireland,
China and Japan is Upper Brook Street,
Africa is in Moss Side so they say,
And if you want to go further still,
Palestine's in Cheetham Hill,
So what do you want to go to Wembley for?
To see United.
What do you want to go to Wembley for?
To laugh at city.
What do you want to go to Wembley for?
Our world is here.
So what do you want to go to Wembley for.

Or:

Law passed to Charlton, Charlton passed it back,
Law took a flying shot and knocked the goalie flat,
Singing where was the goalie when the ball was in the net?
Hanging around the lamppost with his knickers around his neck.

So they laid him on a stretcher, they laid him on a bed,
They laid him on a ten-foot jelly and this is what they said:
Who said United couldn't play, United couldn't play, United couldn't play?
Who said United couldn't play, United couldn't play football?

Or:

I'll be up your flue in a minute or two and I know just where to find it,
It's at the front and it's called a cunt and your arsehole's right behind it.
It's above your socks but below your knocks and it smells like Smithfield Market, Give it a wash or we'll fck off, except for - named person in the group - because he likes it.

Divides opinion that one.

Or:

My Auntie Mary had a canary up the legs of her draws,
When she farted it departed down the leg of her draws, hey.

Always a good song, that. It starts so well and it is such a bright tune but I can't help criticising it, in that it tails off somewhat when it rhymes 'up the leg of her draws' with 'down the leg of her draws.' It really could have done better. Or:

In Melbourne's fair city, where the girls are so pretty, I first set my eyes on sweet Kylie Minogue. As she wheeled her wheelbarrow through streets broad and narrow singing: I should be so lucky, lucky, lucky, lucky, I should be so lucky in love.

Or a whole other range of Kylie songs the favourite, of course, being the one where she says “Twas not so long ago” as it's not very often you can get the word 'Twas' into a song so you have to take advantage when you can. Rennie, the Paul Scholes look-a-like from Abbey Hey, once got us all barred from the Britons Protection in town for ceaseless singing of that. He gets the full pub going and still the Landlord bars us. Some pubs just don't deserve to sell beer. The Britons is right at the side of the Halle Orchestra and still they bar people for singing. Shame on them. I hope their hot nut machine on the bar turns their formerly hot nuts cold.

These Kylie classics could be accompanied by the singing of 'Snooker loopy' as we all can be potting the red, then screwing back for the yellow green, brown, blue pink and black. This might at first seem like a bit of an over used song. It has a secret within it though. You sing the words of

'Snooker loopy' to the tune of the Irish national anthem. Then it is a perfect beer song. Altogether now 'Snooky loopy nuts are we...'

Everyone knows the importance of communal singing to football. The arch under the railway bridge in the speciall pllace provided the perfect echoey acoustics to the mob of Reds who had taken shelter under its bent back. Hands were shook, new arrivals were abused, people were ribbed, people were hugged, cans were spilt over, stories were fair exchanged as fair exchanged is no robbery, coats were zipped up, hair was ruffled, asides were caught, and dropped, laughter was twizzled, knocks were knicker knacker knockered, tomato sauce from fare was left on face, onions were picked off, dandruff stuck, games were re-told, games were re-written, goals got better, once clear events got miasmic, alcy flush got redder, necks got blotchier, legs got stumblier, balance less solidier, jean arses got saggier, morale rose higher and higher, morals went lower and lower, shouts across from group to group got louder and louder.

Whereas an hour before you might simply have walked across the few yards to join that specific niche within the bigger mob, now it was acceptable just to shout your view across. Because you did this, more Reds from a different niche would criss-across you and join in your conversation or shout past you and join in one several groups away from you. Reds unconsciously wanted to find something to physically lean on as the body tried to tell them they were on their way but if someone had said that to them, then they would have denied it as they were not aware they were doing it.

The frequency of leaks once the seal had been broken was accelerating. Dribble stains on crotches from the lags were now growing from an innocuous five pence piece size that would easily dry, to dobbing great big ten pence plussers that were sodden. As the beer goes down you lose the ability to shake it properly and become abandon in the knowledge that your pant fronts will soak up the urine residue. The first button on your fly goes in the second button hole and causes buttony chaos from then on and perhaps, if you're extra sexy, the front tail of your shirt will get to stick out from between two buttons of its poorly buttoned frontage. Classy and hard to imagine any woman being able to keep their hands off you. From this sloppy soup, that's alright to boil and will not spoil, began the first note of a song that would be the birthing pool in the nativity that was the delivery of FC United of Manchester.

Whoever sung it first is lost in beer but the tune caught everyone's attention very quickly as no one had ever heard it attempted at a game. No individual should ever claim it and no individual there that day ever has. It appeared, existed and flourished because of community. It was community created, community based and community nourished. It was a very difficult tune to sing in parts, with one awkwardly tuned line causing particular consternation. The tune was sung at, to, and for, the railway bridge of the speciall pllace as a thank you to its cosseting of us throughout the afternoon, as the downpour caused flooding water to roll past us. Why we should insult the railway bridge with words that have no mention of a railway bridge in them is again lost in beer. That was how it was going to be though.

All the way back and all the way forward…

The Red drunks joined in, familiar with the real words that we have heard many, many times over from the wireless. Under The Boardwalk was badly, sungly born. Its umbilical cord was cut with tenderness, as a torrent washed down from the sky of another country far away from Manchester. It was brought 'down by the sea'ing' to join a mob who howled and hooted and changed the lyrics by the mini minute. We all raised both our arms and swayed them from side to side as we sang it. We were under a railway bridge and telling it that it was a boardwalk down by the sea. I'm sure it would not have taken umbrage. Indeed, our heartfelt singing only ever meant to transport it to a far off sunshiny place as a thank you for its kindness. It knew that, though.

If you'll let us and you want to, we'll take you there one day.

The stand out, lasting shine of all the things that happened on this Cup Final day was the entry into the football-singing world of Under The Boardwalk. For all we were about to face after May the 12th 2005 it would stand with us. It was, for us, MUFCUM's first ever song of unity. The many strands of the intifadah written into its constitution. As far as I know there is only one lad there that day who would not in the coming season go to an FC United of Manchester game. And he will, he's just taking his time. As far as I know, the song has not been sung at Old Trafford yet. It will do, it's just taking its time. The unity that song's emotion brought to our company replicated itself across so many groups of Reds. It played its part in getting so many Reds to experience the new world of the new football club.

So the community that is Basher, Ted, Daz, Blacky, Two Mowers, Dunny, Martin, Simon Go, Peanut, Soya Milk Mark, Donna, Jesus, Kennybobbles, the Ginger Princess, Chrissie Bolton, Stevie 'Justin' Bolton, Seniorie Bolton, Duns, Forrest, Chris 'Mad Cyril' O'Neil, Stanna, Daz's boss, Middleton Daz, Hovi, Matthew Scott, his Dad and his Dad's mates and the others I've embarrassingly forgot - take your place in history. You'd all be too shy to stand up and say it was you as it is not your way but it was you and may this book stand as documenting evidence that you played your part in the history of Manchester United Football Club. Don't be shy; Reds are only ever going to thank you for it, even though you don't want the attention. I'm sorry if I've brought it on you but shyness should never stop us from doing all the things in life we'd like to. If it's not love...

It lashed and lashed down on the way home. The force of the storm flooded through the 17-seater van and our feet were in water all the way back to Manchester. How we didn't die, I'm not sure. The fact we left Cardiff and an hour- and-a-half later, after going the wrong way, we ended up passing Cardiff again didn't help. This time, as we passed Cardiff, we were in pure Arsenal traffic. Some of the gruftier element in our vehicle getting out in the standing traffic and causing mayhem with other Arsenal coaches. But we didn't die because we knew we couldn't. We had to bring back within us the song that we believed would unify the fight. Duns and Two Mowers might have been beery torn that this would be the last time that we would all box together, and we all knew where they were and how they had got there, but the bloodline will never be broken.

We don't know where we're going but we know what we are taking with us. We're packed. Part of us will stay forever at Manchester United Football Club, it could be no other way. Part of us has gathered what we believe to be the soul and wrapped it in the softest of cotton and placed it gently into a treasure chest for its protection against hardship and arrogance, and deceit, and treachery, and slyness.

And the lid was closed. For so many it could be no other way.

There is a plaque at Man United, it's underneath the old Main Stand.

At the beginning of this chapter it was established that my mind wanders. At the end of this chapter my mind now wonders. One little vowel, so much significance.

Like shugborough.

CHAPTER TWO

THE BIRTH OF OUR POWER...

And I'll be here if you should find you ever need me...

Milan always got past me as a city. I know it must be a great city as so many people have told me that it is, but on the numerous times I have been with United, it failed to impress me. Every time I went back I thought that this would be the time I'd become true Milanese and stop being such a thicky and see what must be obvious. Grab in and appreciate what was there. I got as far as the railway station being smart. The Duomo was scaffoldy, the clothes were gay as a gay bob note and it stunk of furry exhaust pipe. I still believe that the next time I go I'll get it though.

The last time I was there with the football club that I fell in love with as a child was to see us get beat by AC Milan on the 9th of March 2005. If you're going to have a last game then the San Siro is not too bad a going away present. Although, that stands in contradiction to our Euro away, experience based, philosophy of 'The shittier the destination, the better time you would have'. It just never felt like it was the last Euro for a while when we were there. One of our party on that trip stated that this would be his last Euro away for a bit as the financial family commitments over the next few seasons were going to cripple him. When he was saying it we all knew that if it really mattered then he'd be there. We'd never played Roma yet. Or St. Pauli. Like he could ever miss those. If the Reds should play in Rome or Abbey Hey he'll be there.

When I've been trying every night to hold you near me. I'm telling you it isn't easy...

How did that AC Milan night of the 9th of March 2005 turn into the Debrecen night of the 9th of August 2005 when United played at home in a European qualifying round? The night that the Glazers first took a seat that was somebody else's in our ground. Somewhere in those summer months we went from only having the footballing cultural problem of saying: "Right, we must understand Milan more and stop being such dimbolinas" to having texts on my phone that said:

> I've just seen my team walk out and it's the first time in my adult life that I am wilfully absent. The flow of four Mancunian generations of Manchester United blood is stemmed
>
> I'm beyond sadness. Them three racketeers are in the ground and I'm out here. I've walked away from the woman I love and it's killing me. I'm not fit for human consumption tonight. Walking on my own down Ayres Road, getting it back to fight tomorrow but tonight I'm beat and they've won.
>
> It feels like we're living through the utter failure of a campaign.

If my non-Vodafone phone could have cried then it would have. It wouldn't as it had more important work to do on that August evening and it couldn't breakdown and cry. It weighed more than usual in my pocket as it carried within it the heavy hearted sentiments of broken sisters and brothers who had fought for so long, to save something they loved so much. It saved their messages so that when I'd stopped blubbering like a little girls blouse I'd shape up. "Don't mourn, organise" had been said at too many socialist funerals for it to be forgotten. Those saved messages and many more had wrought through them the communication that we didn't just go from AC Milan to Debrecen. If we had then many thousands wouldn't have got through that summer of 2005 and would have been lost.

Epiphany? Didn't she sing 'I think we're alone now?'...

On the last night of the last time we were all in Milan I had spewed it early. It must have been about three or four o'clock in the morning but as you know on a European away that's proper Children's Television Workshop time to swerve. I got back to the room and was snuggled down in my bed all cuddly as befitting a gnarled European away veteran of my age. Later in my deserved slumber I heard them all coming back as there was about two or three, possibly four thousand Reds bailing into our room. I was proud of them as the majority were youngsters and were in that 'early 20s, life's great' age. As they bowled through the door they did something that, in other situations and with other lads, might be construed as divvy and callous but in this instance it wasn't. It was meant with affection and appreciation. Of course they'd deny it the twats but I know.

They burst through the door shouting: "Uncle Bobby, come on, get up" and they tipped my bed up. They tipped it from the foot of the bed so that the bottom of the bed was head height. This meant that my head on the pillow slowly slipped onto the floor and my feet were up in the air. They left the bed standing on its end with me still in it in an upside down position. Sometimes you get rubbery boned in beer and find any position comfortable. With a mixture of that, and that feeling you sometimes get when you can just leave your arm up in the air, I was as snug as a bugger. I didn't move and just carried on talking to them all as if nothing had happened. They went about pissing on the toilet seat, brushing their teeth with tubed Brylcreme gel and trying to find a space to get their head down in this small Milanese hotel room.

As time passed and they beerily settled down, the waheyness of them turning their Uncle Bobby upside down turned into concern that I shouldn't stay like that as I might choke on my vomit or something. The choking on vomit concern doesn't really stand up to investigation as being upside down is probably a great way to be if you vom but that inaccuracy was not important. What was important was the care that was shown and the bond behind it.

I was upside down in a room on a European away but I was going to labour with it as I'd been involuntarily put in this situation but I was bizarrely restful. I was going to keep it in collar. I'll corner up and then, if I can, run them in and earn that bonus that piecework brings. I could look up the skirt of things and see them, if not clearer, then from an unfamiliar nosey Parkering point. You always presume, even though your experience tells you otherwise, that life's knickers are there. Visible Panty Life. From a different, upside down, up the skirt position you can establish firmly if the knickers are actually on or not and secondly, if they are there, whether you want to appreciate them from other ways. The boxing glove might bulge at a different level of bulginess or the gusset might be stuck up one side of a flap and not the other or a little two pence sized, wet patch might be visible from an unfortunate but cute mishap or you might be able to smell, because the skirt is funnelling down the aroma, the tuna challenge of an unbalanced flue or even, if her back door is in bits and off its hinges, the discharge of the shite brigade.

If, as you are looking up, life's knickers are not there, then no one is a loser as life's vagina gets the fresh air it craves and that does it so good. And we get to witness a quality blimp. I was getting used to being upside down. There was a possibility that a fondness might form. It nurtures the new.

Loving eyes can never see. Except when they can…

Since May the 12th 2005 our summer had been turned upside down. We'd involuntarily been forced into this situation but we were going to labour with it. It was up to us whether it was going to be bizarrely restful. We were going to keep it in collar. We'll corner up and then, if we can, run them in and earn that bonus that piecework brings. It was up to us how we viewed it, what we made of it and how we came out of it. Not wishing to get too fckn romantic but it was crucial to the whole of football how we viewed it, what we made of it and how we came out of it. The rest of the football world hates us and we wouldn't have it any other way. The divvy faces of fans from inconsequentially towned football clubs laughing at Manchester's predicament and the stupidity of them not knowing the importance of our plight to their existence, will remain with me. It will unfortunately remain as testament to prove my mate's staunchly held belief when he so cruelly, so uncorrectly, but I can't help knowing, however reluctantly, what he meant, when he said: “All football fans are m**gs.” It doesn't help trying to defend the use of a bad word here, which I'm not, especially when it somehow looks as if I'm further condoning my use of it with the sentence: 'Some of my best mate's are m**gs’. As they are. As that's what they call themselves.

If we were going to look after ourselves, then as a political bi-product, we would be looking after a part of football and how it should be. We might very well fail. The coming season, if there was to be a coming season, would see. It would be convenient here to say, well, we'll see by going back to the beginning of our story, but there is no real, definite beginning. It could be voiced that the FC United of Manchester story, and every other football club story, began with the first time a human kicked an object, didn't hurt his/her foot and another human kicked it back. A nearby female cheered and the early monkey man finished up getting a poke out of it, decorating the cake of the female cheerer. The monkey word spread. There is no documented evidence of the first pass in the world and there is no documented evidence of our beginning.

Splash out...

The shites of passage we are now travelling through was always in us all and my approximations at telling our journey and our story could well be different to others. That difference of story should be welcomed and applauded as there has been countless to'ings and throw ins in our short life already. We have all put another giggle in the giggle odeon. What unites the beginning of all the different FC United of Manchester stories, though, was the emotion that all of us have always felt. The emotion that we owned our Manchester United Football Club. It is patently obvious that it was not true but we always felt it belonged to us, individually and as a mass movement. The 12th of May 2005 forced us out to fight. And of the Red friends I knew, none of them were going to door knock.

Governments crack and cisterns fall because unity is powerful, lights go out, walls come tumbling down...

If you are going to start looking at your dialectical materialist history, and learn from the previous experiences of other situations that have adopted a United Front policy, then there can be no other start than Lev Davidovitch Bronstein. Or Leon Trotsky as his stage name went. In Trotsky's 'The struggle against fascism in Germany' he wrote the following about the political situation in Germany on the 8th of December 1931. That's a long time ago, and even Darren Lyons, the soon to be centre forward from the soon to be formed new club, was still a milk monitor at his primary school. They'd just invented primary schools. But, as in so many things written by Trotsky, you can find mirrors and lessons in what is happening today, at whatever scale you want to take it at. It's a long quote but a caressable one in its simplicity. He wrote:

> Germany is now passing through one of those great historic hours upon which the fate of the German people, the fate of

> Europe, and in significant measure the fate of all humanity, will depend for decades. If you place a ball on top of a pyramid, the slightest impact can cause it to roll down either to the left or to the right. That is the situation approaching with every hour within Germany today. There are forces which would like the ball to roll down towards the right and break the back of the working class. There are forces which would like the ball to remain at the top. That is utopia. The ball cannot remain at the top of the pyramid. The communists want the ball to roll down toward the left and break the back of capitalism. But it is not enough to want; one must know how.

Since May the 12th 2005 the ball could not remain on the top of the football pyramid. But it was not enough for us to want Glazer to go away and stop mithering us, we had to know how. We had to get the ball to roll down to the side we wanted it to. Like many, I was honoured enough to know Reds who I would consider part of the advanced section of United thought and punditry. They had political arguments to win and Red clarity to help foist. These were difficult times and the majority of us were all arsing about falling down the pyramid getting bruised and dusty. Or going up a step or two, stopping, sitting down, getting butties out and admiring how far we had come. When in actual fact all we had to do was look up to see how far we had to go. We were cheering ourselves up by rubbing a camel's hoof every now and then at the bottom of the pyramid but what we needed was that ball to fall on our side, into our garden so that Glazer couldn't get a big bad neighbour's knife out to pop it.

Some arguments at the time seemed to have more than a hint of 'Well if he does pop it, we'll just heat up a knife on the stove and melt the plastic of the ball and mend the puncture' about it. As anyone who has ever tried that method of getting your ball back to work then you will know it is sorely flawed. Getting a new ball, however heartbreaking, however difficult to admit that you'd been cuffed, was often the result of having your ball forcefully removed by a bigger foe. For all your courage and valiant efforts to resist you find that sometimes the sheer size and strength of your opponent makes it impossible. However, when you had got that new ball you had learnt a lesson about the evil neighbour and there were countless ways of exacting revenge at your pace. There were allies to forge, debate to be had, windows to break, abuse to throw, locks to glue, race courses to invade, skips to deliver.

Ya turned injun dincha?...

My first ever coming to the conclusion that we could form our own breakaway club was after the derby in February 2005. We'd left the 2-0 victory at The Camp Boo and got off to The Egerton Arms which is a Red pub at the tail end of town off Chapel Street. We all met back there and had more than a dampening down with Holt's bitter. The beer house was jammed and jolly as it would be as we had just beaten the self-aggrandisers. The Benidorm tan came as the bitter went down and life was nice. Later in the evening we moved up Chapel Street to the Rovers Return, a poorly named but nearer pub than the karaoke at The Black Lion on Blackfriars that we were aiming for. We settled in the window of The Rovers Return, a squashed in crew of us. It was whilst there that I first became enthused. Just the right amount of beer makes you dream.

Me and Ted came away that night from the Rovers Return knowing that it wasn't just beer. We'd peeped over the big wall that we had been standing at the side of for decades and had never thought of peeking over. We might have leant against it, or wrote something on it, or painted those nets on it that makes an attempt to make them look 3D by painting the net supports in, but we had never looked over. We had now. We had seen beauty. Cleverer people than me had constructed plans for a breakaway club if Roopy Poopy Murdoch had taken over in the '90s. For me, though, being a dimmylongstocking, it was the first time I had considered it. At the time I was writing a column in the Red Issue fanzine called 'Our home is your home' and in the February issue 2005 I did my full-page column on it. Unbeknown to me the characters involved at Red Issue had also chosen this month to set out in full their ideas for a new club. Theirs made good reading, mine was a bit trite. I get used to that though.

I continued till the end of the season using the luxury that was afforded to me by my column to campaign solely for this new fans' club. You were not pots for rags to believe that with a database at Shareholders United of around 34,000 that we would be able to take, with hard, political, clear, unafraid arguments, perhaps 10,000 with us. The hatred for Glazer and the tens upon tens of thousands who stood up singing 'Not for sale' at Old Trafford meant that when we drank from a cup, that cup had 'confidence' written on it. With hindsight that looks proper knobby but many thought the political commitment from so many thousands of Reds of actually paying their tenner to join Shareholders United, and then more to purchase shares, meant that we weren't just a talking shop. Reds had put their grafted for money into their beliefs. Shareholders United were at the epicentre of this fantastic drive by passionate fans to save their club. It was truly inspiring.

Arguments will ripple, splurge and splat as to why we failed to hold Glazer off but the reality remained that for all the honourable and dedicated input of the volunteers we could still only get a scraping of the percentage of shares needed. The amount of money the fans now owned through shares could probably have got control, or a viable input, at the vast majority of football clubs. At Manchester United it got us a toenail's worth. Perhaps more than a little toenail's worth but not more than a big toenail's worth. Devode. Truly, truly devode. The book on Shareholders United will make a fine and interesting read when it is written.

And when I knew I had to face another day, Maud it made me feel so tired...

The solemnity of the 12th of May 2005 crept into Friday the 13th of May 2005. There was a visit by many of the demonstrators on the night of the 12th of May to town and interruptions occurred at a do organised by a business associated with helping the Glazer deal. I didn't go to town. I went to Alderley Edge. Two very respected members of the Manchester Education Committee approached me and asked me if I wanted to go on an outing. All liberation movements around the world have a separate, clandestine wing. The MEC seemed to perform this role on the periphery of the 'Not For Sale Coalition'. I had previously been to Hereford with them and had enjoyed the racing immensely. I'd also enjoyed the football on my visit to Altrincham. Although, the going on both visits was unfirm underfoot and your footwear was in dire need of a good dubbin'ing afterwards. The mood around Old Trafford on the 12th of May on that Glazer take over night was one of indescribable loss as previously gone into. All I wanted to do was go to bed and duvet the problems into none existence.

My own private eider down...

The duvet lost as I finished up in a knackered car going to the footballer belt of Manchester. We picked up another Beswick lad on the way and finished up, first in a pub to meet 30-odd others and then on the doorstep of one Rio Ferdinand. Actually, it wasn't exactly the doorstep. If Rio has to get a taxi home from town to his front gate then it would cost him a twenty spot. If he wanted the same taxi to take him past his gate and down his drive to his front door it would be twenty five. Grufty men, dressed unseasonably darkly, made their way past houses they were never going to afford, passing parked motor cars that it would take some of them ten years of wages to get. The inner city dwellers had to pass the disparages in class society to get to another working class lad's house. A lad who just happened to be better with a casey than they were. These visitors from the inner city had paid for the mock-in-whatever-period-of-mock Rio's house was mocked in. They were coming to survey their investment.

Rio's buzzer was buzzed on the wall outside his ten-foot, solid wooden gates and a friendly invite was offered to come and discuss his ongoing contract wrangle and his unwillingness to sign. The visitors had a vested interest, as they were all soon to part with half a grand plus for a season ticket. Their working week was going to pay for his working minute. There were substantial rumours that he was holding out for £120,000 per week. That's £6,240,000 per year. If he works two hours a day for six days a week, then that's dead on £10,000 per hour. Or £166.66 per minute. The average pay for Manchester is less than £15,000 a year. If tax and national insurance take 25% of that Mancunian £15,000, then we come out with a net of £11,250. Or £216.34 per week.

So I have to mathematically take back that earlier statement of our working week paying for his working minute, as I was wrong. Our working week of £216.34 does more than pay for Rio's working minute of £166.66. No wonder we were being polite with him. He could increase his reported £120,000 per week wage demand by 23%, which would make it just over £148,000 per week, before our Manchester working week was paying for his working minute. He was being modest and reserved in his wage claims as befitting his reputation for being modest and reserved within the United supporting community. A big cough. And a big ahem. To be fur not many people would come to their gate when confronted by 35 blokes. And to be fur he did eventually come out as we were leaving and talk to us over a ten-foot, solid wooden gate.

For a hundred yards walking down the trying-to-be-quaint, cobbled, country lane outside Rio's as we were departing I thought and said the following: “That him coming to the gate had reminiscences of Keegan on the steps of St James' after the sale of Andrew Cole to us." It was a hundred yards of shame that I have brought on myself and my family. Keegan, however many differences there may be between him and us, faced the disgruntled Geordie mob on open steps. As Reds said around me as we were escorted by the car'red up constabulary within seconds: "Do you think he has not called these?" He came to a solid ten-foot gate, stood on something and looked over it. He's an athlete, if any of us would have tried to storm that ten-foot gate he would have been back with in the safety of his secured home in the full knowledge that the Cheshire police were on their way. He knew that we wouldn't storm him anyway as we were nothing but polite in our requests on his buzzer. He came to the gate because he couldn't resist it, probably in shock that ordinary Reds had the audacity to seek meaningful conversation to answer legitimate queries.

In that brief conversation with Rio over the solid and secure ten-foot gate we had paid for, he managed to say that the two million pounds worth of our money he took in wages, whilst being banned for eight months for forgetting to urinate, had been, and I quote: "A right touch." It was a Thursday night. We had just lost our club to an American businessman with reportedly dubious credentials that even our own, untrustworthy football club board had paid six million pounds in resisting. And here was a man, with his hair in beads, telling us he had been the recipient of a right touch. The Reds who would go on to be part of FC United of Manchester in the coming months are always described in the away fans programmes of the clubs that they visit as 'Disaffected and disenfranchised Manchester United supporters'. The 12th of May 2005 was our DD day. It could not be possible to be further disenfranchised or further disaffected.

Well used Dildar...

That's how, for me, Thursday the 12th of May crept into the Friday of the 13th of May 2005. Beaten. Disaffected. Disenfranchised. Disillusioned. The Red Issue fanzine contributors and sellers were having a meeting that Friday night in the Dildar curry house in Rusholme. This was a regular event for them and had been arranged before any of the previous days doings were done. I'd never been to any before as I'd only been writing for them a season. Whereas I'd been writing for UWS for getting on for perhaps 15 seasons. I'd always gone in and out of reading Red Issue. I wasn't alone in thinking of one of the main characters behind it as a fat, ignorant, grammar school dick and it sort of put me off for a few seasons. I had no conversational basis for that opinion besides a deep-rooted east central Manchester wariness of anyone not from east central Manchester.

I'd got better after the 1992/3 season when the 26 year wait was over. I'd improved beyond recognition after the events of 1999 when I'd be friends with almost anyone. Manchester United Football Club had cured me of my illogical and contradictory bigotry. I was an international socialist recognising no international borders besides that of ones drawn by the international working class of the world. And yet if you weren't from the 11 areas of east central Manchester of Ancoats, Ardwick, Clayton, Miles Platting, Newton Heath, Openshaw, West Gorton, Gorton North, Beswick, Bradford and Abbey Hey then I'd be wary of you until you had been properly weighed up. Collyhurst obviously got honorary membership. And Moston. Sod it, even Harpurhey, Monsall, Blackley, Cheetham Hill and even Crumpsall because it's in M8 and that makes it a friendly place to text from, which goes to prove that I wasn't that bad. Although, all those areas for honorary membership are from the north of Manchester and there is a natural affinity between the east and the north.

I've brought me mate for a weigh up...

The new editor of Red Issue was a fine, fine young man. Pots for rags, but fine. Amongst the people around Red Issue there was Tony Jordan, Jules Spencer, Andy Walsh, Paddy O'Neill and others. Good Reds with something to say that was almost always valid. Paddy O'Neill being the exception as he always talks shite. I'd been invited by the new editor to write for the fanzine. At first it seemed disloyal to UWS but I'm cheap and cheap to keep and the offer of beer money was irresistible. I'd write for both the fanzines during the 2004/2005 season. Being a seller of UWS, we had always seen Red Issue far outsell all the other fanzines at the ground. This was an admittedly big headed opportunity for me to get any views I thought were pertinent to a wider Red audience if anything major arose that coming season. We all knew something was bubbling, we just didn't think it would burst so badly. Andy Mitten, UWS editor, will quite correctly tell you that UWS sells across WH Smiths and paper shops, which bumps up its sales to Red Issue levels. Barney from Red News just smiles and probably has absolutely no idea what Red News sells. He has got a girlfriend, though, and apparently she has not got 'Pallitoy' written on her back, and comes without an adapter and foot pump, unlike his previous ones.

Rusholme scruffy'uns...

So on a warm May evening of Friday the 13th 2005 I went into The Clarence pub in Rusholme, unknowing that I was walking into a meeting that was going to be judged as historic. I was just hungry. There was a few faces in there that I recognised but didn't know the name of. Some people are good with names and some people are good with faces. I don't mean to be ignorant but the early onset of Alzheimer's combined with ongoing specky denial and the legacy of my east central Manchester bigotry, means that I'm shit with both. So if you know me and I walk past you, then sorry for that, I almost certainly don't mean it. I sat in the corner with Tony Jordan, Adam Brown and a smiley-faced cockney that I would come to know as Pete Munday. Pete is an accountant. I would come to call him 'Noel Countwell'. Pete would probably have had his signature brown brogues on.

The four of us espoused opinions of where we were in the formation of a new club, what it could be called and where we would play. I was for the name 'AFC Manchester United' with a return to the east, playing at the ratepayers of Manchester stadium or at least the mini one at the side. I was of the opinion that putting 'AFC' in front of a club's name had attained a political significance as it stood for 'A Football Club'. We had lost the words 'Football Club' off our badge a few years back and that was never going to be satisfactory. I threw in 'Manchester Central' as that was the name that had drawn in votes with 'Manchester Celtic' in 1902 in that smoky room above The Imperial pub. A third neutral party broke the deadlock between 'Central' and 'Celtic' by throwing in 'United'. We'd have to move letters around, though, as MCFC wasn't going to ever breathe.

I also chucked in Manchester 1878 FC. Although, I was aware that the sprayed initials of 'M1878FC' on walls would look more like a car registration plate than a football club. A wise Adam Brown, who was far more advanced than us in legal technicalities of names, allied with a close knowledge of the workings of the politics of sport in east Manchester, knocked back my enthusiasm on both my first choice of AFC Manchester United and also my desired wish of the place we might play. Tony Jordan then said the words I was to hear for the first ever time: "Football Club United of Manchester." FCOUM was poor. FCUM was poorer. The 'of' stuck in there looked gormless but at least it had 'Manchester', 'United', 'Football' and 'Club' even if they had been jumbled out of a big bag in the wrong order.

We agreed the necessity for 'of' would disappear in time like the need for a human appendix. I was impressed'ish. Not too much though. I wanted AFC Manchester United too badly. If you ever want to relive where it was when Tony Jordan first brought the words 'FC United of Manchester' into the universe then it would be in the seats under the window to the left of the door as you come into The Clarence. Tony was one seat away from the outside pub wall if you really want to be exact and sit in the same seat and say it. Wear a black baseball hat. Or you could just start having sexual intercourse more.

Juan Sebastian Veron...

We left The Clarence pub and went into the Dildar curry house. From that point I effectively shut my gob. I JSV'd. Jug Stroke Vessel'd. Red Issue, as previously stated, met on a regular basis for a curry and a parrot. This meant that there was an established political cadre in operation far in advance of anything I was used to. As we sat in the Dildar I sat at the side of the new editor and opposite Tony Jordan for friendly comfort and just listened as things were talked about that I had no knowledge of. 'Backbeat' in Red Issue is at times annoying in its 'Shh you know who' insinuations. The thing is this cadre in front of me didn't need a decoder to say who was doing what at United. They talked about reprehensible acts of corruption and intrigue with alarming normality as they had heard about it before and were past being shocked. I, however, Phil Neville gobbed. I tried to disguise my naivety but also maintain an acceptable standard of decorum. I was also juggling this with my usual habit of quietly weighing up strangers and forming an opinion on them. 'Knob', 'Not so knobby', 'Nice lad'. The people I went into the Dildar liking were the people I came out liking. With a few additions.

These insider, curry'd up conversations around the large table reaffirmed the notion that you should never meet your football idols as they are invariably dicks. It makes matters graver when you know more about their private life and their opinions and dealings. Outside of Andy Mitten, the editor at UWS, whose knowledge of insider shenanigans is vast but private, most of the UWS contributors and sellers are quiet but interesting Reds. United, women, beer. That's not the worse combinations of goals to have. We go out on a UWS Christmas meal most years paid for by Andy and we all get mango'd. Andy would probably say that within that do he is trying to access the mood of Reds but we'd just probably tell him to get his hands in his 40 pockets, the short armed get, and get a round in.

The regular meeting of Red Issue Reds had definitely crystallised their clarity of the situation but it had also part forged them as a force for change. I can honestly say that if all the UWS lads - outside of Andy - had gone out for a beer to discuss the situation we were now in then we would have had a beer, discussed it, got another beer and probably not done anything about it. Subconsciously knowing that we would be part of any fight back but almost certainly not leading it. Just adding weight and support wherever we could. This meeting was beery but different. In fact I only had one beer all night as they all got whacked. I needed my empty vessel to be filled up by this big jug and alcohol wasn't going to get in my way.

The conclusion was that a meeting should be held the following Thursday at the Central Hall on Oldham Street in town. At this meeting the many strands of the intifadah we were now in, would be voiced. A football club of our own provisionally entitled 'FC United' would be a prominent element in the options Reds faced. When Jules Spencer and Andy Walsh kindly dropped me back in town that night they commented on my evening's quietness. I replied that I was a quiet lad. I knew that the work ahead was going to break up marriages with the commitment needed. Form a football club? Form a fucking football club? How? By going to the magic wand shop and wishing one? Excuse me, do you sell football clubs? Can I have one please? I found this football club outside on the pavement. Is it yours? Why take two football clubs into the shower?

Take me for granted, leaving love unsure, makes will power weak and temptation strong...

Although part of me was arguing for a breakaway club, a basic part of me still considered it too woof, bark, donkey surreal. You thought about it but then you went and had your tea and forgot about it until the next time you remembered to think about it. It was only after the second mass supporters' meeting of May the 30th, 2005 at the Apollo that I came right around. The first meeting had seen me on the stage at the Central Hall on Oldham Street in town, on Thursday the 19th of May. The meeting was a coalition of the Independent Manchester United Supporters Association, Shareholders United, Red Issue, Red News and United We Stand fanzines.

I was there to show a solidarity as a representative of United We Stand fanzine. I'd been a columnist for UWS for years and years and because I got the sympathy vote from readers for being so shit at constructing sentences, I was recognised as a UWS mush. My 'Our home is your home' pseudonym in Red Issue fanzine was Francis Marshall as that was the name my Dad used when he was on the lump in the '70s. But I was mostly recognised for just being 'Brady' in UWS or 'Abbey Hey' before that. This was because I always used to sign my articles in the early days in a 'Disgruntled of Didsbury writing to the Evening News letters page' way. But, obviously, using Abbey Hey instead of Didsbury as Abbey Hey was where I lived before coming to town. Obv.

The first Central Hall meeting on the 19th of May 2005 was too whooping and a hollering for me. There was six or seven hundred there and it seemed to be dominated by a few dozen very courageous Reds who had jacked in their season tickets. I knew from my football family that was in attendance in the audience that this was not representative. My football family was that wide a spectrum that it would cover most feelings at Manchester United. I'd not experienced such whooping and a hollering from them. Something was not sitting right. I gestured to Andy Walsh who was chairing that I wanted a parrot. What I would have mumbled and fumbled out fuck knows, but it would have been around the sentence I had been using since the demonstration outside Old Trafford on the evening of May the 12th. The sentence was: "I'll eat my shoe if more than 500 give up their season tickets." As it turned out, Peter Boyle got up and was brave enough to say that he was renewing. Fair play to the porky one. It was too soon for many Reds in the audience that night to wrap up. If you had been going for 20 or 30 years then a fortnight to decide whether to give up or not was just too short a space.

Cleans baths without scratching...

Most of the 11 days between the meeting on the 19th and the meeting on the 30th of May I spent in a caravan in Towyn, North Wales. There was a meeting in the Town Hall Tavern the night before the 19th and a Cup Final on the 21st but mostly I went and hid away from the turmoil like a shithouse. There is something about the faint smell of calor gas in a caravan that shouldn't be, but is, consoling. Obviously the faint smell of caravan calor gas has to be accompanied by you having tomato butties, on white bread, with ready salted crisps, with a vanilla for afters, with a pot of tea and the knowledge that, not too far away, is an afternoon napette on the long settee in the caravan window, with the sun gently shining through and with the caravan door open so as to let fresh, sea air in. Otherwise you're just gas sniffing.

The deliberation over whether to renew my season ticket or not and the annihilation we had suffered from the Glazers had left me a brittle and delicate husk. I had gone off to fathom and was use nor ornament to anyone until I part recovered. In Towyn you can watch turns like Bobby Gold doing his residency at Knightley's Long Bar or Dean Kane at Stones' Social Club. Simple beery pleasures followed by a fish and pea muffin after last orders. Or long walks on the sea wall to Rhyl or to Pensarn from Golden Gate camp. Rooney's Mam has got a caravan on Golden Gate camp as well. Like all of us, the Rooney family will be crossing those ever ageing metal and wooden bridges from the caravans to the sea. Enjoying the May sunshine. Being perplexed by the dichotomy that is Rhyl having non-pollutant-emissioning wind turbines in the bay allied with the brownist, fizziest sea that your foot would putrefy in.

My mate used to be on the shitboats that sailed out of the Ship Canal. The shitboats were full of Manchester's watery waste. They'd legally dump it out in the bay off Rhyl. All the children on the shore would be going: "Look, look a boat." They've built a pipeline to Liverpool now. Liverpool again takes our shite. It seems as though that is what the two cities do. Many years ago we sprayed 'Scouse eat cats' on the wall by the amusements on Golden Gate. The football season had finished and the four bored United fans from Beswick went camping across the road from there. We all eventually got arrested for shoplifting. We'd ragged Rhyl rotten from the clothes we were all wearing, to the tents we were sleeping in. I must have had an angelic little face as there seemed to be nothing I couldn't pick up and take out of a shop. However, Pete Stephenson is a shite shoplifter. He got us all caught. We should put that on his gravestone. In a court in Mold, Basher, who is not pure Beswick as he was born in Harpurhey, had his place of birth read out by the thick Blodwyns. In the cells they mustn't have been able to understand his Manchester accent saying his north Manchester birthplace. He shall forever be 'Basher from Harmony Bay'.

I'd met this girl whilst there and had been doing a bit of courting all week. We were very close. We laughed at gormless things and as holidays do, the time together put us together quicker than on non-holiday time. She was a lovely girl, with a lovely family and we fell for each other in the way only innocent youth can. In a gentle fumble she lost her virginity to me. We kissed and were gripped tight. We were never going to tire of hugging. She had to go back to her Mam and Dad's caravan. Our first night together knowing close passion. We were only 15. The next day, the Police came to the campsite where us lads were camping and arrested us all for shoplifting. They took us off to the cells. I didn't have her phone number; I only knew the approximate area in Manchester she was from. Our life together had been totally Towyn. I'd lost her. She would have stood there waiting for me the next day when I didn't turn up on our arranged date. She would have eventually gone to the campsite. She would have seen our tents gone. Our holiday romance and all the young truths we had told each other would now mean nothing. I'd taken something precious from her and left. She must have felt as if I had treated her like the stolen items we had acquired from Rhyl's clothes shops.

What kind of a businessman are you Willie Baxter?...

From all the exposure to being near water of my latest visit to Towyn, I was beginning to accrue the anger and resistance necessary when I had stopped being mard. Thankfully there were Reds who had not gone off anywhere. They had stayed and organised. The mass meeting in the Apollo Theatre was to be the fruition of that organisation. I got back from north Wales with only minutes to spare before the meeting. It was a hot day and my nads were boil in the bagged. Martin Morris was being United We Stand's representative on the Apollo Theatre stage. All other supporters groups were represented, as well as Tony Lloyd the central Manchester MP, a representative from the Gibson family who had saved United from bankruptcy in the 30s, a fat bloke called Kris Stewart from AFC Wimbledon and David Conn the respected broad sheet journalist.

The meeting approached the 2,000 mark, which for a hot day on a Bank Holiday Monday, after the season had finished, when we had won nothing, when we had been beaten by the American occupying force, was smart. The meeting swayed with arguments we have all heard about what we should do, what we shouldn't do, what we should say, what we shouldn't say. I'd been in isolation in Towyn for awhile, only having people who eat 'five donuts for a pound', who wear frayed tracksuits, with a minimum of three colours involved in its manufacture. Who always put two packs of 20 cigs on top of each other down on the pub table before they start drinking as an indicator of intent whilst wearing greening, bad gold on every finger as company, so this meeting was refreshing. Which was alright considering the unrefreshed state of my plumbolinas. The main organisers thought otherwise. They retired to The Church pub on Ardwick Green afterwards a bit fedster.

Perhaps they had expected more Reds to come or for the whooping and a hollering of the previous Central Hall meeting to whoop and holler even more.

Football Club of Manchester Central...

I got nothing from that yeehar frenzy. At this meeting there was negativity which wasn't negativity for negativity's sake but which had squirmed out of defeat. There was optimism there, which had been released by the defeat. There was practical, assured arguments laying alongside knocky ones. There were bores there who seemed to think that they could disguise that boringness by being ever so contrary. There were bores there who just wanted to hear their own boring voices repeat what other Reds had already said far more eloquently. These bores were only there so that they could bore people later by saying they had spoken. These bores are recognised for the dicks they are.

There were older voices there who compartmentalised the stages we had gone through and were making careful, sophisticated Red guesses of where we should go next to win. We had been 2-0 down at Wolves, 2-3 was always possible. There were young, new voices there who approached the microphone the total Red opposite to the bores. They shyly approached the microphone with a scared child demeanour but left it like MUJACS. The hurt was overwhelmingly evident. It brought tears and a fool might perceive those tears as weakness. What the fool had missed was that the hurt had found something. It had found a shiny knife. As the tears fell from the hurt it mixed its upset with the passing of its thumb over the sharp blade. To me it was my first witness of what the club we were about to form would be like.

The addled, burnt-black-pan of smeared packet soup that all of humanity has evolved from was not an appetising one. Neither was ours. Ours was a strong smelling lump of lonesome, unwrapped cheesy cheesed cheese that you would be aware of as you entered any room it was in. It had obviously fallen on the floor and there was bits of kitchen floor crumbs on it, and tighter, stringier, unfluffy fluff from the corner of the ceiling on the sides. This unfluffly fluff would need careful rubbing off so as not to spread its dirty, dark staining further with the rubbing. There were one or two different coloured, scissors cut, cotton clippings, dampening on its saturated, whiting harder surface. However, the apparently pitiable state it was in was not its lowest point, as it was now no longer on the floor. It had at least been picked up and put on the table. It needed a wash. It needed some very small off parts paring. For those about to be pared we don't salute you due to your retrograde role in our defeat. For those about to bubble, gurgle, boil, ignite and grow we do.

On that night of the Apollo meeting of the 30th of May 2005 a rake of us went to The Frog and Bucket on Oldham Street and then onto Matt and Phreds. We met representatives from the organisers of the Apollo meeting who had left the meeting fedster. I accepted the offer to join the proposed steering committee. Perhaps I was razzed on caravan calor gas fumes but I was the opposite to fedster. It all comes around. Towyn tells you that. All our life all my friends have enjoyed saying 'Harmony Bay' instead of Harpurhey. It's a simple pleasure with a meaning that perhaps not everyone can understand. It's ours. It's made a part of Manchester even more ours.

It comes around. It took a good 15 years after being forced away from my young-holiday-in-Towyn-love, by the police force of a foreign country, before I found her again. I was working for Fearnleys from Salford on this estate out in the hills around Manchester. I was building the garden wall to this property when this pretty, pretty woman came out with a young child in a pram. I knew her delicate face; it was still 15. Her dark hair the same dark hair that had fallen softly on that stolen groundsheet, in that stolen tent, so many, many summers ago. She knew my cement dust covered face. She smiled with graceful tenderness; her eyes opened and let me in. With all she thought I had done, she shouldn't have. I threw down my trowel onto the mortar-board and in a gaping gush of sorries and explanations and trembles, and going back and surrounding sequences, and of where had we trodden and what had we walked, we had come around. We had made something right. She was happy and married and in love and had brought her loved child into Manchester's embrace. And I lost her again.

In the Apollo, in that meeting of the 30th of May 2005 it had come around. This time we had some power within our love-loss to get something back. Manchester United Football Club has been a simple pleasure with a meaning that perhaps not everyone can understand. It's ours. It's made a part of Manchester even more ours. I wanted a go of that shiny knife we had found that was having our thumbs passed across its sharp blade, to announce we were still here. Unmoveable. The knife had a homemade 'FC' scratched in the handle. It weighed nice in the hand. However, all that would mean fuck all if we didn't build a firm enough body behind it for it to be effective in any sodden, desolate entries we may have to continue our conflict in. It wasn't the best protection but it was part of all we had. It wasn't the best offensive weapon but it was part of all we had. Don't mourn. Classify your opposition, categorise it until your awareness of everything it does makes you unafraid. Make it bleed.

CHAPTER FREE

THE DIRTY HALF THIRTY...

It lingered there, it touched your hair and walked with me...

I woke up the next day after the Apollo meeting and opened my emails. There, posted at four in the morning, was the email from the new editor of Red Issue. I was within the new email circle of proposed Steering Committee members. Red Issue's editor had posted at four in the morning as he was off to Spain to go cycling with the editor of UWS. He was later to be reported wearing green cycling shorts, a dark purple shirt and grey socks just outside Barcelona. They were both going to wear luminous tight Lycra together in hot and sweaty conditions for a week or so. Perhaps if editors did have their 'head hit' more often then they wouldn't be as odd.

The re:boot boys...

The e-maelstrom over the next few days showed that the Steering Committee met with three representatives of The Moore and Company Construction Solicitors League. The North West Counties League to us.

Present at this meeting was the NWCL chairman Dave Tomlinson - brother of Rick - who was by far the most positive. The vice chair Mr Farnworth, who was far keener to keep us realistic and Mike Appleby the FA's representative at this level. Basically the FA had no problem with us being admitted to the league as long as we were approved by the clubs at their AGM on the 18th of June. To get that approval we had two weeks and a tidge to form a football club and the 18th of June was our deadline that could not be missed.

We had to have an agreement on a ground with a legal document stating so, not just an 'Oh, me mate said it was alright if we used his ground' verbal one. The ground needed to be of sufficient grading not just a croft with dead cats - which, admittedly, you don't see as many dead cats these days - and burnt out bommy circles. We had to watch out about being tied into a lease for more than 12 months - Stalybridge had an issue around this. We also needed to be big boys and consider things like the share of revenue for match day catering/bar stuff. An anathema to Reds who were walking away from rampant commercialism but it would also be divvy to give what is ours away to someone who is not us. You can be dim and irresponsible but not at other Reds' expense. That revenue would form part of our soon to be formed business plan. Some Reds on the Steering Committee had those business plan forming skills. It's as if we weren't just thrown together - as it felt - it was as if there was some planning somewhere. Although looking at the state of us it looked hard to argue that.

The thick plottens...

It wasn't as if the Steering Committee was just looking at football grounds either, as Sale Rugby Club had not been ruled out at this point. If we were to go there then it had to be a long enough pitch as rugby, as well as handballing it, also cheats by using diddier pitches than football. Sale's pitch wasn't long enough in the end, or it might have been not wide enough, or both, and there was also something about the rugby posts being embedded in 90 foot of concrete or something. I also think the good residents of Sale are alright with rugby fans but football fans have a tendency to smell. As well as finding a ground we also needed to be affiliated with the Manchester FA. This was an obviously vital necessity for any approval we were seeking. We needed to submit information about the structure of the club to them. Basically, it was necessary to allocate titles to Steering Committee members other than 'Cunty bollocks' or 'Cut your eyebrows you could get a good picture on Channel M with some of those sticky out ones' to impress bodies we needed to impress.

The FA needed to know details of the club's limited status without us just writing back 'Yes, we are very limited'. It was laboriously pointed out that there is an issue of liability with a members' club that can be circumvented by writing into the constitution, that the club will not borrow money without the approval of 85% of members. I'm sure that's true, if I only knew what you were talking about. Also, you could only do that 'writing in' to your constitution, if you actually had a constitution to write in. We didn't. Dave Boyle from Supporters Direct was invaluable in wrangling the unwrangleable from the constipation of our constitutional crisis. AFC Wimbledon's existence was also fundamental to us. They helped and cajoled and helped again in these very early times as they so often did with a 'Crowd at Plough Lane when United were there' amount of other things. Their help in these hours cannot be underestimated. They'd roll up information inside a Mitre 5 and then they'd get one of their longstanding fans, who remembered their old style of play, and they would hoof it north. They'd get long ball nostalgia and we'd get fresh and innovative fan based, fan-owning information.

We also couldn't write in our non-existent constitution as we didn't even have an acceptable name. There was an issue of the new club's temporary name of 'FC United'. The name would not be acceptable to the FA or the league due to its lack of geographical identity. We all agreed. Except those that didn't. Whenever anyone says 'United' they always mean Manchester United. Other 'United' named clubs might disagree but however much they do, Manchester United have boxed off the 'United' name. Now with the breakaway club, the political affinity with having 'FC' prominently displayed in our fight back was crucial, as it had come to represent so much. It was like a mini United. No matter how many clubs have 'FC' in their name, in the summer of 2005 saying 'FC' was instantly recognisable as belonging to those who had walked. In our looking for a new name we were becoming powerful of brand. Goodness me.

Don't put your shovel where there's no shit...

The league did not appear to need convincing, or indeed be interested, in the amount of numbers we could gather. That was a shame really as that was one of the artilleries we were going to really impress them with. We hoped we could disguise our other inadequacies behind it. They were far keener on securing a monetary bond that would be used to guarantee our participation for a whole season. Ahh, the romanticism of the lower leagues where football is played for the love of it. If you have a big enough bond. The league was not as yet explicit on the exact size of the bond, but they did mention the precedent of Barrow, who forked out a bag when they joined. I think we paid four bags in the end, I'm not sure, but with the openness of our accounts it would be easy to find out. We knew we had the money due to the generous pledges of the founding members of the new club so we weren't that worried. We just needed a league.

In those chaotic weeks it was a proper daft balance between accepting pledges from those who wanted to give and help, but mixed with the knowledge that the people we needed to convince weren't bothered about our numbers. We needed to keep pledges and offers of help coming in as Reds wanted to help and were desperate to do so. Their enthusiasm would keep us alive. Unfortunately the effective administering of that help would tie up so many, when the blade needed to be pointed elsewhere. I suppose it was emblematic of being Mancunian: We ask for help and, when it comes in its thousands, we moan that it is coming in its thousands. If it didn't come in thousands then we would moan that it wasn't coming in its thousands.

Not a pot to piss in or a patio door to throw it out of...

We had come through Red months of deep, free debate with sincerity and truthfulness being the datum mark for getting us through it. Unfortunately we now had to fib a little. It was very disturbing. It wasn't as bad a fibbing as this lying lad from Clayton who we know, who shall remain unnamed to protect his family, who lied. A lot. Amongst his fibs he had told us, and he was a bloke not a child, was that he had eaten a doughnut, then vomited it up, and it had gone back into its original doughnut shape when it had come out. That his dog had three eyes, even though we could clearly see his two-eyed dog, as it passed behind him on the street. And that he once had fallen asleep on the Rochdale Canal in a canoe and, after making us guess where he had woken up, he had told us "France." Our fibs weren't that bad. If fibs can be honourable then the one we were about to tell came close. We had to convince the league that we were serious about joining them. Of course we were serious.

However, their measure of 'serious' was that we wanted to exist forever. We could not go up to them and tell them we didn't know yet. That the future of this new club we were forming would be decided by its members. We might be looked back on as changing football or we might be minuscule. When Glazer corks it, or is forced out, then our members will decide. Unfortunately, at present, we couldn't tell them that. For the present we needed to utilise the North West Counties League's already existing system to keep a considerable amount of match going Reds, match going. It would not be too strong a word to use and say that we lied. If they wanted us to say that the NWCL was the girl we wanted to settle down with, and not just finger for a few minutes, then they heard that. We all had buckets of water nearby in case our under garments caught ablaze. We also had a few tins of wood preservative ready if any of our noses turned to timber and started growing.

Red sails in the sunset...

If we got league status then it would all be Harry Worth it. Vasco Wackrill, a Steering Committee member, did something in those early first few days that in any other circumstances would be unforgivable. He will argue he did it to take our minds off matters. Vasco callously, with intent and malice utmost in his mind, approached his computer, sat down, tickled his turned up nose, ate his Sunblest crust to keep his hair even curlier ... and sent the National Ground Grading Document to everyone on the email list. Choose death rather than ever read this. It could also be argued that since we didn't have a ground, didn't have a team, didn't have a Manager, didn't have a kit, didn't have a badge, didn't have a league, didn't have any fans that weren't electrical, that we should all get together. The formation of a new club deemed it crucial that we all meet to discuss those little technicalities that we were missing. It had to be this season. Next year would be too late. However, the real reason we all physically met for the first time as a Steering Committee was to kick fuck out of Vas for sending that National Ground Grading document. We were going to meet on Monday the 6th of June 2005, upstairs at The Seven Oaks in town.

The poverty of theory...

Me and my Gailly used to have a theory of the 'Three Ps' when it came to wine choosing. We'd always drank beer but being lazy in the house we decided that going for pint after pint from the home brew barrel was hard work. If you had a bottle of wine it condensed the alcohol into a tight pack, thereby aiding settee'ing by reducing pissing visits and promoting comfyness. I heard Paddy Crerand at an IMUSA meeting once say that he only ever drank wine from being young, even in Georgie's company. No wonder he was a hard get as ordering wine in Manchester in the 1960s must have called for bravery. The tougher pubs he went in must have had only a close approximation to what wine was ie you ask for wine and you get a barley wine, a dirty look or 20 Senior Service. Along with this was the beer drinking clientele of the '60s who thought that washing your hair with anything but soap was gay. Even though the soap they used was usually a loaf sized, green block called Fairy.

Our 'Three P theory' on wine was brought about through lack of knowledge of what wine was. We didn't know much about it; we just knew we liked it.

So we had to devise our own skills to get us to where we wanted to go. The first 'P' of the 'Three P theory' was price. You're faced with shelves and shelves of wine. Where do you start? You start with the first 'P' of price and don't pay more than three quid. It was the '90s so I suppose you could push that up to four now. The second 'P' of the 'Three P theory' was percentage. Anything less than 12 percent was not worth the elbow injuries encumbered around uncorking. If you had found your wine, and it fitted the first two P's of the 'Three P theory' of price and percentage, but there was more than one wine that hit the first two P's, then the third 'P' of the 'Three P theory' came to the fore. The third 'P' of the 'Three P theory' was picture. If you had a rake of bottles, all three pound, all 12 percent or more, then obv you would go for the stronger percent one. However, if you found that, even using this method, you had different wines that tied - then you would decide by the power of the third 'P' and choose the one with the nicest picture on the front. Obviously this was very subjective but all art is subjective, but you still have to fund the arts and this was our way of doing so.

Love is the tender trap…

Unluckily, no one on the Steering Committee had an 'O' level in club formation. We had to split the single cell of where we were now and burgeon. Top swot scientists recognise the ideal, life giving conditions, of bacteria and hot springs. They acknowledge the random forces that have shaped the geography of the world. Now it was time for us to do so. We had to break out from being a presumptuous cadre and build like a bugger. Our 'Let's get a Steering Committee theory' on how to firebomb the formation of a club was brought about by a lack of knowledge of what football club forming was. So we had to devise our own skills to get us to where we wanted to go. We didn't know much about football; we just knew we liked it. We didn't know much about a fan owning football club; we just knew we'd like it. We were not just faced with a shelf full of wine that might all be the same or might all be different. We were faced by a warehouse full. It felt like a world full. If we were going to do anything then we had to bind tightly.

There was no one, single Eric amongst us coming on in the second half of the main road derby when we were 2-0 down at half time to orchestrate a 2-3 victory. Our strengths, if we had any, were in numbers and support and graft and organisation. We wouldn't have been a pleasant side to watch. Or would we? We were trying to play football the way it was meant to be played. We just weren't that accomplished at it but we pushed forward when we could. Smiling when possible and trying to involve.

We want our sun drenched, windswept, Ingrid Bergman kiss…

The Steering Committee met for the first time on the 6th of June 2005 at The Seven Oaks pub in town. It was never a beer house I was enamoured with thus its nickname of 'The 11 jokes' because you never seem to find anyone joking in there. We had the following, alarmingly humourless, agenda:

1) Ground.
2) Affiliation with FA
3) Name of club
4) Situation re: pledges
5) Initial roles within the club of the steering group/ structure of club
6) Membership structure/voting issues
7) Constitution
8) Staff situation
9) AOB

I felt confident with point number 7 as I had always had quite a good constitution. I've only ever been sick three times on beer and one of them was when, on reaching my sixth pint on my 20th birthday, I decided to have a vodka for every year of my life so far. I vaguely remember that one of my legs belonged to Shakin' Stevens, and the other to Max Wall. I've also never had a hang over which can make you a bit unpopular. I wake up still drunk if I don't get enough sleep but if I get seven or eight hours, I'll just get up and play the trombone and eat fried food. I can't play the trombone but if there was one at the side of my bed then I could. This is not a hint for what to get me for Christmas. However, point 7 was not about how good we were at alcohol recovery, so my strongest contribution to the discussion had been taken away. Unless I got it in AOB.

Not knowing me, not knowing you…

We sat around a big table. Luc Zentar, by virtue of having a pen that worked and a proper notepad instead of an empty utilities envelope to write on, was elected Chair. I sat next to a wheezing bloke who had a gas canister at the side of him. Internally I tutted, as the first ever Steering Committee was no place for him to be bringing a gas canister, so that he could occasionally let some out and get a caravan smell. He wheezed away and I thought: this inappropriate fckr has come here with his caravan gas canister but is cracking on daft for some sort of ex-miners, can't-breathe-properly-me, compensation scam. Eventually I got used to him as if you listened carefully, he involuntarily wheezed a diverse medley of popular chart music. He didn't mean to, it was just that he had a spazmattron chest that wheezed erratically. He was stronger with 'There's an old mill by the stream, Nellie Dean' than he was with 'The bump' by Kenny as I thought he lost the mood of the record on that one. His 'Tiger feet' by Mud was passable but his 'On top of the world' by The Carpenters was the one he played the crowd with. I had just met Russell Delaney for the first time.

Mike Adams was introduced to the meeting along with a 'Carphone warehouse' voiced Irish man called Phil Sheeran. They had not been on the circular email list as yet but they were seen as important to any future dealings by other activists. I had no issues with anyone inviting anyone, as Martin Morris was sat at the side of me for no other reason than he owed me money and I wanted to keep an eye on his whereabouts. As had been said many times before - we can make no apologies for being self-elected at this period, as we had to first get together. I had seen Mike's mush many times at games over the years but that 'I've got enough friends why do I need anymore?' ignorance prevented me from ever saying hello. Mike really has got one of those faces where you say: “I know his kite” or “You'll know him if you saw his face” sort of a face.

Phil Sheeran looks as if he should have a permanent, big knit, multi-coloured scarf casually thrown around his neck that falls casually off the shoulder, so you would never, ever want to let on to him at games. He had a tight fitting, tan leather jacket with him. Even in Ireland that can't be acceptable. It was obvious he plays the women with the 'Come and mother me, aww, will you just put that pie in the oven for me whilst you're up? Will you wash the pots while you're there? Oops I'm from an island far, far away and me knob's fallen out - will you touch it?' card when courting and it almost certainly works.

The wheezing fella at the side of me decided he'd had enough of wheezing out 'Oh the crystal chandelier lights up the paintings on your wall' and contributed to the meeting. He was a fucking cockney. I am one ignorant Mancunian bigot bastard. It was a Monday night, in town, no one minds them at the game but what is he doing here on a Monday? You have to remember that around the time of Russell's first ever contribution, at the first ever Steering Committee meeting, I had not got used to the 'Name that tune' entertainment of his wheezing and just found it annoying. Consequently, when he first contributed, he just went on and on and, being the sometimes bigot that I am, I just stopped listening after a bit. I sat there unthinkingly thinking 'Cockneys always live up to the loud-at-the-poolside-on-holiday cliché, of dominating conversations with their listen-to-me opinions. And wearing big, bright shorts'.

The cavalry twilled trousered philanthropist...

Except Russell wasn't wearing Bermuda shorts. It would have been funny if he was as there wasn't a pick on him. He certainly wasn't overloud. He was going on at length about FA regulations, ground regulations, grounds, players' registrations, necessary insurances and what seemed like a million or more minute matters. But only minute in the way that a billion stars appear minute within the vastness of your looking up. My mind had wondered off as my Mam had always accused it of, but Russell Delaney's adept way of tying a whole raft of niggling, annoying issues together in a tidy, eventually succinct, bundle was playing itself out in front of my eyes and ears for the first time. The reason Russell had to go on so long was because he had done so much. None of us knew what was going to happen. Anything almost could. Russell Delaney had got out the wooden easel, he had stretched the bare canvas across it and he was beginning to daub with primary, glooping, vivid oils, all the eventualities. We could catch the splashes if we wanted to.

There was unkempt slashes that scared you, there was still calm outlines, there was scribbling overs, there was annihilating overs, there was a bringing back of those things that had been covered only seconds earlier. There was a big achievable background, there was a rushed and hurried foreground, but he'd painted a bow around them all that we could loosen or fix. There was structure and pace and serenity mixed with order and unruliness and mayhem. A lot of people go off at a tangent and lose you, we all do. Russell would go off at a tangent but it wasn't a tangent. He would be saying: "Well this might happen in this situation, if it does then we can do this, if it doesn't, then we can do that or this. If that then happens then we can do that. If this happens then we can do this." Because things were hurtling along we did not know where we all were. Real, graspable things had become nebulous. If someone had asked at that first meeting if we were all sure that we were sat on a chair, then I would have had to look down at my chocolate button to check. There would have been a few of us doing it. We could now look up from looking down at our arses and look at the easel. Russell's influence had arrived. We have a chance at being alright. The cockney bastard.

Over the coming months we would thank Russell for all his efforts by meeting at venues that could only be arrived at by stairs. The man had a chronic chest complaint, that required a permanent oxygen tank to be carried around with him, and that's how we repaid our debt. We should have just met on the top floor of the CIS and told him the lift was broke. He'd have still done it, the awkward get. It was always my honour to carry his oxygen tank upstairs to any meeting or back down to his dilapidated, crumpled car but only when you could cop him doing it, as he would never ask.

Grounds for divorce...

There did not seem to be a ground in Greater Manchester that we had not contacted about ground sharing. Not wanting to cause any lumber, or get sued in the small non - league shircles we now operate in, but there was a reason most got binned. I argued at the first Steering Committee that there were only two grounds within Manchester's border as far as I could see. The mini boo camp at the side of the dustbowl at Johnson's Wireworks and Abbey Hey FC's little ground. Abbey Hey's ground could just about hold a thousand. I had fallen well down from my goony days of writing in Red Issue that with 34,000 Shareholders United members then it would be possible, with the right amount of leadership, to walk with 10,000 Reds. I would now have been made up with four or five hundred. Therefore, I argued that we should go to Abbey Hey.

I'd had conversations with Tony McCallister, who was involved heavily with the workings of Abbey Hey FC. He is a season ticket holding Red and was more than helpful in anything I had ever asked of him about knocking a club together. The lad has spent such a large part of his life working at the lower end of the leagues. When I first told him we were going to form a club I felt a bit of a get as he told me instantly that we could do it, and we would be successful. That meant a lot then as we were faced by much conservatism from the lower league establishment. Conservatism of the 'Don't be so stupid, don't you realise what it takes to form a club?' variety. Abbey Hey's ground used to have old seats that had come from the Stretford End. However, they'd been burnt, as the ground is easily accessed and easily vandalised. I'm sure if the seats had advertised widely that they had come from the Stretford End they would have been safe from destruction.

The first Steering Committee meeting was in a whooping and a hollering mood and I got a shoe'ing for my unlarge thinking. I argued back with Irish history. I told them I was getting that it is 1916. It's Easter time. I'm in Dublin. I'm in a Post Office. Call them and they won't come. Who was going to volunteer to be James Connolly and get strapped to the chair? I was beaten back with tales of the couple of thousand pledges that were electronically plugging themselves into our new club circuits. If anything could be volunteered for, then the electrical volunteers were volunteering for it. The goodwill was spellbinding. It would appear that the volunteers would volunteer to be strapped to any chair to be shot for what they thought was right. If we were to be representative of that force then we had to earn it. We were going to go for something bigger than Abbey Hey's ground. That's if Abbey Hey would have been good enough to have us.

Stop whacking off in my tool shed...

The ground options were one-two'd about. Stalybridge was too awkward to get to but we'll keep in contact. Leigh RMI would have finished up 'Leigh MRI' as it was moon shuttle distance, and it would have hospitalised our supporters to get there regularly, but we'll keep in contact. Other grounds, that would have required our fans to get in that bulk carrying, green coloured Thunderbird craft to get there, were also discounted for their distance. Other smaller clubs fell the same way as Abbey Hey's ground, in that they would be too small.

Droylsden came very close at one stage but it was something like, they couldn't have a ground share agreement under the terms of their lease with the council that finally saw that drown. That's the story I'm sticking to anyway. It came out in the press that we were going there and all the Steering Committee knew that we weren't. We had nothing to gain by denying it, when we still didn't have a ground to go to. So if the press thought they were being clever by outing our destination then we let them cling to it whilst we furrowed away. Droylsden held about four thousand, with the talk in the summer of 2005 of upping it to six. I don't know if those improvements went ahead as planned but if they hadn't, we would have come very close to capacity on many occasions with at least a couple of lock outs.

The new ground in Ashton, that we would later beat Cheadle Town 5-1 in the cup in October 2005, was also an option. We were of the opinion that Tameside council were pretending to not want us, to improve their hand in negotiations but really they were desperate to fill their new venture. We always knew we had them to fall back on so any cheeky getness on their part was always forgiven, as we were juggling. If things got desperate then we could always bail in there. I didn't mind that ground really. It was a bit out of the way but it had good motorway links and the buses up Ashton Old Road are frequent enough.

The covered side would have generated a good atmosphere and it had a few seats for those nearing death. I am biased, though, as it is very handy for the east Manchester Reds. It was a bit short of beer houses nearby. Having said that the pub where the future Tameside branch organised for that cup game was a good one. There was also a little social club right by the ground that looked a treat with its selection of turns for Friday and Saturday nights. However, with the ground being brand new it did have that feeling of 'Ikea' no tradition, flat packness and nobody wants to have a screw left over, bin it, then have the end fall off. Added to that Ashton town centre has got the 'Wild West in polyester' about it. There is a reason that on one side of the small section of the snipe that divides us, we talk like Mancunians and on the other side they go a bit funny like in the gob department and turn Lancashire'ish. They like being on one side of the snipe, we like being on the other.

Give me your tired, your poor, your huddled masses yearning to breathe free, the wretched refuse of your teeming shore. Send these, the homeless, tempest-tossed, to me...

Andy 'Juan La Janet Street Porta' Walsh turned up late to the meeting as his industrial neck hair had grown around, and over, his Joe 90 glasses and he missed. Adam Brown had a copy of 'Whopping Great Big Gazonkas' concealed within his brief case as he had just come straight from the University. He claims he only buys it because it smells of the programme. Jules Spencer and Phil Bedford smoked. Tony Jordan wore a cravat. With a matching muffler. Vas Wackrill denied his full name was 'Vaseline' once again. Martin Morris tapped me for another tenner. Pete Munday said: "Stick it in your family album" and "My business plans a dustman, it wears a dustman's hat" and thought this would impress us. Andrew Howse said that that the Latin for 'albino' was 'Albania.' Tony Pritchard, a Red with a high level of commercial and company management, looked on us with disdain. We were all he had to work with. We were fucked. Luckily enough, we weren't important. As the last line on the first ever FC United leaflet said: 'In the meantime, FC United will exist for disenfranchised Manchester United supporters as long as there are disenfranchised Manchester United supporters in existence.' That was you, you tempest tossers.

Comedically named and shamed...

In the first week after the meeting at the Apollo, the unconventionally-named-outside-of-Portugal, National Ground Grading Document sending, Vasco Wackrill got together our first email list of supporters. These were Reds who had gone online and expressed a support, be that moral, financial, physical or sexual. Some of those Reds might be reading this now. Some might have dropped out for whatever valid or invalid reasons. There were 437 names on that first ever list. I know that because I counted them by hand, as I kept the print out from the email. There were 55 names on the first page, six pages with 56 names on and 46 on the last page.

Counting all the names on that list might, at first, appear to be a tedious task. Not if you are looking for funny names.

Top of the list for no real reason as far as I'm aware was Andrew Tester. Not really a funny name to start with Andrew, you let us down there lad. Although, the coming months were going to be a tester. Last name on that first ever list was John Berry. Again not a funny name John, but I suppose it was a dyslexic spelling of where we were going to finish up playing our home games. So I suppose we'll just about let those two names sandwich all the other names in for their portentousnessyness. Of the other 435 names on the list this is how they appeared page by page, but picked out for their unusual nameness. First page: Mark Rampling: Not that funny a name but we expected a slow start and you would with their Charlotte. Jamie Fake: Not sure, could have Cadbury's fake if pushed. Mark Baldwin: Close enough to being called Mike to get my attention. Martin From: His ear to eternity. Martin Greenup: North.

Stop arxing about...

Page two saw Lee Duddridge: 'Dudds' and a 'ridge' all in the same name. Ryan Butt may have been funnier pre-1992/3. Brendan Brennan presumably from Brentford was there. Kurt von Arx could have done so much better if that 'x' was an 's'. Steve Cummaford would not get past the decency censor on the email at Manchester Council, so I presume he doesn't work there, but if he did, no one would know as he couldn't email anyone. He could live in Chorlton-cum-Hardy though. Connor Murphy and Darragh Duffy only went on the list because Brendan Brennan was on it. Lee Swettenham: Ham that's sweaty. If Lee Swettenham had a gay marriage with Lee Duddridge they could be the Swettenham-Duddridges. Page three saw Dean Birtwhistle and Jake Folkherd-Hobbs squeeze on before Christoph von Arx: Hold it that's the second Arx on here.

Nuno Pinto drove us off page three onto page four by having two names that are both cars. Page four was quite dull and only gets Nick Duckett to represent the page as there was no one else there. Page five was much the same if it wasn't for the outstanding Rick Awdas: Dick Oddarse to his family and friends. Page six had a Joe Royle and a Robert Reckless but cummafording after Dick Oddarse they were always going to suffer. The same comparisons hindered page seven's Ron Snellen and Peter Clack's progress. The matter was made worse for these two as they surrounded a Kevin Hunt in the list: K.Hunt. We limped onto page eight to find Geir Finstad Gotvassli which we have all said when pissed. We by-passed Samantha Hood hoping that her middle name was 'Clitoral' and finished with Arfyn Ruhonah and Mahbub Alom, who were at the side of each other on the list, and only go to prove that people just make names up.

Loneliness of a long distance runner bean...

Perhaps we had no real funny names due to the seriousness of the situation. No name is going to be slow-burningly-funnier than 'Adam Dunne' anyway. Unfunny named or not, these were some of the 437 Reds at the beginning, on that first ever list. Vas might still have it. If not, I have a copy. You could never disgrace yourself. You're part of the way things are going to be. And when they are, you'll have been pivotal. Proud of you. The future has a chance of being yours, go and write the present. Give me the youth not the tired old men of 30. We've not got 'Green bean love' in that we don't have to eat it quick before it goes cold. We can take our time as we did with all our Steering Committee meetings. And we did take our time. That first meeting at The Seven Oaks on the 6th of June 2005 ended, as every future Steering Committee meeting would end, with us being escorted from the premises by weary bar staff, with our hair resembling a bear's couch and our eyes Marty Feldman'd.

Move the pencil and write my heart...

It felt like most of June 2005 was spent in The Town Hall Tavern pub. I didn't mind it there as Ernest Jones, a leading character from The Chartists movement, used to have his offices on Bow Lane, which runs at the back of the pub. It meant something nice had happened here before. We'd meet at least 69 times a week. In there, various members of the Steering Committee would report back on what they had done in the intervening few moments since the last meeting. Sometimes the room beamed bright with a 'Rob McCaffery's whiteness of teeth' just-brushed-brilliance, as if the chirrupy, football broadcaster himself had pulled up in his car on the road outside the pub, and his luminous installations had shone an approving light all over us through the pub window. Sometimes we dulled each other to near death. Some ideas were so excruciating that you wanted to beat the executor of it to death, dig a big hole for them, put them in it, refill the hole, come back a few weeks later, dig them up, put them on the side of the hole and then batter them again. But not before you had rung the local branch of the Necrophilia Society to inform them of the body's whereabouts.

There were so many rhubarb ideas that it would not be nice of us to pick one out. Picking one out would mean that the worst idea we ever had as a Steering Committee would be forever down in print. No one would want that. That's just terrible. So I won't. Oh, go on then: We nearly had a scouse manager: Who was a borderline dwarf. Apparently he was very accomplished and a very nice man. If somewhat not as large as other people. And somewhat Liverpudlian. He guaranteed us that he would get us promotion in our first season. At the NWCL there are enough good players to fill the side from Greater Manchester. Only at the higher Unibond and above level do you start getting players from further away. I was told this numerous times by existing activists within the NWCL.

At NWCL level, bringing players in from further away resulted in expenses being paid and resentment in the dressing room. This is what I was being told by experienced NWCL workers. We didn't know any different at the time. A successful scouse manager would want to bring in players that he has worked with. They will have been subject to the unwritten NWCL 'local' rule and would therefore be overwhelmingly scouse. Therefore, the scouse manager would bring scouse backroom staff and scouse players. No one would expect him to instantly produce a team, without that team consisting of players he knew well. The Steering Committee listened as the three members of it, who had met the prospective Liverpudlian manager, argued for his appointment. They said, of course him being scouse and hot-wash-shrunk made him two-nil down before they met him. However, his experience, his record and the quality players he assured us he had the influence to get, made it a three-two victory. They understood our reluctance but please trust them. He was the man for us.

To each according to their needs and from each according to their ability...

There was another candidate. An Ancoats Red who was untried in management. He was only 34. He was normal sized. His name kept coming back to us from very trusted sources, but he was an unproven risk. A Steering Committee member, who was absolutely vital to the existence of this club, spoke on the matter. You cannot over emphasise this Red's calming influence. The way he would lay back and watch as we went on. Most of us couldn't even spoke proper England. He'd let you all finish, then he would clay together the ten-million-tentacled ramblings, into chewable chunks. He got the ingredients out of the air of the meetings, he put them together, and then he made them very edible. It's all about the presentation. And the taste. It was all served on a silver service tray for you. It is not a surprise this Steering Committee member makes his living in food.

However, on this occasion he gave us an off egg, with that blood in the yoke that could be the hint of a tiny foot or arm of a chicklet. He had put it on a stale muffin, dipped in cold gravy browning that had been made with vinegar. And not that nice chippy vinegar but that sharper, stronger wiffing, stuff. And then it was served to us on creased, empty bread wrapper, grease-proof paper. He said: "Karl Marginson. I've met him. He's a great lad, a great prospect but he's not for us. I've got this feeling his arse would go if we lost three or four games on the bounce." With a Mancunian grief in his voice, he reluctantly recommended the scouse manager. So did the two other Steering Committee members who had met him. You had to trust these three. Within a Steering Committee you have designated roles. You are sent off to achieve and then report back. Like Lassie with less fur. We were working piece-work. We had to trust. These were very trustworthy Reds.

There was silence in the meeting. Then fire. Within this room there were sussed Reds who knew that we had far more in common with sussed Liverpudlians than many of the thumb rings who do nothing but take from the game. However awkward it is to say, the two cities are very much the same. The lads from Everton's 'When skies are grey' fanzine are worth meeting, outside of the day we play them. The Liverpool Echo in 1999 contained an advert from the Evertonian fruit and veg barrow boys, congratulating us on our historic treble. There had been an article for Reds to send money to the striking Liverpool dockers within the pages of the UWS fanzine. My Dad got on well with Eric Heffer, the old Liverpool labour MP, back when he was a joiner on the tools and not an eventual collaborator. I even crossed the apartheid that exists between the cities by loving my Gailly for so many years.

A betrayal of two cities...

This room was full of Reds who could see over the football divide and into the social, economic and political reality. The three lads who had visited the prospective Liverpudlian manager, had done what so many had done before: When good stock from the two cities meet, we realise the enemy is elsewhere. Except on match days. Unfortunately, forming a football club was going to have lots of match days. We could not just be leaving a season with Manchester United where the song was sung to the backwards of "You're just a team full of scousers" due to them having Fowler and McManamanamanaman in their side. And then appoint a scouser as manager. With a scouse backroom staff. And overwhelmingly scouse players. It could have been argued that it was very brave. That we were taking on ancient inter-city bigotry and pointing to the actual enemy elsewhere. A fresh club, a fresh start. Unfortunately football is not like that, it would have killed us before we had put on any liniment.

You SCART bastard...

In Matt and Phreds after the 'scouse manager' Steering Committee meeting, I was in rounds with Andy Walsh and Martin Morris. I said we had so much else to do and argue for without saggling ourselves with a rogue incendiary device that didn't need to be there. We were in the process of creating a beautiful young vision. We were asking Reds to come across to try to love her. If the most beautiful woman had walked through the door and into Matt and Phreds I'm sure we would have all taken a sneaky peak mid-conversation. However, if that beautiful woman had a big cold sore on her lip then that is how we would have defined her. That woman could have been beautiful both inside and out. That little cold sore affliction wouldn't have changed that but on first meeting, that's all you would see. Fit or not we would have been waiting for that cold sore scab to come off and float on the top of her drink. Cruel, but that's the way at prez it goes. We were asking Reds to come across to a beautiful vision. We were giving it a flapping lip with a crust.

Art begins with the slightest of touches...

The 34-year-old Ancoats Red, who was untried and whose manhole cover might leak in a crisis, re-entered the betting. We could not sling accusations of untried at anyone. Like we were tried club formers. Joz Mitten, our soon to be centre forward who would drop down from Conference level to join us, rang Karl Marginson. It would be great here to say that 'Margy', as he would come to be known, was having an all-over-wash in the sink or was training Saint Bernard's to do inner city rum rescues or was doing voluntary services overseas, helping blind children in Africa to improve at kerby or was taking malt loaves to the starving in Darfur. The reality is that when Joz rang him he was playing golf on Flixton golf course with Steve Tobin, a fellow Flixton FC player.

Margy was, and still is, a fruit and veg deliveryman to the elderly. He used to be a winger for such notaries as Rotherham and Macclesfield. Our knowledge of non-league players could be written on the back of an Alpine-home-delivery-American-cream-soda-mineral bottle lid with a pasting brush. His knowledge couldn't be stenographed across the surface of the Isle of Man without using the dance floors on the ferries as extra writing space. He also got, immediately, what this new club wanted to be about. He got it because that was what he wanted for his children, and the youngsters of east central Manchester Ancoats where he came from, who could not now afford to go to Old Trafford regularly. Weeks later he was announced as our manager to the waiting press on June the 22nd 2005 at the Midland Hotel.

The Midland Hotel used to have Albert Tatlock from Coronation Street living there full time before he died. Royce met Rolls there and they went on to profit from car workers' labours by producing a petrol swallower for the rich and shallow. The hotel now has little Olympic flame type holders all around it that are lit, and bare flame away into the open air. This at first appears as if it is an immoral waste of energy resources like the Rolls Royce. The hotel has changed though. Those little cradles of flames that surround the hotel are lit so that the homeless of Manchester can go and do baked potatoes in them if they want. This time, though, when we, the football homeless, wanted a press conference, we entered inside its decadent, high ceiling'd extravagance; we weren't staying outside, alfresco cooking starch. We were storming Manchester's Winter Palace. We built it, we should be in it. Someone else will have to pay for the beer or rag the till, though, as it is fckn scandalously priced.

Manchester in bloom...

Me, my Dad and Tommy the carrier built the dressing rooms in Granada Studios for the actors on Coronation Street in the early '80s. We used to go in the staff canteen for our brew. We were mortared up but we stayed quiet in the corner, harmless and polite. The cast stayed at the other end of the canteen and were very nice. We could go: "That Elsie Tanner doesn't half cane the panstick" and they could look back at us and feel contact with a less pampered life and appreciate their escape from it. After a week or so Albert Tatlock came on set after being away. Immediately he complained to the canteen management, not to our face the tory twat, that we had no right to be there. We were forced to leave and have our brew around cement bags for the rest of the job. We were building his forthcoming, dressing room luxury and he had no grace. He would hate us announcing our new club's democratic existence within his last home of the Midland Hotel. We're in the process of writing our own soap story where those dirty of neck are getting their tidemarks removed. We're leaving our residue on the plated taps and ornamental washbasins of the idle and the indolent.

When Margy first entered that Steering Committee meeting to be introduced to us all in The Town Hall Tavern pub and also on his date with the media on the 22nd of June, his back door was coming off its hinges. They were the only two occasions that was going to happen to him in the coming season, outside of having an iffy curry from the Curry Club we were going to set up in the ground to feed supporters. Many months later Margy told me he was made up to be entering the Steering Committee interview room where people talked proper. It made him less scared to be amongst his own and he flourished. Later, after saying “basically” a dozen times in his first interview with the media, he carried on that Manchester bloom. At the Stalybridge Celtic friendly a month or two later, one of the proposers of the scouse manager sat at the side of me in the pub after the game. We watched as Margy handled the drunken Reds in there with time and courtesy. The scouse manager proposer said to me: "I'm so glad I argued for Margy as manager." I smiled to myself. That's how quickly Karl Marginson won us over. He brought Phil Power, an ex-Macclesfield player as Assistant Manager and Daz Lyons as future Player Coach

Badge'r de-baiting...

Of all the other arguments at Steering Committee meetings one of the most vitriolic was the argument for the design of the club badge. Tony Jordan worked endlessly on kit design and sieving through badge designs. Forcing a straight man to go on about fabric and co-ordinated colour schemes was just too tempting. The red, white and black home kit we have now sort of chose itself, as it is a very good one and stood out. There were some fantastic badge designs; however, the one we have now wasn't always the favourite. It seems to have gone down in FC United of Manchester folklore that we always wanted the Manchester coat of arms on our badge. This wasn't always the majority view. It was in the end but it took some arguing. We all eventually agreed the final badge should come from some sort of amalgam of the coats of arms with the three stripes for our three rivers, the boat, perhaps a few bees and a phoenix. Just as an aside. It always surprises me that the backwards, with their three stars on their shirts, rather than say they stand for nothing, haven't said they stand for the Manchester's three rivers. I'm sure they will. Laugh at them when they do.

All contributors’ attempts at Phoenix's looked like Orville. We were told we might struggle with the bees as Boddington's had trademarked them. United had trademarked the red devil in all its forms and the brewery that was pulling out of Manchester making Mancunians redundant - including Gordon Derward, a Beswick Red and future FC United of Manchester member - had done it to the bees. There you are, I've just sat you down and told you a 'birds and the bees' story. I wanted a train incorporated somewhere to show our origins and our present day preferred form of transport, but I was on my own so I shut up. At one stage some were so sure of the success of one of the entrants that it was always referred to by them as the new club badge. I thought it looked like a Bacardi advert.

The Steering Committee tried to be as efficient as people in a hot summer room can be when whittling down the finalists to be eventually voted on by the entire membership. It was all very subjective but we had to do something. We couldn't put every single contributor out to be voted on, as some were so embarrassing. Actually, that would have been a good reason to put them all on a website. We put the printed versions of the various designs on the upstairs bar and praised or ripped them accordingly. The present club badge only got to the final stage due to the persistence of Luc Zentar, Martin Morris, Adam Brown and the bloke who failed with the train option. It very nearly didn't make it. Many thought it a bit too plain, with not enough subtlety. It's a badge not a scone.

Copyright, right, right...

The club's name 'FC United of Manchester' won the democratic members vote by a distance so great that it rivalled the distance of an unrolled roll of free school dinner tickets at a Clayton primary school. It beat AFC Manchester 1878, FC Manchester Central and the ridiculously poor Newton Heath United. Howsey had done a lot of the work on trademarking. The lad went from knowing only about skidmarking to being a bit of a boffin on trademarking due to the graft he put in. It took awhile but eventually we were refused our prospective name and prospective badge by the Patent Office. They argued that it was too close to four earlier registered trademarks by United and that our recent applications were likely to be confused with them. There is a story in here about our ongoing application being delayed even more, as it was stuck in a Post Office due to it being 5p short on its postage, but I don't want to frighten you further with our inefficiency. The only way around it was if United agreed to let us have them both. Apparently if we wrote to them they could say they weren't bothered and we could proceed or they could refuse us. We always knew that if we challenged United for the name that there would be a lot of press interest for the underdog. We were prepared to take them on. So was our membership. We will never know the discussions that went on within the confines of Old Trafford. We received this email back from them on the 28th of August 2005.

> Dear Tony,
>
> I refer to your email dated 12 August 2005 which David Gill forwarded to me as I am responsible for the protection of our intellectual property rights.
>
> I have had a look at your badge on the website fcunited.co.uk. I confirm that we have no objection to the badge nor do we have any objection to you registering the mark "Football Club United of Manchester".

Kinds regards,

David P Beswitherick

Director of Group Services & Company Secretary

So the badge and name debate finally came to a close on the 28th of August 2005. That was obviously very late to have our trademark confirmed but the metabolism of legalities is a slow, meandering one. Combine that with our gormlessness and the 28th was a miracle worthy of pilgrims putting candles around it. It got there in the end. I remember Beswitherick having a moustache on the top table at the last Manchester United AGM. His name also contains 'Beswick' within in it.

This time it's personnel...

On the 25th of June 2005 we held open trials for players in the carnival atmosphere of the Armitage Centre in Fallowfield. It wasn't exactly open. We had put out a message saying 'Do you want to play for United? Well now you can'. 930 had registered an interest. They ranged from experienced league players to a bloke saying: "I have a manly physique and Restless Leg syndrome" to someone saying: "New carpets smell nice but don't let any of your new players do sliding tackles on them" and a bloke saying: " I've got one of Barbara Stanwyck's leather waistcoats that she wore in The Big Valley, can I have a game wearing it?" We knocked it down to 230 on the day. 17 would go on to the glamorous surroundings of training on Tuesday and Thursday nights at Parrs Wood playing fields. The 17 included Adie Orr, Rob Nugent and Mike O'Neill. The only agents these lads were going to see would be the one selling them a Daily Mirror or a strawberry Mivvi. They'll be paid in mis-shaped Penguins, as we happen to have a founding member who works at McVitie's on Stockport Road and he can get boxes of them cheap.

Roaming numerals...

So we now we had a manager, a league, the nucleus of a squad, a kit, a name and the soon to be voted on badge and board. Two things were missing: Fans and a ground. The meeting on Tuesday the 5th of July 2005 was where it was all going to go alchemistic. It was to be called an Extraordinary General Meeting. It was decided that we'd go back to The Central Hall on Oldham Street. When I went to book it there was an old bloke in there called Gordon Jones. He was putting out all the seats out on his own for the bottom bit of the hall. I went through with him what would be required for July the 5th regarding tables and chairs for the stage. I almost said don't bother with getting out all the seats for the bottom bit when we come, as there will only be the Steering Committee there. I was wrong, as always. It was packed. The fans were no longer just electrical. FC United of Manchester got its constitution, its badge and its new board. Unbeknown to the rest of the audience, we also got our ground at Gigg Lane, Bury that night. The audience would have seen Tony Pritchard come onto the stage and start a whisper into the ears at one end of the Steering Committee. It spread up the row to be met with fist clenched glee. We had a ground, the formalities of which would be finished in the next few days.

Reds always have an affinity with the number seven. Seven core principles were voted on that night of how the club will operate and how they will be protected by the Board:

1 - The Board will be democratically elected by its members.

2 - Decisions taken by the membership will be decided on a one member, one vote basis.

3 - The club will develop strong links with the local community and strive to be accessible to all, discriminating against none.

4 - The club will endeavour to make admission prices as affordable as possible to as wide a constituency as possible.

5 - The club will encourage young, local participation - playing and supporting - wherever possible.

6 - The Board will strive wherever possible to avoid outright commercialism.

7 - The club will remain a not-for-profit organisation.

Many of those who had been involved with the club's formation went to The Castle on Oldham Street for a post meeting pint including Margy and some of the lads. We were in the middle room where the piano is. The lid was down. If only one of us could have played piano we could have opened that lid and got a song going: And the reason is clear, it's because we like beer, it's the nearest thing to heaven that we'll see, we're on the top of the world, looking down on creation...

Form is extemporaneous, class is permutable...

The first ever board meeting of FC United of Manchester took place on Monday the 11th of July 2005. There were 11 board members. I'd argued at a Steering Committee meeting that there should be 11, as that would represent one member for every player. It's probably a bit too big to be workable long term but the romance for now will suffice. I think the only other thing I ever did was to argue that under 18's at the new club should get in for £2. At the time Gorton Showcase Cinema was charging youngsters £2.50 to get in. All Mam's and Dad's want young teenagers from under their feet whilst they're going through that moping stage. In east Manchester, Mam's and Dad's could throw a few quid at their offspring to go to the pictures and they would have a bit of peace from the prem necks for a few hours whilst knowing where they were. Also, with the £2 in at FC United of Manchester, a guardian can take other families youngsters if they delegate it between themselves. The 'five wage packet thinners for a tenner' theory was born. Our prices are based on an east central Manchester mood, as they should be. £2 is within the spending power of spends for all Manchester youngsters. They can go and grow as they want or require.

Here's a fiver, now fuck off...

In the voting for the board I came twelfth. Anyone who wanted to become a board member had 100 words to get in by the 28th of June 2005, to say to members why they believed they should be. Martin Morris had been advised by Andy Walsh that putting 'I have also shit in a fridge at maine road' within his 100 words was not advisable. He did shit in a fridge at maine road. I know this as I was there when he did it. It wasn't good. It was a proper splatty one. He was only trying to be honest about his feelings on both occasions. I didn't believe I should be a board member as it is hard work and I'm not that keen on the worky word. I finished up in my 100 words going on about winning the League Cup in 1999, the under valued Lincoln biscuit, people who say: "Not three bad" and "To some tune", my channel five ghosting and that I, not unsurprisingly, live alone. Apparently I comfortably got on the board from votes counted from members at the EGM. I didn't get one single postal vote.

I was right about that saddle though…

As in board elections as in life, I came twelfth. I wouldn't have it any other way. The twelfth man on the subs bench gets to sit down a lot. He can brim with happiness for the people out on the pitch doing the graft for the greater good. He can also sometimes get the chance to come on and change things near the death. But not too much as I get a stitch easily. I went to the first ever board meeting of FC United of Manchester on Monday the 11th of July 2005 as an invited guest, as all the Steering Committee members were. It was pertinent that the old should meet with the new. The agenda had the delights of electing a Chair, an IPS update from Russell Delaney, a ground update from Tony Pritchard, a business plan from Pete Munday, the dishing out of responsibilities for the board to accommodate membership, finance, communications, operations, commercial, club development and community and external relations. And finally we got to discuss the team. If Victor Kayam had been passing with his wallet open, we would have had to watch out, as he would have liked us so much.

There were two new board members voted on by the members. One seemed very nice. Very articulate and very demanding. All necessary. You can only get so far being thick and willing yourself to be cleverer as was the want of many a Steering Committee member. The other new board member I just didn't take to. That's okay as that happens. He might not like me. Hopefully so, as by your friends be known. Before the meeting he asked me what my name was on the Red Issue message board. I told him I wasn't on the internet. He still told me his and to look out for him. He told me he thought he had canvassed well on the build up to the EGM. I told him the only thing I know about canvassing was that sometimes temporary accommodation can be made of it. It might be a tiny strain of the 'Lenin recommending Trotsky and warning of Stalin' in me but I wasn't comfortable. We had gone from clammy, swirly carpeted rooms above pubs to an air conditioned boardroom. Symbols of making it in business are not going to impress anyone of any worth. My instincts were being knitting needled. Sometimes when you're out you get the feeling that you might be in the presence of someone, who has in the past, and probably still longs, to say the word "Pants." Or "To the max." Or "You's guys." I had a very quiet meeting. I was weighing him up. He wouldn't have noticed. I have no right as an invited guest into a FC United of Manchester board meeting, to comment further on what I saw and heard that night from the new board member that I was player camming.

We might very well make it as a football club to a size of minor significance. As we develop the club will have to be wary of people who have an alarming lack of basic, basic knowledge of what the ethos of this new football club is, and of the love for Manchester United Football Club that has defined us as fans. We will be tested. Interlopers can disguise themselves and learn quickly and knock out superficialities. Peter Kenyon very promptly dropped saying "Man U." There is a tendency in football for a small number of small businessmen to seek to get in at boardroom level at a football club. Not at this club's expense they're not. No one is rinsing out our equally owned, equally shared, equally fought for democratic till. Any new member to the board, voted in by a one member-one-vote system, has to be embraced. The Red quality of that Steering Committee that was left behind, and which formed the Red rump of the new FC United of Manchester board, was enough to keep any court jesterisms in abeyance until it either changed or exposed itself to the members.

I'm almost glad the meeting had this to face. It was a bare footed, bare arsed step into a walk-in freezer to wake us up. The world isn't full of tombolas and rock buns. We're not an edition of The Bunty where if we hip-hip-hooray enough then all will be well. Lots of Reds know where they were when Beckham got sent off for England against Argentina in the '90s. It was my birthday on June the last. I was watching a lovely French film at The Cornerhouse called 'Ponette' as I can't stand all the little Englander shite around any World Cup. The film is about a young child who misses her dead Mam so much that her wishes to see her again come true, and her Mam comes back to hug and kiss her. It'll make you cry.

That's only a nice film though. Nothing comes back by just wishing for it, we have to act on it. After not commenting on that first FC United of Manchester board meeting, I observed the reactions of dozens of younger home and away Reds who came into my company. They will ask of anyone: "Who are you? Why have we not seen you at any of United away games? Where have you come from? We're your age and younger, why don't we know you? Or know of someone who knows you? Why have you got a flat-top?" In the end there is no decision other than to let the membership decide. I chose from that early moment to ignore, letting others have the patience to engage. I knew all I needed to know. Actually, I can't call anyone for knowing the price of labour across Manchester as I pointed out that Manchester Council was the biggest employer in Manchester. Its Senior Officers, on scale SO1 and SO2, who were just below the Principal Officer Management level, were on £24,000 to £26,000 a year. Therefore, we should have a workers' general manager on a workers' wage set around those levels. I do believe we now have.

Viraj mend it with a new one...

When Glazer took over there was a fumbling promise to get a fans' side together by August 2005. It had been done. A life of shopping on Saturday's at The Little Book of Furniture or buying wooden toys from Daisy and Tom's had been avoided. An advent calendar lets you open a little cardboard window, one at a time. There is not one large window but a series of little ones. You can open the window and enjoy the goods but it is impossible to properly close that opened cardboard window. It never closes right. Everyone can see you've opened the windows and acquainted yourself with the pleasures inside. We have opened a load of little football windows and we may never be able to re-close them properly. I'm reminded of 'The cross-eyed hod carrier and the three cross-eyed bricklayers' joke. The cross-eyed carrier says to the first cross-eyed bricklayer: "Do you want any mortar?" The second cross-eyed bricklayer says: "I don't need any yet." The cross-eyed carrier says: "I wasn't talking to you" and the third cross-eyed bricklayer says: "But I didn't say anything." We've opened so much, and let so much out, and bathed in it all that our eyesight can be impaired if we don't concentrate. It's time to butter the brick, corner them up and run them in.

CHAPTER FOUR

THOSE THAT BELIEVE ARE NEVER ALONE...

Leek CSOB versus Football Club United of Manchester, Saturday the 13th of August 2005. Kick off 3pm. Except you can't leave all the friendlies out as they were part of it all. So we won't.

I go through all this, before you wake up...

This new football club will encompass a fat caravan's worth of different ideas. A thin caravan would just not suffice. No one wants a thin caravan. They're just too thin. Instead this fat caravan will be so wide-of-waist that on closer Inspector Hornpipe'ing it will be found to be a ringer caravan, with a load of caravans all welded together seamlessly and not so seamlessly. To in some way represent these different ideas and opinions within the caravan, I have drawn together five of my favourite United writers to have a go at it. They'll recount their day with FC United of Manchester over the pre-season friendlies, up to and including, our first ever league game against Leek CSOB. This is dangerous for an author as they are all better writers than me. I'll recoup my limited literary credibility, though, by using the AFC Wimbledon friendly as an excuse to squeeze in a load of quotes from other Red acquaintances. These Reds are a bit dimmy and can possibly not string more than a sentence together. This is a sort of equal oportunities policy for the book in that I positively discriminate on behalf of the thick. When you read the AFC Wimbledon bit think: 'You're sorry you wagged it so much now'.

Leigh versus FC United of Manchester. Played Saturday the 16th of July 2005. FC United of Manchester's first ever game. By Mike Duff...

A get's up this Saturday mornin an I've got nowt on (figuratively speakin). The missus Marie is out all day shoppin, an it's only nine in the mornin. The phone goes, an it's me daughter Kerry
-Dad have yer got me that phone yet?
An a promised her a mobile, an a mate a mine gets em.
A reiterate me promise to her an a ring up Danny Phones, an a sez
-Any chance of a phone?
-No problem sez he, call down.
So he lives in Alkrington, which is twenty-minute walk from where I live, so I walk it. An when a get there he's de-branchin a tree wid a bow saw. So typical Tom Sawyer fashion a give him an hand. Then we stop an have a few cans, he tells me the phone's in a box in the livin room an to take which ever I wanted. His brother Terry drops me outside an off license near me flat.
While am in there a bump inter Donny an Donny is a big Red, an we chat a bit about football, an he sez
-You heard about the new United team?
-Yeah, a say.
-Playin terday at Gigg Lane, he sez, -a might give it a coat a watchin. Beginin of history, he adds
A smile an think nothin of it
A get four cans an prepare ter have a quiet afternoon in.
Wrong, the phone goes, an it's me eldest Liam.
-Dad can yer lend me a tenner.
Him an his cousin Paul are livin in a flat in Monsall an are always skint.
-Better than that, a say, get here within an hour an I'll take the pair of yer out for the day.

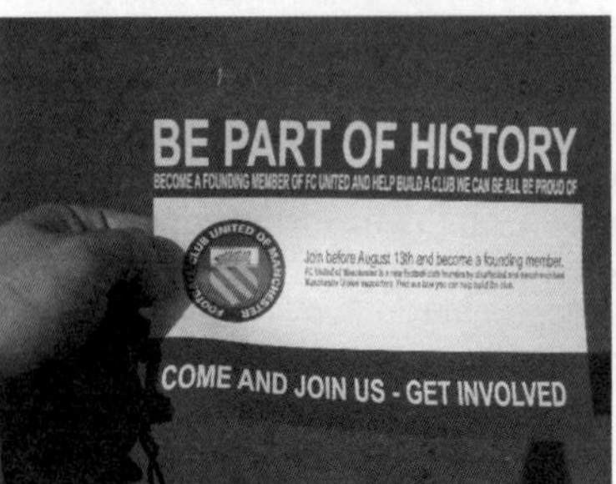

A roll a weed, open a can an wait. They turn up an hour later, an we jump a 163 ter Bury. They're 18 an 19, so a let em have a can or two wid me, just nice ter be goin ter a game wid me kids. An we get to the "Staff of Life" for two o'clock, an no sign a life
-Time for a pint, I say.

So a takes the pair of em in for a couple a pints a piece, an then at ten to three we take a nice leisurely stroll ter the ground. An it's fuckin deserted, so a pull this fella walkin by
-Thought this new United team was playin here today?
-FC United? No, he sez, playin away at Leigh.
A look at Liam an Paul, adventure over, a think.
So we walk back up towards Manchester Road, an I'm thinking, fuck it bus into town, have a couple with em in the Kings on Oldham street, then get off home.
Anyway as we're walkin up, a taxi stops, an some people wid suitcases get out.
-Right Paul, a sez, blag him fifteen ter drop us at Leigh. We'll catch the second half. So the three of us surround the taxi driver.
-How much mate Leigh? A say
-Only got fifteen, sez Paul.
-It's an emergency, sez Liam
The Asian driver looks at us an sez
-Twenty-five pounds
-No way, sez Paul.
-No? he sez, cheapest price.
-Fuck it, a say, don't matter.
An we start ter walk away
-Twenty last offer, he shouts after us.
An we turn an get in, an a notice his name badge, Khalid his name is.
-Fast as yer can Khalid, a say, the game starts in five minutes
-This is a taxi not a space ship, sez me new mate but fair play we are bombin along.

We finally get ter the Station road ground an we can hear the roars, an a chant of "Red Army" is ringin round the end an side of the ground. I'm pleasantly surprised there's gotta be two or three thousand here. All the gates are locked at the front, so we stroll down the side, an spot a piece of wall not barb wired up. Liam jumps on top an Paul hurls me up an the three of us are in. (Sorta swings an roundabouts for the additional taxi fare). We drop down into a space back of the toilets, an amble on in. Liam askin the score an me askin if the bar was still open.

It's nearly half time so we decide to have a quick walk round an a pint. There's a dinghy bein sung about, an we get in the bar under the main stand just as half time is blown, so a shout six pints in. We're stood there an the bar fills an it's a buoyant atmosphere, this young kid next to me starts singin about FC United bein the only team in Manchester not in debt. An it's contagious a find meself singin along with him. Paul an Liam are soakin it all in. When Robbo a lad a know comes over with a couple of others I'd not met before (Loki an Bret) an we're havin a drink an a laugh.

Robbo introduces me to Conrad who writes the music page in the United We Stand fanzine.

An I'm stood there listenin an thinkin all these people are here, an two an a half thousand others. They can't all be wrong. I hadn't taken it serious up until this point. An a think of somethin Arlo Guthrie said "If one man stands up for something he believes is right, they will say he's a lunatic. If two men stand up for what they feel is right, they will say that they are gay. If three men stand up, they'll say somethin's goin on here? An if four men stand up for right then you have a movement." An a look around me an a see this movement. This is about right an retainin wot is ours. It's about not givin in to oppression. It's about everythin Manchester's about.

A song goes up all around us "Barrow Barrow- we are goin to Barrow", an it's so apt. These men who have travelled the football grounds of Europe are swappin the San Siro for Accrington Stanley an the Nou Camp for Nelson. An they aint cryin about it they're lauhin an singin. An it's great to be a part of it. An the second half we're behind the goal at the opposite end to the main FC contingent, an it's a real top day experience. An I aint a man that can give you flowery accounts of free flowin football, but it was enjoyable stuff. An songs about hatin Blackpool Mechanics, at this point I'd never heard of em. An at the end a mass game of football on the pitch.
Two hundred goal hungry bastards tryin to get the ball into the net.

A first game tunnel, a future General Manager and a pitch invasion…

An we do two or three pubs around the grounds an bump into Mad Cyril an Meric an it's like a Wembley in the middle of nowhere. Somehow we're at a bus station an we board a bus back to Manchester it's hammered out wid Salford Reds. An Liam throws up over his self, an Paul stops the bus while he has a piss on a main road in full view of any one who cares to watch. An it's non stop song.
Once we're in Manchester a don't want the day to end so a take them in the Kings on Oldham Street, an as usual the clientele consists of people who look like they belong in a Pogue's video. We sink a couple an it goes hazy.
Next we're outside the Big Issue office an a song comes into me head. A song a stole a long time ago from Woody Guthrie an I aint sung it in years.

An a start singin:

> An one bright mornin
> In the shadow of the steeple
> By the Big Issue office
> A saw my people
> They stood there homeless
> I stood their wonderin
> Does this land belong to you an me?
> This Land is your land
> This land is my land
> From the Wythenshawe forum
> To the Heaton Park island
> From the Vale of Clayton
> To the Monsall heartlands
> This land belongs to you an me.

An Liam an Paul are laffin an it's bin a beltin day. Today I'd recaptured a belief in my City, today I seen a spirit that a thought had long since gone. Manchester sayin "fuck it" to the world. I'm pissed an the lads walk me to the bus stop on High Street.

-Not goin home? A ask
-Not yet, sez Paul, have a mooch. Check the birds.
An a go home happy an smiley.
An a wake up next morning an Marie is sorted
-You were drunk last night, she sez.
Then it starts comin back.
An the phone goes
-Dad it's Kerry, have yer got me phone yet?
-Fuck, a think to meself- left it at Danny's.
-Not had a chance yet Babs, a say, don't worry I'll sort it today.

Leigh versus FC United of Manchester. Played Saturday the 16th of July 2005. FC United of Manchester's first ever game. By Duns...

Saturday 21st May 2005. The FA Cup Final in Cardiff and a minibus containing 17 of the best mates I have made through watching Manchester United. All in high spirits as we were about to watch our team play it's biggest game of the season. A joyous occasion surely? But this was the saddest of days. This was the last time we would all attend the match in each other's company. A great change had taken place, and this upheaval caused me to shed real tears throughout the second half. It didn't really matter that we lost, as the great lament was for a bigger issue that day.

Monday 30th May 2005. A huge rally at the Apollo theatre. You could almost feel the sands shifting beneath your feet. Tuesday 5th July 2005. The inaugural EGM at Central Hall. Hard decisions to be made all round. Deep down though, I knew I'd be at Everton come August 13th.

Saturday 16th July 2005. Leigh away. FCUM's first ever game. It was a beautiful sunny day and I was looking forward to it immensely, but in practice the whole thing sat uneasily with me. I don't normally like football at that time of year, it doesn't seem right, and perhaps this contributed to the whole dichotomy of the day. On one hand I was delighted that something I could definitively call my own was now there before me, but on the other it all just confirmed the divorce and extrapolated the seismic changes occurring within the Manchester United family.

On that day, too, I had to meet a mate to give him my hundreds to pay for my season ticket at Old Trafford, an irony not lost on me, and one I was intent on keeping under my hat (the irony, not the money, though I do have a Mickey Pierce moustache.)

The Haircut-with-Stella fella…

The game was a poor goalless draw - a brace of streakers apart (not that I'm gay, not that there's anything wrong with that), with Leigh clearly superior albeit residing 4 divisions above, and as a first ever game together, FCUM did well. To see a team that I helped create run out was a buzz, but I doubt I got the same buzz out of it as some mates who had invested their entire being in this. I was still torn twixt my heart and my head, eventually settling somewhere between the two. (My gullet? Well, I've lived most of my life with my gullet ruling both my heart and my head, so why change now?)

I can remember really wanting FC to score, as I knew I'd miss the next couple of games due to holidays, and I'd heard AFC Wimbledon's Kris Stewart wax lyrical about what it was like to see your team score their first ever goal. I didn't want to miss it, though I did in the end. Even if we'd have been beat 8 – 0 it wouldn't have mattered to the 2,500 there, as this was more a day of symbolism than anything else. This was highlighted when thousands stormed the pitch at the final whistle, carrying their new red-shirted heroes off shoulder high.

There were one or two unsavoury incidents. Leigh's keeper copped a few beer cans, hundreds jibbed it over the wall, and apparently a steward got floored. However, an overflow of testosterone is what gives football its edge, and thus its appeal, or at least it did before it was sanitised by the government in the 1990s, and isn't the sterile version of the game what we wanted to leave behind?

As much as Leigh was a good day out with valued friends, it represented a lot more to me, and in that it saddened me. At the time I was probably still hoping that my mates would rejoin me at United, but I suppose this confirmed everything that I had feared. Or maybe my non-enjoyment was a manifestation of some sort of deep lying guilt – that this was purity and that I knew I was unclean.

Those feelings have since subsided, and sadly, a lot of barriers have gone up around both Uniteds. I have attended both frequently, though with priority given to the millionaires from M16, and I believe the two clubs can co-exist – they have to, as when Glazer fucks off we need to be able to get our United back and our mates back and one day there will be another minibus taking me to Wembley to watch my football team with all my friends – united.

AFC Wimbledon versus FC United of Manchester. Played Saturday the 23rd of July 2005. Kick off 3pm...

Matthew Forsure...

The decision to temporarily leave home wasn't an easy one, having listened to the arguments for and against in the Apollo I was drawn by the persuading tones of, I'll say this in a nice way, a big fat bloke from Wimbledon. Bernard Manning's posher and slightly better looking love child spoke with the passion of my Cub Scout leader when she told me my knots were the best she'd seen in years. The daft get Kris Stewart seemed to think that football clubs should be owned by the people that actually put there hard earned, or Manchester Council earned money into them. His line about "Just wanting to watch football" struck a chord, the bollocks surrounding the last few months at Old Trafford had taken from us everything that had been ours, the simple pleasure of just watching football had seemed a distant memory.

Despite containing at least two cranks and an albino, the Steering Committee with the graft and passion that shapes our city, pulled it off and we had a Football Club that was ours. When Kris Stewart, he of Bernard Manning look-a-likey fame spoke, he urged anyone who cared to get involved with our new club and help out where you can. I couldn't be bothered with all that gayness so I just kicked back and waited for some mug like Brady to book us a minibus for the trip to Kingston Upon Thames, where legend has it the locals picnic next to rivers and have them bikes with a basket on the front. An unnamed newly elected board member had other ideas and the lazy twat roped me into organising the coaches for the season, I'm not saying I'm easily swayed but when the title of "Travel Secretary" was mentioned I was in, the perks included sitting and the front of the coach and talking to Steve McLaren type figures behind the wheel as they discussed the pro's and con's of the M6 toll road, smart didn't even come close.

I'd never volunteered for anything since the aforementioned cubs leader made me stand outside Sainsburys in Prestwich cleaning people's shoes for the fun of it, this helping out my Football Club would be slightly different, mainly because it would be morally unacceptable to put the money in pocket rather than the bob a job tin, before you start I went to confession whilst still in my neckerchief so I'm pretty much above reproach on that one. In the end it was a pleasure to sit at the front of the bus, mainly because its quite difficult after years of feeding the ducks to see the subtitles on the small screen. The trip to Kingston was a great experience, the strippers in the pub before the game was a lovely touch and reminded many of us youngsters of why we knock about with perverted, older Reds in the first place. As I stood and drank and sang, I did so with the same people that I'd stood and drank and sang with in far flung places like Barcelona, Bordeaux and Bolton. You looked around at the people that were there and you couldn't help but think that maybe we'd made the right decision, just maybe we might be doing something that makes sense.

Martin Morris...

My mate Howsey is an albino. His eyes are pink, light shines through his hair in discos and he has a terrible temper. He lives in Stockwell, South London, though he was raised in Newton Heath. I have a picture of him, taken outside Kingstonian's ground on the day of our game with Wimbledon, in which he is standing with Board members Spencer and Delaney (Red In Peace). I also have a picture of my mate Beddy, who when looking for Tottenham tickets might ask: "Have you any spurs for Spurs?". He's wearing an inflatable duck on his head and behind him the albino looks like he's interferring with a small ginger haired boy. What stands out for me from FC United of Manchester's first competitive game? It has to be the bailliff from the electric board turning up at Howsey's flat only to be told: "He's the one with the white hair that's coming down the stairs now mate".

Lynette Cawthra. Is a bespectacled, Josephine 90, Shareholders United activist. She was conceived in Chorlton, born in Withington hospital but moved to Bramhall. That's posh. Her father, Cuthbert Snodgrass-Blenkinsop, won the 'All England Poshest Name In The Empire' Championship for five consecutive years in the 1930s. She is the only person at FC United of Manchester to still have a scullery maid. However, her poshness does mean she can get away with saying: "Glazer makes me very cross. I'm hopping mad with what he has done."...

After you have picked your nose on the settee in your own at home there is often the problem of what to do with it. You can, but you don't really want to, put it back. It's alright at the game to wipe it under the seat as it is your seat, with the added bonus that you can have a sweepstake with your near seated mates, to see how far in the season each one will last. In your home it's tempting to have a special crow corner where all crows are thrown. However, your flat would soon start to smell of ageing crow and that is never acceptable. Instead use your TV guide. If you're ferreting up there on, say, a Tuesday, then wipe the crow on Tuesday's telly page of your TV guide. By the time it is Wednesday no one is going to open your TV guide to go back to the Tuesday page. By the end of the week your TV guide will be defunct and you can recycle it and your crow waste. Clean and green'un green. The crow I wiped on the side of the metal uprights at the back of the little United end at AFC Wimbledon was the last one I have ever left outside of my property.

Andy Brennan. A Moss Side born Red. He's very emotional. Every time he sees a moving motorcar he cries as it reminds him of Princess Parkway. He doesn't cry at parked cars obv.

I didn't go to Wimbledon as I'd just discovered that if you read '1961' upside down it still reads '1961'. I'd also discovered that if I had a child I could not call it Kevin Norman Oliver Brennan. If you've got it, flaunch it, as blokes who point chimneys say.

Stuart Brennan. He's an investigative journalist with the Manchester Evening News. He is also no relation to emotional Andy Brennan...

If you rub a gold ring on your powk it will cure it. Soap doesn't have a sell by date. That's why you never see off soap. Only women bleed. And radiators. Wee is warm. However, if you accidentally wee in your face when you're in the bath it feels cold. Never buy a house that is on the turner-over bit of an A to Z. You see, there is fuck all I can't investigate. The common bathroom usage of fanny flannels has declined over the last two decades. I was reminded of this last piece of investigative work I did when journeying on the coach to AFC Wimbledon with Spike and Swampy. They are a right pair of fanny flannels. They should be called 'Ronald and Frank' the De Boer'ing bastards. Yates wrote of a female acquaintance that she had too much beauty for love or luck. Those two must have a lot of love and a lot of luck in their lives the ugly fuckers.

Lasse Lukacs. He's from Oslo but living in Manchester at the time...
I was really looking forward to going down to the Wimbledon game, but on the day, as I sat on the bus, my girlfriend rang and she said my cat was ill. Although I tried to beg her to take it to the vet, she had to go to work and my mother doesn't have keys to get in to my flat, so I just had to get off the bus and make my way back home. We were only 45 minutes away from Birmingham. When I walked in the door, the cat lie lifeless on the floor, so I rushed it to the vet. When we got there, the vet had a look at the cat and it said it was in a sort of coma. The cat had found a lump of hasjis that had fallen under the sofa in the livng room and swallowed it, then done a trance dance for my girlfriend, before keeling over. Anyway, cat's fine, but I really should be careful where I leave my stash next time. Don't want to miss one of those games again...

Portia Vale. She's from Kent...
It doesn't rain near me. It does near you. The Health and Safety Executive view football as consensual violence. Me and Himey Spartacus, my altruistic Jewish friend, took the valve out of the ball after AFC Wimbledon scored the winner in this game to avoid further lumber. I hope that, for a comeback, FC United of Manchester is not a Kevin Rowland'er.

Alan Hargreaves. A Miles Platting born bloke with a beard...
I didn't go to AFC Wimbledon as I was in France. I was checking whether there is a tanning cream called 'Collyhurst Road' in St Tropez.

Farrell. He's got very floppy hair for a Mancunian...
I missed AFC Wimbledon as I was in The Dutch Pancake House in town. I fancy Betty Stovah.

Andrew Howse. He's from Moston and likes cheeser conkers...
Can I just reiterate - they're not shin pads they're calipers. I went to AFC Wimbledon on The Variety Club Sunshine coach. I got unloaded by Goonersaurus, Arsenal's mascot, on the way down there. I hate that

mascot. It's not fair. Unlike my albino arse that I can use to find my lost keys in the dark.

Adam Dunne. He's from Prestwich. His favourite team is Red Bra Belgrade. His favourite song is 'Charlestown Multies sing this song do dar, do dar' and 'The stubby index finger' song from the film Evil Roy Slade. His favourite joke is the 'Dyslexic dying of a brian Haemorrhage' one. His favourite role model is Top Cat as when TC tips the concierge at the beginning of each show, the coin he puts in the concierge's hand is on a piece of string. His favourite toffee is the toffee cig as it reminds him of a nude ginger female...

Tears are alkali, saliva is acid. No time now for tears. Spit. We can welder's flash our way into football existence.

Stalybridge versus FC United of Manchester. Played Saturday the 30th ofJuly 2005. Kick off 2pm. By Two Mowers...

A bridge not too far...

It's Saturday morning 30th July and today I'm taking my lads Ryan and Tom to Stalybridge a.k.a. Stalyvegas to watch the third game of F.C. United of Manchester's history. I leap out of my Les Sealy and open the curtains and good morning Openshaw it's a brand new day – a -bee-bow-bow-buppa-b-bow-bow[1]. I look out across the trees and greenery and Ripley's believe it or not I can see some geese and a couple of ponies in gay abandon on a grassy knoll. Yes, I've just spilt a pint of Tag-Lag bitter all over your water colour picture of life in M11, unless of course you live next-door or back-to-back to me in which case you'll have the same bewdiful view and have probably seen me stood at the window bollocko loads of times. My weather forecast is mainly sunny with a maximum of 19°C and a minimum of 53°F. You see since deciding to flog my season ticket on the way to Cardiff my heads been in bits, thus I'm fluctuating between old and new which has affected my metric and mint imperial systems. For instance the window I'm looking out of is 150cm by $30^{1/8}$ inches. The peace is shattered by next-door's quad bikes and your picture is restored. Anyway people if you wanna be happy come to Vegas with me – a-bee-bow-bow-buppa-b-bow-bow.[1] For me it's a local a game as I'm gonna get so I'm hoping loads of familiar local red faces turnout. I don't think any of the lads I usually go to O.T. with are gonna show any interest in "Snyde United" but I respect their reasons.

Even though we're only a bus ride away Martin Morris is giving me a lift cos I've been minding his camera since Wimbledon and I'm giggling to myself cos whilst in London I got a tube ticket all-dayer and went round all the sights, Big Ben and that big wheel fingy etc. getting my picture took with his camera, in a Palin-esque kinda way. I also took a pic of a cable I laid in the hotel at Vauxhall. Plans change on the last minute though, Martin's late but Kev me brother-in-law and good red phones up cos he wants to take their Sam and is offering a lift. It's the first time I've been to a match with both my lads, junior football aside, since Boca Juniors at OT a couple of seasons ago. I'm happy with that, going to the match with me lads. It's not the reason I'm going to FC but it's a good supplemental reason. It's what I wanted to do at O.T. but could never do without a load of fucking about. Kev tries to find a parking space near the ground and we end up parking in an undulating secluded lane. I get out of the car. Fook me he's parked on the side of a fooking mountain I thought as I almost tumble down the pavement they've managed to construct on the rock face. How do people live round here? How do they learn to ride bikes and play on space hoppers? What happens when they get pissed? How do they get home? What happens if you've got mates round for a cheese and wine party, when it's finished do they just open the front door and fall off the cliff? All those ambulance chasers hanging about Piccadilly are in the wrong fookin place. They should be round here with the slogan "where there's a hill there's a solicitor's bill".

We abseil to the ground and try The Hare & Hounds for a swifty but its chocker so we go into the ground. I buy a programme for ten bob (that's shilling to you youngster) that looks as if it's been made with a John Bull printing kit and one of them duplicating machines with the big windy handle that they used to have at primary school. The proceeds of the match are going to Myra Mandryk a long serving member of the Stalybridge back room staff who is severely ill so it's all in a good cause. We get in the Mottram rd. end behind the goal with most of the other reds and we're stood right at the front watching the team warm up. I shout Jozzer and he comes over for a chat. He looks a bit fooked already so I'm just about to offer him me seat before remembering I'm on a terrace – a fookin terrace for the third Saturday on the trot – unlucky Joz. At kick-off the stand behind the goal is pretty full and in full voice with a mixture of classic United songs, newborn FC songs and songs In the final stages of labour breaking into the brave new world.

My lads Ryan and Tom love the atmosphere. The rest of the ground is sparsely populated with the Celtic fans congregated behind the opposite goal in the Joe Jackson stand and it sounds like they need Joe himself in there to start a fookin song off. What first appeared to be a fine day typically brought rain and as we're in an unsheltered bit and not dressed for it I suggest we move to the new Tom Pendry stand, Brady without his kwik-save bag to keep his hair dry was already in there. Ironically Pendry, former sports minister and MP for Stalybridge, once favoured the reintroduction of safe standing and here we were, off to sit in him. Ryan, 12, and experiencing his first proper sing-song at a football match wanted to stay put so we leave him there. I was glad cos the view I had of a packed stand of reds constantly singing and having fun and my own lad at the front of it all, joining in and buzzing off it was moving stuff and it reminds me of why, after my first few games as a kid, I carried on going. I was always gonna be Manchester United, my family had saw to that but the main reason I wanted to keep going, on my own if necessary, was the being part of a crowd singing songs, making up new ones, funny ones, thinking that one day maybe I'd start the singing off or I'd make a new song up that everyone would sing. I could see him there getting hooked on the same experiences I'd had.

The Under the Boardwalk tune took off properly that day and with the whole stand joining in with swaying arms aloft it felt really special cos Brady and me were both back at Cardiff under that bridge in the rain where the seed had been planted. We looked at each other, if you didn't know the story you'd have thought we were couple of gaylords eyeing each other up, but the look didn't mean 'ooh hello sailor', it meant 'ooh they're playing our song'. It was a moment of real pride.

The game itself was quite decent and FC matched Celtic, 5 divisions higher, for most of the game. An FC United player got on the scoresheet for the first time but the unfortunate Rawlinson had deflected it in the back of his own net. The introduction of the numberless sub, Rory Patterson aka Mr. Mystery set the theme of new choons for the whole afternoon and there were reds still trying to invent mystery related choons into the night and the next day and I've got drunken texts to prove it. Celtic wrap up the game with 5 minutes to go. A 2-0 defeat but a decent display from the reds. We've still not scored and for me strangely it feels good, it's like the ache of extra-long foreplay or you know the feeling when you're tied to a chair and…erm..well you know there's gonna be an explosion sooner or later.

Our Tom gets a lift home with Kev and Sam but I'm off into Vegas centre for a beer and I'm taking Ryan to show him that the fun doesn't end in the ground. We get a lift down t'hill with a couple of familiar faces. A flame-haired boy called Mad Cyril who sells UWS and a flesh-haired boy called Forrest, the star of the BBC's FC/Leek documentary. We have a couple in the Mill Pond and then go in a Wetherspoons pub called the Society Rooms. It's rammed with reds, familiar faces and there's a good atmosphere with loads of good-natured singing. I meet an apathetic Droylsden "firm" in there and one of them comes up and says "I'm surprised at you". The lad thinks I'm a traitor and he's helped me make up my mind because I don't value his opinion much. Another red saying it might have been different but when I make assumptions about what his principles may be, I know I'm right. Plus, his dad once tried to electrocute me in the shower (another story). The manager of the Society Rooms decides we're a disgrace to society and shuts the bar so it's back to the Mill Pond and we're soon joined by Margy and his galacticos who promptly join the fun. I'm glad we never got Redknapp he'd have just fooked off home for a glass of wine with his missus. Ryan's having his picture taken with Margy and I reflect on what a good time everyone's having. Potentially we could be in for a return to the good bits of the good old days every week and I'm reassuring myself that I'm doing the right thing. Isn't it what Mancunians do when faced with injustice and the choice to conform or rebel? We question and protest. Isn't this the Mancunian way? But right now we're getting pissed and we've just been beat 2-0 so let's wreck this fookin shithole – hang on a minute that was the bad bit of the 'good old days'. "Landlord, 568ml of your finest cask ale please"

Flixton versus FC United of Manchester. Played Tuesday the 2nd of August 2005. Kick off 7.45pm. By Tony Howard...

We'd had some top days out already with our new flame, but after three dates and much flirting we still hadn't scored. From day one I thought the moment when the ball first hit the back of the net would be the point I would finally discover whether I'd made the right decision to bin my season ticket. Morally I knew I had, but what if when they scored I felt nothing? If this FC United really was just something to pass the time during the American occupation rather than a 'love thang'? I've been told it's a similar question women ask each other when they kiss their new boyfriend for the first time. "What did you feel? Is it the real thing?" Well at Flixton we all got the answer.

A mate sorted us out in the upstairs bar of the clubhouse so we were set for another session. The guest passes were used liberally and with some creative accounting we got a load of us in to beat the throngs in the downstairs bar. Our number included some FC virgins who'd come due to the close proximity. Even me Dad was on it. It was a strange one breaching the FC subject with him. He'd given his season ticket up after the Millwall cup final having finally had enough of football's rampant commercialism. But he'd followed the reds over five decades watching all the greats and surely he wouldn't be interested in this 'other' United – a team that wasn't technically his beloved Manchester United.I was shocked to discover he was buzzing off it and after making the journey to Leigh for the first game he marked Flixton down as his next. Fifteen years since I regularly went to matches with my Dad, here I was doing it again. Me mate brought his Dad as well and while we discussed whether to watch the match from the balcony or the things that looked liked bus stops on the far side, the old men waxed lyrical about seeing Best score six at Northampton.

Raise high…

We opted for the balcony due to the ease of access to the bar and looking across Valley Road with its backdrop of electricity pylons was a surreal sight, especially after copious amounts of Guinness. We spent a few minutes discussing whether we'd played against Flixton's number nine on a Sunday at Hough End, or if it was his brother. And after deciding it was him we felt a bit smug. A game of vocal tennis had broken out around the ground. Those who had named themselves 'the bus stop boys' wished rain upon those in the uncovered 'terrace' behind the goal. They in turn took out their hydrophobia on us on the balcony by untruthfully claiming they could see us eating prawns. The lying bastards – the buffet was top but there were definitely no prawns involved.

Then it happened and I nearly dropped my vol-au-vents. Steve Torpey picked up the ball near the halfway line and ran at the Flixton defence jinking one way then the next. He beat a couple of men, swerving to his left as he went past the latter, before unleashing a thundering left foot strike that ripped into the top corner.

We went ape shit and nearly fell off the balcony. We'd got the answer we wanted and it is a feeling I will never forget. I felt like I must have done when I kissed a girl for the first time (it was only two years ago but I still can't remember). It was a bit like waiting weeks to get a shag from your new girlfriend and finally getting there (without the bodily functions of course).

I was made up – because I felt so genuinely happy. Like a father probably feels when his son wins the 50-yard dash on sports day. I felt pride in watching 'my' team that I helped form, and I was so relieved that I felt that way. And to my right was my dad – the man who'd introduced me to Old

Trafford 20 years earlier. I'll never forget the smile on his face. And everyone around us was smiling too. That game for me was the true start of a genuine love affair. The moment I decided FC United was 'the real thing'. Whenever I stand freezing at some backwater like Darwen I think back to that moment when Torpey scored 'that' goal and I never doubt my decision.

Leek CSOB versus FC United of Manchester. Played Saturday the 13th of August 2005. Kick off 3pm. By Linden Burgess...

I reflected on all of it on the way down to Leek. All the antecedents, the precipitating factors and the weight of history that had put me here.

She knitted her own scarf. What a teenage girl was doing knitting I don't know but it was the fifties. She showed tenacity and early jibbing prowess when, not having enough for three lots of bus fares plus three in on the gate, she got her two younger brothers there for two o'clock, sneaked in via a compassionate workman and managed to stay in and watch the match. He was just as bad. He thought an away programme constituted a romantic and insightful gift. It was when he found out about the Bobby Charlton scrapbook that he knew it was something special.

I didn't appreciate any of this until I was 10. It was 1979. That game. When Arsenal scored the winner he punched a hole in the internal lounge door. You could hear it going off next door as well as the dividing wall was just as crap. She went in the kitchen and shuffled a few pots and I sobbed silently on the couch as witnessing any domestic mither when you are little makes you think there's a divorce on the cards. I needn't have worried. It was about loving United.

If the naive glee of a sojourn to Old Trafford or staying up late for Match Of The Day had been exposed as having a painful side it was nothing compared to the shattering of the innocence of adolescent family life. It was 1984. That strike. He was on strike as well as was Silentnight on the same industrial estate and there was an abundance of secondary picketing as Agecroft was a scab pit. I cried watching the Battle of Orgreave as I tried to make sense of the brutality. I wore a 'coal not dole' badge to school and read the political papers he brought home. From then on I would always challenge, question and on the advice of my Dad, I would never let anyone piss up my back and tell me it was raining.

It was unsurprising therefore that events at Old Trafford over the last fifteen years would not sit easily with me. The corporate greed, apparent contempt for working class people and the Hello! magazine lifestyles of our players left me feeling disillusioned and alienated. It also meant not being able to sit or stand with family and friends, which was unforgiveable. The worst thing though was the social breakdown that was happening in our communities leading to some of the worst poverty and deprivation in the country. Next door to the richest football club in the world. They should have cared.

In the end it was like the final throes of any long-term relationship. The love, passion and inspiration went years ago and resentment sets in when they reach for you and you have to pull away. You're left with a comfort blanket of companionship and you have to get out before you're too old to hope for something better. United had turned into everything I hated and I could smell piss.

The thing is though coming out of a long-term relationship can be very liberating as you discover your sense of identity again. It was with this invigoration that we set off from Stamford Street. We talked, we were silent and we laughed and although we didn't admit it some of this was nervous anticipation, as we didn't know if we were going to a party we weren't invited to.

Free minutes to free…

We were dead late and were still in Macclesfield at the official kick off time as the traffic and weather had conspired against us. It was half past when we dumped the car and ran the few hundred yards to the turnstile. It was too late though, the tickets were piss wet through and stuck together on account of me cagoule being bobbins due to an unexpected lack of waterproofing. The turnstile bloke wasn't arsed, he had a right gid on. "Anywhere you like and it's 1 - 0", he offered, enthused by the turnout. Being 1 - 0 down was unimportant but 'anywhere you like'. Magical. I want them on a t-shirt or a banner me.

We jogged over to the nearest stand, well corrugated shed. It was overflowing. Full of the floatsam and jetsam from the Glazer debacle and well before. Songs established from the friendlies were being sung and there were smiles on faces. I soaked up this veritable cornucopia. It was warm and pervasive and I liked it. There was also a game of football going on. We'd not actually missed that much as there had been a late kick off due to the huge crowd so we were there to witness our first league goal for 1 - 1. We jumped, hugged and savoured. Ten minutes later we took a dreamlike lead. It had become one long party by now in our stand and the Leek equaliser before half time would not curb it. It was not pivotal but the chants of "We don't care about Rio" were and summed it up succinctly.

The whistle went and we wandered pitch side revelling in our new found match day freedoms. There were familiar faces, older faces and families with kids but the resonating commonality was the Cheshire cat grins. The t-shirt said 'Our club our rules' and the banner said 'It's a love thang'. People were having fun. At the football. Fuckin' hell. The DJ was as well. After a bit of Status Quo and Meatloaf, Foreigner's 'More than a feeling' came on which was inadvertently appropriate. More than a feeling, I should coco-pop. It was a sense of belonging, of relief, of shared concerns and responsibilities and of making your own history. I'd have put Issac Hayes's 'If loving you is wrong I don't want to be right' on as surely something this good had to be. This was more than a load of pissed off football fans it was a grassroots movement; the floatsam and jetsam had become a comradeship of heroes. Me cagoule had dried out as well which was a bonus.

Unfound fiends…

The second half was underway. After a slow start it all got a bit watching Brazilish and it wasn't just the kit. We started to dominate and turn on the style. New heroes started to emerge on the pitch as Spencer and Torpey both scored for 4 - 2. The years of over officious stewarding and resultant sterile match days had left me inhibited but by now my first FC United of Manchester game had knocked that out of me and we celebrated with childlike delight. Chants of 'lets all have a disco' rang out and we were spoiled by a fifth goal just before full time. After the final whistle it all went a bit surreal. If I could have put it to music it would have been something suitably psychedelic, probably 'Let the sunshine in' off the Hair soundtrack as it wasn't so much a pitch invasion as a sixties love in. Men embraced other men in a 'here's me hand here's me heart' fashion normally reserved for three in the morning.

It was a priviledge to have been part of the day and I will hold the memory dear, it was much more though, it was an embryonic journey. The wit and exuberence off the pitch and the energy and attacking football on it was in the best spirit and traditions of United and long may it continue.

There was only one thing missing. Me Mum. She said she wasn't ready, it wasn't for her. That's alright though because love isn't just about the obligatory joy and pain, it's about patience and timing. Whenever you're ready, bring your scarf.

Come into the garden Maud...

If that was our first ever game, our first ever non-friendly competitive game, our first ever pre-season and our first ever league game, then you have just literary'ly had it. Nothing is going to stop our chubby caravan now until the last game against Padiham away on the 29th of April 2006. We'd better start with the first home game against Padiham, though. We've got a caravan and we intend to use it with intent. We've got up, got dressed and gone in it. It's got a reconditioned engine and it's acting like a Winnebago. It's got net curtains, that we've glow-whited, we've got a pull down table to eat on and a comfy, cushion-covered-cushioned settee that pulls down into a bed for napette'ing, a little fridge that can get a surprisingly large amount of smart stuff in and we're carrying our own calor gas. Shelter, warmth, food and clothing. With our four basic necessities provided for we can now concentrate on producing the cultural high art. Almost certainly.

CHAPTER FIVE

OUR HOME IS YOUR HOME.

Our ways, our conduct, our lives established 1878…

Football Club United of Manchester versus Padiham F.C. Saturday the 20th of August 2005. Kick off 3pm.

And I look across at smiling eyes, that warm my heart and greet the morning sun…

This was our first home game at our new, temporary accommodation. It would be nice to think of Gigg Lane as home but that would be, for many, pushing it. However, it will be our accommodation for the season, we will have 'Home' written on the players' door and other teams will have 'Away'. So home, however ill fitting at present, is Gigg Lane, Bury. That's Bury. The bit of a town to the slight north of Manchester but housing, for a season at least, FC United of Manchester.

Before this game I had only been to Gigg Lane once to see United. I had been as a youth to Bury itself, to go to their big baths which has an arse twitch inducingly high diving board. It wasn't as if the pretend hard party of youth visiting from Beswick were ever going to dive off it. We found ourselves there as Basher Brayshaw's cousin, Mark, lived nearby in Whitefield and he had invited us up. Whitefield, like Hattersley, Gamesley, Houghton Green, Langley and The Miners and the Moston Mill estate in Moston, had been the home to Mancunians slum cleared from east central Manchester in the 1960s.

The Brady family found themselves on the Moston Mill estate in north Manchester as it was the only overspill council estate offered to us within the city boundaries. My Mam and Dad weren't being some sort of early day Manchester United bigots having a problem with out of towners and refusing to move out to mingle with all the josskins in the humpty-back hills, they were just being very prosaic. Or pragmatic. Or both. I could sort what they were by getting my big dic down from the bookshelf and looking up what the difference between prosaic and pragmatic is, if any, but I can't be arsed. Actually they were being pragmatic, as prosaic means dull and lacking imagination. If you knew Doris and Francis Brady then you would know that those words could never be latched onto them.

My Mam and Dad had two children to skulldrag into decency and they both needed to work to keep the boy in itchy, roughly hewn, wool balaclavas - that in later years might have been handy at West Ham if I'd not left them on various buses - and to keep the girl in editions of Jackie containing full colour posters of The Monkees over three issues. Issue one starting with The Monkees legs, so all three had to be bought to finally get their heads sellotaped onto the wallpapered wall. None of them could drive, my Mam and Dad that is, not The Monkees who might very well have been able to, so Moston, being the least furthest flung of the far flung, represented the least time spent on an orange and white SELNEC bus.

My Mam used to get two buses to the Rotunda rubber band making factory in Clayton, east central Manchester for her shift starting at eight in the morning. She did this by getting up about two or three minutes after she had gone to bed. If we had moved to Whitefield she would have had to get off the bus half an hour before she got home from work and got back on the bus taking her back to the Rotunda to be just in time to clock on again for the next mornings shift. My Dad, being a bricklayer, and this being a time of building industry boom, could find sites close by that were easily attainable by local bus. 'Local bus' being the key words there as the overspill estates didn't have any. At this time overspills were just new houses with gas warmed, blow air heating that blew through a grill in the wall, usually where you wanted to put your settee, upstairs toilets that had a brand new black toilet seat with white emulsion speckled over it and a kitchen with a serving hatch.

Now, admittedly, serving hatches are fckn great and I have no idea why their popularity has waned, but serving hatch or not your new overspill house was just plonked in a field with new nishlington all around them. Nish all around them besides mud and high-blood-pressure-faced farmers devode that the value of their country retreats, with original hard wood sash windows through out, were now plummeting. The inner city proletariat had come to give his children impetigo, watch his wife getting undressed in the upstairs bedroom window and to pre-bum any burgeoning, vestal village brides. Moving to Whitefield was never going to happen until that Star Trek beamy uppy thingy that transports people about really, really fast was invented. So the Brady's didn't move there.

P.A. Barabus...

All these years later, I find myself on a dreaded sunny day on a bus passing through Whitefield on the way to our first game at Gigg Lane, Bury. We've been invited to do the P.A. for the day. When I say 'we' I mean me, Peanut, Martin and Simon Go. We haven't a jar of glue what P.A. stands for. All we know is that we have to get some of that popular music together to play and to announce anything that needs announcing. Realistically you'd think that four people could share that not so substantial load. We can smile about it now but at the time it was terrible.

I'm on the 135 bendy bus that takes you to Bury. This bus has always intrigued me. As far as I know it is the only bus in Manchester that bends. It's not made of rubber or anything, it is just that in the middle it has a move'y bit that enables the longer than normal bus to bend as it is going around corners. I don't know if it has been an engineering success but as has been said - there are no others in Manchester. The Jaap tram was an option to Bury but I went with the bendy 135 bus as it has an unusual destination on the front. The 135 bus passes through Cheetham 'Joe' Hill which is an area in north Manchester. Instead of putting 'Cheetham Hill' on the front of the bus, as you would expect from a reliable and respectable bus company, they have abbreviated it to 'Ch'Hill'. Proper indahouse, pure time and down with the hoodastocracy. It's forcing you to be chilled when you really are not quite comfortable being so. How can you 'Ch'hill' when the fckr bends in the middle? The driver at the front has bent around onto one road and all the people at the back are still on a fcknother road.

I had a gun once, as a kid, that was called 'A gun that bends around corners.' It was quite self-explanatory. The barrel bent at a 90% angle and fired soft rubber balls around corners. It was cat shit. That's probably why they don't have them now. If guns that could fire around corners were a major and worthy success then they would still be around now. They're not and there is a reason for that. Impractical shite being the favourite. However you have to forgive the gun that fires around corners as it was only a children's toy. Its manufacturers tried the market to get the attention of not right children - it obviously had some success as I bought one - but it then found that the number of not right children was not so great as to make them economically viable, so it dropped out of the 'guns that bend around corners' business.

The bus company running the bendy bus should have applied the same logic. They were making us live through an episode of Bullseye. When the programme Bullseye used to be on television at Sunday tea times whilst you were having your salmon paste sandwiches, I could never really watch. It wasn't so much the smashing, super, lovely'ness of it all, it was more that I had been disturbed from the opening credits. The opening credits showed Bully, the programme's cartoon bull mascot, driving a single-decker bus. The occupants of the bus were all jolly and laughing and loving the fact that they were being driven along, at speed, by a cartoon bull. The hilarity and matey, dart throwing togetherness of the programme was encapsulated in those short, opening credit scenes.

Unfortunately, just as you are enjoying the oche-inspired camaraderie and are considering that darts may not just be for sta-press-trousered blokes with wispy long underarm hair that disconcertingly comes out of the ends of their shiny sheened, short-sleeve shirts, Bully does no more than smile at the camera and then fly out of the driver's seat, grabbing onto a big dart that is inexplicably passing by. No camera shot ever went back to the faces of the occupants of the bus. High on treble 20s and open-poured, nose blackheads their cartoon lives were about to end due to the wanton neglect of their cartoon bull driver.

I run for the bus dear, and whilst riding I think of U.S. dear...

From my back seat of the 135 bendy bus I could see the driver quite clearly on another road to my right. We at the back of the bus were quite clearly still on the road the driver had just left. I listened for the unbuckling of the driver's safety belt as he awaited the big cartoon arrow's arrival for him to do one on. The occupants of the back of the 135 bendy bus were not for flapping. They were veterans of Ch'Hilling. I was a Ch'Hill virgin about to receive my first rough poking. In that moment of panic I found a 'gun that fires around corners' bond with the fellow bus journey'ers. Their steadiness was telling me that FC United of Manchester wasn't going to be a clichéd roller coaster ride that Ronan Keating could sing about - it was going to be a very Manchester/Bury specific bendy bus ride full of pissed twists and gurning turns, of oh-aye-highs and tremor lows. When sometimes, we are going to feel as if we have been left behind in the bus stop with its glass protection smashed in and affording us no shelter, but really we won't have been.

We're just giddy on goodness but can't help expecting things to go wrong because of the pushed in pessimism that besets so many Mancunians. We will journey, we will arrive, we might stop and start and start and stop, we might be able to shout "Move along the bus" and 'dddrrring' the bus bell to let more join us or we might lose some on the way, but whatever way it is going to go we will have all bought a ticket. It'll get crumply in our pocket, mixed in with the grey fluff and loose change grease, but it will be ours. Keep checking your pockets - don't lose the ticket. It's your ticket. You know it is still in your pocket but keep checking. Get it out and look at it. It's real. If it was a bone it would be fide - it exists - your eyes haven't eye-sticky opened from an afternoon napette to find it was all in your fever'dly happy box, when your sleepy away time let you dream on and dream of love.

That was a lot for bus passengers to be saying to me especially when any outside adjudicator might just view them as blokeys and lady blokeys just sitting there with their shopping bags going home.

I'd rather live in this world than live without them in mine...

Clutching my newly acquired £112 season ticket the journey passed and I became a bendy bus old boy. Actually, I had two season tickets. One for me and one for Martin Morris, one of the 11 board members at FC United of Manchester and one of the four of us on the P.A. today. He helps to bring a new football club into the world but he can't get around to going to town and buying a season ticket for the club that he was instrumental in forming. So I purchased one for him and I'll add the cost to the ever-increasing debt that the man owes me. He's still paying me off from United's Champions League Qualifier trip to Zigandzag of Hungary a few years ago. It is a very good job he is not dealing with anything financial within the club or we'd be dickymintmaximus. And it would be a very foolish person indeed who'd want their club to be dickymintmaximus.

I was also clutching a bag of CD's containing a vast array of popular music to be played over the PA before the game, at halftime, and after the game. 'Vast array' might be exaggerating somewhat but there are only so many CD's you can get in a polly bag. If a polly bag could be brimful then this polly bag was brimful. It was sat on my knee threatening to spill out all over as the bendy bus bent and bended, as its bendy bus status so intended it to do.

It was a boiling day and I really should have worn shorts but I had a pair of cheeky Roy Keane's on and I was roast'eny post'eny. A full, non-sweat absorbing, unforgiving polly bag full of CD's against my already sweating body was making me sweat more. However, now I had found Ch'Hill standing in my life, I was not going to let such matters as a threatening to burst polly bag, a mobile and season ticket combo not fitting in my front jean pocket properly, or the first movements of an uncalled for semi, get me down. This was the home fixture that we never, ever, thought was going to arrive. And here it was.

If I could have blown up a balloon and set it free I would have done. The process that has come to pass that says that the blowing up of a balloon, and the setting of that aforementioned balloon free, somehow represents an act of celebration mystifies me. And, yet, here I am on the day we are going to play the might of Padiham FC in our first home game still wanting to set one off. The fact that my brimming polly bag did not have the room to contain a balloon blower upper pump, or that to blow up a balloon with my gob would take two hands thereby meaning I would have to take my hands off the CD brimfilled polly bag and they then would spill, or indeed the fact that I did not actually have a balloon on me, prevented me from blowing up a balloon and setting it free in an act of celebration of how far we were just about to come at 3pm kick off time. I celebrated in a 'background, wallpaper' way that so many self-respecting Mancunians do. I did the following...

Such a little thing, but the difference it makes is great...

I departed the bendy bus at the nearest stop to Gigg Lane, but not before doing something that anyone from a great city should do. Manchester's own balloonless celebration for the well intended but shy. There are many ways a city can be designated as a great city: Great architecture, its immense history, its political heritage, its pulsating cultural present, its reputation for music or food or hospitality or warmth, its fashion sense, its lack of fashion sense, its beer, its continuing ability to grasp the changing nature of the world and interpret it to the positive, encapsulating movements and changing them with its own form printed on it or taking the swelling rank and file initiatives and making them its own. All these things undoubtedly contribute to what makes a city great. It's not a slide rule measurement, which is a good job really as very few people can use a slide rule so the measurements would be wide open to accusations of inaccuracy, but shirley a great city should possess at least a sprinkling of the above, if not a smeared-on smattering.

For me, what makes Manchester the sweetest city or place I have ever had the pleasure to be in - and I've been to Talachre - is the apparently mundane but soul floatingly uplifting, eye-glistening fact that Manchester has the highest ratio per head of population of any city in the world that says: "Cheers driver", as its population gets off the bus at the end of the bus travellers' journey. Manchester's very own balloonless celebration for the well intended but shy - I "Cheers driver"d the driver as I got off at the bus stop that would be my footballing home for the next 12 months. I had thanked him in a way that appeared so background, so unintrusive, so lowest of low, low keys that if Trevor McDonald's 'Tonight' team would have done an in depth investigation, they wouldn't have discovered anything that would have aroused any ITV 'Tonight we reveal all' suspicions other than that of a bloke getting off a bus with a full polly bag. Away with their shite investigative journalism as they would have missed a "Cheers driver" that was everything. It had all the loving tradition and habitual meaning that I clasp closest, and that my city clasps closest.

However, despite our giving instincts, we don't wave the bus off, as that would be just too three socks odd.

As a city Manchester does not only "Cheers driver" at weekends when people might be doing joyous things on buses like going to town for a swifty latchlifter or visiting dear friends, as I'm sure even the most grim of places - Stoke - could do that. Mancunians say: "Cheers driver" as they are going to work. Not coming back from work as even Stokians might do that. If they're not called Stokians then they should be. Mancunians show their politeness to the driver when they are at their lowest depth. A Monday work plummet and still, amidst all the horror and puss soreness of everything that is going to torment them for the next five days, they still somehow manage to knock out a "Cheers driver" as they bade farewell to the public motorised vehicle and wander off to work, away from their family and friends, to have the surplus value extracted out of them by some rapacious employer. An early Monday "Cheers driver" might not be as chirrupy as say an early Friday one but it is still there, it is still uttered, it is still meant. It defies politeness.

No city should have to be that polite on a Monday morning. Any city can be excused a bit of being obnoxious at such a demoralising moment in the grind of the working week but not Manchester. It carries on 'Cheers driver'ing because that is what it does, that is what makes it smile, it understands that as in topless women's pillow fighting, it is not the winning but the competing that counts, that we make you look, we make you stare, we make the barber cut your hair, he cuts it long, he cuts it short, he cuts it with a knife and fork, that it is not possible to carry on bouncing a super ball at the same time as having someone coming up behind you to pull your trousers down, that Billio's good at everything - running etc, that whereas other cities accept that 'going' doesn't rhyme with 'boing' or 'sand' with 'wand' or that 'liquorice' is pronounced 'rish' instead of 'rice' we question it, that lobby doors are always open in soaps even when it is winter and you'd have to be potty to be sat there in the George Raft but oh, no, there they are having a parrot about something soapish and no one ever says: "Oh, hey, it's proper Fergal Sharkey in here, shut the lobby door", and if we had to tell you one thing that would improve a non-Mancunians life then that would be never go in a pub that doesn't give you a tray if you're in a big round. That is what it understands, that is what makes our city great. It's Manchester's gentle tone of kindness.

Admittedly, not all residents of our city do “Cheers driver” as they should but this can be put down to the high number of southern students that come here to study and stay. Many of the city's downsides can be attributed to this 'southern students coming here to study and staying' factor. It's Manchester's 'Get out of Strangeways' card that we can play when outside, aggressive commentators are having a go.

And, also, I take back the views just expressed about Stoke as being grim as Stoke is the only city I know that has 'OK' written in its middle. I'm thinking, but having thunk, I can't think of anymore. Also, if you took the 'O' and 'K' out and put an 'E' and a 'V' in there to directly replace them, then Stoke would be called Steve. So it can't be all that bad - despite every single thing that I have ever heard about it telling me that it is. We're playing a few sides this season from around the Stoke area. FC United of Manchester will try, in a North West Counties League division two fraternal way, to debunk the myth that all people from Stoke have black and white pictures of Laurel and Hardy on their parlour wall doing something funny.

Little Malcolm Glazer well he tried to ride a bike, but he fell off, it made him cough, and the buttons on his trousers they fell off, and he showed his dirty bottom to the boys and the girls ...

So it's one o'clock on Saturday the 20th of August 2005 and I am approaching Gigg Lane. The last time I was here in that pre-season friendly with big United I was beered up and perhaps approached it from a different way, but it looks different. It's not as ramshackle as I remembered. There is no bommy-night-wood stands or rickety, patchwork, railway sleeper timber fencing outside and no one is selling hot, roasted horse chestnuts in paper bags with accompanying music from a greased-moustached, portly bloke in a white collarless shirt with a black waistcoat playing a barrel organ. I must get a prescription for this Sepia vision.

The barrel organ man might have had a monkey somewhere with him but he's keeping him hidden due to an overly keen Environmental Health Officer. After all it's a given that few people like monkey fur in their food so you have to have some sympathy for the Environmental Health Officer and his enthusiasm to catch the barrel organ man for letting the monkey run all over the top of his barrel organ. If he sold hot roasted monkey nuts the Environmental Health Officer might not be as keen, as a monkey near monkey nuts being sold would just perplex him. And in his perplexed state the portly bloke could play a barrel organ tune from his '20 barrel organ greats' album and by way of good music, lull the EHO into not prosecuting him for any monkey related misdemeanours. Or not.

Signed, sealed, delivered it's ours...

Bury FC have a small, neat, compact football league ground. They might be taking us around the corner charging £5,000 a game but they have got a product. We're in the North West Counties League division two where it's a matchday bonus if a sausage dog doesn't short-leggedly meander onto the pitch and turn out a mix in the 'D', or someone is not wearing a Peter Storm wind cheater behind the goal. This small, neat ground is a ground that belongs to a Football League side. A proper, existing side that gets announced on telly every week by the Pools Panel. The Pools Panel bother to set what results they think Bury might get if they have a game postponed due to over excessive brown/grey plaid trilby hat wearing by their home crowd, or there's one of those regular outbreaks of consumption that often besets the town. Bury FC is a breathing bone that forms the blown up ball, backbone of the professional game. You say "Bury" to any football fan and despite thoughts of smallness, they never the less will take them serious and their position in the football pyramid as just and valid. When it comes to FC United of Manchester there are more than a bucketful of occasions when we have sighed: "Will everybody stop taking us serious. Stop putting us in proper leagues, stop putting us in proper grounds, stop making proper matchday arrangements. Just because we said we wanted to be a real throbbing football club doesn't mean to say that a) we meant it and b) you should not just dismiss us as mouthy dicks." For mouthy dicks is what we are, in parts.

The mouthy dicks were now renting this ground. The ground's a bit dark blue which is understandable as Bury play in dark blue, but for now it's got everything FC United of Manchester needs to meet our league requirements - transport links, stands, roofs, pitch, toilets, corner flags, pubs nearby, roomy forecourt so that we can be comfortable during the match day lumber when we play Flixton etc. It's not faultless but it's all we have, so if it is all we have then we will have it. When I say: "We will have it" I mean that we will be having it in a normal sized manner that could in no way be misconstrued as us having it large. We will be leaving 'having it large' to people who find themselves, and their posse, being enamoured with Radio 1's DJ Spoony whilst wearing unacceptably high levels of multi-coloured placcy wristbands. This is not to imply that any level of wristband wearing is acceptable as it is not. I'm sure this fad will fade. When it does, remember who did. Wrists are for watches and self-certificated firing one off. And sometimes darts if you survive Bully's coach journey.

Red and Bury'd...

The outside of the ground is swathed with familiar Red faces that have 'I'm doing an important job, don't mither me' written across them. Mark Stopford, otherwise known as 'Soya Milk Mark' due to him being a vegetarian, is leading the delegating of jobs. He had been a staunch J Stand lad but had wrapped up his season ticket after May the 12th. Don't have a beer with him and get him mooney eyed as he is over fond of telling you of how he was in Crumpsall hospital as a child and Stuart Pearson, United's centre forward from the '70s, came in to visit him at his hospital bedside. "You wouldn't get that now", he'll mistily eyed say over and over again, looking into the bottom of his pint pot in town before getting his £8.50 Stagecoach Megarider weekly bus pass out and getting the last 23.23pm 219 back up Ashton Old Road to home. No one really has the heart to ruin his drunken party 'seven' piece and say: "Actually, Mark, I think they probably still visit hospitals." No one likes to see a grown vegetarian cry.
So we say it when he has gone for his bus, leaving him to his own state of mangoed'ness and talking cracker crumbs. If there is such a mythical perception as that of a 'Man's man' then Soya Milk Mark would fail the mythical perception of the 'Vegetarian's vegetarian.' He's a gruff central Manchester voiced, broad shouldered, shaven-headed knockerouterer who you wouldn't like a crack off. He's originally from Cheetham Hill in north Manchester but has been residing in Openshaw, east Manchester, near my Mam and Dad's for the last few years. If you had to visualise him then think of Uncle Fester and sing: "The Adams family started, when Uncle Fester farted, he farted through the keyhole and paralysed the cat." Except, only visualise and sing it when you are far enough away to out run

him. And, also, Uncle Fester will have to have a Clash tattoo on his arm in your visualisation.

We were in a police escort back to Lime Street a few seasons ago after United had been playing the Mickies and a scouser shouted from a bus stop: "Hey you, yeah, you" to get Soya Milk's attention. When he had got the attention he had so required, the scouser said coldly and clinically straight across the escort divide and into Soya's eyes: "You ugly fucker." The scouser himself was no oil painting, which increased the insult many fold. I'm sure he wouldn't mind me saying that. Actually, he probably would. Having said all that, he who laughs last, laughs last, longest laugh, last long, last and that - he's turning in with the lovely Donna and her plumptiously full and bouncy mellodians and equally plumptious and spankable backdoor. And we're not.

The Ulcer Volunteer Force...

Anyway, Soya Milk Mark is delegating to a myriad of excited kites near the reception area outside the ground. They have puppy-energised mannerisms and I fully expect them to run around like buggers for a full ten or 15 minutes but then feel the need to have a nap on top of each other in a big bundle of wet nosed Redness.

But stay on the grass...

For the time while they are awake though, I have no idea of the nature of the jobs they are doing but they look busy. Not in a Manchester Council 'quick get a clipboard and look busy the midnight mass from next door is coming' way but in a way that you know they are up to some good. An amorphous mass of little tidgey people adding up to a big achieving blob for the greater good. We are many, the mistakes they'll be few. Co-ordinated unco-ordination, everyone a probable amateur at what they are now undertaking but doing it with a Red community verve that will not accept not achieving as an answer. Gates will be personed, programmes will be sold, scarves will be flogged, corridors will be patrolled, players will be chaperoned to their new dressing rooms, matchday secretaries will matchday secretary, balls will be pumped up, the media will be satiated, flags will be apportioned positions, tea will be brewed and an all round swill of good humour will wash us safely to our first 4.45pm. All except the Fuckle Brothers doing the M.C'ing on the P.A. Never in the field of human conflict have four such nodgering nodgery nodgers met on the field of play.

F.C.M.C...

In our M.C'ing defence the P.A. at Bury FC is a smoked-glass Aiwa midi stack system. The sort a teenager in the late '80s would have been embarrassed to have in their bedroom. If we had found a silvered, cardboard hard, wank sock and a bit of a Nirvana poster blue-tacked underneath it, we wouldn't have been in any way surprised. It only has the facility to play one CD at a time and you have to turn the sound off before you can use the microphone. And that's about our defence. We're going to prison if the prosecution try to convict us on gross misconduct and improper use of all that is upright. We tried to get the sound right, we wandered to the furthest ends of all the stands we were using when the ground was almost empty and asked scared punters if they could hear the sound system. On reflection though, if you're just sat there on your own and a random nodger comes up to you and randomly says in an overloud voice and with a too concerned face: "Can you hear the sound system all right lad?" You are going to think that this is some poor chat up line and your answer is almost certainly going to be: "I can, but don't ask me for a date as you smell of chipsticks. And you're a bloke."

Hit it with a big stick...

Peanut's positive presumptions along the lines of: "Uncle Bobby B, don't worry, it will be all right" were beginning to win me over. I should not have been so foolish. The P.A. sound, although tinged with a gloop of surgeons paper mask muffle, was indeed quite audible if you sat there and really listened. Really listened. Unfortch football fans don't really listen, they have to be heartily hailed at or they will just blabber on about inane things between themselves. We can't have that. Our inaudibility was compounded when more and more FC United of Manchester fans came in. When the ground wasn't too full we'd had the volume setting on 12, whatever that means. We were not backward enough to not know that it would need turning up when the ground was full due to bodily absorbtion of sound and general hubbub and bub hub. What we didn't know as yet, was that when you put the volume over the mark on the volume knob saying '14' it went whacky. And not in a

Timmy Mallet whackaday good way. It hadn't done it earlier on when we had the luxury of messing about with an empty ground. We had "tested, tested, one, two, three" until the cows had gone home, heard our "testing, testing, one, two, three" and come back due to the cow-magnet clarity of our set.

Our smoked-glass Aiwa midi stack system had chosen twenty to three to start going bandit on us. Frantic technical messing about by Martin who has a 2:2 degree in technical messing about from Salford University proved fruitless. We got the word 'goosed' then we got the word 'arama' then we put them both together and collectively decided we were goosedarama. The sound would go no higher than 14. Having the sound at 14 was alrightish if you were in the Main Stand just behind us. The Main Stand was proving to be like all Main Stands in that it was getting the more placid, football appreciating, less vocal of the support. In the Manchester Road End behind the net where the chanting was non-stop you could hear, as a German Red might very well have said to us if he was in attendance on that day, "Fuckensy all'ensy."

If the Manchester Road End could hear fuckensy all'ensy then there was fuckensy all'ensy that we could do about it. We were stuck with Radio 4-calming noise levels, but that's all right as who wants to hear a P.A. anyway? They had done nothing but play 'We will rock you', 'All we hear is radio gar gar' and 'We are the champions' over crowd atmospheres for decades. We concluded that it was fitting that in FC United of Manchester's first home game that the P.A. should be relegated to inconsequential background noise.

Lamont Dozier 'Baby, don't leave me now' or Jackie Wilson's 'Whispers are getting louder' or 'Something smart' by the Something Smart band featuring MC Smart...

We played some nice music for eclectic tastes which included Donny Hathaway's soul classic "You were meant for me, no one else can come between this love I know," a 1940's Frank Sinatra, who was still ours at the time, singing: "When we first met, I felt my life begin, so open up your arms and let this fool rush in." Take That singing: "And we're still so young but we hope for more." Diana Ross and Marvin Gaye's 'Include me in your life,' Beautiful South's "Let it rise up in the morning and take you for a walk, let it do the talking while we're too tired to talk," a dedication to our non-goal scoring centre forward, Joz Mitten, of Morrisey's "Yes I am blind but I can see. Evil people, prosper over the likes of me and you always." The Stone Roses' singing about a reservoir having an erection. Bob Dylan forecasting that others should not criticise what they couldn't understand as here were sons and daughters beyond their command. Joy Division's 'Atmosphere' or was that Russ Abbott's? The Carpenters eulogising "Such a feelings coming over me, there is wonder in most everything I see." Aretha firmly stating: "Till you come back to me, that's what I'm gonna do," Edwyn Collins fully intending to "Rip it up and start again and I hope to god I'm not as dumb as you make out." The Dubliners' 'Pub with no beer', Nick Drake's 'Northern Sky,' Lamb's 'Burn like a good bonfire in whatever you do.' And Percy Sledge's 'You're pouring water on a drowning man.'

A board meeting of FC United of Manchester had decided that the team should come out to Happy Monday's 'Wrote for luck' and if you could hear over the feedback, the pitch invasion as hundreds and hundreds from the Main Stand decided to go to the Manchester Road End stand via an invasion of corner of the pitch, the roar of the crowd as FC United of Manchester came onto the pitch for the very first time, then Happy Monday's 'Wrote for luck' was what we came out to. Almost certainly.

Maths explains the universe...

We would learn over the coming games that to co-ordinate music with the teams on pitch arrival you have to do the following: The referee, at exactly 2.55pm, will call the teams into the bottom of the tunnel. At approximately this time we will put 'Wrote for luck' on, as it is six minutes long. At 2.56pm the referee would have done his jewellery check and under orders from the board of FC United of Manchester, knocked out any FC United of Manchester players wearing sovereigns, etc. As he is doing this I am on the pitch by the top of the tunnel looking down at the players. John England, the Matchday Secretary, will be at the side of the players at the bottom of the tunnel but in my eye line. As soon as the referee has done his jewellery check and says: "Right lads" to bring the players out, John England signals to me.

I then signal to Martin who is in the glass P.A. booth that is pitch side, by the tunnel. Martin then has to knob-twiddle with our Aiwa smoked-glass, sex machine, midi hi-fi, turning the music off and turning the facility to have the microphone back on. He then signals back to me that the microphone is ready. In those intervening seconds the teams will have heard the call from the referee to organise themselves to be going onto the pitch and will be just starting to walk the 15 yards from the bottom to the top of the tunnel. After receiving the signal from Martin that the microphone is on I say, and trying not to rush it and trying not to be too nasal'y Mancunian with my accent, "Sisters, brothers, Red, white and black, open your soulful souls and welcome onto the pitch our opposition and FC United of Manchester."

That sentence is about 15 yards long as by the time I have finished it, the teams are passing me out onto the pitch. Its still 2.56pm'ish. I give it several seconds to let the cheering proletariats in the crowd calm themselves and then announce the away team and then FC United of Manchester's. This team sheet has been filled out by John England in accordance with North West Counties League rules. On receiving the team sheet in the last half hour before the game starts, I check whether there are any awkward names to pronounce. If there are any, I approach the opposition's staff for clarification. And try not to giggle if one of them is called Gary Goodhand.

During the game the four of us should manage to rustle up some semblance of order to make sure that at least one of us is not going to the tool shed for a squirt or rambling on so that we miss who scores any goals. We do not have the privilege of any action replays. If we miss it we cannot invent a time machine and go back and replay it. It is missed and we won't have a Scooby who scored. Our professionalism cough ahem comes to the fore and we keep an orderly, attentive house at all times. You see, fuck all gets past us. Except when it does.

We're on top of the world Ma...rgy...

It came to pass. But not without Sure Shield...

Padiham came to our temporary home having won both of their first two league games and were therefore league leaders. Our new team faced a foe. A sombre start to proceedings was the immaculately observed one minutes silence for Nick McCool, a Padiham player who had died at only 20-years-of-age whilst playing five-a-side. Football's importance in the world was firmly put in its place by such a tragedy. The roar at the end of the minute's silence became a noisy, thundering celebration of life.

The whistle to start the game went and our home journey was off. Rory 'How the fck does he get a game, the man with no name' Patterson was butty'fied by two Padiham defenders in their box in the 26th minute and a penalty was ours. Was our first goal at home going to be a boring penalty? It was. Except it wasn't boring. Rory 'I shall remain nameless' Patterson chipped the ball into the middle of the net as their goalie, Rob Batty, dived to his left. If you're going to score a penalty then at least make it a cheeky one.

Reds have taken to the un-named one and I can see why. Unfortunately he has a lot of work to do to win me over. One reason is because my Doctor on Mill Street in Clayton is called Doctor Mistry and there is only room for one Mr Mistry in your life. The second reason is that when he scored on his debut in the friendly at Stalybridge, actually we didn't score there so it must have been just a reaction to a crowd chant or something but anyway, the un-named Mr Patterson in that game did that divvy footballer thing where they turn around and point over their shoulder with both thumbs at the name on their back. The fact that there was no name on the back of his shirt, and thus that's why he was doing it, is irrelevant. We haven't forgiven Giggs for doing it in the 0-3 victory over Juventus at the Del Alpi so we are not about to start accepting such cliched histrionics from a new boy. Shape up - this is FC United of Manchester - no hats with little bells or associated goony derivatives.

After 73 minutes Phil Power, FC United of Manchester's Assistant Manager, got a game. That's not strictly true. There was a flash point as FC's bow-legged Adie Orr clattered into Liam Denning of Padiham and their players, quite justifiably, reacted. Mr Power decided that his presence was needed and steamed in along with the rest of the FC team. This will be officially interpreted as building a close team spirit when in actual fact many of them just like a bit of a box. Joz Mitten, despite being seen in The Garrick in Urmston on the Friday night before the game drinking water - that's water - still didn't score. We hope Joz does not take this as an indicator that beer will work where United Utilities' finest fails.

The game finished 3-2 to FC United of Manchester and saw us going merrily to the top of the league. It can only be down from here. The attendance was 2,498, that being larger than Bury's previous two games. Some of those in attendance had done both - meaning they had left Old Trafford and whizzed up to do the double. We are as one. I have yet to see anyone who was in attendance that day who had a big enough face to contain the smile that went across it. You can be too happy, you know.

Definitely the last Red event of the day we played Padiham FC in our first home game was the birth of Sean Anthony Roper at 23.59 and 55 seconds. He just squeezed his birth in at the near post to be born on the day of our historic first home game. He was reported as perfect and even at a month premature he still weighed six poundss and three ounces. He's going to be a fat get like his Red, J Stand Dad. A gurgling, bib wearing, soup-consistency bizzing, off-milk sick smelling celebration of newborn life. A fitting metaphorical match as the loving parents are a meeting of being born in east Manchester - Abbey Hey and Newton Heath - but now living in Blackley, north Manchester, as is FC United of Manchester: Born all those years ago in 1878 in Newton Heath in east Manchester and now temporarily playing to the north of the city. The police helicopter that flies so regularly over east central Manchester to check on its residents with its big high-powered searchlight is known as 'The Openshaw moon.' No twinkle of stars or state sponsored neon light bulb could outshine the warm light that was illuminating within the Reds who had just been at the home birth.

CHAPTER SIX

THE HOODED CLAUSE...

Winsford United versus Football Club United of Manchester, Wednesday the 13th of August 2005. Kick off 7.45 pm. Played at Northwich Victoria's ground.

It's the simple understanding of the way you hand it over and hold on to it, too...

You would think a town with 'Wins' in its title would be more successful than to be in the North West Counties League division two. Apparently not. So much for American motivational video methods where you name yourself a winner, therefore you are a winner. It might just be that someone was called 'Winnie' and she was the first to own a Ford, and that was such a big event in a town where someone without a glance in their eye is considered a bit of a Bamber Gascoigne that they named the town Win's Ford. Before that it was called 'Mamwhy'smebrothermedad?' and twinned with Little Windscale-cum-Hardy

We might never know why Winsford is called Winsford because we are not going to be playing there. This Wednesday's game against them and the next Saturday's game against Ashton have been moved to Northwich Victoria's ground. Apparently Winsford is seven miles from Northwich.

Bolton and Manchester are eight miles apart but this seemingly short distance might mean a lot. After all J Stand used to sing: "Only eight miles, two different worlds" to reflect our differences with Bolton. Personally, I always thought the fact that Bolton called themselves 'The Trotters' was enough to give the world a cultural clue. Who knows, Northwich might look down on Winsford as not fully formed or Winsford might look down on Northwich for wearing leather waistcoats. Or they might all be bestestist of mates and go Gymkhana'ing together, exchanging family photo albums for sexual purposes later.

Openshawshank redemption...

Our trip into the dark ages began being in the dark ages. We were picking Two Mowers up at his home in Openshaw and there had been a massive power cut across the city due to the Kenny Inclement weather. We live in a city where it rains.

It rained.

And the fridge went off.

We cannot call Winsford if we carry on like this. Two Mowers got in the car carrying a bag of part-melted, frozen, mixed veg in case we got hungry on the journey - he didn't want to waste them. Tight get. While he munched cauli floret lollies on the backseat and we had carrots julienne lollies in the front, he told us a lovely story that had happened to him that week.

Two Mowers had dropped Mrs Two Mowers and two of their young lads off at Manchester Dental Hospital just outside town. Mrs T was in the arms, legs, knees, handbags, elbows crowded waiting room with the two young lads. As well as living the overcrowded indictment of the state of our NHS, they were also suffering that intense mixture of thumbed magazine, of 'Is one of these primary school children baking one as I can smell the top of the turd?' boredom, and of the parping it that dentist's waiting rooms specialise in. Even if you can get past the 'Primary school child baking one in class till the bell' smell, then you are still cruelly taunted by the underlying, stinking, threat of the black, thick rubber of the gas mask. You can hear the high pitch, sectionable wurrr of the plugged in Black and Decker that they put in your mouth and pretend to you that it's white heat technology dental equipment, when you can still clearly see the B&Q barcode on it. You're fluxxed by the cordite cordiality of the lingering waft of drill-bit-burnt mercury filling and new nylon carpet. No feet clench like the clench of dental feet.

In this calmed and relaxed atmosphere sat the scrunched up Two Mowers family. The door opens to one of the dentist's rooms. This means that your time of meeting the Big D is drawing nearer. You want the door to open and someone to leave so that you can get it over with and go back to having a normal, not running for a bus, non-derby day half time, heart rate. But you also want the door to open and hear a professorial looking bloke say: "You'll never guess what they've just invented whilst you've been waiting here. You can all go home. Your teeth's troubles have been cured, you don't have to do anything anymore, they just cure themselves." The waiting room looks around to the recently opened dentist room door. There is to be no saviour in the form of a professorial looking bloke. Let's give him a buttoned up, crisp, white coat to make him sartorially, as well as professorially, accomplished as that might help him along with his inventions. No. Even the addition of the crisp, white coat in our imagination has not worked. Instead out walks a small black lad. The room closes in on itself, in shitting-itself silence, as one of us is going to be orally Roger'd and we all know it. We came into this world alone and we walk to the dentist's chair alone.

Because they are young and daft and thinking about how slack their trousers are or pizza toppings, the two Two Mower children have not seen the small black lad open the door and enter the waiting room on his way out. Because children today have such a short attention spa... they forget to be thinking about the step that eight of them later will be sitting on, sharing a high strength, two litre cider and look up. In unison - that's together, they've not just grown up quickly and joined the public sector union - the two Two Mower children bluster out, whilst pointing over loudly: "It's Adie Orr, Mam, Mam, it's Adie Orr. Adie, you're Adie Orr. Mam, Adie Orr, there, Adie, just came in, there, it's Adie Orr."

Adie Orr is one of FC United of Manchester's strikers. The two Two Mower children have done well to spot him, as he is that pacey on the pitch that very few people have got a good look at his face. Adie Orr, born 22.02.1984 looks all emb'd, shocked at his new Manchester youth cult status. He smiles and runs off quick. This is in Lee Sharpe contrast to the players after our games as they always come to the pub with the fans and share a pint and an autograph. It later transpires that Adie had done well to smile, as his face had been big needled to buggery by the dentist. Karl Marginson, our manager, had made Adie have new, lightweight teeth fitted to make him that little bit faster in the final third. When other players are tiring after carrying a full, heavy set around for 90 minutes Adie will be there to take speedy, helium / titanium toothed advantage.

No one will be calling Margy then for his stern dental policy towards the players. Everything will be all smiles. Except for Adie, as he can't smile that often as his newtons might float off, as that professorial bloke we were talking about earlier has not quite satisfactorily completed his revolutionary dental work to British Medical Association standards. Margy realises that this is a bending of FIFA governing body rules concerning teeth but he has not strictly broken any. Show me the rule book, show me the page. Also Adie, on his visit to the dentist that day, had done a little brown stripe in his trousers because he was scared and he didn't want the kids to be disillusioned, so he had got on the toe train and got off quick. No one wants a role model who soils his grubbies. At least the origins of the 'Primary school pupil baking one till the bell' smell had been sourced.

Chute to kill policy...

We got to Northwich town centre but we all had to admit that we were lost. We knew that Northwich did salt, and every time we went into a chippy we thanked them for it, but outside of guessing that there probably wasn't a Southwich, we knew very little about the place. The positives were that the roads had tarmac on them. The negatives were we didn't know where the tarmac went. Ironically, we could see tarmac but could smell asphalt. We realised that we also didn't know the difference between tarmac and asphalt. Tarmac was easier to spell and that was about it.

This wasn't helping us get to the game though. However, like a rescuing white stallion with a large exhaust pipe that an Amsterdam video production company might want to use, the vision of the white, Hayton's company coach appeared. Hayton's coaches were taking Reds from Manchester to the game. We'll follow the coach to the ground and everything will be smart, we simply assumed. Doubts in our simple assumptions were soon realised when the coach pulled up outside Northwich Magistrates Court two minutes later and Reds spilled off and began to piss in its manicured gardens. Dripping Rhododendron petals rained down like wet confetti at a watersport fetishists wedding as desperate men, desperate for a damping down, blew the petals off with excessively high speed bladder empty'ings. This was bad enough, but facing the Magistrates Court was Northwich cop shop.

Injury lawyers 4 the U's...

They're all going to have convictions for indecent exposure on their criminal records. Breach of the peace or armed robbery is self-explanatory. A criminal record for indecent exposure would always have to be followed with the sentence: "There were no kids involved or out, I was just having a lag outside Northwich Magistrates Court. Oh, and Northwich cop shop which probably, on reflection, explains why I got caught."

Whether the authorities CCTV'd this synchronised FC United of Manchester fountain and later used it as a theme for a new town water feature we will never know, but this drive by chuting did not result in any criminal convictions and after several detours we found the ground.

The Ginger Princess' scheme to get into every away game on a junior concession, even though she was 26, was successful tonight with entrance gained at the reduced rate. This jibbing of lower league club funds can be legitimised as when she was going past the programme sellers she heard them say: "What should we charge for programmes tonight? We can charge what we want as these dicks will buy them. Let's charge two quid." Unfortunately, we are seen as a butty to the clubs we visit. This is well understandable as they, if things go well for us in the promotion stakes, are going to get one kiss off us and one kiss only. They have to make it a good one, so inappropriate tongues and abusive brushing ups are predictable. The programmes sold out at two pound a pop.

Googie Withers worked within these walls...

The first half against Winsford was what I had always thought I was going to be watching this season: Poor fare football, with legs swinging wildly at balls they were going to miss or, if they connected, they would Nicholas Butt off at all angles. It was 0-0 at half time and thoroughly unentertaining. The second half was everything the first half wasn't. We fell behind to a wobbly goal in the 51st minute but this did not detract from the increased pulse of the game. The atmosphere was building up as the United fans, mostly congregated in the Danebank Terrace alongside the pitch, presented their presence with a wall of noise. Of all my years in the building industry, I have never heard a peep out of a wall. The characters that named that wall wailing were, I fear, prone to exaggeration.

I'll work with the analogy though, as this is a match report and there are certain restrictions you have to work to within the match reporters' guilds. Let's settle on a proper wall of noise being a nine-inch solid leaf of engineering brick in a Flemish bond of a stretcher, followed by a strengthening header, followed by a stretcher, followed by another header and so on. And all backed up by an eight-inch thermolite block wall behind it. We were never that wall of noise noisy but for a crowd of 2,220 it was at least a wall of four by two timber studded, sound-insulation filled and plaster boarded over with a neat skim finish to the plaster. It was a sturdy enough wall to accompany Torpey's 72nd minute equaliser.

This was quickly followed by Adie Orr making it 2-1 three minutes later. Let's re-run that. It's in the last 15 minutes and Adie Orr scores. The other team are tiring and Adie Orr scores. Whatever the board invested in Adie's new lightweight Newtons was proving to be a sound financial investment. And he had only had them done that week as witnessed by the two Two Mower children. The one worrying aspect was that after he scored he high-fived everyone behind the net. He high-fived the Ginger Princess. Now, she might have jibbed in on a junior concession but she is still entitled to an opinion, be that only a concessionary one. Her opinion was that he was not high-fiving but using the hands of the fans behind the net to keep himself from floating off. Teeth can be too light you know.

A four legged friend…

The fans celebrated Adie's goal with a passion. Many years ago we had come to classify goal celebrations. There is the normal one of fans jumping up and down shouting: "hoorah." There is the second, more passionate one, of jumping up and down, shouting "hoorah", but legs being witnessed in the air. If you can see shit in the treads of trainers then you are witnessing a goal worth celebrating. The third and most passionate of celebrations is where all the first two descriptions are followed but they are accompanied by crutches up in the air. If you watch the United end in the 3-2 victory over Juventus in the European Cup semi-final in 1999, in Turin, then you will understand the crutch shortage at the MRI. This is because either United have a very limpy following or other Reds agree with our analysis and bring crutches with them even though they do not need them to get around. They're just glory limpers.

Been boned, been binned…

I saw crutches when Adie Orr's goal went in. There was also a pitch invasion where they ran onto the pitch and re-kicked the ball into the net.

You understood their wanting to do that but you also had to want them to get off the pitch before getting us banned. Sinister people are watching us closely and we needed self-policing discipline if they are not going to take advantage of us. Mind you, earlier in the game the hooded young men from Moston were heard to mute: “Has anyone ever dragged a wheelie bin onto a pitch and just left it there?" That would be hilarious. There was an internal fight going on within founder members - that's a great idea, ain't nobody not going to find that scant regard for authority funny, it shows we're inventive and unafraid to arse about. Too long have we been heavily stewarded, too long have we been herded. These feelings waged indignant war with the feeling that if it had happened, and a wheelie bin had been wheeled on the pitch, then the bad, bad press and, perhaps a ban, would do us serious damage. A young Moston man being wheeled onto the pitch, inside a wheelie bin being pushed by several other young Moston men is an event that's been lost to football. It's a poorer place.

That loss, and the loss of our third goal that never came. Winsford equalised and the result finished 2-2. Our first dropped points of the season but a marvellous football spectacle. Made the more so by the introduction of our midfielder from Urmston, Ryan Gilligan, late on in the second half. The Danecroft Terracing witnessed another football quandary. Do we condone or condemn the following behaviour?

Ryan Gilligan came on as a substitute in the second half and was dominant. He's got a shaved bonce and a horse-shoe-shaped veins protrude across his temples. Dentists would be frightened of him. The Manchester Evening News took a poll and it was decided that people would be less scared to meet him in a dark alley because at least in a dark alley you could pretend that he wasn't as frightening as in a light alley way. But he is. He had played a fantastic ball through to Steve Spencer, a midfielder who was playing at left back, who in turn played the ball to Adie Orr for that second FC United of Manchester goal. But also, late on in the game, one of the Winsford players went all 'Paraguay versus Uruguay'. He rolled about after an innocuous tackle as if his foreskin had been hand sewn to a casey and a Dave Bassett managed team had played a long ball game with it. The referee and line runner ignored the soap dish and got on with the game. Ryan Gilligan approached the 'My Lord, he doth protest too camply' player as he was getting up. Gilligan calmly looked to all sides of him and saw that the game was elsewhere. As their player Gary Bear'ed about thinking he was on Match of the Day and a later post-match video was going to vindicate his fey claims, Gilligan came up and kneed him straight in the kite, giving him something to moan about later.

The advent of the song sung to the tune of 'The candy man can' seems to conclude from the condone or condemn debate that we like our football laid out on the counter, with the blood soaking into the swollen, wooden chopping board and splashed up the white emulsion walls:

> Who can knee your teeth out?
> Put them in a can.
> Store them in the back of Margy's fruit and veg van,
> Ryan Gilligan can, Ryan Gilligan can.

On this same day the unemployment figures in Manchester went up by 25 as Glazer made 25 local workers redundant from the staff at United.

CHAPTER SEVEN

WE DRINK TO THE DAY WHEN THE LAST BUSINESS MAN IS STRANGLED TO DEATH WITH THE ENTRAILS OF THE LAST BUREAUCRAT...

Ashton Town versus Football Club United of Manchester, Saturday the 3rd of September 2005. Kick off 1pm. Played at Northwich Victoria's ground.

All I've known, all I've done, all I've felt was leading to this...

As long as you're having a nobble...

Having a nobble at FC United of Manchester remains paramount within the temperament of the fans and the board. The signs for quality nobbling time were looking very good today. The sun was out, United weren't playing due to an international against Wales in Cardiff and Wednesday's FC United of Manchester game, despite the storms, had attracted an excellent crowd of over 2,000. As me and JP got the Jaap to Altrincham to get the 10.08 train from there to Northwich, we allowed ourselves to get cocky. Today would be the day we broke past 3,000 for the first time. Such wanton acts of happiness emanating from me are minuscule in number and I wasn't cumf but I really, really believed it. I'm blaming JP for my misguided confidence. JP mixes grumpiness with boingyness. The boingyness gene in him is strong and can be seen at its most unrestrained in his younger brother, Found-a-Fiver.

Found-a-Fiver is so called because he always looks as if he has just found a fiver. He's constantly grinning and prescription drugly happy about most things. He could find a 20 spot but he's just as happy finding a fiver. There is no cup half full with him; he's ecstatic that he has a cup. He'll show you his cup going: "Wow, have you seen this cup, the chip in it is top." He will say 'top' though, which is very Andi Peters but you forgive him because he's so contagiously effervescent. When he dies the future board of FC United of Manchester are going to make a fortune as they have already secretly put him on the Stock Exchange. They are going to donate his body to Steradent so that older generations can have their false teeth cleaned by his dead bubblyness. There has got to be at least a million tablets in him.

They can't cremate him, as that would be like putting an oxyacetylene bottle on a bonfire - he'd just go up, dead or otherwise. You couldn't bury him either as he'd just boing and boing until all the occupants of the other graves got up and left, and there are enough people in authority who don't like our existence without having accusations of encouraging zombies thrown at us. With the money FC United of Manchester get they'll build and name a stand after him at the new ground where the price in will be forever fixed at a fiver. It's from that boingy gene pool that JP gets his boingy side that was predicting the 3,000-crowd barrier would be broken today. We shall see said the blind, and quite possibly over optimistic and boingy, man.

From Northwich, it's the quiz of the week...

There were about 60 on the early train. I didn't expect it to be rammed as it's a proper traipse from either of the two train stations nearest to Northwich Victoria's ground. Cars were going to be big today. We got off at a station called Gralam Lostock. That's not even a word. A bloke doing his front garden on this quiet country lane went Phil Neville gobbed as we all walked past him. He lived just before Arthur Street which made me glad there were no cockney Reds with us as they would have surely said: "That's not Arthur Street, it's a full'un." And then proceeded to buy it with the spare shrapnel in their London-weighting pockets. We walked down country lane after country lane. Many had not seen as much green since the pre-season friendly at Old Trafford against Celtic a few years ago.

Jules Spencer, the board member from Rochdale, brought his quaint country ways with him. He did a bit of blackberry picking, as it was just the right time of year for them to blossom on all the hedgerows we were passing. He'd brought a little wicker basket with him, which had a red and white cotton gingham cover over the top. His missus had brought an air rifle and she shot a rabbit for tea. They skinned it there as they were going to hang the skin over a crush barrier in the ground to dry, as later they were going to make matching rabbit fur thongs out of them as all the glitterati in Rochdale have them. They had plenty of time to do this because they are from the hills and they found all this hill walking normal and as a consequence were miles out in front of the wheezing city folk at the back.

Jules became media spokesperson for FC United of Manchester only after the board had made him sign a piece of paper pledging that he wouldn't wear his family heirloom tweeds all the time in interviews for the telly. When you hear him interviewed on the radio he is wearing them. He has a dark greenish tweed jacket with brown leather buttons and the matching green tweed trousers are that pantalon style that just comes to the knee. He wears cream coloured, knee length, thick wool socks with a pair of sturdy, brown brogues to finish the ensemble. When his older brother was in possession of the family tweeds he had sewn a badge onto the jacket saying 'After Manchester United I like sex best' on the left hand side of the lapel. If you look closely you can still see the cotton marks where they picked it off. When Jules is wearing his tweed suit he will always try to stand to the right of you so that you can't see the evidence of his older brother's shame. Jules' great Grandfather invented workhouses and they still live off the profit from that all these years later.

You think your tired feet were fire proof...

Just when it seemed as if we were going to die, as these country lanes were never ending, we spotted The Slow and Easy pub on the corner. I recognised the pub from the previous Wednesday and excitedly shouted I knew where we were. In that instant I went back 12 months and imagined myself 12 months later knowing a pub that was in Northwich, near Northwich Victoria's ground, because that is where my team were about to play in a competitive league game. No jump of the imagination could have been asked to jump further. Except if it was.

This change of culture was grasped further when we reached the Witton Albion Social Club, which is only a few hundred yards from Northwich Victoria's ground. Northwich haven't built their social club yet. They're building the ground before the pub. Confirmation again that people are odd. Billy Brayshaw, his missus Caroline, and their 18-year-old son, Jack, were already in the Witton Social Club from 11 o'clock that morning. It was five past now. I sat down with a pint of Guinness that was obviously the first pint from the pump, as it tasted like socks. As we were talking inane nonsense I got a phone call from Andy Walsh the club Chair or Secretary or Chief Executive or whatever he is called. It's the toppest swottest job at the club and Andy had deservedly and democratically found himself with it.

He had just had a phone call from Karl Marginson saying that the players were stood whistling whilst waiting for the coach. It seems that someone at the previous Wednesday game had told Andy that for an advert in the next programme they would provide a coach for free today. Andy had told Luc or Luc had told Andy, who had told Martin who told Luc who told Andy to tell Martin to tell Peanut to cancel the coach from the usual source. Peanut had cancelled the usual coach company as today was freemans day. Unfortch the freemans coach had decided that they wasn't going to turn up. A testicle had been Paddy Roche'd. But was it really of 'Paddy Roche putting it in his own net in that game against Arsenal in 1977 and costing us the league' proportions?

We're all sensitive skinned people, with so much to give...

I am sure there will be recriminations and shouting and bawling between board members but realistically everything was fine. So what if occasionally the players have to get in their motorcars to get to an away game that is only half an hour away? They got there. If anything, it might have reminded them that they are only North West Counties League division two players even though the crowds might be old fourth division size. We are a club that smiles and so should they. And they do as they know that so many want to play for us and they are as privileged as the fans to be part of the scream. In 1877 in Newton Heath, players standing around must have gone:

"Should we form a club? What do you think? We probably could. We would save a fortune on testimonials, as the average age of death in the inner cities is 31 so it would be a bargain if we had local players. Next year it is then."

The myth about the Scottish being tight only came into being in 1967 when it was discovered that the European Cup winning Lisbon Lions and their 'All born within 50 miles of Glasgow' fame had only come about because the board thought they were all going to turn up their toes early. That quest for a bargain gave us our birth in 1878 so it was a quest for a bargain that made us go for the freemans coach in 2005. It's all linked, it's all bloodline.

Of course we want to appear professional and turn up as all other clubs do with a coach and players wearing club blazers and ties. But are we like anybody else in this league? We're not. We're an Industrial and Provident Society, a one member, one vote ride. No one small businessman with used dental floss breath and a carroty-coloured third wife with furry face issues that are highlighted in sunlight, owns us. Outside these grounds we are visiting we are seeing parking spaces designated specially for the Chairman and a few other supposedly distinguished apparatchiks. That will be replicated across all the leagues. Little men with cantilever extended egos and unreported penile dysfunction problems, as it must be her fault, park up. They have thought it important enough to delegate a job to someone to go and paint out their own parking spot. That will never happen at this club. If a democratically voted in Chair wants to get on any of the club parking spots then they should get there early enough. He or she has got graft to do, so get on with it. No flouncing.

Have you ever had your knackers in a rat trap? In a mangle? Or in a knot?...

Every F.C. United of Manchester fan in that Witton Albion Social Club before the game was not in anyway concerned that the players they were about to pay seven pound to see were at this present time packed four to a car and passing Lostock Graham. It was idiosyncrasies like this and the rejection of sterilised synchronisation that made so many walk towards the infant we were now all rearing. We laughed and loved it. We looked forward to the game more, knowing what we knew. For the second time in the day I jumped myself back 12 months and imagined myself back to this day and I was a fuller, fatter person for it as those around me were. We were still being flung by the big bang and things are going to get bumped into. We're in the sparkle of seeing a club form in our form. We're not perfect. We try and aspire to be but everyone is lackadaisical at times. Some more than others. As a club we'll try to be less gormless than others but a club with out any gorm to have less of would be a dry club. If we were a turkey at Christmas we could never be accused of being a dry bird.

Pack a packet of Parma violets it's going to be a long day...

The players slummed it and got to the ground in their cars. They managed to put in a paltry performance and wapped in four and kept our first clean sheet of the season. The game saw our Assistant Manager Phil Power make his 'official' debut after his 'unofficial' on pitch debut during the fracas at the Padiham game in August. The surprise though, was the crowd. I was convinced, as were many others, that today would be our first 3,000 barrier breaking game. It never came. As we all left the Witton Albion Social Club to go to the game we went the not so secret, secret route on the path through the fields. When this path hits the wooden bridge and you cross it you can see the relatively large terrace that runs along the side of Victoria Stadium. It was not as full as Wednesday night and the game was five minutes old. The turnstile that we had gone through five minutes into the game at the Wednesday match was also shut, as there was no one milling about late. The 15 or so of us in our company were the only ones outside. We were baffled.

It was a Saturday, United weren't playing, the sun was out. The only things a good crowd attendance had against it was that it was a one o'clock kick off, it was the last real weekend for family holidays before the kids went back to school and England were playing. None of them were insurmountable. We could have at least equalled the 2,220 crowd of the Wednesday night game against Winsford United. Instead we got 1,424.

We learnt a few things from our two close proximity visits to the Victoria Stadium. The first was that we have to get used to and understand, acts of crowd up and down'ness. Crowd up and down'ness might well be our signature tune for this and coming seasons. If we make coming seasons. As we play away against Ashton on the 3rd of September 2005, we are a club two days shy of two months old. Our first home game against Padiham saw us playing a side that was born in the same year as United in 1878. We can't count in days of existence what most clubs can count in years. We would be very foolish and tittily naive to believe that our trajectory was only ever going to be upward. That would be lovely to believe. It would also be divvy.

The second thing it taught us was democracy will continue to reign. I spent too large a part of the game discussing a flag with Tommy McKenna and Steven Wood from the Supporters Group. Not a corner flag or why they don't have halfway line flags anymore, or a flag with edgings and a kerb, but a flag. Tommy and Steve had been instrumental in organising the fund for the first ever, fans paid for, flag of FC United of Manchester. Fifty or so internet-based FC United of Manchester fans had chipped in and an 'Oooeerr Mrs, that's a big one', sized flag had been ordered. The fans internet site www.fcunitedofmanchester.co.uk had decided democratically on what should be said on the flag. They had short-listed three and a winner had emerged from that. The new, first ever fans paid for flag for FC United of Manchester was to say 'Manchester's finest' and have the badge with 'Born 2005' near it.

Two large problems there for me. The first, and as I kept repeating to Steve and Tom, was the '2005'. If the first ever, fans paid for, flag for a club said '2005' then it was forgetting many things: The anti-Glazer campaigns of the last year, 1999, the anti-Murdoch campaigns of the '90s, the formation of IMUSA and Shareholders United, Ron's leather, the derby pitch invasion, the wooden seats of the Stretford End, 1968, the 1958 Flowers of Manchester, Eddie Colman's walk to work, the bombing of our home in the war and our time at Maine Road, the Gibson Guarantee, The Outcasts, Bank Street, and the railway working, early age dying blokes from 1878 who first said: "Now football is a precious game, played in the sun, played in the rain."

The house I live in...

The first ever, fans paid for, flag should have '1878' on it. Anything less is collaboration with Glazer and the giving him of something fine from our finest collection. If all FC United of Manchester Reds lived in the same big house then all the above examples from our finest collection would be stored in a display cabinet in our living room. They'd all be a bit squash'd but we'd do it. We'd have that photograph of Duncan Edwards tucking his shorts in as they lined up for their last game against Red Star Belgrade; there'd be cuttings from Stuart Pearson's feather cut; a beer mat from Jim Holton's pub with R.I.P. on it; the white Admiral shirt with the black stripes down the side; a piece of broken deckchair and a pickled and preserved donkey's ear from the Red Army's visit to Blackpool in the '70s; a piece of the big six, asbestos roof that the lad fell through at Norwich; the actual dart that went in that Red's nose at Liverpool with part of his nose still on it; some of the netting that Middlesbrough put up between rival fans to stop darts flying across; one of Denis Law's snot stained sleeves with a congealed crow hardened in the cuff elastic; a Carlo Sartori ginger pube; a birthday card from Brian Kidd's 19th; a pair of soiled ladies panties from George Best's first Mancunian conquest; one of the touted tickets that Bobby Charlton got prosecuted for when he was caught trying to supplement his modest, Manchester United playing, England starring, media working, soccer schooling wages by a process of over charging the Reds who had paid his wages for years; the old wooden 'J' stand sign; video footage of the United mob that walked from Glasgow town centre to Ibrox in revenge for their visit in the '70s, "No surrender" very quickly turning into: "Oh sorry, we give in"; bulbs from the old electric scoreboard arranged in such a position so as to spell 'Cunt'; some red and white picket fencing from in front of the post-war Main Stand; a downloaded copy of 'Why footballers who plan goal celebrations should be hated and despised and have two pairs of pliers put either side of their sheriff's badge ringpiece and pulled in opposite directions so it looks like Farah Fawcett

Majors' smile and then have a wicker place mat from Habitat placed in it and then they should be hated and despised some more.' It's got a very long title but it's a succinct read. Basically goal celebrations equal Bellamy bellendery; a bottle containing the essence of programme smell; the rusted screws that held the 'Wonderfuel Gas' sign up over the Stretford End. And that's just the bottom shelf.

All the above are our fine bone-china tea sets that are not to be taken out of the display cabinet and used mid-week or for anything frivolous such as visits by unwanted aunties or distant cousins with calamitous kids who are only coming around because they have no friends and we're too polite to tell them to piss off. Our treasured bone china tea sets are there on display. There would be a rota of Reds in our big house to keep the display cabinet polished. No rhubarb aerosol spray polish would be used but a deep, creamy bees wax. We'd polish its glass frontage with vinegar and water from a washing up bowl and use newspaper to get that appropriate finish.

The focal points of the majority of houses are the telly and the fire. In our big Red house where we all live, the focal point would be our display cabinet with our Manchester United Football Club history in it. We might have a Nottingham lace doylie on top of it with a fruit bowl on it. My Mam once said: "I don't like fruit in the house." When we asked her why she said: "Because it makes the house smell of fruit." What else was fruit ever going to smell of Mam? In the Brady house we would have tinned pears with Christmas Day tea, with Carnation cream. That was the Brady's input of vitamin 'C' for the year from fruit. The irksome smell of fruit safely contained within a shield of smell resistant tin.

Catarrh'ed and feathered...

In our new big Red house where we all live we would have plentiful supplies of organic, fair-traded fruit to keep our Roddy McDowell's in order. And there'd be a chippy next door that did smart chicken and cashew nuts. And a papershop next door to the chippy that would make you say "chocolate bar" every time you bought some chocolate as saying "chocolate bar" sounds so much better than just saying "chocolate." Our display cabinet containing all our history from 1878 would be as part of and as intimate to us, as is the window-shaped shine from the window that you get on your erect bell end. If it's bulbous enough, ie so much so that you could use it as a mirror to have a shave with - you can see if the curtains are drawn or not in your bell end, window reflection. To consider giving something so integral to your being away to some undeserving gnome would be deserving of the sentence passed down to all collaborators: Head roughly shaven and a tar and feathering.

Kingdom of Fevver...

And not even with some nice big feathers that, say, Samuel Pepys might have quilled his ink with or one that some native American Indian might have ran around and around and around a circle of wagon trains in his hair with. I am not going to actually achieve any military value by just going around and around and around your circle of wagon trains while you Winchester the fuck out of me but look at me feather, it's smart. No, the collaborator would receive some real shitty feathers found on a lorry squashed pigeon on Back Piccadilly. Or from our older, founding members of the club who would have organised a collection point for feathers from their leaky, old Eider downs. And the collection point for these feathers would have been one of their old piss buckets. And the tar would have been bulk bought and of poor quality thereby reducing the costs to the club for paying for your tar and feathering. Costs will have further been reduced due to the high amounts of founder members catarrh that was introduced into the tar.

Nothing matters Grey Mare'y when you're free...

Not putting '1878' on the first ever, fans paid for, flag would also be an insult to the old Grey Mare pub in Miles Platting. The Grey Mare pub in Miles Platting, affectionately known as Poodles Bar due to the Landlords less than straight hair, was a Red pub of the highest last order. It was bears arse but hilarious. It deserves a book on its own to do justice to the reckless rumbustuousness that went on within its sectionable walls but what it did have was The Busby Suite. The Busby Suite was a room off the main pub filled with Red memorabilia. In the pub itself anything could be bought, from packets of rindless back bacon with Arabic sell by dates to angle grinders. If I was a crime cracking police officer and I read about some gullible American being sold a bridge or the deeds to Jodrell Bank, then I'd suspect the perpetrator to have come from The Grey Mare. I wouldn't accuse any frequenter of the pub with my crime cracking feelings, as no one wants their name with the word 'Grass' painted after it all over the estate. I'd have accused some snot from Hale Barns and have framed them using all the police framing skills that have been used on our class over the years. And then in an 'Alias Smith and Jones, Hannibal Haze and Kid Curry' moment I'd have turned to my crime cracking partner and said: "What we gotta get Haze, is outta this business", and leave the police force as we were only in there in the first place so as to facilitate that last analogy.

It never rains in the vault...

But amongst all this petty and not so petty crime in The Grey Mare, amidst all the forehead scars and ladder length charge sheets, amongst the saws that could reduce barrel lengths and the unusually named Housing Benefit books, one thing remained sacrosanct in The Grey Mare pub: No swearing in The Busby Suite. It was a place to pay respectful homage to the man who changed Manchester United Football Club into the love we all fell for. Putting '2005' on the first ever, fans paid for flag would be like going into the Busby Suite and saying: "Lathered tit wank, fuck mop doc twateulogy." No, it would be more. It would be like going in there and saying "Lathered tit wank, fuck mop doc twateulogy and whilst we're at it, those fine bone-china tea set analogies and that bees waxed display cabinet we kept them in - I left them out in the back yard in all that bad weather and they finished up looking fucked. So I put them in the middin and the Corporation carted them off. I've ordered some nice MDF/Formica mix, corner cabinets and some Pyrex plates from the catalogue. That organic pomegranate from the fruit bowl on top was nice. Do you know there are exactly 365 seeds in a pomegranate? I've never counted them like but apparently there are. Thinking about it though, who would have counted them? We could be having our hat properly nailed on here. I retract that statement about there being 365 seeds in a pomegranate as it is unconfirmed and could just be a Ronald Rumour.

You'd be beaten severely and deservedly so. I'm not suggesting Steve Wood and Tom McKenna our first ever, fans paid for, flag organisers should be beaten severely, although Steve would probably benefit from a good hiding. What I did suggest to them, as FC United of Manchester were whacking the shite out of Ashton behind us on the pitch, was that it was not too late to argue for the flag to be changed, as Barmy Charlie the flag manufacturer was notoriously slow at producing flags. Whilst I was arguing this I brought in my second problem with the flag. By the glazed yet dismissive look in Steve and Tommy's eyes, I could see that they had hoped that I had forgotten about my second problem due to the first problem being so long and meandering. The second problem I had with the flag was that it was going to have 'Manchester's finest' written on it.

We are patently not Manchester's finest. Not only that, but in the fans meeting in town the previous week some attendees had stated that some Manchester United fans were hardening against us. Chris from Stretford had made an excellent point that the situation we faced was like concrete.

Concrete takes time to set. The views of the very, very small minority of United fans who were hardening against us were only hardening. Nothing was set; unity was the only way forward for us all. If that agreed on strategy of unity was to be adhered to, then didn't the flag stating 'Manchester's finest' stand in contradiction to that mood of unity? That was also not taking into consideration that the statement 'Manchester's finest' lacked subtlety and wit. If any statement was backslapping, Manchester city in context then 'Manchester's finest' was it. I'm bending the stick a bit cruelly there as I'm sure the dicks at self-back slapping city could come up with a far more excruciatingly embarrassing, self-aggrandising 'Did I ever tell you, we're great us' banner than that, as self-aggrandising is what little Manchester city excel at, the stone-washed denim suited, pippy snot swallowing, brown cuticle'd, finger smelling, artex ceiling'd, copper-panelled chimney breasted, ornament buying oafs.

But to have the first ever, fans paid for, banner of FC United of Manchester be at risk of being divisive was a point worth labouring over. And over. And over. Poor Steve Wood and Tommy McKenna had taken to wearing false glazed over eyes glasses to disguise their even more glazed over real eyes. But that first flag would always be the first flag. You don't get a second chance with first. Steve and Tommy's argument was that the fans who had paid for it had voted for it and decided. They had other options but 'Manchester's finest' was the chosen one. My argument was that it had been voted for in the very, very early days of our existence. Fuck me, we weren't two months old now but things had moved on at a Fireball XL5 pace. Arguments that were deemed relevant last week were now worthy of being archived in that big warehouse where they put that biblical box that killed all the Nazis at the end of Raiders of the Lost Ark. Our membership was growing and learning. If the argument could be put out there on the internet site that perhaps 'Manchester's finest' was already outdated and not fitting of the Unity Offensive we were now engaged in, then the membership, because everything was so new to us, would reconsider their earlier vote for the flag and change it to something else more pert and pertinent.

If nothing else I can look back and say I tried. No one will probably give a shite. With not being on the internet I couldn't do anything about internet debates but I had put my three pence in with people who were and if there was no resonance then there was no resonance, but at least you had put on the shirt, been proud to wear it and tried. Football fans rarely ask for more than that. I'm a democratic centralist. You cannot have democracy without centralism. You vote democratically and then you all abide by it. If you don't like it then you argue more vociferously the next time you get the opportunity but in the mean time you go along with what the majority have decided. Otherwise there would be no democracy. It would just be a big vote that you could do what you wanted with or choose to ignore. Like the Labour Party Conference.

The unbearable likeness of Lisa Scott Lee'ing...

The third thing that was learnt from our two visits to Northwich Victoria's ground was the importance of ground configuration. More specifically, toilet facilities. There is not a ground in the premiership that I have not been into the toilet. That doesn't single me out from anyone else who goes to the game and wants a squirt. What does, perhaps, make me slightly different is the fact I have also been into and used the women's toilet during the game of every single Premiership ground. What you get in the women's toilet is cleanliness and the chance to be next to the cubicle where a female is pissing like a horse. A dainty little spinnerooney type female goes into the toilet but when she pulls down her draws she reveals a urethra not too dissimilar to an emergency chute on an aeroplane. The sound of her dispensed urine hitting the toilet water at horse piss thickness and horse piss speed is noisier than Noisy Bodine. And we all know how noisy Noisy Bodine was. I'm not saying you get a lob on, but. Actually, I am saying you get a lob on. It breaks up the tediousness of some Premiership matches where the opposition think they can play 10-0-0 against a Manchester United side and think they'll bore a draw out of us by wooing us into deep slumber. Silvestre often falls for it, the nodding get.

Of course, you can get it wrong if a big piano shifter comes into the cubicle next door and fires out a mix and you find yourself unwillingly wiffing the biz of a big'un but mostly it is worth the risk.

The cistern chapel...

It's authority's fault I go in women's toilets. Many years ago a bar called Bar 38 opened up on Canal Street in town. Our mate, Besty from Clayton - who held the dubious award of being the youngest out of us to lose his virginity, age 11 - was the doorman so we could always get in for a drink no mattered how kalide we were. It was the first bar I knew that had mixed communal toilets. The first time I went in it I didn't see the sign to say it was mixed, I just thought, as had been my whole life experience, that if you saw a bloke coming out of a toilet - Martin Edwards aside - then that meant that the toilets were for blokies. When I walked in all the cubicle doors were shut but the four sinks by the door were being pissed in by four blokes. As one bloke left the sink another would start pissing in it. I was desperate to go so I joined the sink-pissing queue. When it was my turn I started pissing in the sink but turned the tap on, as I wasn't dragged up.

Unluckily just as I had started all the three blokes at the side of me zipped up and left. In the next few ensuing seconds a rake of girls burst into the toilets and, at the same time, all the cubicle doors opened to reveal women leaving the trap. I was mid-piss and was left to be the centre of disgust by a toilet full of women. My argument of: "There was loads of blokes doing it so I just joined in" sounded as feeble as it was under such female attack. One bloke came in during the abuse but, as I probably would have done in such a hostile environment, he stayed right out of it and queued politely for a cubicle. I left shamefaced and scarred. And from that day forth I always went in women's toilets at away games. If the Manchester Licensing Authorities had not allowed Bar 38 to be so liberal with its pissing piss policies I might have been normal.

United wee stand...

As you probably wanted to know, Blackburn is by far and away the best women's toilets in the Premiership. Though, Derby's a few years ago, before they went down, were nice. The worst were Southampton's old Dell toilets. What Northwich Victoria brought to the proceedings was a toilet design so breathtakingly obvious that you are at a loss to think why it is not at every football ground that has ever been built. I was going for a burst during game and was on my way to the women's as I thought that I might as well do every women's toilet in the North West Counties League. My ever so funny friends decided to shout at the nearby police officer that I was on the way to the women's toilet and that he should watch me. He did, so I had to go into the blokies. I'm so glad I did. Northwich Victoria's toilets at each end of the ground have a window above the piss stones. Nothing too unusual there. If a toilet didn't have a window it might be dark.

What makes Northwich Victoria's windows so different is the fact that they are at head height.

And they open outwards.

At the Victoria Stadium you can open the window and watch the game in progress whilst you are pissing. How simple. Nothing needs to be missed. Obviously, if you are a dwarf it might not be such a good view but they deserve a bit of bad luck for their regressive role in the campaign to bring back safe standing into football stadia. The midget, bosses men, bar stool sized bastards. They're not that daft though, as Reds might call dwarves but they win out again as they are always breast height when dancing with any woman at weddings or birthday do's. Just watch the dwarf. They waddle up to the bar at any function and get a half as it looks like a pint in their hand, so they can mug everyone that they are knocking back pint after pint. They'll forget about the half pint rule, though, when it's your round. They stand there and eye up the female contenders to dance with. The woman with the largest table polishers will be sure to be called upon for 'Come dwarf dancing' later. It could be your wife or your daughter or your sister who goes home with dwarf drool all over their mellodians.

Manchester United at the back of their stands have executive boxes looking out onto the pitch. If there was ever another reason to hate executives and their corporate swilling, then that is it. If we ever get to go back into Old Trafford, victorious in our fight against greed and big business, then the exec boxes are being ripped out and toilets with head height, opening windows looking out on the pitch are being put back in. Juan La Porta didn't promise half as much and got in at Barcelona as Chairman. We'll piss it. We don't need the dwarf vote.

Daz ultras...

The fourth in a long, long line of things we learnt at Northwich Victoria was the acceptable face of dog masturbation. That sentence really will need some explanation. Two out of the three buses that left Chorlton Street in town for the game stayed behind at the Easy and Slow pub in Northwich after the game for a few beers. They were joined by many more in cars, including those cars driven by the players. Reds were being mithered by camera Monsieurs from French television. They were begrudgingly accepted, mainly due to the fact of who they weren't. They weren't some knob from Sky who cannot seem to film anyone who isn't wearing a football shirt or a team coloured wig. They were also more accepted as the beer went down.

They went live at one point with the lights for the cameras searing down on Rory Patterson. The cameras whirred as the broadcaster asked serious questions of our talented forward player. There was a silence around the pub as the questions and answers Agincourt arrowed about. At this point our Daz leaves our company and goes up to the side of Rory Patterson and into the intense glare of the cameras lights. He starts to nudge Rory's arm going: "Rory, Rory." The interviewer continued like a professional and so did Rory ignoring the bowling ball armed, interview intruder. The intruder was not going to go away. "Rory, Rory." The nudges turned into gentle shakes that turned into persistent small scale shoving that resulted in Rory Patterson sort of 'D Day landing craft' rocking as he tried to answer the live French television questions. It was only a matter of time before they would have to accede to the intruder's request for attention. It came seconds later.

At an impasse between French question and FC United of Manchester player answer, there fell a silence where it was impossible not to have been worn down by the intruders insistence. Rory Patterson turned to Daz, the French live cameras turned to Daz, the French interviewer turned to Daz, the French lights turned to Daz, the amassed Red clientele in the pub turned to Daz, the rest of the assorted FC United of Manchester players, management staff and board turned to Daz, our corner containing all his mates turned to Daz. What was so important that he had to go up and pursue and pursue the socially unacceptable unpursueable? In that moment of dead air television that is interminable Daz puts on his most sincere voice, his most quizzical stance, his most interested face and confidently long balls out into the world the question: "Have you ever wanked a dog off? Two dogs, two hands."

You can't comeback from that and so no one tried. French-Anglo relations hit Eric heights. On the coach back into town afterwards the song was sung, to the tune of 'Sloop John B/ We paid for their home': "Two dogs with two hands, two dogs with two hands, dog pleasuring Patterson, two dogs with two hands." This was accompanied by the placing into the air of both hands and traditional masturbatory hand movements being played out. If ever a one-all equaliser was scored by fans getting Mr Patterson back for that game at the pre-season friendly at Stalybridge, where Rory had done that thing where players point over their shoulders to the back of their shirts with both their thumbs, then that was it. Hopefully we will never see its thumb pointing like again.

Coach potato...

That coach home was also to be the first place I ever conga'd up the aisle of a coach. Much to the chagrin of the health and safety conscious coach driver. This was also the first time that the 'Free Barrie George' tune came out. The tune being Diana Ross' 'I'm coming out.' There was no mention of Barrie George on this occasion as that was to come in the next week. This time the words to the tune went: "He's coming out, he wants the world to know, he wears a sheepskin coat" in homage to the ridiculously obscene sheepskin coat with hood that the health and safety conscious coach driver was wearing. It was a mere three days out of August and he was wearing a sheepskin coat. With a hood. Presumably just in case it got three days out of August exceptionally cold. As it so often does.

Admittedly, "He's coming out, he wants the world to know, he wears a sheepskin coat" is not the longest or most refinedly worded song but it really accepts itself to conga'ing. But because it suits conga'ing so much it brought forward the old 'Conga on a coach' paradox. The essence of the conga is to try and get as many people to join in. On a coach, the more people who join in, means the less you can conga as you go through the coach window, so you actually want less people to conga on a coach. Even though you cannot help saying: "Come on" to everyone in a jolly manner to goad them into a foot-flailing frenzy. So there we were, stuck right in the middle of the 'Conga on a coach' paradox. The most conga friendly tune you could hope for but coming at the time you were on a coach.

As in most things Football Club United of Manchester, we did all right. We alcy flushedly balanced the importance of numbers in a conga with the acceptable length of line to stop us crashing and dying. Crashing and dying always being something to be avoided as it moots the atmosphere a morsel. When we got too many in number there seemed to be a 'subs in a five-a-side game' voluntary dropping out of one or two from the line as enthusiastic conga'ers volunteered for a breather. Only for them to reappear at a later stage in the sheepskin shong as others took the bath. And all co-ordinated with a communal shout of: "Turnaround" as those at the front of the conga recognised their lack of coach length to dance in and in a one word instant, went from being at the front of the conga to being at the back. Self-policing at its Football Club United of Manchester best.

We won 4-0 at the game by the way, as I'm not sure if I told you that. We continue to be top of the league.

CHAPTER EIGHT

PARTY LIKES IT'S £19.99...

Castleton Gabriels versus Football Club United of Manchester, Saturday the 17th of September 2005. Kick Off 3pm. Played at Radcliffe Borough's ground.

It's just the thought of you, the very thought of you, my love...

Before we start this chapter it's essential that you are made aware of the Moore and Company Construction Solicitors League and Non-League News round up Number 3 regarding goalpost safety. More specifically metal cup-hooks. As you would expect numerous enquiries have been received by The F.A. mostly from Club and Match Officials seeking clarification on the subject of metal cup-hooks on any part of the goal. To date, two Non-League matches have been postponed by match officials. Having now referred the matter to both The F.A.'s Legal Department and Referees Department, Steve Williams, National Facilities Manager can confirm the following procedures should be undertaken by the match referee…

> It should be the responsibility of the designated referee to point out to the participating clubs or the pitch users before the game that any metal cup-hooks on either the goalposts or the crossbar could constitute a danger. This could constitute finger entrapment due to the wearing of a ring or create severe neck injuries due to other jewellery being worn such as earrings or necklaces. Whilst the Laws of the Game clearly state that jewellery should not be worn during any part of a match, such dangers also exist prior to, or immediately after matches, where nets need to be fitted or removed by any user or club personnel.
>
> If both teams are prepared to play, having had this fact pointed out to them, then it is The F.A.'s view that the referee can be considered to have done as much as might be reasonable in the circumstances.

Basically The F.A. are saying that you, as the goalie, can't come out onto the pitch with your brew and, as you're a professional and want to keep an eye on proceedings as the match progresses, be legally able to put your cup on a hook. It's because you care so much about your fellow professionals that you don't just want to put the cup in the back of the net where someone could trip over it. You want to hang it on a metal cup-hook out of dangers way. The very use of the cup-hook has cleanliness written into its existence as it means that you would have washed the cup out with the water from your bottle, as no one wants a filthy brown ring. Washing your filthy brown ring away is a positive. If I went back to a woman's house on a first date and she presented to me a filthy brown ring, I would not think as highly of her as I might normally have done if she had no evidence of uncleaned browness. This would obviously depend on how desperate I was to drink out of her furred up cup.

Hanging the cup on the metal cup-hook holders also means that the cup will now drain and dry efficiently and be ready for its next brew. Nothing but hygiene and player safety are the winners from metal cup-hooks. And now they are being banned from all levels of the game at the commencement of season 2007/2008. We came down ten divisions to escape such illogical and mind befuddling, nonsensical bureaucracy. You can't even have a brew now. Steve Williams, the F.A. National Facilities Manager, should really look at his decision and the far-reaching ramifications it will have. Again I fear FC United of Manchester will be at the fore of this fight because if the referee comes up to us all lar-dee-dar pointing out that if we are prepared to play, despite the presence of metal cup-hooks, then we will take that challenge as these colours run from no one.

Café come home...

This anger got the power breakfast off to a moody start but dissipated when we found we could say the sentence: "We're playing Cassy Gabs at Raddy B's ground." And we did annoyingly say: "We're playing Cassy Gabs at Raddy B's ground" a lot during the day. Far too often to be considered acceptable. To say 'power breakfast' would also be overstating history. A decision had been taken that before we went to see Cassy Gabs playing at Raddy B's ground we would all meet in the restaurant bit of BHS in town and have a breakfast before getting the Jaap. Eight items £2.29 with a piece of toast thrown in freemans. Bargain. You could have ten items for £2.59, but like the Oxy 10'd lad at the till is going to know the difference between eight and ten items when it's a Jackson Pollock of beans, tomatoes, both tinned or fresh, scramblies, bacon, sausage, mushrooms, tater hash browns, fried bread and thumb-plaster residue.

No breakfast is complete without the Assistant putting her thumb plaster into your bean juice as she is holding your plate. Of course she must suck her thumb immediately after she has given you the plate. This means that her saliva will be there for the next time she thumb-plasters the next plate. It's this bacteria that makes us strong. All these Detox'd work surface generation of children with asthma should just get down to BHS in town for their unlicensed cure. Throw those inhalers in the middin you wheezin, over-protected gets and go and lick the knobbly underside of a burnt black frying pan or scrape your fingers down the outside of the stove and suck the crumb-dripfluff, wetwax gelatine and cheese combo from under your fingernails. Don't come to us with your note saying: "Aww, Sir, I can't do PE today, it's me chezzy", just rub your head in puddles more often than you do now.

It might only be 30 pence saved from £2.29 to £2.59 but it is the jibbing principle and again the thirty pence is better in our paw than that of a large department store. We'd had enough this day of large departments with the decisions of the F.A.'s Legal Department and the Referees Department on metal cup-hooks. FC United of Manchester's fight back against those laws had started with those procured 30 pences. Steve Williams beware.

Having breakfast at BHS around nine or ten o'clock will probably become a tradition over the coming season as it fills you up for the coming frivolities. As John Travolta so sagely sang, grease lining your stomach for any alcohol excesses that are going to rear their beautiful, adorable, frothy heads. Nine or ten o'clock is not too early a time so that it is horrendous as in an early start to get to Southampton or Charlton, but its early enough so that you know you are going to an away game otherwise you would still be in your feather. But it is also late enough for you to not worry too much on the Friday night about going out. BHS serve breakfast till 11 so if you went out and got to bed at two'ish on the Friday then you could still theoretically get nearly nine hours sleep before you had to get to BHS.

Of course you could leave it later and go in either Koffee Pot in Stevenson's Square or Koffee Pot Two on Great Ancoats Street for the all day breakfast and sneak in a later nosebag, but you need some structure to your footballing life and 11 o'clock is not a bad structure to adhere to. If it becomes a contentious issue we could always raise it at the AGM of FC United of Manchester and resolve it by a show of hands. Also Koffee Pot and Koffee Pot Two have been known to contain a whole Assistant's thumb plaster in the breakfast. A hint of thumb plaster is tasty and, as proven, a healthy addition. An actual fallen off thumb plaster, where the sticky bit to the plaster has gone rubbery black and unsticky curly and the yellow good for you bit contains a thick outlined stain in the shape of Wellyphant, and all this taking place under the snotty bit in your egg, is a bit too queasy for some. Not for me though because if Wellyphant is on it then it has got to be safe.

I say theoretically get eight or nine hours sleep if you come in at two o'clock on a Friday morning, as everyone knows an alcohol induced sleep is not a very good way of getting a good bo bo's as it is not a quality sleep. So your eight or nine hours achieved after coming in at two would be of a poor quality. Strange that, though, as you can sleep on a stairwell landing when mango'd but you can't when not. I've had some eminent nods upside down in a bucket with only Swarfega as a pillow.

We all rounded off our full breakfasts having established who was a bacon fat cutteroffer, who broke their yoke with the traditional toast or the end of the sausage and who was an egg and bacon eater. 'Egg and bacon eating' is the process whereby you attempt to get as many items of your breakfast onto the same forkfull so as to take in all the tastes of the breakfast. You quickly realise that the hardness and the flatness of the bacon goes last onto the fork as if you poked the bacon onto the fork first and then attempted to get a soft, white piece of the egg on after it, then the hardness and flatness of the bacon would squash the egg and make it impossible to fork up.

Better then to get the egg on first, it being the softer, say followed by a soft bean or two, then a bit of tomato, then firm it all into place on the fork with a soft inside of the sausage, but a soft inside of the sausage enveloped in the harder exterior of the crisped sausage skin to prove you're on the road to semi-firmer upping, then some toast then, and only then, go for the piece of bacon. Adding the bacon onto the fork will serve the purpose of pushing all the other previously forked breakfast items further up the fork, compressing them into a meaty mouthful that is steady on the fork and going nowhere but gobwards. That is the style of eating a full breakfast that is known as 'Egg and bacon eating.'

It is not the best-named style of eating, as obviously the crux of 'Egg and bacon eating' is to get far more than just egg and bacon on your fork. The reason it is called 'Egg and bacon eating' is that the style of eating is easily transferable to other foods. That is you can 'Egg and bacon eat' a Sunday dinner for example. You can start off your forkful with, say, some softer cabbage or some mash, then follow it with some peas, then replace the 'softer interior, crispier outer skin' role of the sausage in the full breakfast, directly with a roast potato that has all the 'softer interior, crispier outer skin' qualities of the sausage of the full breakfast but this time its role has been transferred to the Sunday dinner plate and its skills have been taken up by the roastie. Then on your Sunday dinner fork you can put some bread or a carrot or broccoli and then finish off with the piece of chicken breast that replicates the harder, flattening role of the bacon in any full breakfast 'Egg and bacon eating ' scheme. It's the style of eating in attempting to get as many items from your plate onto the same forkful that gives this particular style of eating its distinctive characteristics.

But back to BHS. Our column of full breakfast nosebag should be that secure on the fork that the sweeping through of plate juices with it is easily achieved with no loss. I'm sorry if I have mixed the thought of a full breakfast with the thought of a Sunday dinner in the last few paragraphs as the two don't really mix and can lead to quease in some Reds. That's why I am ill at ease with the cockneys use of bubble and squeak on a breakfast plate. It's cabbage and it is potato. Wrong time of day, dickheads. I also blame them for the increasing use of tater hash browns on breakfast menus. I know it's an American invention but we all saw it first many years ago eating breakfasts down south on United aways.

But back again for a second time to our full breakfast column of nosebag on our fork. It should be that safe on your fork that at this point in your eating you could easily enter in conversation about being slightly concerned that Gareth Ormes is the only left back in the FC United of Manchester squad or how much nicer it would have been if Kevin Elvin, our main right back, would have been called Kelvin Elvin. Or Kevin Evin. Or if Gareth Ormes played for big United and he had a good game then the Mirror would have a headline of 'Great Ormes.' Being confident with the secure nature of the breakfast items fixed to your fork affords you the time to luxuriate over deep football talk. We luxuriated away the morning.

Rennies at the ready we eventually got on the Jaap. The majority of away games in this league are within close proximity so you can be at home but also be going away. The North West Counties League dichotomy. This trip to see FC United of Manchester play Cassy Gabs at Raddy B's ground was one of those home but away dichotomies. We got off the stop before Radcliffe, at Whitefield, and went in the pub right opposite the tram stop called The Church. The lads from around Prestwich said that this was a fine boozer and we'd get a quiet drink whereas if we went closer to the ground we would have to push and shove and shout over singers.

The Church is a Holt's house and so you expected the lager drinkers to say "It Shimla Pinks in here." And they did. There is something Capstan Full Strength and ear hair about Holt's houses but really it's a case of fck lager drinkers as there is enough places now that only do lager and shit smooth bitter. We have to suffer their 'bar' culture enough times, so wrap it you bellends and see what a proper beer is like. Mmmmmmmmm. I had my first drink of Holt's bitter at 11.59 a.m., just getting in a swifty swig before the second finger hit 12 so that I could say I'd been on the beer since morning time in case I did anything pissed up daft later in the day. Reds always let you off for doing something daft after the daft event if drinking since breakfast time is involved. It's a Red understanding alcoholic family like that.

The lager drinkers moaned, ordered a pint of Diamond, coughed, gurgled, spluttered, said a couple of "Good Jesus'es", moaned again and then went on bottles. The vault in The Church crowded up with us all. It was not just us though. Connections with connections meant that the quality of drinkers in that pub, that was so far away from the ground that it had nothing to do with the coincidence of passing drinking, was of the highest standards that Manchester United Football Club had come to expect. Banter, beer, bollocks, the 3 B's of football fans pervaded every percale pleat of the pub curtains. It's still so early in our FC United of Manchester days but having Reds around you who had gone through the same decisions and heartbreak as you made the bearing of the loss that tidgey bit easier at wholesome Red times like this.

I looked around me at that crowded pub and there was no one who I wouldn't go for a beer with outside of football. The 15 or so in our company safely ensconced themselves in the big bay of the vault window, with the clatter of the vault bubbling behind us. We took in a few pints of relaxative and let the comfort ease us through the early first hours of the afternoon. The sun shone approvingly through the big bay window at such an angle that it went from the bay of the room to the pool table at the back. It lit up the faces of the righteous men and women who had hurt so much that last summer but who were still here smiling and holding onto peace. I was in the shade by the sidewall of the window.

The people who were in that pub would rage against being called righteous as all of them to a manly man, womanly woman, manly woman, womanly man respected the decisions of all Reds in whatever decision they had come to over the summer but sometimes an outsider, sitting in the shade, has to say it for them. These were good, good people. All across north Manchester that day on the road to watch FC United of Manchester play Cassy Gabs at Raddy B's ground there were good, good people. In The Last orders and The Colliers and The Lord Raglan and many more, the light that wouldn't go out was having a go at brightening everything up.

These people had deprived themselves of watching Rooney grow into the player they knew he was going to be. And they did it whilst being nothing but proud of the Reds who had stayed behind. Knowing the hurt that was crucifying them. Knowing it because they had racked through it themselves and if ever the 'Social Services seminar' word of empathy had any resonance in a situation, then this was it. Take off their small enamel pin badges, be that an FC United of Manchester badge or a Manchester United Football Club badge, and use the fastening back pin to slice their skin and they all seeped the deepest, deepest of red. Nothing could break the bloodline. It might have been the Holt's, it probably was, but here my heart knew calm.

Until a respected, honourable and deeply admired Red came in and disturbed my visions of FC United of Manchester forever. I could never be the same again after what he imparted to me. Just as my heart knew calm it vaulted.

We come in peace for all mankind...

We took the lead after 11 minutes against Castleton Gabriels. All our dreams of that day had come true - we were now watching FC United of Manchester play Cassy Gabs at Raddy B's ground. Jozzer Lead Sock's big daft head played a lovely header down to Rory Patterson who serenly placed the ball into the bottom left of the net as the goalie came towards him. The Oljabols in the crowd were predicting ten. Castleton Gabriels had a lot of fat, tough blokes at the back who did that thing we had seen many times before when teams from a lower division had come to Old Trafford in cup competitions. The fat blokes at the back started the game in the first

20 minutes shouting and bawling the bestestist of games. Their demeanour was that of 'I could of made it, I just didn't get the good fortune to get noticed.'

There is a truth in that for some. Not for all. Castleton Gabriels' back four were probably in that last category. In the first 20 minutes the adrenalin whizzes around the not so skilled giving them previously unpossessed talent. It is never going to last and a biffen stripping always ensues. The unvanquishable demeanour of the first 20 minutes is slowly replaced by a hunchback and a resignation brought on by the realisation that Darwinism can almost certainly be applied to association football and the heights you attain within it. Our second goal came from Ryan 'Scarsky and Hutch' Gilligan. The third and final goal I missed because I was parroting. That is going to happen to a lot of people a lot of times this season.

Malcolm Glazer's banks and sons came to take away our funds, but everyone must stand behind the Reds behind the wire…

There's just too much to discuss and our get-togethers are an ideal time to discuss them. Unfortch the match is on at the same time. Castleton Gabriels' goalie, Mark Canning, had been having a great game up until the third goal. A corner from Rawlinson had caused confusion in the box. In this kerfuffle young Mark somehow managed to help a Rob Nugent effort into the net by way of him overhead kicking it in himself. If that sounds confusing it is, because it was.

It could be argued that because the score remained at 3-0 then the fat blokes at the back didn't do too bad. They were clapped off and deservedly so as no one should be so red-faced and not be appreciated. Not wishing to get all 'Chariots of Fire' on you but the only unsporting part of the day came from us lot at the side of the pitch. Dave Chadwick, Margy's 'run through brickwalls' signing, decided he should share his specialist brickwall ignoring gift with Castleton Gabriels' number ten Denny Khan. Very kind of him. Chadwick 's momentum in the challenge on Khan saw Khan taken for an unwanted waltz right into the brickwall at the side of the terrace. Because we were right where Denny Khan hit the wall, he disappeared out of our sight as he was escorted by Chadwick's body into the welcoming, if unforgiving arms of the wall.

The wall bulged as Khan's head battered into it and the clump noise was sickening. This was very serious. At that speed and at that angle he must have broken his neck. The noise as he hit the wall silenced everyone at a level not seen since the David Buust incident, when Buust spilled his broken bone blood all over Schmeichel's 18-yard box. Everyone silently prayed that there was a doctor in the crowd. And not a shit one that did it in music or something shit like that.

The last thing FC United of Manchester needed at this time in our early infancy was a body bag. Obviously you'd feel sorry for the boy and his family but fck, a dead player is not good press. As the heavy hush dominated, a voice from our company shouted "Get up you fckn mard arse, you won't melt." And like Lazarus with a bump that was in dire need of witch hazel, he did. Denny Khan, out of our sight as he had hit the wall below our sight line, had hit it with his shoulder and not his bonce. Smart.

We had to go on the post match piss to have a few blood thinners to celebrate life. Denny wouldn't have wanted it any other way if he had passed away. The fact he lived to sample a lifetime of Tia Marias was a Brucey bonus. We now know though that we have an attempted murderer in our team in the bulk that is David Chadwick. He is a Wigan blue though, so it hardly came as a surprise to the Reds that were present.

We left the ground and went to the nearest beer house in stark red, white and black contrast to our previous pub out in Whitefield before the game. Ohh you just don't know where you are with FC United of Manchester, we just won't be compartmentalised. The pub was called The Victoria and was Faz's local. It was ten deep at the bar. It should have been called The Nil by Mouth. Faz is a ginger get who wants beating with a big stick to keep him restrained. The only reasonable thing about Faz's existence is that he is a gravedigger. He tries to tell you that he isn't but nothing else but extensive shovelling up explains the amount of Elizabeth Duke gold on his whereabouts.

He does something in graveyards anyway as he is always in them. Whenever you ring him he is always in a cemetery. In actual fact he's a Stonemason that specialises in death. He engraves headstones for a living. That's not a job, that's an Amsterdam fetishist pastime. Getting back to the only good thing about Faz though, is the fact that he engraved Matt Busby's headstone. And for that we all love him.

For everything else we wish him nothing but orange freckles on his ginger face and that his ginger eyelashes get even lighter, giving him that fiend look that means that even if he gets picked up by the police for a minor traffic offence, then he will still serve life. None of us would go to court as a character witness to save him. We might send him a cake with a file in when he is inside. This might seem kind on our part but it would be a cake with just an actual ring binder file in it so that he could document, and neatly alphabetise, the amount of times he's been illegally entered and by whom. Some people alphabetise their record collection. Faz, with a lifetime of prison in front of him for the crime of being a 'glow in the dark' headed, 'moth attractor' skinned, male ginger, could do it with his grufty lovers. They would nail him and then pull up his jumper to reveal his translucent skin, to enable them to energy efficiently read their books on monster trucks and wrestling in the cell darkness.

The Victoria is Faz's local by the virtue of the fact that if you went out through the backdoor of the pub - which you can't because there isn't one, but if you could - then you would be at Faz's front door. He was rambling on as he does. This time it was about how great it all was that FC United of Manchester was playing virtually on his front door step and how he could get gassed and just fall over and be home. As he told this story over and over again to the different Reds that came into our company we hit saturation point. We plotted. A squad rotation system was devised to ensure that at least one of our company feigned interest in Faz's repeat story of how handy Faz's house was to the pub we were in.

As these brave martyrs had 'Faz story punishment' inflicted on them a small but elite squad of us went outside and rearranged his garden. Childish but funny. He was right though; he was very handy for the pub. Faz's innocent face as we Charlie Dimmocked him was worth living through his boring story of how some graves that had previously been designated for four burials could now only accommodate three due to subsidence over the years. Being involved in graveyards and all things dead meant that he had two giant slabs of marble in his garden. Why we are not sure but they were there. They became a very heavy doormat if I remember correctly. Everyone's chippy papers were posted through his letterbox with such things as 'We hope you get calcium deficiency spots under your nails' and 'If you're walking around the countryside on a pleasant summer evening we hope that any gnats flying about will mob up and always be at head height and annoy you' written on them. In an act that might actually go beyond humour and into the realms of the reckless, we also fitted metal cup-hooks around his front door casing.

This game also witnessed the first airing of: “Free Barrie George, he wants the world to know, he didn't kill Dando.” The song's words adapted to the

'He wants the world to know, he's got a sheepskin coat' tune. We know it was its first airing because we had only just told Found-a-Fiver the words in the Raddy B's clubhouse. As the Wig Wammers wigwammed that day, we could see him from across the pitch, both pre and post Denny Khan dint in the wall, bouncing up and down quite contentedly singing on his own. Lenin started with less. Almost certainly.

CHAPTER NINE

SPIRIT, PATIENCE, GENTLENESS…

Eccleshall versus Football Club United of Manchester, Saturday the 5th of November 2005. Bumfire night. Kick Off 3pm. Played at Stafford Rangers' ground.

Too long have I loved, so unattached within…

The Saturday before the Eccleshall away game on the 29th of October, FC United of Manchester had a Saturday off from any league fixtures. It was deckchairs all round as the box of toys could put their cheesy bottom ends up and rest awhile, pleased with their deserved top of the league status. Not with our board. Inheriting frightening Glazer tactics, they decided that we had to play a match that was purely a mechanism for making money. They played a friendly behind the not so substantial prison walls of Thorncross Young Offenders Institute.

Ryan Gilligan, our miscreant midfielder, had once served time in there when he was younger as he had robbed a kebab shop. Unfortunately he robbed it whilst driving his works van with his works number on it. As Margy said on the day: "He was never in the top class. He didn't get English 'O' levels as he couldn't spell 'O' and he didn't get Maths 'O' level as he can only count up to the amount of testicles Hitler had." The loot from his not so well thought out robbery was apparently buried on the playing fields of Thorncross Young Offenders Institute. Our board reasoned that under the guise of playing a community orientated game, against lads who had mischieved slightly but through football could achieve a higher standing in society, they would get into Thorncross. Whilst distracting the authorities with fluid four-four-two football a crack team would dig up Gilligan's buried treasure from his youthful heist. So we were putting out an 'Oceans Eleven' 11 to build up club funds in a way paramilitary Red rebels have done for years.

The team, the programme editor, the referee, the wife of the referee, the wife of a board member who came to the game because she's mates with the wife of the referee, a journalist from the MEN and a 'session in Mulligan's and O'Sheas the night before' me, set off from outside the White Lion in town. I'd never been in a prison before. I've been to court and convicted three times for Breach of the Peace, Drunk and Disorderly and Shoplifting but only ever got fines and bound over. As it turned out, any reservations that we were going to get bullied and bummed - as you always remember where you were when you heard that Elvis had shot Kennedy and where you were when you watched 'Scum' - were soon eased. The prisoners were frightened away by the new FC United of Manchester tracksuits the team were being forced to wear.

Dearest Tony Jordan - no wonder you were never allowed into Moston's 'Fanny Licking Belt Whipper' gang with such poor designer tastes. They don't even have YKK zips. I suppose it was a good job really that TJ had designed them that badly as FC United of Manchester's firm that day, due to her majesty's crowd restrictions, was me, the wife of the referee and the wife of a board member who came to the game because she's mates with the wife of the referee. The black tracksuit bottoms alone with the red 'Sally Army' stripe down the leg was enough to put off Thorncross Y.O.I. lads. Although, if it went off I'd get right behind the wife of the referee as she looked a right handful.

As the team got changed the wife of the referee and the wife of a board member who came to the game because she's mates with the wife of the referee walked around the pitch we were about to play on. They showed me which mushrooms were magic and which ones weren't. The wife of the referee is responsible for the food in The Curry Club at our home games.

We thought we were just being right on when we added a vegetarian option to the meaty curry menu but it is now so obvious why the mushroom Bhunas are such a big seller with Reds. It would also explain why the atmosphere in the Manchester Road End is so wired.

The programme editor had gone all fancy on us and was getting himself a game, as the records will show that we only took 11 players to play. I was also offered a game, so in the unique environment of retrieving stolen kebab shop takings for club funds, it wasn't that hard to play for FC United of Manchester on this day. I refused on behalf of my deaf legs. My head plays a crisp, neat, passing game mixed in with speed and invention of movement with that unbeatable mix of craft and graft. No ball is too high or too fast to bring down and kill with one touch, no defence unbreachable, no defender unknockdownable, no opposition player not teararsepassable, no goal glory unattainable. Unfortunately this doesn't transfer to my feet that consistently go hard of hearing when my head tells them to do good stuff.

The Never Was'ers, never was'ing…

In footballing terms, my head would have gone to Manchester Grammar sporting a freshly cut short back and sides and wearing a school cap, and carrying a brown leather satchel that contained a wooden pencil case, with a sliding wooden lid, that when slid back revealed a protractor and a compass inside it. However, my feet would have gone to Belle Vue Backwards in Gorton in wellies in summer. Or possibly done basket weaving or Harvest Festival card making at Ten Acres Special School in Newton Heath. Reality deemed that I played on the right wing for North Manchester High School for boys and peaked there, never fulfilling my potential to play for The Never Was'ers from The Vic on Grey Mare Lane in Beswick as my Dad, his brother Arthur and our Christine's godfather Kenny Fowler had done.

The records will also show that the first ever programme editing, ex-Steering Committee member to take to the pitch in an FC United of Manchester kit was also the first programme editing, ex-Steering Committee member to score a goal. It was an all right goal described by some as the best of the seven in our 7-1 victory. The programme editing, ex-Steering Committee member will just tell you it was the best goal ever. What the records won't show, and I'm here to tell the world, is of the two worst misses that association football has ever seen. The programme editing, ex-Steering Committee member showed proper 'Life sized, charity plastic boy, outside paper shop with calliper and slot in head to donate change through' skills. If he tries to bore you with his great goal story then just get him to go through his two misses. As he was going onto the pitch as substitute to replace some - cough ahem - new player I shouted him back and said: "I've got something for you." When he enquired what, I reached into my pocket, took out an empty hand and gave it to him saying: “There's some skill.” There is a reason he edits programmes and doesn't play when we're not doing an undercover heist.

The match gave a few squad members the chance of a run out. I saw our new second goalie for the first time. As many of you will now know, he's not thin. He's no size eight. You wouldn't get on a seesaw with him, as it would be really boring being stuck up in the air. You also wouldn't want him to stand on your foot. Margy was heard to say: “People think I sold Phil Priestley our previous second goalie but in actual fact Melville just ate him."

The game was just really windy and was only notable for the amount of abuse Darren Lyon's heading skills came in for and for Margy actually telling, not one, but two funny jokes. This really was an unusual day. Here they are. Usually I would tell you to look away at the threat of a Margy joke but this is Margy doing alright:

> This bloke is the best wasp noise listen to'erer in the world. There is not a wasp noise he has not listened to, does not know or does not recognise. He is walking down Market Street one Saturday and he sees an advert in HMV's window saying 'The album of the best wasp noises ever.' He's intrigued as any wasp noise listen to'erer would be. He goes in and asks the Assistant if he can borrow the shop's headphones and listen to the album. The Assistant agrees and puts the album on for him. He listens to the album all the way through. He's perplexed. He goes up to the Assistant and says: "I'm a world renowned authority on wasp noise listening to'ing and I have listened to the album you have just put on and I don't recognise one single wasp noise." The

Assistant looks at him then looks at the album and says: "Oh sorry mate, I put the Bee - side on."

That's is by far and away and by far and away on a bus, the best joke that Margy has told. It goes down hill with this next one. Actually a hill is not a steep enough incline. They found a defunct volcano on Mars that was three times higher than Everest. It could go down the side of that. After standing on top of it on a box:

This bloke goes into a Psychiatrists and goes: "Hiya Doc, I'm having these dreams where I'm on a desert island. Only the beach is blue, the sea is crimson and the sky is scarlet. Can you tell me what it all means?"

The Psychiatrist turns to him and says: "That's easy. You've been marooned."

You let this man manage your club.

To help you take your mind off Margy's jokes, why don't you ask what happened to Ryan Gilligan's buried treasure from his youthful kebab shop robbery? It was the reason we played at this prison after all. It turned out the buried treasure was only a couple of chicken kebabs, three steak puddings, a large tray of donna meat, a dog's dick shish, two rogan joshs, two pillau rices, four jumbo sausages, a fish in curry sauce, eight spring rolls, six chicken breasts, 11 tubs of peas, 16 tubs of gravy, 19 scallops, a garlic naan with cheese and a diet coke. Phil Melville ate them before we got back to the prison car park. He left the coke obv.

The crowd that day for all you statisticians? Only I counted them so I was made up with myself for being bright. I nearly let on to the fella from the MEN what it was but he was a blue so it wasn't going there. The crowd was 33, which included me, the wife of the referee and the wife of a board member who came to the game because she's mates with the wife of the referee. She also came because her board member partner was playing rugby. I'll just repeat that - playing rugby. You might want to consider that when the next AGM comes along and you have the chance to vote.

In the game we had felt sorry for the prisoners when it got to 6-0 so we started playing two-touch, so we didn't have to score again and show them up too much. The poor sods were still going to be banged up whilst we were in the beer house later. Unfortunately we did score again so started playing five-touch and that calmed it down and they even got one back. We felt particularly sorry for them as tonight the clocks went back. The poor gets would wake up at two in the morning thinking that their sentence is dragging. Then the clocks go back an hour and they have to re-serve that hour all over again. We were to go through the same dragging sentence a week later in the Eccleshall away game. Except we had to re-serve an hour and a half in a tedious, dragging 0-0.

Let's get ready to crumble...

Eccleshall were reformed in 1971. We know this as it says so at the top of their programmes. Reformed from what? Alcoholism? Criminality? Bestiality? They did make a welcome announcement about wishing Best well in his most recent illness and the travelling Reds were very appreciative of their gesture. This possibly proving that there is a bit of Bestiality in most Reds. However, the consensus of opinion in The Joiners Arms pub later was that criminality was the unsocial behaviour that Eccleshall were reforming from. This was based on no deeper science than that we had beat the lads from Thorncross YOI 7-1 and that we had also beat Eccleshall 7-1 in August, at the start of the season. There's an illicit link there in those samey scorelines that Bluey or Frank Cannon would crack within the first half hour of an episode.

Eccleshall's team had a rake of changes to the one we had beaten so severely in that early, sunny summer. Their manager, Mark Askey, said this defeat was because we had met them a month too early due to injuries and holidays. The predominant consensus in our company was that the use of the word 'holidays' was another way of saying 'just missed their parole dates.' The imprisoned players from August had obviously paid their dues back to society and had learnt a discipline inside, as the performance they put in today was tight, organised and restrained. Despite increasing pressure from the FC United of Manchester's players and increase in noise from the fans in the 2,011 crowd, Eccleshall maintained their control and gripped us till the 90 minutes had been served. They gained this deserved point despite the hardship that some of their players had in trying to put shin pads down their socks without knocking off their tagging device.

You can't dislike Eccleshall. Their reserves play teams like Fegg Hayes, Ball Haye Green, Florence and Foley. Their first team's initial season in 1918 saw them play Gnosall, Chebsey, Chance and Hunt. It is never dwelt upon but Hunt might have been the home of their stalwart from history that they like to go on about. He was a strong, defensive wing half called reverend Kenneth Hunt and it wouldn't be too much of a guess to say that the reverend Hunt came from Hunt as there is a right load of Hunts in Hunt apparently. Rev Ken not only had a name that time had been cruel to but he had also played for Corinthians. This always adds a bit of 'goalie in wool polo neck' class. There is also a song at FC United of Manchester that is sung to the tune of the 'Ryan Gilligan's one times table' song. Otherwise known as the 'Hitler, he only had one ball' ball tune. The song goes:

> FC, they've only got one ball,
> The other was nicked by Eccleshall,
> Margy's mother,
> The dozy bugger,
> She popped the other,
> And now we've got no balls at all.

This song came into existence pre-season when most Reds thought Eccleshall was just a big meeting hall in Eccles that had such a cavernous floor space that they formed a football team in there. That way they were a team named after the distinct area they came from. Like Newton Heath being part of Manchester or Everton being a part of Liverpool, so there was a hall in Eccles that Eccleshall played in. They drew their local support from admin staff upstairs in the building and from the large family of the catholic fundamentalist maintenance man who insists on practising the rhythm method. Their out of towners were the bin men who came to empty the bins from Turn Pike House depot. We had come to this conclusion when it was fathomed that Eccleshall wasn't pronounced 'Eccleshawl' but more like 'Stuart Hall' or 'Ecclesfuckall'.

We were right about the club's pronunciation but wrong about its location. Eccleshall are from Staffordshire. What we were also right about though was the words of the song. The main reason amongst all the reasons that Eccleshall were chosen for that above song, infact the only one, was the fact that 'Eccleshall' rhymed with 'ball.' The thing is, if you know your Eccleshall history, which you should, then you will know that in a game against Stone Christ Church in 1919 an unusual thing happened. Eccleshall, who by a dual virtue of being granted a free entry into the next round of a local cup competition and a recent drug scandal had gained the nickname of 'The E-Bye-Eccs', were beating Stone Christ Church by a 5-0 scoreline. Or a '10th of November 1994' as it is known today. Many teams beat other teams by a '10th of November 1994' so that is not the unusual part. What is the unusual part, and what made the new FC United of Manchester song so spookily pertinent, was the fact that with ten minutes to go in the Stone Christ Church game the ball burst. The replacement ball then also burst. The game had to be abandoned, as there was no other ball.

George Hayden, our kitman and match ball provider comes out in a rash every time he hears that story. He tells it to our ball boys at Halloween to shit them up, as it is the scariest story he knows. What he continually makes people aware of is Eccleshall's criminal, reformed in 1971 maybe, but still criminal, past. They have a reputation for nicking a ball at every game they go to. There might be justified reasons why they do it that can be traced back to that game against Stone Christ Church in 1919 but no one, besides Hitler, should be a ball down. You would also think that in 1919, and with the recent drug scandal that they had just gone through, that Eccleshall would have stayed away from playing a team called Stoned Christ Church.

United reform church...

But this is not 1919 this is now and as said earlier, you just can't help liking Eccleshall. The day had started with rumours that only a 17-seater bus had turned up for the FC United of Manchester players. Actually no it hadn't, the day had started with a ten item breakfast at BHS in town but disappointingly they had changed the flavour of the sausage from the delicious, traditional over-salted, additive laden, burnt fat taste to a herby tasting one. Ever since people did not stand and fight the introduction of apple in sausage it has been this way. The disappointment of the new tasting sausage - which had resulted in only one and a half sausages from the two sausages served being eaten - had left me sympathyless for the players plight.

This was compounded by the fact that the rumour of the players requesting a coach with tables would not go away. As one member said at Chorlton Street Bus Station as they waited in the rain for the three supporters coaches, without pisspots, that would take them to the game: "We'll put fckn mirrors on it as well so they can fckn fancy themselves while they're playing 'Four-of-one-three-of-another' the twats. Shape up." Harsh possibly, but these are very close days to the days of just walking away from pampered pisstakers and all players have to be exemplary if they are to hold onto their role as representatives of FC United of Manchester. On the players part this must include an incredible modesty and an all round, humble 'We do alright' attitude even if we are top of the league.

I wouldn't be too harsh on the member being harsh on the players, and only basing his harshness on rumour, as it shows anger towards the state of Bellamyship football. It is an anger that is trying to direct a perceived wrong in the right way, pushing it towards an attitude that we can all cuddle and perhaps in a 'We do alright' modest way, show off about sometimes when we can't hold it in any longer. There is an old tune that my Mam always sings to her children when she just can't keep her love inside her anymore. Either that or when she's had a couple of gills. It's a lovely tune but I don't know where it's from, so I can't tell you what it is, so if you don't know it, you'll just have to believe me. If she's singing to our Christine she sings: "There's my girl, take a look at her, she belongs to me." It was proper embarrassing when you were a kid, as she'd usually accompany it with a public bear hug. Perhaps a Boo Boo sized one and not a Yogi sized one but that's only because my Mam is petite. She'd give us a 'Grizzly Adam's mate' sized one if she had the strength.

That tune is what we want to sing about our team. "There's our team, take a look at it, it belongs to us." Everything we ever do is leading us towards that day when we can. And when that day gets here, everything we do will lead to the day after that day when we will vigorously try to maintain it.

House Un-American Activities Committee...

The way it is happening at FC United of Manchester, happened a couple of hours later when Joz Mitten, our centre forward, walked into the Joiners Arms pub we were all in. It was 1.15pm. Dearly. He was wearing the new tracksuit and so looked a bit of a Rev Ken but a player coming in and sitting with his mates for ten minutes before a game at this level definitely stirs you to singing: "There's our team, take a look at it, it belongs to us." You're torn, as you want to buy him a pint but know that even though that would be great, and a story to tell when he's retired, for now, we have to be professional and fight like fck in every game we play. I suppose we could buy him a pint of the horribly nicknamed, but unfortunately based on fact, wifebeater. Pints of that would ensure the on pitch fight occurs. He had a Red Bull which, seen as how the brave carthorse leads the line, is very applicable.

No one can decide which country the scar on Jozzer's head reminds them of. If only we'd concentrated more in geography. If we'd concentrated more in maths we would have recognised that it has hints of the parallelogram about it. It's the way it adheres to the parallelogram rule. That is the finding of the resultant of two vectors by constructing a parallelogram with two adjacent sides representing the magnitudes and directions of the vectors, the diagonal through the point of intersection of the vectors representing their resultant.

So Margy said.

He said it before the Cheadle cup game so we were a bit dubious at first as we thought his mind might have been on the forthcoming game. I had to get my big dic down from the bookshelf when I got home before I could agree with him about the parallelogram rule but that's why we employ him. He has an instinct for these matters way before anyone else can see it.

As it turned out, Jozzer's Foo Foo was in actual fact an ever-changing flux of alopecia.

Joz's leg that usually gets over...

The big, good looking get even has a medical condition that makes the women love him even more as it appears as if he's got a big, rufty tufty, battle scar. One that he might have got at the police-televised Leeds confrontation in those quiet back streets when we went to Elland Road in March 2001. Or they'd think he might have got it by doing city after 900 of them came out of The Temple of Convenience in town, or he did it on the pitch scoring a last minute winner for the glory boys. Whichever way the women thought he had got his battle scar, their knickers were going kneeward.

He doesn't even work in re-tail but he'll still tail you twice girls...

But it's a scar like a henna tattoo. It will go in a bit, so that in years to come when a scar is no longer sexual to women it will have gone. Then he'll just be back to being a plain handsome bastard who women want to bone. And re-bone. Bastard. The only thing I would say to these women to put them off and to therefore put us grots in the picture for a bit of slopsies, is to look closely at his cuticles before he fingers you. He's a plumber; he's had his paws in and out of shitters all week. Think of that when he's giving you a fisting. Smell them. You know and I know you're smelling the inside of a bag of Cheddars. If it makes you hungry then you're his and he's going to be bending you over and pushing you past your Mam's before you can say: "Good Jesus you could have at least washed that tomato pip and bit of sweetcorn off them before you Spocked me." If you're not that fit then he might bend you over and push you past the post office in the mist. If you are, as he'll describe you, a borderline boiler then don't worry. He'll just wait to bend you over and push you past Primemark when it's foggy and dark with no full moon. With a Margy mask on. Whatever you are, you'll get a good servicing, as he's Corgi registered. Let this also serve as a warning to male Reds to never shake hands with him on a matchday as he does his foreigners on a Saturday morning.

That's the wonder, the wonder of glue…

We were playing Eccleshall at Stafford Rangers ground. If I had to choose a treble of things about it I'd say: "There's a Bostik factory very close by. They did crinkle cut chips. They also sold Hubbabubba." I'd never had Hubbabubba before. I saw it advertised on the menu for 25p and thought I'd have one with my chips because they were cheap. It didn't matter if it tasted like grid, as it was a bargain so you could sling it. It turns out Hubbabubba is chewing gum that makes it easy to blow bubbles. They're missing a marketing ploy there with West Ham. The youngsters had a load of them. The Ginger Princess blew one as big as her head. Peanut couldn't do this as he has got an unreasonably sized head and no Hubbabubba invented could stretch to that distance. Apple Hubbabubba is luminous lime green and tastes as if it is. Awful. Cola Hubbabubba is different in that it is brown but the same as in you'd rather put your penis in the mouth of an adolescent pike that is screaming for Bonjela for its toothing problems than eat it again. I'm still glad I tried it though.

There would have been a time when I wouldn't have tried them as too much experimentation is not a key element of my genome code, but after you have dared to walk from the club that you adore nothing intimidates you. 'Walking away' is not a good enough explanation as that implies you have turned your back on your love as you go off. We're doing nothing but stepping back. We're walking but we're not walking away. We've not turned our backs; we're moving a distance but fully facing what we are leaving. Fully facing what we are leaving and in constant, constant contact with those who stayed to Alamo. We're fully facing and cheering and encouraging the Alamo'ers. The Durutti Column'ers. Our walking eyes and their Alamo eyes are fixed on each other during this joint skirmish with darkness. Our fixed eyes are telling each other "I won't let you down." The other eyes are staring back, saying: "I know you won't, only fools would believe that. This is our fight that we'll win together. It could be no other way. We've been through dark and stormy weather but always been each other's friend, we've been through troubled days together and thought that they would never end, but through all that went wrong, we stood proud, we were strong, we're United, Manchester United."

If anything we might not even be stepping back and contrary to our frantic appearance, might even be standing still. It just appears as if we're moving as in when you're on a static train in a station and a train at the side of you slowly moves off. You have to look down and pat your legs for some illogical reason to check whether it is you moving even though you know it is not. We're making a stand and viewing a love being dragged off. At this time we're not powerful enough to do anything about it but we know that even in this terrible circumstance we are not powerless. We're still in close, close contact. Like Sinatra in 'Von Ryan's Express' when at the end of the film he is chasing the train that every one of his allies is on. He's trying to get on the train by grabbing the hands of his fellow comrades who are reaching out to him. Except this time in our Manchester United Football Club film, Sinatra will make it. He might still take the bullets the baddies are firing but no one gets left behind. For we made a promise to follow the voice. We know attrition is our biggest strength. We've got a proper beast on our case and it is looking grim but we're like fckn vandal paint, once we mither you there is no way you can get us off. Attrition and an in-built Mancunian twattishness to fight you will see us through this.

All the used Hubbabubba in the world gets taken to the Bostik factory by Stafford Rangers' ground. They re-mixed it, as we asked them to do, with one part Hubbabubba, one part Bostik, one part aggression, one part knowledge, one part spirit, one part patience and one part gentleness. They then stuck it all in a big pot with '1878' stamped on it and stirred it. The supporters' coaches that had left town were to pick up the mixture before going into the game. We're going to take it back to Manchester regarding it as another concoction, another part of us, with which to fight the occupying force. We're going to stick it in the gnome's beard. He'll try to cut us out with scissors but we'll still be there and ready to reload. We'll stick to his drapes and his carpet and go black, shiny and hard, and even that stuff that smells like pear drops won't be able to get us out. We'll stick to the bottom of his sneakers; we'll stick to the fanny of his pants every time he sits down in our city. If you stick all our Hubbabubbaness together then we'll finish up like Steve McQueen in The Blob - even though I've never seen it - and we'll blob him away. Hubbabubba Glazer into history. Make Glazer Hubbabubbered. We're not walking, we're sticking around.

And while we're sticking we'll sing songs to raise morale as all wars have war songs. We'll sing songs for us and for our Alamo'ing comrades. FC United of Manchester will not have one Gracie Fields but a concrete terrace chorus. In the grinding, 0-0 draw against Eccleshall today I saw an over-large carrot being waved in honour of Margy's fruit and veg war army and heard songs about us being able to see in the dark. And all this whilst abhorring swedes. To the tune of Abba's 'Fernando' our goalie, Barrie George, was serenaded with: "There was something in the air that night, our goalie killed Jill Dando. Did she work for ITV? Or the BBC? We don't know" for the first time. The previous Barrie George song first sung at Cassy Gabs when they played at Raddy B's ground now an established terrace favourite. The ageing, 37-year-old Darren Lyons also got his first song to my knowledge. To the tune of 'In the jungle, the mighty jungle' it went:

> Down at Bury, at Gigg Lane Bury, Darren Lyon plays tonight.
> Down at Bury, at Gigg Lane Bury, Darren Lyons plays tonight.
> Heeeeeeeeeeeeeeeeeeeeee's old and grey.

This last line might also be changed to:"
FCCCCCCCCCCCCCCCCCCCCCC home and away."

I know this because this last song didn't get sung at the game. It got sung at Scu Bar Two near the United-friendly Zumeba Bar on Oxford Road. I believe it was first aired by George the Kit man at an after game do with the players. Scu Bar Two won out this night though, as they were doing a very United friendly eight bottles of any beer for eight pound.

Where did you get them from? I got them off Kilter...

It might have been more obvious to have put the Aretha Franklin words 'Got to find me an angel' that are placed at the beginning of this chapter at the beginning of the previous chapter. The relevance being that in the previous chapter we were playing Castleton Gabriels with Gabriel being an angel and all. However, I put those words at the beginning of this chapter, as this was the week, between playing at Thorncross Y.O.I. and Eccleshall away, that Russell Delaney died. You are going nowhere but upwards youngster and there'll be a full squad of angels out to look after you, even if you are wearing your FC United of Manchester baseball cap that you looked a bugger in.

CHAPTER TEN

IN A FAR OFF FIELD NEAR FARNHAM...

Russell 'Rascal' Delaney's London away on Tuesday the 15th of November 2005. Kick off 11.30. Played at All Saints Church, Tilford that is somewhere ridiculously posh in Surrey. Actually The Smiths recorded 'The Queen Is Dead' at the Jacobs Studios in Farnham. We've also got Darwen versus Football Club United of Manchester, Saturday the 19th of November 2005. Kick Off 3pm. Played at the Anchor Ground. Which is their ground and not somebody else's for the first time this season.

We've come too far to turn around, be as you are...

The piss taking, respiratory challenged, cockney bastard. This funeral is Russ Delaney's way of getting us all back for all the times he had to drive all the way north to come to the countless summer Steering Committee meetings. When he got there he'd discover that we'd gone out of our way to choose a pub that had the meeting room upstairs. He'd then have to drag his oxygen tank wheezily up the stairs on his own before we found him. And then he'd have to face two of the Steering Committee smoking like beagles who'd met on the Beagles Re:united website, got a job with the council who have a 'No smoking' policy and so they'd smoke like buggery when they got to a Steering Committee meeting to make up for it. Russ thought he was in the Woolworth's fire when he was surrounded by those two ignorant gets. His whacky, quiffed back hair attracting the secondary plumes off the plums.

The morning of Russ' funeral saw me leave ours at half five in the morning. Let no one tell you that Manchester is a 24-hour city. There was not a bus or a taxi anywhere. It was dark and proper Chinese chippy and I nestled up in my coat for extra warmth but it was a summer one and a bit inadequate. An FC United of Manchester fan without a big coat? Never. There was a reason, though. I was going to wear a suit today but at the last minute I thought that I could pay no bigger sartorial compliment to Russ than to search out the exact clothes I had worn for the FA Cup Final, when we were all together for the last time. I know I was going to look a bit of a Russian Front later on when everyone was in suits but I know Russ wouldn't have minded.

I was on my way to Adam Brown's house which involved a traipse through Hulme. I was going to go with Martin Morris who, as well as having flu, also had a baby that was poo poo sausage. He'd left it as long as he could but at half 11 the night before he had texted me telling me he was agonisingly spewing it. The thing is, I was already asleep by the time the bongs had gone on News at Ten so I didn't get it till five o'clock in the morning when I woke. My only way of getting there now was to walk to Adam's who was going to Andy Walsh's, who was taking them all. I knew Adam was leaving his to get to Andy at quarter past six so I had a first half's worth of time to get there if I left at half five. I didn't want to ring Adam and cadge a lift and get him to come and get me, as I wanted to leave him in bed, as he might be one of those people who get up two minutes before they have to leave. It was going to be a long day so I didn't want to rob him of any feather time. I regretted my decision 20 minutes later.

We all face an El Guapo. Our El Guapo just happens to be El Guapo...

I left ours and walked down Portland Street and then down Oxford Road. If you don't know the layout of Manchester then there is nothing I can do about you being a bumpkin so you'll just have to bear with me. I walked down Oxford Road and it was proper throwing out time at the Sally Army doss house which is based just on the edge of town, off Hulme Street. There was no one else around besides ratchpots, as the days of people working the six-two shift and getting the bus to town to get one out again to Trafford Park or wherever have long gone. They all have cars now. So there was probably only me walking about who'd had at least a cat lick of a wash. I walked under the Mancunian Way flyover and approached the park opposite the Poly at All Saints. The gates to the park were open and a light lit the path that went across it from one gate to the other. The rest of it was coal cupboard.

A diddy path lined with pitch-blackness and rustly bushes. During the day it is a nice park where in the middle were all forms to sit on. If these forms were sat on now then they could see a lonesome figure enter the park in an inadequate Lacoste coat that they'd only be too obliging to alleviate me of. I couldn't see them, as I was entering darkness from a lit Oxford Road, but they could see me. For a few approaching seconds it was one those life decision moments. It would be more sensible to spend an extra few minutes to walk around the park. If I did that then I would have to admit that I had left behind me the days of the unfrightened. I could never utter the sentence: "I'm from Beswick, I'm frightened of no one" again and mean it. Fuck them and fuck their families. I'm going in. We've lost enough over this summer without volunteering to lose even more now.

I'm not ready to accept old age yet. I have seen more Christmas's than I have got left but I just wasn't ready to crumble. Especially not on this day when we were saying good-bye to a life. I couldn't extinguish an inner city pilot light in me that was always ready to flame up when asked. I want to but not just yet. It would have been disrespectful to Russ to do it today. The training of Stanley Park night games were having their benefits. If approached, no asking, just twatting. It can be a better world than that but try telling that to a Mickey who has brought the suitable equipment to peel you and who is intent on taking the peelings back to Tuebrook to make a lamp shade. If there's more than one, dig the one at the front and get off on the toe train. I bowled into the park as if I was walking past The Arkles in United's mob. From entering the first gate in All Saints Park to leaving the second gate at All Saints Park I was at the game. I left the darkness behind me; glad that today was not the day that I entered Cardiganshire.

Afterwards, as I approached Hulme Bridge and the adrenaline had gone down, I felt like a proper scare mongering, Daily Mail Tory. If there were any lads there in the dark of All Saints Park then they were probably all wrapped up lying on the forms going: "Look at that potty sod in a thin summer coat, the dick. It's the middle of November. It must be a Geordie doing Big Boned Galloot Studies at the Uni." If they were lying in a freezing park at half five in the morning then they must be going through desperate times. If they had asked for my coat to keep them warm then they could have gladly had it. It was only afterwards, after hearing even more stories of the rascally'ness of the 'Rascal' that I realised Russ was being buried at a church named All Saints. I had to go through an All

Saints to get to an All Saints. He was loving this the cockney bastard. If I could invent a time machine I'd go back in time, take up smoking and join the two beagles at the side of him.

We all have one last set of dancers to go up...

It's never good burying a 47-year-old. Especially seen as 'The geriatric bomber', as Russ called his mother, had now buried three of her five children. That's just not right. We found out that Russ was born on the 12th of February 1958 only six days after the dark snows of Munich and only nine days before Duncan Edwards eventually accepted he had to go and play for another side on the 21st of February. Tumultuous times for a Red to be born in. They might well have shaped Russ' life.

Two weeks before Russ' funeral I had been at Seanie Rafter's Dad's funeral. The Rafters were from the end house on Bosworth Street in Beswick next door but two to ours. Seanie was from a family of 11 children. Thirteen Rafters in a three-bedroom house with one of the bedroom's being a boxy type one. No one outside of the Rafter family has ever discovered how they all fitted in. At Christmas time some families play charades. In the Brady household we try to name the Rafter children in chronological order within two minutes. I always get the younger ones around Karen and Wani and our Christine can get the older ones around Margaret and Terry. It was at Seanie boys Dad's funeral on the 27th of October 2005 that I came across the following piece of writing. In words written by an unknown author, before Seanie boys Dad was laid to rest at Gorton Cemetery to be with and to take care of Seanie's young son Liam, we all cried at the passing of life and at the cruelty of how it sometimes comes.

> Miss me, but let me go.
>
> When I come to the end of the road.
> And the sun has set for me,
> I want no rites in a gloom filled room,
> Why cry for a soul set free?
> Miss me a little - but not too long,
> And not with your head bowed low.
> Remember the love that was once shared,
> Miss me, but let me go.

A few weeks later and I am at Russ' funeral. His three match-going mates enthral the mourners in the church and shock the staid female vicar with

United jibbing stories and tales from the back catalogue of 'Rascalness' told from the pulpit. Lucinda and Joanna, Russ' daughters, get up and no female in the church is left dry-eyed. Every bloke is looking at his shoes wanting to whinge but not wanting to be the first in this football funeral. We all know that the first to blubber will be grassed on by Russ with a ghostly shout of: "Wahey, mard arse." Then from nowhere the girls repeat the above passage that appeared at Seanie boys Dad's funeral and I knew then that my quandering at whether to use the words in the book, were being answered by the Wheezer Geezer.

Even at this moment of heartbreak the 'Rascal' still had us had. He had made sure that the organ player had learnt his trade at the Les Dawson School of Music. The 'not quite as masculine as he might have been' organ player was also wearing an unrealistic polyester wig that had just blown off the vestry roof. Was this the first time that FC United of Manchester had been mentioned within a church? We don't know but in a final nod to all things FC, when Russ' brother attempted to turn the music centre on with the turneronerer, it wouldn't go. It was meant to be playing 'Time to say good bye' by Katherine Jenkins but it wasn't having it and as the seven, that's seven for Eric's shirt number, pall-bearers lifted him up to take him out of the church there was still only silence. Proper FCMC'ing. It stayed silent until the mourners were at their most worried and then it burst into the lovely song. If you listened very carefully as the music came on there was a wheezin cockney going: "Wahey, got you."

The seven pall-bearers were enormous 'Sorry mate no trainers' sized doormen look a likes. The fact they were carrying Russ who was a proper tin ribs looked odd. Having said that I think most people in the church were just glad he had not ordered seven scantily clad females whose knickers would go knee ward whilst they were carrying him. The beauty being that because they were carrying him they could do nothing about it. Because if you didn't know Russ, as I hadn't before the summer, then you certainly had been entertained by him. It was he who organised the pre-Wembley dos at the Wilsden Green Irish Club. Or that one at Villa Park at that semi against I've forgotten who. But there's no disgrace in forgetting that, because like the 1960s, if you remember it, then you wasn't there - so it was with Russ' dos.

We all went back to The Barley Mow pub on Tilford Green. It couldn't have been more quintessentially English with a cricket pitch outside. Of the nine of us who went down from Manchester only Margy and me hated cricket. I went through how I thought it was a shithouses game as 11 against two was proper Leeds hitting scarfers. Margy recounted how in his only ever cricket game played for Moston Brook against North Manchester, my old school, they were all out for 16. He wasn't in anyway arsed. What's fair about a game where a load of blokes throw a piece of wood at you? Margy's arse also twitched as he heard Dave Boyle from Supporters Direct and AFC Wimbledon, who had come down with us in our car, recount the story of how they sacked their manager even after a 60- game unbeaten run. Strangely Phil Power really liked the story.

As the beer went down we discussed the legality of going and digging Russ up and bringing him the short distance across the green to the pub for a session. We could see the church from the pub window. It had only been a couple of hours so that really doesn't count as desecration. We could probably collect bits that had fallen off him, grill it and eat him on a muffin, as he had to taste better than the buffet. Then we thought that he was better off there as Margy told another of his jokes:

> David Blunkett walks into work. His secretary goes: "What are you doing here? You've been sacked." Blunkett replies: "Well I wish someone would tell this cunting dog."

That last joke didn't really happen at the Barley Mow pub but there were other bad Margy ones that easily replaced it. That last joke came through as I was writing these words back home in Manchester. I was just getting to that last paragraph and thinking what poor jokes Margy had told at the funeral as an example of why Russ should be left in his grave, when Margy texted me with the Blunkett one. Russ thought Margy was fucking ideal for us and that timed text was too eerily timed to be coincidence. The hairs on the back of my neck are spookily tingling.

Me and Martin Morris from the board have had many discussions of how it would be impossible to sack Margy, he is just too nice a fella and if ever things got ropey we just wouldn't do it. We started this together and we'll finish it together. He can take us to any level we want to go. I think our only problem will be league clubs after him if we carry on getting promoted. He is just everything FC United of Manchester want and need. He's one of us. His east central Manchester bloodline is clearly written in the red blood that it needs to be. At the funeral I was telling Margy that the fact that Cammell Laird had done the treble in our league the season before, meant that there was no real point in doing it again. Therefore, don't worry about our Cup exit of the previous week to Colne. Promotion would be what we would be remembered for. Everyone had enjoyed a great day out at Accrington Stanley's ground and we were unlucky losers at 2-1. Margy couldn't have it. He was devastated that we had lost. Truly devastated. From the timing of that Blunkett text I'm taking it as a sign from the 'Rascal' reconfirming what we already know. The 'Rascal' saw in Karl Marginson everything he needed to know. It's all right for Russ, though, as he's turned up his toes. He doesn't have to put up with his shit jokes.

Russ died, as others have before him, at too young an age. If an analogy could be made with the babes who died too young, then Russ was the Duncan Edwards within a mainly superb side of the FC United of Manchester board. There was fuck all he couldn't do. There was fuck all he couldn't have done. He deserves a stained-glass window somewhere in the new ground that we'll get, as Duncan has at St Francis, his local church in Dudley. Russ would hate the attention. Good, you awkward cockney get, we're getting our own back. There is going to be a minute's cheering at the next home game as a silence would be snide, as Russ just could not stop parroting and would never be quiet if something needed to be said. His mother put his North West Counties League Board Pass into his grave so that if he ever wanted to come to a game he could.

Russ with two mitherers…

As we were about to set off back to Manchester I went on a lone trip back to Russ' grave as I know I will never be going back there again. I thanked him on behalf of every single FC United of Manchester fan and on behalf of every other football fan who would want to thank him if we are successful in our fight back against the commercialisation and sanitisation of our game. He was all tucked in and the gravediggers had put that rolled out lawn turf on top of his grave. If I'd have had a ball we could have played a miniature game on it. I would have won obviously. Mostly due to the fact that Russ was dead. It was a freezing night but just as I had not given those imaginary lads in the dark at All Saints Park in Manchester my coat that morning, so I didn't leave my coat to keep Russ warm on his first night in All Saints Church. I wish I had. And that's where we can all learn from Russell Delaney, as he really would have given you the coat off his back and made you feel as if it was you doing him the favour. The only consolation I can take from my selfishness is that there is no grave big enough that Russell Delaney's warm heart couldn't keep warm. Leave those debilitating oxygen tanks behind you youngster and go and make more people happy with your smiling.

Philosophers have only interpreted the world; the point is to change it...

As I was leaving to get back to the car where the lads were waiting, I pissed in the porch gate of the poshest house I could see in this stockbroker belt area. However sombre the occasion, you should never change your class hatred of the inequalities in society and Russ, for one, wouldn't want you to. The rich are rich and live in places like this because they have exploited the labour of others. For every time you go: "Aww, that's nice" when you see a lovely thatched-roofed country retreat, be that Cheshire or Surrey, think of the employees of the person who ran whatever company the owner of that country retreat ran. Think of the employee with no index-linked pension and, after a lifetime of work, no discernible income to be able to afford to put a gas fire on during cold nights such as this November night when FC United of Manchester said good-bye to Russ Delaney. With blankets around them they die alone. Used whilst they were economically viable, discarded when they were not.

They hate our class enough to exploit our working day and willingly watch as we scratch our way through life going from debt to debt, never really attaining the material things we want for our children or us. Any benefits or advancements we have gained have been wrenched from them by the power of our collective will. They will take those gains back at anytime with no compunction if our recognition of their hatred for us falters. Therefore, until the contradictions in capitalism are worked out, let the rich be afraid of their gravedigger that will come in the form of us, the international working class of the world. It is a 90-minute game. They have a clear lead at the moment but we outnumber them by millions to one. Even Margy could get us a result with those numbers. Almost certainly.

A Darwenian experiment...

Did you know that Darwen was the first club to use professional players? Once reached the final of the F.A. Cup? Has provided four England internationals? Got beaten by Arsenal 11-1? That they wouldn't allow concessions to the travelling fans of FC United of Manchester meaning that children and OAP's paid full price in 2005?

That last point was to mar the game for many. Reds had relished playing such an old established side, whose last league game in 1899 was against Newton Heath, at their own stadium and they found Darwen's excuse of not giving concessions because it would lead to "big queues at the turnstiles" a bit spurious. Many concluded that the financial cuddle they were about to receive from us was being exploited further. No one likes to feel that they are being taken the piss out of. Many did. Still, the day had started as many previous trips to Darwen had - The Party Train from Victoria. Going to Blackburn Rovers had involved getting off the train at the stop before, at Darwen. We'd then drink our way down the main drag to Blackburn's ground. This year instead of getting off at Darwen for Blackburn we would get off at Darwen for Darwen. I'd suppose if we had followed the logic of the previous visits with big United then we should have got off at Blackburn and worked our way back to Darwen.

Heartbreakingly, we paid on the train. It was only a fiver return but it was the principle. It was Basher Brayshaw's fault. Never try and jib any form of transport with him near you. It started a few years back getting the free Fireman Sam to United. No one pays on the last few trams to Old Trafford as they get that rammed, that no guards ever get on. Not with Basher. As you're waiting on the platform for the tram to arrive he starts. "Are you paying?" "No." "Why not?" " No one is Bash, it's the free tram." "Do you want an efficient transport system for Manchester?" "Yes." "Well you have to pay for it." "But everyone is jibbing it." "So you don't want an efficient transport system for Manchester?" "Course I do." "No you don't." "Yes I do." "It's a couple of quid, if you wanted an efficient transport system for Manchester you'd be glad to pay for it." "But." "But nothing, this city needs an efficient transport system but you don't want to pay for it, she is - he usually at this point points to an innoffensive looking granny - but you won't." "But." "Why do you keep saying 'But'? Does this tram system keep Mancunian cars off the road, reducing pollution and congestion?" "Yes." "Has it been beneficial to the city?" "Yes." "Go and get yourself a ticket, you have no shame." "But." "There you go saying 'But' again. There's the ticket machine, go and get a ticket."

It's hard to resist his onslaught. It's easier to capitulate. It has reduced his travelling companions to the game, as you get a ticket, get squashed to fck on the tram and get off without even seeing a guard. In Basher's world you're somehow meant to console yourself by keeping your unused tram ticket as an 'I was there' memento. He doesn't even work for the Greater Manchester Passenger Transport Executive. Thinking about it though, there was this weedy kid that went to Moston Brook High School with Basher - before Margy went there - who was called Sammy SELNEC. There was a Tommy Toe Cap when Margy went there a few years later which goes to prove that Moston Brook has been consistent over the intervening school terms in teaching you about wagging it as well as the appropriate use of alliteration. Sammy SELNEC's Dad worked for South East Lancashire North East Cheshire buses that dominated the city at the time. Sammy SELNEC was a cult as there was not a bus route across Manchester that he didn't know the destination, departure and arrival time of. It was a bizarre but effective way for a scrawny-specky to stop getting bullied but it worked for him.

From the science classes every week, instead of messing with iron filings in Physics or turning the gas on in Chemistry, Basher's class would watch Sammy SELNEC's unvaliant efforts on the football pitch outside the classroom window. One week Basher's class were having a chemistry exam. They ignored their exam papers and watched, as Sammy SELNEC took to the pitch in a white long sleeve T-shirt with matching white shorts and socks. That all white strip sounds as if he looked as if he had just come out of a washing machine but he didn't as he was one of those ragpicker children that always look driven from home. He was everything off-white should be. It was freezing and the under-nourished, narrow backed but-good-with-buses buffoon was suffering. His loping run and fuzzy black hair were playing their usual on field tactics that was a futile fusion of aimlessly goal hanging cunningly sliced in with running away from the ball incase it hurt you.

He had done a few miskicks and raised classroom titters but there was a recognition from the chemistry test taking class that Sammy SELNEC's side were pressing for a winner regardless of the pipe cleaner'ed ones Kes'ishness. It was late on in the game. There was a goalmouth pinballing of the ball in a ruck of knees, comic book dust clouds and elbows. From the war in this furore came the ball. It sedately popped out of the close Comprehensive School confines of the mass goalmouth battle. It bobbled gently along the goal line to Sammy SELNEC's quarter-to-three footed, goalhanging feet. There was nothing else he could do; Sammy SELNEC hit the ball with everything his sugar buttie'd bones could call up. Sammy SELNEC scored the winner. He'd hit the ball on the line with all of his 'knowing the price of a bus pass' powers and it still didn't hit the back of the netting, but it was still in.

There was mayhem. Books, pens, paper, litter bins, porn magazines, chairs, tables, XL crisp packets, lone Swizzells, one vent baratheas with silver buttons up the sleeve and a candlewick bed spread all went skyward. The din echoed around the unlagged lofts of the surrounding homes. The gas fire was blown out in the caretaker's house and had to be re-lit with matches. The glue holding down the formica on the counter at the local branch of William and Glynn's bank unstucked and got floating ten bob notes gummed to it as they came down from the Sammy SELNEC goal cheering, disturbed air. Harry Dunk, the teacher, didn't know what the fuck had happened. It was a joyous, spontaneous, pupil power revolt. They were the many, the teacher was the few.

All these years later and Basher cannot let his city's transport system go underfunded because of the effect the great goal scoring deeds of a specky, scrawny child, who knew about buses, had on him. This didn't help us lot, though. The specky, scrawny, bus route-knowing twat has cost us a fortune over the years due to Basher's persistence around 'To not pay is to fail'. Including the Harold Melvin we had just paid the Hector on the Victoria to Darwen train. We were somewhat pacified when we got off the train, and at The Railway pub right opposite the station, we saw that 'Jamie' was on that night. That makes the loss of not going to see big United at Charlton a lot easier. Who is going to say: "Oh, Jamie is on tonight I must go out to The Railway and see him" unless you're his Mam or he owes you money?

I have a soft spot for that pub though, for a few reasons. They once palmed us off with the worst snide fiver ever. It was just about a fiver on one side but just all white on the other. It was that bad that it deserved a round of applause. Which I think it got. The pub was also the scene of a sing song so mighty after a game that the Transport Police came into the pub with the intention of getting us all on the next train back to Manchester. The pub was that packed and the sing song so loud that Reds were running up and down the top of the bar singing and dancing. The Landlady poured on, oblivious to the dancing feet around her pumps. The Transport Police stood there open-mouthed for a second or two and then pissed off. Before we had finished the conversation of why Blackburn and Darwen Council call themselves 'Blackburn With Darwen Council' we were drinking.

The first pub we went in was The Marigold, which, Windy Miller assures me, is Darwen's only nightclub. It said 'All drinks £1.75'. We'll do all right in here then as the pub might have had the air of 'Strippers on a Tuesday dinner' about it but we'd have them over for the cheap Guinness. I got two drinks and sure to their Darwen word all drinks were £1.75. Except I got a Guinness and a coke so I got charged £1.75 for a can of coke. What is it about Darwen with snide fivers, dear coke and no concessions? We left before they charged us per hour for the use of the pub stools and went to The Anchor by the ground. I needed to get there as I was fed up of carrying a bag containing 500 IMUSA/Shareholders United leaflets and at The Anchor I could unload them off onto the volunteers who would distribute them.

You're one, twice, an 11 fingered lady, and I looooove you…

The Darwen game saw the introduction of a couple of lads waving large flags at the front of the main FC United of Manchester end in an Italian derby style. Some Reds liked it, others saw it as a bit Kop'ish. I thought it was well worth trying although you'd feel a bit of a balloon waving it constantly. It has hints of those poor lads who stand around Market Street with those wooden billboards that say 'Cheap rugs this way' on them. It also saw the introduction of songs that included:

> Darwen sing, I don't know why, coz evolution has passed them by.
>
> Coz Darwen are a massive club. FOOT.

There was also the Lionel Richie one about loving the 11 fingered lady, the Darren Lyons 'He's old and grey' got its first match outing, the one about their number nine being so tall that he got Channel Five with the top of his head, the Darwen youth giving us abuse from the sides were regaled with: "We know what is going to happen to you at tucking in time tonight when your Uncle visits but just leaves the landing light on"[i] and the longest continued, aerobic rendition yet of the all singing, all dancing, all scarf waving "Oooh FC United, Hoi." I haven't a jar who made up the "Ooooh FC United, Hoi" song and it shouldn't work but it does. Whoever made it up must have been worried to fuck when they first said: "Hey, I've got a new song" as with one person singing it for the first time, on their own, it must have sounded Mark Robins. If nothing else it will encourage a younger following, as it will kill the older Reds, as it is too bouncy for sustained singing. It beats the tedium of any "Red and white - put in any teams colour here – army" extended nonsense.

Mr Brown scored the opening goal in our 2-1 victory. Apparently, if Margy has to bollock the team at half time for a poor performance, he rips into them for only a very short time and then him and Phil Power walk quietly away. Really, when the players think they have walked away, they're Inspector Hornpipe'ing about how the players are reacting. Listening for any comments or leadership. Surprisingly, FC United of Manchester have no real dressing room shouters as yet. I find it very hard to believe that the Ryan Gilligan's and the Chadwick's are quiet but I'm assured by the management team that this is so.

Then along comes Mr Brown and his debut scoring ways. Mr Brown is a Fog Horn Leghorn of the lower leagues. Not for him the subtle football arguments of: "Did the 1974 Dutch Total Football Side have a shouter in the dressing room? Or were they just exquisite footballers with a total grasp of their trade and how to apply it on the pitch to perfection?" No. Mr Brown would have nullified any Cruyff silkyness by simply shouting very loudly at him that he was shit. Did anyone ever try it on him? It could have worked, we'll never know. Big United have the Megastore, little United have the Megaphone. I doubt very much whether Mr Brown has high phone bills as he usually just opens his windows and shouts to his mates. It saves him a fortune when he's in Fuengirola. Cruyff could probably hear him in Barcelona. You never see Cruyff and Brown on the pitch at the same time so perhaps Cruyff's arse went.

Darwen's ground is on a great site. Exposed but great. Again the only relief from the cold, though, is being set on fire. As you look down the valley from the ends you can see all the factories still belting out smoke from various sites dotted all around your view. There is no need for this smoke as they are computer companies. It is just that as part of the planning permission granted from Blackburn WITH Darwen Council you have to have it as they insist on Lancashire authenticity. With the Holland's pie factory nearby at the cup game with Colne FC last week and the chimneys all around us here this week, we feel as if we have fallen into a 1960's black and white BBC 2 documentary about correction boots and chasing a runner around the surface of a nit comb trying to crack it with your thumb nail.

The consensus of opinion when we went back to Scu Bar Two in town for the '8 bottles for £8' promotion again was that the crowd noise, especially the last 15 minutes, willed the team on for that late winner and made a difference. We also concluded that we were glad that we had done, but saddened that we had to, in boycotting Darwen's fare inside the ground due to their intransigence on the issue of concessions. We also concluded, as it was a six-hour evening beer session so we had plenty of time to conclude, that it was the first time we had seen a woman breast-feeding at the game. And as we watched Rooney pass to Ruud for his goal at Charlton on the big screen at Scu Bar Two we knew that not a game goes past without it killing you, that the football team you fell in love with as a child is somewhere else. It can be no other way. It has to hurt. The loss is excrutiating so, therefore, the pain and the hurt will be excrutiating.

CHAPTER ELEVEN

WHY AEORTA…

Cheadle Town versus Football Club United of Manchester, Saturday the 26th of November 2005. Kick Off 3pm. Played at Stockport County's ground. It's got carpets at the back of the stand. I really wouldn't want to Hoover it after we've been there.

And there beneath the stars I'll leave you, before you go of your own free will. Go gently…

Russ Delaney's one minute of noise on Wednesday the 23rd of November 2005 at our home game versus New Mills AFC was the first time I had heard about or witnessed such an occurrence. A Celtic mate assured me that they did it to mark Jock Stein's passing but that was to avert any sectarianism as they were playing Hearts. As far as I am aware this was the first time that love was the law. The same practice of one minute of noise occurred when, later in the same week, Georgie passed away on that Friday the 25th at 12.55 pm. Manchester again seems to have popularised a practice that will become standard in football custom. You will have read a Brazilian rain forest about Georgie's life. Fitting, as he liked a Brazilian. But for all the things we have read and knew about George, a United feeling on it was summed up on the 27th of October 2005 on the United We Stand fanzine website at uwsonline.com. The article read:

> He's on his way out, I think we can all see that. I have just read a few contributors debating the rights and wrongs of Best's wrongs and rights and whilst I take on what some say about Georgie's partners walking into doors and his other mishaps, he'll always be a hero. And that's football - pardon the cliché - through and through isn't it? I've wanted United to win every game against every team, always will, since before I can remember stuff and it makes no odds who's in red as long as it's the red of Manchester United.
>
> My Grandma used to live in a flat off Simonsway in Wythenshawe. She died in 1985 and me and my Dad went to clean out that flat. He made me chuck out a box of his stuff, old programmes and that. But I wouldn't let go of his 68 European Cup Final programme or the ticket stub inside. And I began to ask him questions, not about his dead Mother or her things in her flat but about watching United win the European Cup.
>
> He tells me about doing a sicky with a twisted ankle from his job as a plumber with Manchester Corporation in May 1968. "How's the leg?" He was asked when he got back in work. "Still sore" my Dad said, to which his gaffer replied "Well, you managed to get up those steps at Wembley last night on it so you must be on the mend." And he goes on "The second was scored by wee Georgie Best, the crowd they all shouted, but I never did, the third was scored by young Brian Kidd." We've sung that walking home drunk a thousand times but I heard it first in that flat on Simonsway.
>
> And that's where the name Georgie Best takes me back every time I hear it, not to all the sorry places I've heard his name since. So in the same way that Manchester United Football Club will always be Whiteside in 85 or Ole in the Nou Camp, rather than Martin Edwards and Malcolm Glazer, George Best will always be a hero. So when it is your turn George - and it could be soon - rest in peace mate.

Cheagle Royle'ty...

It has been quite an eventful week or two for Reds at all sorts of levels with Russ dying and then Georgie dying. The triumvirate was finished off with Roy Keane leaving and an era dying. I decided to get the 192 to the Cheadle game. I couldn't get the train as I've got no platform shoes. The 192 is a long, bumpy bus ride but ideal for reflection. That and it is cheap as I can use the Stagecoach Megarider bus pass that I use for work. Bargain. The only problem being that every week when I give the driver the £8.50 for the bus pass I have to avoid saying the word 'Mega'. That's not as easy as it first appears. The driver, subconsciously or under orders from management, always tries to get you to say it. You ask for an £8.50 weekly ticket and they always say: "You mean the Megarider mate?" A reluctant nod and a shitty face from me suffice for my answer.

I'll be pleasant as I get off, so I'm not too worried about appearing ignorant. The appearance of being ignorant is worth it if it helps stop the word 'Mega' from seeping into our language at least once a week. If they called the bus pass the 'Sorted Saver' or the 'Top Ticket' then passengers might protest at the T4 Pop World word we were being forced to use. 'Mega' seems to have slipped by unnoticed. It is a matter of choice whether you are divvy enough to say divvy words but when you are forced to use a word you don't want to, by the virtue of the fact they have named your weekly bus pass with it, then no 'doth' can protest too loudly.

The box of toys were at it on the beer from 11 o'clock in Didsbury but I knew it was going to be a late one so I did Brady family stuff in the morning. I just missed a 192 in town but another one was waiting. That left after a minute or two. In this short space of time 14 FC United of Manchester fans had got on the bus in several different groups. That might suggest a big crowd might happen today. Or it might not. Just before I had got on the bus I had been told a story about this United fan from Monsall called Rigga. He's part of the 'Regeneration of Monsall Mob' that is the crew who are going to FC United of Manchester games. Rigga's in his late 40s but the mob who have re-found a love for football are all youthful. Many of them are feeling, for the first time, an inclusion at little United whereas before the love was there for big United but it didn't feel reciprocated. And as I always tell women who love shoes but who find that their shoes hurt them - love should never be unrequited. Just find the good gollies that love you back and everywhere you go you'll be taking that love with you. From your sole upwards.

The story I was told just before I got on the 192 involved Rigga buying a parrot for £300 in The Queens pub on Monsall estate. I don't think it makes me unusual in that I am not aware of the market value of a parrot, but if £300 reflects the 'two thirds off' price that shoplifted goods go for around the area, then a parrot might be worth £900. If it's not then Rigga has been taken around the corner. Unless there are grades of increasing quality of parrots, as in diamonds. A ten-caret parrot. Whatever the caret of Rigga's parrot the 300 clicks were worth it for the following:

The parrot was taken home from the pub after rather wisely refusing the insistence of the clientele there that it have a cig. I blame Tib Street Joke Shop because they sold smoking monkeys and so from an impressionable age residents of Manchester thought that the majority of mammals liked a smoke. They weren't being cruel in The Queens pub; they were just being animal friendly. They'd offer you a cig so why not the parrot? Anyway, Rigga takes this parrot home and, refusing to conform and just teach his parrot to swear or to put the kettle on and we'll all have tea, he teaches it to react to visitors. Not in a 'Geese make good guard dogs' way but in a way that when any body comes to Rigga's home and starts parroting - sorry - the parrot turns around and says -actually it might not turn around and say, as it might be already facing the visitor who is talking in Rigga's home, but whatever way the parrot is facing, when a visitor comes to Rigga's home and starts going on the parrot says: "As if."

I chuckled to myself about the unluckiness of the parrot to come from a warm climate to Monsall but then thinking it was also lucky to have found Rigga and, as sure as I am that this sentence has never been said before, so I am sure that Rigga will make a good parrot-dad. I was still chuckling when I sat upstairs on the bus and the half dozen FC United of Manchester lads on the back row started to tell a joke between themselves. About a parrot. Two parrot jokes in the space of ten minutes. If there's a parrot section in the Guinness Book of records then that's shirley got to go in it. It was a good parrot joke but I have to warn you that the lad telling it said that it was told by Bobby Ball on 'I'm a celebrity get me out of here'. Or Tommy Ball. The one with the braces anyway. I am sure that no FC United of Manchester fan watches 'I'm a celebrity get me out of here' - even the Red on the bus said it was his missus who heard it and told him - so none of you should have heard it. The joke that I am sure Margy will tell sometime over the coming season went:

> A woman goes for a piss in this pub. As she's going to the toilet there is a parrot by the door. As she passes the parrot says to her: "Hey you, you fat twat" and then, unlike Rigga's parrot who will face any visitor, it looks away. The woman goes to the toilet slightly perturbed as she does indeed carry a bit of cladding on her. When she comes out of the toilet and passes the parrot it says: "Hey you, you fat twat." The woman now knows it is her the parrot is addressing. The woman goes to the toilet a further three

times and each time she is passing there and back the parrot says: "Hey you, you fat twat."

The parrot has not picked on any other portly pub person who has passed, just this woman. She's getting upset, as you would be, and she thinks rather than let it put her off her beer she'll tell the Landlord. She waltzes up to the bar and tells the Landlord. The Landlord then leaves from behind the bar and goes right up to the parrot and says:

"Hoi, twatty parrot-face Davies, I hear you're calling this woman a fat twat when she passes you. She'd take some turning in with I'll give you that, one hump and you'd be off, but if you abuse her just one more time I'm going to reach inside your cage, pull you out by your raggedy neck and squeeze it until your eyes pop. Then I'm going to pluck you by running you over with the Flymo. Then I'm going to put you in the oven, roast you and give your burnt body to Tiddles. Alright mouthy?"

The parrot definitely understands. Half an hour passes and the woman is desperate for a wee. She's been putting it off as she's been emotionally scarred by her encounter with the parrot but she has to go before her Jack and Danny bursts. She gets up and approaches the toilet. So far silence. She is getting closer. Still nothing. She passes the parrot and is just about to go into the toilet when the parrot says: "Hey you." The woman looks around and the parrot, not facing her but looking away, says quietly: "You know."

If you've heard it then you watch 'I'm a celebrity get me out of here' so you'll have to crack on daft that you haven't.

I need to be in the town where they know what I'm like and don't mind…

As the bus passed the Apollo Theatre I was giggling again. My Gailly had told me that on the freezing night of last Wednesday, as FC United of Manchester were playing New Mills AFC and giving Russ his send off, Elbow had played at the Apollo. The lead singer, Guy Garvey, had come onto the stage limping and using a walking stick. His Dad used to be the reprographics fella at Peanut's school so we don't mind them. 'Reprographics man' presumably being someone who did the photocopying. In fact our softish spot for Elbow meant that 'Station approach' had once been our half time record of the week at a Gigg Lane home game. It was a week before their 'Leaders of the free world' album came out so we thought we were really 'on the edge' and groovy by using a burnt copy. We weren't, obviously.

Anyway, Garvey hobbles onto the stage at the Apollo and eventually says: "There are two stories how I got this leg. One is that I fell over. The other is that we were kicking tramps in town and I got a frozen one." It lacked in any parrot references but it was still alright. Elbow are from Bury but living in Manchester. FC United are from Manchester but living in Bury. We both have urban genie things going on, bread and Buddha issues with mace.

A man's notebook is his castle...

The Robinson's Brewery End at Stockport County's ground holds 5,000 apparently. As we were coming through the turnstile with a couple of hundred Reds still behind us just after kick off, the head turnstile man directing crowd control shouted: "40 more and that's it." There was also the Main Stand to the side, which had a fair few hundred in it. The crowd was 3,373. Someone at Stockport has been wagging maths lessons on 'sums' day so we didn't break our North West Counties League record attendance of 3,808. Not so alright. It was the first ground we had been to with an electric scoreboard so we saw our name up in lights for the first time. Alright. The pitch had Rugby markings on it, which many found not right, as we had walked away from that at Old Trafford. Not so alright.

This was made up for, though, by the fact they did pie, mushy peas and gravy to an excellent standard for £2.70. I placed myself behind the Ginger Princess in the queue as she uses her Big Un's to get to the front, it's crude but effective when you're hungry. At first I only saw the pies and thought I'll have one. Then I saw them dishing peas. Then gravy. And all in a big tray with sizeable portions. Alright. Chris O'Neill reported "Pub standard Guinness." Alright. The only thing that made me come down was the fact that when we had withdrawn from the queue with our fare I saw that for 60p more you could have had mash with it. Not so alright but alright because the pie, mushy peas and gravy were alright.

The game was as up and down as our alright and not so alrighting. It finished three all. Chadwick, in the last minute of normal time, headed in our equaliser after we had been battering at them. The day had been Best emotional and no one really minded the dropping of two points as it had been a class encounter and a class day. The "12 Miss Worlds and no World Cups doo dar, doo dar" song reflecting the love of Georgie's lifestyle. No one also minded dropping two points for two further reasons. The first being that Padiham and Winsford, our two main rivals for promotion, had been playing each other and had also drawn three-all. The second was that Dean Martin and Vincent Braine scored for Cheadle. I hope they're playing when I have to announce their names when we play them at home in April. If Vincent has a skilful brother, and he got a game for them, then the Cheadle manager would be in the enviable position of being the man with two Braines.

In the twist of separation, we excelled at being free...

At the final whistle I went up the side of the pitch with Tom the photographer to get a good picture of the electric scoreboard with our name and the result on. If the photograph is in the book then you'll know it was a success. If it's not then don't book Tom for your wedding unless you have a really ugly family and they'd benefit from having no-headed wedding pictures. We both retired red-nosed and cold to the bar as we were going to get on the coach with the players for their Christmas party above a curry house in Rochdale. Barrie George, our goalkeeper, didn't fancy too long a night as he was working next day in Tesco in Northenden stacking shelves. There's 5,000, sorry 3,373, Reds singing your name on Saturday at 3pm and on the Sunday you're putting cling-filmed brisket into a freezer display unit.

That sort of makes you very proud to associate with these ordinary lads. Whereas with ex-United reserve midfield player Mark Rawlinson's moth eaten effect T- Shirt and Margy's salmon coloured jumper the feeling of 'proud to be associated' was not so strong. All the players sidled onto the coach that had brought them to the game but this time it was going to take them for a Len Murray and a bucketful of Britneys in Rochdale and then back into town to go to Funkademia. Margy, perhaps because we were going for food, decided to tell a food joke:

> Two cannibals eating a clown. One says to the other - at this point the company he is talking to all say to him: "Does this food taste funny to you?"

It could possibly be a longer night than Barrie George expected.

In one ear, nose and throat and out the other...

Forrest, who is not a volunteer or anything whatsoever to do with any role at FC United of Manchester besides one of falling over intoxicated whilst he is following them, had somehow managed to get himself on our coach. He had brought his nasally mate, Charles, and it looked as if they were going to get weak-bladdered a lot all night and visit the toilet together. Not for me or anyone else here that, but we'd have to pick up the residue of him later. His outside energy source saw him taking on the role of compere at the front of our coach. The only positive being that whilst he was compering he was not driving the coach as Forrest is the lad, if you remember, who drove us to our last game altogether at the F.A. Cup Final against Arsenal. More than welcome.

The noun that I love so well...

The driver of the coach rather un-Forrest like, got us to our curry house uneventfully and safely. This was probably the last uneventful thing of the evening as the upstairs of the curry house had been booked for our use only. We'd all chipped in twenty-five a piece and that got us a nosebag and the opportunity to embarrass ourselves on their karaoke machine. We unfortunately took the opportunity.

George the kit man, who has been in the army since long bows were our only surface to air missiles and their army R and R meant going out for mutton and mead, used to sing in an Irish folk band whilst he was serving in Northern Ireland. He was telling us that if his army bosses had found out they would have killed him. It was pointed out by an Irish lad on the coach that if the 'RA had found out they would actually have killed him. Dangerous times. The innocence of George telling you how he joined the Irish Regiment because of his Irish Mam and Dad without realising the political consequences or the innocence/suicidal tendency of him wearing a Celtic shirt alongside hardened UDA members is a story worth hearing. He tells it with such a smiley face that the 'fuck that was insane' truth of the situation is lost behind his jolly demeanour.

George's folky past meant he was not shy at hogging the mic. This later resulted in the singing to him of "Georgie, Georgie they call him the kit man George." The players presented him with a collection for the amount of graft he has put in for them. You just know that some of them are going to tiger stripe those white shorts whilst they are giving their all for the club and George has to deal with that. George thanked the lads for the collection; he said it was very kind of them but that he was going to give it to the Junior Supporters club. It was an emotional moment. With the beer going down I did well not to well up as George's gesture closely followed a gentle aside with Martin Morris. I had asked Martin who he was discreetly texting in an 'Oh, aye, who are you texting?' copped you, way. I wasn't prepared for the answer. He told me that he still texts Russell Delaney with the FC United of Manchester scores. Martin had always texted Russ the scores whilst Russ was in hospital and he saw no reason to keep his fellow board member uninformed just because Russ had been filed in the big filing cabinet under 'H' for 'Have you got any Anadin's? I'm sure I'm coming down with something.'

You would think that George's unshyness would have made him be first to the mic. Not so. In speed that FC United of Manchester fans have yet to see, Joz Mitten was the first up. He sang the Luther Vandross/Alexander O'Neal - for surely they are the same person - song 'Never too much'. You just know he uses it to get to see a woman's crinkle cut chip, as he never looked at the karaoke machine screen once. Unluckily for him there were only men in the room. So female Reds, if he comes anywhere near you and you hear him quietly singing: "I still remember in the days when I was scared to touch you, how I'd spend my day dreaming, planning how to say I love you." then super glue your grubbies to your waist girls otherwise they'll be off before the Manchester Road End can say: "He's an intelligent player both on and off the ball. I've seen things formaldehyded faster though."

UTB and UTD...

George the kit man sang 'Under The Boardwalk'. Margy and Ryan Gilligan sang 'Brown eyed girl'. Then the shaven-headed Ryan got up again with the equally shaven headed Rob Nugent and sang a Right Said Fred number for all the baldies in the world. Adie Orr sang the Adie Orr song with Josh Howard and Barrie George and got stage mobbed. Adie said: "I wish" as the 'He's indestructible' chorus came up. The song also turned into all the players singing "Phil Power's bald" to the same tune. Margentina sang Georgie's favourite song 'Vincent'. For a singer he's a good manager. I refused to sing 'Fairy tale of New York' with Martin Morris as he always manages to wangle out of singing the girls bit and palms me off with it. Tony Jordan stepped in and resolved the situation forever by making sure that both sing both bits. Obvious when you think about it. A collection of the supporters got up and all sang: "My eyes have seen the glory and my heart as felt the pain, while Glazer's at Old Trafford I will never go again." 'And number one was Georgie Best' punctuated every song. We rounded off with everyone in the room singing The Smith's 'There is a light and it never goes out FCUM' long after the DJ had turned off the music. Kevin Elvin was told by a board member, that copped him trying to sneak in the queue at the bar, that he'd had enough of that sort of nonsense with Giggs trying to sneak in at the Sugar Lounge. The boy was bemused; he just didn't see the ribbing.

There was much merriment on the coach that took us back to town. We all walked into Funkademia uncomfortably like the Russian Mafia as Dave the FC United of Manchester supporting owner had arranged for us all to get in late on. He might not have been so generous if he had heard the words to 'We're off to see the Mitten, the wonderful Mitten of Joz' or the new words to 'In '77 it was Docherty and Atkinson in '83, now it's the Darwens and the Daisy Hills, the Holkers and the Leeks and the fckn New Mills, United, little United, we're the boys in red and we're on our way to Hattersley'.

Will we be handsome? Will we be rich? We'll tell them tenderly...

We are playing no teams that are from, or that are near to, Hattersley. But if we were we would not be frightened to go there. As stated earlier in the book, my family did not want to go to Hattersley in the late 1960s, as it was an overspill estate and too far out from town. Now they would not be bothered. They'd travel anywhere. Anywhere has been a pleasure to visit this season. We couldn't have known that in those dark and sometimes lonely days in May, June and July 2005 when we had nothing but a head full of enchantment and un-conjured words, that days like today would happen. A roaring crowd, a fine, if badly dressed, set of footballers, a footballing ambience that Reds were finding compelling and a defiance that had stood against a far greater foe than it should have had the temerity to stand against. Smiling and singing whilst we were doing it.

Malcolm G said to Matt Busby, I've bought your club and its history. No said Matt you gnomey twat, you can buy Old Trafford but you can't buy me, you can buy Old Trafford but you can't buy me, you can buy Old Trafford but you can't buy me...

In the Big Brother house on telly all the false contestants always pretend that it's great and they all get on in the first few days. Then there's carnage. FC United of Manchester might be open to accusations of having a big free love in at the present time and there is a tickle of truth in that. Of course there are dicks at FC United of Manchester. We're all dicks in our different dick ways. The spectrum of our support is almost as broad as that at big United. At this early stage, though, we have no Glazer apologists as we have changed European and Premiership football, for football that is ten divisions different. The reasons were vast but there was a unifying core of 'You can fuck off'. And it's this unifying core of 'You can fuck off' that is ironically giving us the appearance of being softy sausages. We show enough aggression to fight back. This aggressive fight back results in cohesion of the aggressors. This aggression somehow translates to the outside observer as us being a United hippy commune who have patchouli oil butties for tea every night and homeopathic hot rubs for afters.

We might crack on that we are, but we're not so daft as to be naively innocent. We might be enjoying the innocence of football boingyness as we perceive how it used to be but we align it with the irreplaceable advantage of coming from a city. You cannot purchase the awareness that that upbringing gives you. We know for example that next week we have to travel to Barrow on the train. We could very well meet the Nationwide'ness of Bolton or Preston. After the cup game against New Mills a rake of us got on the 9.10pm train at Macclesfield. Burnley were at the back on their way home from their Southampton game. On Hector avoiding duties a couple of us walked into their carriage. We knew who they were, they knew who we were. They didn't feel confident enough to make anything of it and we couldn't be arsed as we had experienced the infectious pleasures all day of owning your football club and boxing was irrelevant. The tens upon tens of 'On double time taking the piss' police who met the train at Piccadilly and made us get off a carriage at a time might not have thought so, but they had just met the caravan of love. We'd be naïve to believe that we won't have to organise in future seasons but not yet.

Oxytocin 10...

For now everything we are supping is sumptuous. We've escaped from tithes that the majority of other football fans haven't. No wonder people love cuddles - cuddling can reduce heart disease, cut stress and promote long life. Apparently the effect is related to a health-giving chemical called oxytocin. This hormone makes us feel loved. We're not having a club sponsor on our shirt. If we did, though, it should have that chemical splayed across the front. From Oxy 10 to the Oxytocin 11 in the team. We could have been isolated, separated grains, numerous and potentially vociferous but spread harmlessly wide but oxytocin brought us close. It is making us feel as if we are not going to vitrify and shatter. Glass is made of sand. Mortar is made of sand. It's in our control, in our influence, in our eager new palms to unify the transparency, the bonding and the strength.

CHAPTER TWELVE

GIVE THEM THIRTY NINE YEARS OF MY LOVE...

Holker Town versus Football Club United of Manchester, Saturday the 17th of December 2005. Kick Off 3pm. Played at a rugby ground in Barrow. It was that cold my knob froze, fell off and rolled to the front of the stand. A steward nonchalantly picked it up and put it in the bin. We could only deduce that they're used to body parts falling off at will in Barrow.

And always be by my side if I am wrong or right...

Holker Town is the furthest destination FC United of Manchester are going to this season. Holker is somewhere up in Cumbria, way past Lancaster. If you get to Scotland you've gone too far. You'd also miss the game even if you found Holker as the venue was switched from Holker's ground in Holker to Barrow. It is five coats colder up there. If it wasn't for the warming effects of the nuclear power plants around there everyone would be a lolly. I'd been battered with flu all week and wasn't looking forward to it. The night before the game I had gone to bed with a tea cosy on my head, bed socks, a vaseline'd up conk, a hottie and a gongler count registering record scores on the Gonglergeigercounter. There was proper one pence chews in them. Of all the times to be feeling perished then now was not it.

I'm normally nesh but this was going to be walking into the arms of a fridge. And a good fridge as well. Not one of those Hallé-ballet-booshka make ones you get cheap at Comet or Curry's in the sale that are cheap for a reason. The reason being that there's not much between them and a stove. Barrow was going to be one of those big American fridges that could freeze a family sized tin of Fiery Jack. There is no Burns Unit at Barrow Royal Infirmary. There is a custodial sentence dished out to people who scald themselves as they are seen by the locals as just trying to defrost on the sly. John Thaw, the actor and Gorton Red, never played in Barrow as they fucking hated him. And Paul Scalds.

They invented the wheel in Barrow...

I'd been to Barrow before in the very early '80s. My cousin had met someone from up there on a family caravan holiday in Morecambe. I'll have to repeat that last sentence again. A family caravan holiday in Morecambe. Even writing it a second time it doesn't seem believable but we did go to family holidays in a caravan in Morecambe. That didn't drag.

Anyway, she met this fella from up there and we went to Barrow for some sort of family function. It was 1981 and over a million workers' jobs had gone to the wall that year alone. Thatcher was rampant and cities were being decimated. Not in Barrow. They all worked in the shipyards building nuclear submarines and the town was booming. Their council had Basil Brush's catch phrase translated into Latin on the town's coat of arms. Manchester had seen the onset of pubs being empty with the Thatcher years. The 'We'll go out early and save you a seat' era had come to an end with her election victory as everyone was coppering up for a latch lifter never mind going out before your tea had settled or your Just Musk or Paco Rabanne was dry. We were about to see whether Barrow was still as prosperous or whether their windows were now boarded up as ours were. Or 'Openshaw curtains' as timbered up windows are accurately called.

Farah, Farah, Farah, because United are going to Barra...

At the FC United of Manchester Supporters Group Pre-Christmas bash the other week I'd seen the members drunkenly singing:

We've got a ticket to Hyde, we've got a ticket to HHHyde, we've got a ticket to Hyde and it's a snide.

We've got a ticket to Holker, we've got a ticket to HHolker, we've got a ticket to Holker, we won it at poker.

That's a shit song. 'Polka' rhymes with Holker not poker. Still, goodness me, we should let them off as at least they were trying. Paul Weller tried to rhyme something badly with 'Donkey carrot' once so that was a lot worse. The thing is the 'Poker/Holker' song was annoyingly in my head all week. It was annoying me as much as the 'Follow, follow, follow because United are going to Barrow' song. And that was annoying. The 'Follow, follow, follow, because United are going to Barrow' song had been around from FC United of Manchester's first ever match against Leigh RMI in July.

By train or charra to Barra...

It was boiling Bodine back then so how out of context it all was to be talking about Barrow. Or 'Barrow - the home of the frosted foot' as all the road signs say as you drive into Barrow. But that wasn't the annoying bit. The annoying bit about the 'Follow' song is that nowhere, ever, never has 'Follow' rhymed with 'Barrow' in a Mancunian accent. No one pronounces 'wheelbarrow' as people were now singing 'Barrow'. We say 'wheelbarra'. There will never be a time when I will concede to the protestations of Geordies that they are the greatest supporters in the land, they patently are not despite the amount of times they try to tell us that they are.

What Geordies did get right once, though, was that song where they rhymed 'Peter Reid' with 'Has got a monkey's head'. Said in a Manchester accent that sentence, apart from its obvious observations about the nature of Reid's top end, means absolutely nothing. Said in a Geordie accent it is very funny. If you're ever in the company of a Geordie then pass the time by trying to get them to say 'Perpetrator'. However, if you are in the company of anyone from Liverpool and you want the time to pass then you should try to engineer it to get them to say 'Fazackerley' or 'Glockenspiel'. The night will go a lot quicker. You'll never get a Mancunian to say 'Barrow' if it rhymes with 'toe'. If someone from Manchester came up to you and pronounced it 'Marrowfat peas' not 'Marrafat peas' then you'd think they were dolly. And you'd be right.

It's not Friday, it's not five to five, it's Jack Kerouac-a-jack. On the road…

We wasn't getting the charra to Barra, we were getting the train. The 8.45 direct train to Barra from Piccadilly had been designated the party train. Once a train gets labelled with the moniker 'party' before it in the Red world then it has lost any real chance of it being a sedate train. I'd like to make the apology on behalf of my fellow Reds to all the other travellers. Trains are usually quiet at the time any party train leaves so the travellers mithered will be small in number. The thing is, we're not usually small in number and that's why I think we're not as annoying to them as say a stag night outing.

A stag night outing might be ten or 15 lads out for the night. They will be loud and obnoxious, as if you look closely at their lives they will be having their 'One night away from the missus' night that happens to them say once or twice a year. They will regress and try to shout their way to the world's attention. Manchester town centre suffers at Christmas with this with all the Christmas party gimps. All the dicks get let out for the year and shout, fight, collapse and vomit. We people who go out every week wish for January the 2nd when we can reclaim our socialising. Seasoned travelling Reds have been whipping up and down the country every other weekend for seasons on end. If they are noisy it is not from giddiness in the main, it is from an attempt to get heard over the larger throng or because there is something important to say and because we are such a large party, the person you are saying it to, is seats and seats away.

If any innocent travellers get caught in the middle of a carriage with us then they might get a bit wary at first. Large numbers flooding onto a train is not easy to cope with. They soon realise they are not in any danger as the Daily Mail would have them believe and it is my experience that they enjoy the friendliness of the flow of conversation. This is because the banter is not aimed at them. If it was a stag night then the shouting and showing off would be there to attract other passengers so that the 'One night away from the missus' ers could show how zany they are. Innocent travellers would feel obliged to force a smile at the zanyness presented before them otherwise a) the zany 'One night away from the missus' man might try even harder and louder to attract their attention and b) if zany 'One night away from the missus' man's desperate need to show off fails then he might turn to bullying as they are ten or 15 strong.

With a party train any other traveller will just melt into the proceedings and enjoy any lewd or unusually funny tales that ensue. They often don't get seen by other Reds as we are all on a journey of importance to us and our travelling community. Because it is normal for travelling Reds to be travelling then they become the normal human being that they are. And the normal human being that they are is one that is usually polite. Therefore any innocent travelling passenger, if seen, will be treated with courtesy if their manner so demands it. If they are an 'Outraged of Hale Barns' then it is they who are being impolite and condescending so they can go and get their head fitted for a bowler hat. I hope it's ill fitting.

It's just that something so good...

So here we are on Piccadilly train station at 8.30 on a Saturday morning. Sometimes, though, you have to remind yourself where you are, not physically but mencully. Big United were playing at Villa Park today in a game moved for Sky to the traditional football kick off time of 12.45. I was on Piccadilly going north when the team I fell in love with as a child was going south. So I reminded myself with this song I heard: It's to the tune of the Irish song 'Go On Home British Soldiers' -

> Go on home Malcolm Glazer, go on home.
> Have you got no fuckin home of your own?
> For one two seven years we've fought you and your peers,
> And we'll fight you for one two seven more.
> If you stay Malcolm Glazer you will see,
> You will never defeat the MEC.
> So take your fuckin debt and the Edwards and Cheshire set,
> And go on home Malcolm Glazer, go on home.

If you ever need self-validation, just meet me on Store Street by the railway station...

There had been talk of some FC United of Manchester fans getting on the train at Oxford Road rather than Piccadilly. This was to avoid any potential conflict or heartbreak with meeting Reds going to Villa. Oxford Road station might suit people who come down the Oxford Road side of town but as far as I was concerned Piccadilly was Manchester's train station. I had nothing to be ashamed of from my decision in May of 2005 in that I just couldn't give Glazer one pence of my wedge. Nothing had or could change that. No one had anything to be ashamed of in any decision they had made, both in staying or going. The only decision that was worthy of shame was the Glazer apologists and there are no friends of mine, both who have stayed and who have gone, who are that.

Walhalla in winegar...

As it turned out, I finished up walking up the station approach with a Norwegian lad who was going to Villa. I have got to know more and more Norwegians recently as a Norwegian couple had been staying at ours for the last year. Dotty and Lasse had wangled their way into my house under the pretext of staying for a fortnight until they found accommodation elsewhere. As of today's date that fortnight had turned into one year and three months. How I've remained unpickled is a mystery. There is nothing that Norwegians don't try to put in vinegar and preserve. I've woken up early with empty jars at the side of my bed where I've copped them mid-pickle attempt on me, but you sleep with one eye open if you share with Scandinavians.

Dotty's first breakfast at mine was pickled sheep's head with raw onion. Breakfast. The eyes were pickled, the ears were pickled, the gums were pickled. No wonder Scandinavians are always naked and bang at it as they've pickled their jumpers and jeans. I don't mind Dotty walking around the house bare arsed, her being a girl and all, but I had to be firm but unfair with Lasse as no one wants to see reindeer balls. Which is another thing they pickle. I have actually had reindeer balls for tea once, as Lasse is a chef. If you're going to share with anyone try and share with a chef.

Football is a precious game...

Especially a kleptomaniac chef. He was working in town at a venue that will have to remain unnamed as I persuaded him to rag it rotten over the last year. I told him that as an honorary Mancunian he has to live by Mancunian laws - if it's not nailed on, nick it. No food or drink was left unstolen. I have forgotten what shopping is like. I have had a year of Jack Daniel's, Smirnoff, bottled real ales with odd names; he even nicked Pimm's once. You can be too criminal. I've been stuffed with beef medallions, salmon, chicken, lamb and all cooked and accompanied with mange touts to asparagus. I don't like asparagus but Margy sells it according to the song so it would be disloyal not to have a go.

I'd be home from work and Lasse would come in with his bags laden with gear. I can only liken it to a parent who has a child coming home from Primary School with a painting that they are desperate to show their Mam and Dad. He had this big 'Look what I've had away' smile on his face, as he couldn't wait to show you the produce of his nickerypokery in his bag. Last week I was cruel for no reason. He came home with a bottle of Jack Daniel's, stating that work was having a stock check. He'd reasoned that if they were having a stock check then they didn't know what was there, so he'd nick this bottle of Jack. Taught him well but could do better. I told him, casually, that if they didn't know what was there then why didn't he nick two bottles? He left devode. But that shows you how far he has come in 12 months. Without practice you don't get better. Every football fan knows that. He'll probably nick Norway when he goes back.

So many Norwegians have come to see Dotty and Lasse and stayed at mine over the last year that I have RNLI written on my front door. Robert's Norwegians Lost Institute. It is on tier three. If I stood for Prime Minister in Norway I'd get elected as I'd mop up the 'Hey, I have been staying at his' vote. The Norwegian who I had been walking up station approach with, on our way to our two different but related games, had never stayed at mine as far as I am aware. Although he might have done as there have been so many Norwegians the Manchester Tourist Board made us put a fixed, laminated sign on our living room wall telling you the directions to the toilet. It reads: Turn left at the third Norwegian, go straight on for nine Norwegians then do a sharp right at the tenth. Follow the tenth one round and you'll see seven Norwegians in front of you. Go past these and do a right by the ill Norwegian who is not carrying anything pickled. At this point be careful not to fall over the stolen contents of Lasse's bag. By the eighth Norwegian you will be able to stop and ask him for further directions. Unless he's naked.

I got the friendly Norwegian I was with to say “Aston Willa” without him noticing it, just for pure personal pleasure and I left him by the ticket office. He was going to meet Big Bernie from J Stand. Bernie is an honourable man who just loves United so much that he couldn't let them go. I'm proud of him for that. I wanted to see him on the platform and say: "Give them 39 years of my love" but we were on Platform 14 via the walkyfasty bit of the far side of the station and I never got to see him. I am also acutely aware that I have never got Dotty or Lasse to say 'wentriloquism' or 'waricose wein' as I set out to do when I first met them. I've made a right wulva of myself with that failure.

Anne Coates Red...

The week before the Barrow game we had beaten the Castleton Gabriel's side 10 - 2. We'd turned them into time. And us being three o'clockers not ten to two'ers. At our forthcoming AGM our excitable board would, therefore, be able to proudly pronounce that we had invented a time machine. The members would realise that we hadn't but at least they'd now know that when we sing the song: "We often score six but we seldom score ten" that we will have actually had done the more difficult 'ten' part. That wasn't the outstanding feature of the day though. Before the game Margy had conspiratorially called me over to the boot of his car in the car park at Bury's ground. His boot was open as I approached him and he was looking shiftily into it. The angle I was coming from meant I couldn't see what was in there.

He's from Ancoats; it's going to be a body part. It'll have foil around it or it will be in Tupperware as he's not rough but it will still be a body part. Body parts might voluntarily fall off in Barrow but in Ancoats they are forcibly removed despite the owner's not unreasonable remonstrations. I momentarily checked the contents of my stomach and found that they would easily be able to deal with any MDF human abattoiring that I was about to face. I was the cultural attaché here for Beswick; I couldn't go all big girls blousey and faint like those trainee police officers in the credits at the start of Quincy. If you want to enjoy Quincy more by the way, then have a sweepstake with your fellow Quincy watchers about how many minutes into the programme you think Quincy is going to say the word 'Contusions'. But outside of the world of mid afternoon telly what I was going to see was what I was going to see.

I'd seen worse dished out by Ryan Gilligan on the pitch. Actually Ryan had just moved on to play for Flixton, as he couldn't get regular first team football. Fuck me it was going to be Ryan Gilligan in the boot. You never leave FC United of Manchester without a contusioning. As I approached the car boot Luc Zentar, the club's acting secretary, arrived. That was good news as if I did faint I'd land on Luc as the lad has got a bit of keg on him so I wouldn't damage myself. Margy's "Psst psst over here" turned out to be a car boot full of Coca Cola. Ancoats Corleone. Well I say Coca Cola. It was Turkish Coca Cola. There was not one decipherable word on them that didn't look as if it had not fallen out of a casbah. They might very well have a good Coca Cola plant in Turkey I don't know but my apprehensions were soon backed up when we noticed that all of the bottles were out of date.

Margy's assurances that the 30th of November 2005 wasn't that much out of date, seen as how it was only the 10th of December and that it would be alright as it was from The Shamrock pub in Miles Platting, somehow didn't make us anymore thirstier. Luc tried it, but as has been said, there are touches of the Phil Melville about him. A car boot full of out of date, Turkish Coca Cola. You let this man manage your club. Trevor Francis tracksuits.

Calmer Sutra...

It was with this recently in mind that I found my phone ringing on the train to Barrow. It was Margy. He's probably got a crate of Croatian Stork SB he wants shifting. It was a terrible line as reception was not that great as we were near Cark and Cartmel station and everyone knows how poor reception is around there. You say “Cark and Cartmel” to anyone around the globe and even if they don't speak English they'll mime a 'Poor reception on a phone' sort of a mime. Although luckily enough every 'poor reception around Cark and Cartmel' conversation I have had in my life has been with someone who can speak English, so I don't actually know what a 'poor reception on a phone' mime would be like.

Margy wanted to tell me that the ground staff at the ground we were about to play at had left the rugby posts in behind the nets. He thought that this would be a good point to make in the book. Good point Margy, well made. The fact it was on the BBC North West programme the night before taking up more time than the report on Liverpool in the World Club finals and the fact we were all about to see the rugby posts sort of didn't make that inside information. He'd been on the Turkish cola and it wasn't even ten o'clock.

Margy had disturbed mine and Two Mowers' peace. We had found a nice quiet spot on the train and was oljerbolling the two hour journey away. Two Mowers was telling me how he had got a digital camera and had persuaded a fat blue he works with to pose for a series of photographs entitled 'Fat blue'. This involved the fat blue in his city shirt posing outside a cake shop or outside a Kwik Save with a trolley full of Sugar Puffs and Butterscotch. It was an ongoing project. We'd also discussed the false owl in the hole in the wall at Silverdale station. They'd made a hole in the wall just to put a false owl in. That if people in wheelchairs who lived in Arnside formed a team then they could call themselves the Arnside Ironsides and that if your missus had to get any debilitating disease when she got older then it would have to be Parkinson's for the noddy blow jobs. The grannies that like to say, “Yes.” Get in there McClair.

Two headonism abounds…

We got off to find people in Barra were not as luminous as expected. I suppose they stand as a perfect, peaceful metaphor for the ending of The Troubles as they are an equal mixture of green and orange. Always worry when they say "Orange Wednesdays" in Barra. They also seem to sing "And we're all off to Dublin in the green, in the green" with a passion not seen anywhere else. You could tell that things had progressed since my last visit here in the early '80s. They now had sautéed submarine and periscope Panini for tea. The first pub we came across open at our 10.45am arrival time was the Wetherspoons. It was ten deep. We left. We passed, and were visually unimpaired enough to see, the blind shop which had named itself, in big, big letters The Blind Shop. It didn't sell blinds. It did sell, right by the door and in an awkward, customer unfriendly way, a large section of china and porcelain goods. Someone is taking the piss out of someone somewhere there. We eventually finished up at The Continental, which was showing big United on large screens, and we parked our arses accordingly.

Can't make it all alone, I built my dreams around you…

It got fuller and fuller, as you'd expect as time got nearer dinner and kick off time for big United approached. When Ruud's goal went in the place erupted in a swathe of beer, uproar and joy. I had to text Margy at the pleasure of what we were seeing. I wrote:

> The pubs are rammed and bouncing Margy. We've left ten divisions behind and still gone potty over Ruud's goal. Psych those lads up so they know what it is to wear that FC United of Manchester jersey. Our hopes are your hopes youngster. Do your bestestist as we know you will…

We had come north to a nuclear coastal town when the team that had formed our youth and childhood were in the Midlands. We knew why we were here for this team, but we also knew why it was inconceivable that we could ever be defined in any other way than that of a Manchester United Football Club fan. Those FC United of Manchester players, however good they are being, have to constantly be reminded of just who we are and of what we have given up. They know it. We just have to keep saying it to them so that we continue to know that they know it.

We're going to miss Cliff Rescue and the Helicopters who are playing the Cross Keys pub, Barra on the 29th of December 2005...

We concluded that the queue at the bar in The Continental was getting too big unlike Caroline Brayshaw's arse that was getting fitter as she gets older, so we went to a quieter pub called The Cross Keys by Debenhams at half time. It was there we discovered a real ale called Tag Lag at 4.4 percent. It was going bandit. It reeled us in. Micky, one of the lads behind the dinghy that had first appeared at Leigh RMI away was there with the original dinghy in a polly bag. It had been under his mate's bed for the last five months but he'd retrieved it from its sticky sitch and put a puncture repair kit on it. The story behind the blow up dinghy was supposed to be a sort of 'United, not for sail' romance. In actual fact the lad just thought the design on the dinghy was a phoenix so he bought it, but when he blew it up it was an eagle. If you ask Fletcher Moss then he will tell you it is a mosquito or a dragonfly. I hope you all quickly conclude not to ask Fletch what was on the dinghy as it is obvious he just likes naming insects. The dinghy is to be looked after so as one day it can be presented to any future club museum. It had an outing at the beginning; an outing now in the middle and it will have an outing at the end of our very first season. It will sort of be the same checking on the progress of Caroline Brayshaw's arse. Join in, Billy Brayshaw won't mind.

Hold it, reeled in, the dinghy, the lads at the cup game against New Mills at Macclesfield's ground rowing across the empty stand in the pouring rain, Andy Walsh our acting club Chief Executive saying on radio four this week that if you put a frog in a pan of hot water it jumps out, if you put it in a pan of cold water and warm it up slowly it just suffocates. There's a watery theme developing. We're linked to the water of the Ship Canal. As it should be. We craved water that much we dug the ship canal to bring it here.

Good King Restless last looked out...

We left the pub singing to the jukebox. We sang “I'm leaving on a jet-plane, don't know when I'll be back again. Five o'clock” and made our way to the ground. When we had come around to Barrow's ground there must have been about 20- odd of us all with no colours and dressed darkly. We had walked past the queue as it looked enormous and thought there might be another turnstile around the other side of the ground. As we were walking past the main gate one of their stewards shouted to quickly open the gate and let us in as FC United of Manchester's lads were coming past and they didn't want any lumber. We went straight to the front of the queue, circumventing the need to go through a turnstile and through this opened gate. How embarrassing. I apologise to anyone who was waiting in that queue that we jumped but we didn't make your wait any longer. We were just presented with small town divvyness and took advantage. In the ground the 'I don't have to sell my soul' banner was unfurled for the first time paid for by a rake of lads.

First Blood had with him a red, black and white scarf from AC Milan that had 'io non ho cugini' on it which means 'I have no cousins' in reference to their sharing of their ground with Inter and their disassociating of themselves from them. As I walked past the far corner of the ground there was a banner with a second bit of Italian on it from the Yorkshire Branch that had 'ad initio mmv'. That would be great if that meant 'I have cousins' it being Yorkshire Branch but it probably just means ' Formed 2005'. Two bits of Italian in such a confined space, though, shows how cultural we are. Or daft. MMV is probably Latin as well. We don't even spoke good England so a second language is smart. Although, I am bi-lingual by virtue of the fact I talk English and I also talk shite. Although, the ladies have been known to say I speak the language of love. That's what I'm maintaining anyway.

With a goal from Simon Carden if he plays...

The crowd of 2,303 saw FC United of Manchester beat Holker Old Boys 2-0. The surface of the borrowed rugby pitch we had to play on was firm, uneven and dead. It didn't help the game. However, the long journey with the early start meant that the vast majority of the Reds there were too inebriated to notice. We missed a number of chances and if I was a reporter for one of the broad sheets I'd report us as being 'profligate'. If you're going to have a gate you might as well make it profli. It was 0-0 at half time and we all concentrated on staying alive. The half time break was punctuated with on pitch entertainment of a band, a bloke in underwear with safety boots on and the dinghy. That dinghy was named well as it is called The Explorer as every time it comes out it explores the pitch. Every time Simon Carden comes out he scores. His goal to break the deadlock in the 64th minute was his 114th goal in three appearances for us. Adie Orr's lightweight teeth again enabled him to take advantage as the home side tired for our second goal. This tiring out of sides is quite prevalent this season. It is not a tactical advantage that will last if we go up divisions. Still shouldn't moan. Oh, go on then, I will.

Stephen Spencer was again the man for me in the game. He never stands out and grabs you, say, as some of our forwards or more robust defenders or midfielders do, but he whacks out the graft and the skill in equal proportions. Without his presence we would lose that timed motion that keeps the momentum above the necessary thump. The great thing about him, though, is that he could be sat at the side of you now if you're reading this on a bus or in a motorcycle side car and you just wouldn't recognise him as he's got one of those non-descript mooeys. If, however, you're reading this in bed and he's sat at the side of you then call the police.

He'd make a rhubarb ghost when he dies, as he wouldn't scare anyone, as you wouldn't notice him. He'd be grafting like bleeding hell 'Wooo woooing' and shaking manacles in your face and taking his head off and putting it underneath his arm and we'd be just sat their going: " You can tell its Eid there's a load of repeats on the telly" or going: "Was there a bloke whose job description was 'cig lighting man' in those beagle laboratories? I bet his thumb was red raw as they can put them away those beagles." If Stephen Spencer gets injured the club should send Brolly the club photographer out into the stands with him and photograph him at the side of unknowing fans in the Manchester Road End and have a gallery of the unknowing in the next match programme. He's had to have cards printed with 'It's me, love' written on them to give his wife every day when he gets home from work to stop her following through when he frightens the fuck out of her when he walks in the front room.

I'm spinning around, move out of my way...

The magnificent ballet of the adult May Fly only lasts for 24 hours. There is absolutely no reason why I should know that besides the fact I was watching the history channel with Alan Titchmarsh the day after our Barra game, recovering on the settee, and he said it. His name does begin with 'Tit' though. Mind you, mine begins with 'Bra' so we're equal if anyone ever announced a 'Gormless beginning to a second name' competition. FC United of Manchester were now approaching the shortest and the darkest time of the calendar year and we were showing no signs of limping off the parchment pages of football history. The ball was still at the ballet.

I've never seen an adult May fly being magnificent. Almost certainly I never will. It would probably take a series of coincidences involving me being at the side of a river in May and Alan Titmarsh walking past just as a May fly was donning a pair of those soft slippers that ballerinas wear. Alan would then, after un-invitedly interrupting my company, have to tell me to look around and see the May fly having a magnificent ballet dance. I'll have to settle for other forms of 'magnificence' gratification. The form this gratification took for me on this occasion happened on the way home as our train carriage burned with the following song, sung to the tune of 'Burn, burn, burn, the ring of fire':

From Newton Heath to these days unknown,
From Newton Heath to these days unknown,
We formed a club and it's all our own,
We formed a club and it's all our own,
Burn, burn, burn, FC on fire, FC on fire.

CHAPTER THIRTEEN

THE GUNS OF FLIXTON...

Flixton versus Football Club United of Manchester, Monday the 26th of December 2005. Kick Off 3pm. Played at Flixton's own ground, which is made of 100% pylon.

The only thing different, the only thing new...

I work with a lad called Jimmy who was a Young Guv'nor in his time. I do believe he was referenced in Mickey Francis' book on the same subject. That unsurprisingly, however, is not the reason I'm mentioning him. Jimmy is now a very good Shop Steward. He also likes fruit cold from the fridge. Not bananas, of course, as they go on the turn if you put them in the fridge. It's Jimmy's love of fruit that has cheered me up this Christmas week, before the Flixton game. I'm not that clever with fruit. I'll eat it but I struggle with it and only persevere because I know it's good for keeping your backdoor WD40'd. A Caramac is always going to win in a fight with a kiwi fruit for my affections. This week Jimmy showed me how to eat a pear properly. You'd think I might have already known.

What you do is you pull out the stalk, bin it and then bite a five pence piece size off the top of the pear and bin that. You are then free to eat all the pear downwards. Pert-breast-cupping the pear in your hand until you just leave the bottom belly button bit. If you start eating it in the middle, as I always have, then a collapsing occurs as you get to the end of the pear. The top stalky bit and the bottom belly buttony bit fall in on each other because you've eaten the guts in between and pear gets everywhere. In eyebrows, on shirts not necessarily your own, along olfactory canals, across light fixtures, up kettles, inside sandals and so on. But no more. I now know how to eat a pear. If you get it wrong it collapses in the middle. If you get it right it doesn't. You get your pear goodness and the carpet or any other number of soft furnishings doesn't.

We had played Flixton in a pre-season friendly as written about by Tony Howard in chapter four. Five months later we were playing them again in a big boy league. We had learnt simple lessons and we were still here. We seem to have handled it all relatively alright. Not great but alright. We'll always take alright, it's just how we are. These last few months towards the changing of the year to 2006 were our potential pear middle where we could have done things a lot more unwisely than we have, but because we were handling it alright, we were showing no signs of collapsing. We had played Flixton right at the very beginning of our existence, scoring our first ever goal, and now were playing them right in the middle. From this game onwards we would be in the second half of the season and on our way to May. If we were not continually learning simple, humbling lessons then we would not be here. It doesn't have to collapse in the middle. As with other clubs before us, we were proving that we had not let our hearts fall into careless hands. However, to play Flixton you had to find it first.

Farewell to this lands beerless marshes...

Flixton's a little bit of Runcorn or Widnes come to the outskirts of Manchester. It's all pylons and chemical works and disturbingly worrying marshlands. It's at the back of Brother Beyond. If beyond was a warehouse then you would enter the big warehouse doors into beyond. There would be the front bit of beyond. Then there would be the middle section of beyond and then right at the end of the warehouse would be the back of beyond. If you got to the back of beyond and then kicked the fire exit doors open and ran out into the dark for ages until you got a stitch then you would find Flixton's ground. Almost certainly.

Oh shut up we enjoy it...

Infamy, infamy they've...

I have time for the film 'A Taste of honey' from Shelagh Delaney's book. Very few people haven't. The opening scenes show Rita Tushingham playing netball in Gresham Street School in Beswick with Barmouth Street baths in the background. I was born at home, in the street behind Bradford Park and Barmouth Street baths. Our Christine persists with the rumour that as she saw them filming it that day then she is one of the people gawping in the background. She could be making it up, she might not be. Just into the film Rita Tushingham and Dora Bryan are doing a moonlight flit from their rented room. They get on a bus. That bus then takes them past Albert Square, then back to the Transport and General Workers' Union offices on Oldfield Road in Salford and then back past the statue of Victoria in Piccadilly. It's a proper arse about backwards journey that makes no sense. Welcome to getting to Flixton. Despite Ted's - who's a taxi driver - protestations that it is just past Trafford General Hospital and you can't miss it, you can. And we keep doing, as this is the second time we've been here and missed.

I was getting a lift from the Ginger Princess as getting the 256 from town on my Megarider bus pass was a no-goer as it was Boxing Day and sod all was running. We drove down Chester Road past Old Trafford as big United were playing West Brom today. Thousands were walking to the ground. Big United were kicking off at three and so were little United at Flixton. As we crawled past White City in the congestion we knew that all the fanzine sellers would be grafting away on Warwick Road. It was opening day for the fanzines with a fresh issue out. You could tell it was opening day by the weather. It was lashing down. The most important day for a fanzine to be sold is the opening day. All the arguments, ideas and opinions are at their freshest and all the regular readers are at their keenest. If it's pouring down, though, the readers just seem to rush by as they want to get out of the rain and into the dry of the ground as you would.

Blacky would be on the J Stand bridge organising the selling of United We Stand but mostly woo'ing his harem of women. Faz would be at top spot selling very loudly with Dom, Dan and the youngsters. Howsey would be at the side of them selling Red News with his 'I'm Moston's only albino, you can see my pubes for a pound' T-shirt on and the rotating Red Issue sellers would be outselling the lot of us. The United We stand sellers had lost me, Martin, Dunny and Tony Howard to FC United of Manchester games out of the dozen regulars who used to sell UWS. We weren't very good, I'm sure if Blacky had just organised four hat stands and put them where we stood they would still have sold the same.

That bloke isn't funny anymore...

In my early years of selling I used to find out what was in the fanzine and then try and sell it around that. Often trying - very poorly - to introduce a bit of humour. The thing with that is if you shout out something that you perceive to be funny - and passing people laugh - then you feel a bit of a cheat saying the same thing again a few minutes later. Even though there would be a different crowd going past and they might very well laugh, as with the first people to pass as they hear your joke. You still, somehow, felt a bit of a swingler trying to pass off a throw away line as if you had just that second thought of it. That's how fraudulent comedians are. They have to act and deliver lines as if they find it funny and fresh. You know they're mugging you, they know they're mugging you; it's just the degree of mugging going on. I couldn't do it and soon reverted like every other fanzine seller to “UWS, new issue out today.” It still sold the same. What that tells you I haven't a jar.

So keep it up, quench my desire...

Over the top of the Ford showroom's roof I could see J Stand getting its new coat of construction. I'd been in J Stand since Alex's first season. I'd taken our Christine's lad Ben along to the game on and off for the last few years but he was nine now and I knew the family importance of going to the game. So I bought the two of us League Match Ticket Books in J. To anyone who is reading this who is not a United fan then don't even try to fathom out what the difference is between an LMTB and a Season Ticket. We can't and we're Reds. Our Ben was growing quick as a bugger and you can miss out on so much of their lives.

One day you're gingerly, two fingeredly taking his bib off to avoid contamination from what's on it as surely he didn't eat that, whilst all the while knowing that your next concern is how to open his wet, clutching mitt which is holding a semi sloppy Rusk with a soft spit hat on it and the next day they're beating you at Connect Four before waltzing off out courting with a girl in a training bra. Getting seats together would mean that at least once a fortnight we could spend the afternoon talking tripe. It wasn't as if it was all that dear. I think the seats cost £86; it might have been even cheaper. I was on £80 a day foreigners that summer so it hardly killed me. My last season ticket for the 2004/2005 season cost £513. By the marker of money earned on foreigners per day you can see the increase of going to the game. And £513 is apparently not too bad by other clubs standards.

I'd secretly got our Ben this LMTB in Alex's first season. I'd received our two tickets in the post at our house. I went around to my Mam and Dad's with the brown, A4 sized envelope containing his ticket with his name on the front. When I got around to my Mam and Dad's I spotted him trying to hide a cricket ball. Bad, firm but unfair, uncle I may be but I was having no close relative of mine playing cricket. I used to hide his cricket bat under the duvet in his bed so that a) he couldn't find it and b) it would hurt him as he got in bed, therefore in a Pavlov's dog way the last thing at night it would teach him was that cricket was a spiteful, hurtful game that should only be played by Winker Watson types. He would only ever thank me in the end; he would look back on those cricket bat induced spinal injuries in a fond way.

It never worked. I don't like any other sport. I'm not even that keen on football if United aren't playing. I lose interest after 20 minutes and just want to see highlights. Our Ben now will actually watch or participate in any sport - snooker, American football, darts, Grand Prix, swimming, athletics, anything. This comes in handy, as now I can gladly not see a game throughout a whole European Championship and just glean the salient bits of who United are after and how they played from him. He's very rarely wrong. Although there's possibly only him and Alex left on the same side in the Darren Fletcher debate.

Anyway I went around to my Mam and Dad's with his secret new LMTB in the A5 brown envelope and copped him before he could conceal the cricket ball he was carrying. He was parping it. I shouldn't be proud of that but I am. I told him it was alright that he had a cricket ball and that he should show me how good he was getting at bowling. He wasn't having it. I'd done too good a job. If a nine-year-old child can have an incredulous, 'Fuck off you're having me over, what you up to tricky bollocks?' face on then our Ben had it. I persisted as I knew that this was the child who had too much energy and who we used to say: "Go and run right over there and comeback and see if you can do it before we can count to ten" to. And he would. Which was bad enough but when he got back we were all going: "Nnnnnine, te... oh, just made it, see if you can do it again." And he would.

I would play this flaw in him as no previous Brady, to anyone's knowledge, had such high energy levels. We are a family of settee/arse/arse settee'ers. That's why the front cover of this book has that picture of our Christine and me at Blackpool on it. It's one of our favourite family photos. The ball is in the air. I'm not getting it. Our Christine's not getting it. She's saying: "Aww you get it." I'm saying: "Aww, no, you get it." The ball was almost certainly never retrieved. The only unanswered family question is who had the energy to throw the ball up in the air in the first place? If our Ben was alive at the time of that photograph then he would have got it and ran around the caravan a hundred times to celebrate that he had got it. Then he would have ran around it a hundred times more to celebrate running around it a hundred times.

I carried on with as sincere a face as possible asking to see how good his bowling had got. I went out into the garden and walked to the end of it and put the A5 sized brown envelope with his LMTB in and his name on against the washing line post. I told him to see if he could bowl the ball and hit the envelope. He cracked. He had energy to dissipate. If that request had been asked of me or our Christine at the same age we would have gone: "Why? I'll go and wax a lemon at the same time so I can be doing two life-fulfilling things. Dick." Bennyboystrousers, however, wanted to bowl and bowl and bowl. And bowl. As it turned out I mustn't have been doing too bad a job at terrorising him out of playing cricket as he was shit and kept on missing. He'd bowl, miss the envelope, go and retrieve the ball, bowl, miss, go and retrieve the ball, bowl. My Mam, Dad and our Christine were now in the garden watching Ben bowl as they had thought I had invented a new 'count to ten' game to tire him out. After several hours he eventually hits the envelope with his LMTB in and his name on. He has to go and put it back up against the washing line post so that he can carry on bowling. Goodness love him. If, indeed, we had have just invented a new form of 'count to ten' game then he would probably still be there now.

There's no cure for being young and daft except for being old and daft...

Ben went to put the envelope back up against the post. As he's doing it he sees his name on the envelope. It might have possibly been his first ever letter, I don't know. "My name's on this." "Is it?" "Yes." "Oh, that's funny. Open it then, it must be for you." "What is it?" "How the bleeding hell should I know, I can't see through envelopes." He tears the top of the envelope off and pulls out the LMTB. It's left him totally befuddled. He knows he can see an LMTB, it's got his name on it but the realisation that it is actually his has just not flopped into his consciousness. "It's yours, it matches this one here that's mine." We all as a family jumped up and down in the garden as we all realised what we were living through. To this day it is the most energetic thing we have done. There were tears. The east central Manchester bloodline from Ben's great grandad going to Bank Street was about to be continued. Another wander, another lifetime intensity, another eyes seeing, another aorta cramped. This was our club, this was our city, this was our family, these were our gifts. You cannot amend the unamendable. You cannot alter what is not going to let you alter it. Born a treasured Red. Nothing could ever change that. Nothing.

You can never stop me loving you, you can never stop the way that my heart's beating too, you can never stop me loving you, that's one thing you'll never do...

And so we drove past Old Trafford as Manchester United were about to play. We remembered J Stand and Stevie Newall, Old Vinny, Coops, Potty John, Little Paul, Alex The Heart Attack, Straight-Haired John, Davvo who I had gone to school with and who nearly filled me in once for calling him "Chunky." Not because he was carrying keg but because he looked like Clement Freud's bloodhound dog called Henry from the Pedigree Chum advert, who was advertising chunky chum with chunks or something. We had all sat together, with so many more, for so many years. I knew Vinny's wife had died this last year but I'd not seen him to give him my condolences. Vinny, an ex-steel erector, had not been too clever as he was on the touch line of being 80 and had missed a few games at the tail end of last season through ill health.

I'd only seen Stevie Newall as he waved as he drove past as I was carrying a large wimberry pie across Droylsden precinct. Stevie's one of the finest Manchester United supporters you will ever meet. If you can't get on with Stevie Newall then you cannot get on with anyone. There is nothing he wouldn't do for you. If Glazer made tickets a hundred quid he would still have to go though. I'm proud of him for that as when they have got you that deep everything hurts and if it hurts it's because you care. Yvonne, his Mrs, is just as nice although I wouldn't go in a drinking competition with the pair of them. I've been on dialysis since our pre-season in New York a few seasons ago through them.

I'd seen Straight-Haired John on Oldham Street for ten minutes one morning as we were going to work. He went from laughingly calling me

"Judas" to ten minutes later saying that when I come back into J Stand he is going to stand up in the aisle and be the first to shake my hand. And it will be my honour to shake his. That's what it will take over this season. Patient explanation of where we are and how we got there. If we all do that with our football family, because we cannot speak to everyone, then those who are close to us will get to know, and if that then is replicated for every FC United of Manchester fan, then only Glazer will lose. Burying many emotions we drove past. We've come too far to turn around; be as you are. I'd not seen Coops since last season. That was the only positive I could draw as the ghost of Stretford Trades and Labour Club was passed and the right turn off Chester Road to go past The Robin Hood into Urmston was done.

We've got a Ford Cortina that just won't run without gruel...

We found Flixton's ground by turning left after falling off the end of the earth. As we got out of the motorcar a few lads walked past in flashing Father Christmas hats. All very festive, if somewhat Boltonesque, if they had just had that. Surreally, though, they accompanied the hats with black balaclavas over their faces. And there were tens of them. Blokes in total black balaclava facemasks were going past each other and letting on. How did they know who was under the balaclava? Normal everyday conversations were going on between blokes as if it was normal to concur in dark disguise. Only if you're in a TSB with a firearm should that be so.

The reason they had worn them was that apparently the clump of lads at the previous Barra game, who stood on their own wearing all black, had inspired an internet debate that concluded that balaclavas were the next step to darkness. I also heard the rumour that Reds wore them, as they could not tell the Rio story of that week without blushing with embarrassment so they covered their faces whilst telling the story. Rio had apparently told the press that they were going to win the domestic treble this season. With Chelsea so far in front that was taken as either the musings of a brash cockney, big headed idiot or of someone who was just dolly. He then compounded any dislike for himself by adding onto the end of the statement that they would win the domestic treble for the new owners. Not the fans. The new owners. Aww, such a nice man. I can see why the Rio chants ring out so loud and so often across Old Trafford.

Well so could anyone...

Pampered roofy bastards…

We were going to take our place behind the net where we were when FC United of Manchester had scored their first goal. We took one look at the dark balaclava wearing sky and concluded that the New Mills cup game was enough wetness for one season. We went in the seats. We stood up, but on the very edge where the stand finished so as not to get in anyone's way. The game was dominated by Two Mowers and his family talking about the octopus Danielle had received for her birthday earlier in the year. A nice but somewhat unusual birthday gift. It costs a fortune as you have to feed it biros and felt tips and when it comes to Christmas presents she has to buy it four pairs of gloves. She called it 'Andy'. She saves a fortune on socks, though; as Octopi are that footloose they have no feet.

Danielle Two Mowers had bought Father Two Mowers a George Foreman grill for Crick. It seemed there was nothing they had not put on it over the last 24 hours, from warming their slippers up to cup-a-soup. We discussed if it was possible to do a pie on it and agreed that only by the use of carrots acting like stanchions in the old Bramhall Road away end at Sheffield United would the job get done. I told them that the key to a George Foreman grill was having a damp cloth ready at the side of it as part of the cooking process. As soon as the food came off, you cloth the grill otherwise the fat congeals. None of this waiting till after tea business, cleaning was part of the cooking process pre-meal. You don't want any of your neighbours complaining about you not keeping a clean George Foreman grill.

One armed Bab…

We had a neighbour once who we called Barbara Goodword because she never had a good word to say about anyone. The girl could moan. If you didn't keep a clean George Foreman grill then everyone would know as

Babs blabs. She lived opposite us with her husband Bill Three Sheds. Why he had three sheds no one ever quite discovered but he did. If he'd have had two sheds I'm sure no one would have bothered but he had to go and push it and acquire that third and get himself a shed reputation. A passing student might have said that he had a shed load of sheds. Anyway Barbara Goodword once got me and my Gailly on our doorstep. She came up with her cig dangling out of her smoke-dried face and her skinny frame hunched into a question mark shape and we prepared for the usual gripe about someone or something or both. This day she gets us and goes: "Hey, did you hear about the fire on Harrop Street? They've been burnt out of house and home. She's had to move herself and her kids in with her Mam." At this point me and my Gailly are going, right, here comes the moan now. There's been a fire; she'd like the distress that's caused; now she's got to apportion blame to someone's inadequacies. We stood there for the onslaught. Babs Goodword was about to regurgitate her bile on the community. She goes:

"It's a shame that as she's a nice woman. Looks after her house and her kids are always spotless."

It didn't register with me and my Gailly. For a second or two we stood there heavily perplexed. Barbara Goodword had just said a good word about someone. As it sank in me and my Gailly looked at each others shocked face. This was not our globe, these were not the parameters we ensconced ourselves in, something had just changed and it's leaving us fucked and unsure. Stop it, we don't like it. We want to go back to where we knew where we were, and what to do, and what to expect, and we could see things coming, and from that semblance of sequence we could ascertain a reassurance and ease.

For those few seconds me and my Gailly knew fear. We shouldn't have done. There was something nice happening around us but it was just so new that we couldn't see it yet. As the silence after Bab's good word went into further seconds the shock was beginning to turn into pleasant realisation. Of all the deliverers we had not expected Babs to deliver us to a nicer place. Me and my Gailly no longer looked at each other in shock, we looked at each other with eyes that said:

'See, we always said it was a nicer planet than some make out. Shame on us two for doubting that Barbara Goodword could not be won to the beauty of the world. Rosa Luxemburg in her book 'The mass strike' has written about the ability of workers to change in the struggle of the strike, as in that within that struggle they had to face the inequalities and injustices of the system they are forced to operate in. In facing those inequalities and injustices, so they could see the contradictions and horrors of capitalism.

The miners' strike in 1984/5 had done this, schooling so many previously uninterested activists to the reactionary role of the state and to the pitiless nature of the market. So the fire on Harrop Street had changed Babs.'

That was a lot for two sets of eyes to say to each other in so short a time but we were in love and lovers can do that.

As we were getting used to this new world Babs turned her head to the side, looking contemplatively off down the street. She took a drag of her cig, swallowing everything. Slow seconds later as the exhaled smoke came out she said sagely, in hushed appraisal, with wistful reflection:

"Mind you, he's a right alcoholic."

She was back. Only going to prove, as the onset of Stalinism did in Russia after October 1917, that you can have happiness for a bit but darker forces in the world will snatch it back off you if there is not enough of you to defend it properly. You can't have socialism in isolation, in one country or in one individual. We all have to jump together or at least a fair clump of us. Enough to win the arguments with those left behind. If the German workers in their post-World War One upheavals had been won across to the ideas of the Russian revolution then the Glazers would not be here today. There would have been enough of us. We would have won back then and be well on our way to a classless, egalitarian society. The German workers' movement at that time was the most advanced in the world. It was fighting back and was large enough to get the British Prime Minister, Lloyd George, to write:

> 'The whole existing order, in its political, social and economic aspects, is questioned by the masses from one end of Europe to the other.'

In non House of Commons speak his arse, and that of all the ruling class, had gone.

However, Russia, unlike England and Germany, had a combined and uneven development in its economy. This meant that you could see the biggest, most technologically sophisticated factories in the world living alongside the backwardness of a 'horse and cart' peasant economy. For example, the Putilov engineering factory in St Petersburg/Petrograd in 1917 employed 27,000 workers, equalling the numbers employed in Metro-Vickers in Trafford Park in the same period. This advanced nature of industry was mixed in with the vast majority of the Russian population being land working, isolated peasantry whose ideas of developed society was not pissing in the puddle where your rag wrapped feet were.

The success of the Russian proletariat in the cities of wrestling control of the means of production was only ever going to be temporary without the aid of their more advanced sisters and brothers from other industrialised nations such as Germany and ourselves. Indeed, there were gunboats on the Mersey in 1919 as even we threatened to erupt in those tumultuous revolutionary years. Mind you, many Reds would say they should keep gunboats permanently on the Mersey, but that's a football matter.

Joyeux noel...

We had jumped in the summer of 2005 and we were scared of the new at first. We were scared of the new and that there wouldn't be enough of us. We were as scared as me and my Gailly had initially been, when Barbara Goodword had been the deliverer and delivered me and my Gailly to the temporary, fleeting world of her niceness about her burnt-out neighbour. As always, we can learn from our class history. We know that without sufficient forces with us that our enjoyment might only be temporary. It was only the 26th of December 2005. Five months is fuck all but a flicker in football history terms. The community around us is our 'German workers of 1918-23' that we have to make constant calls to, to rescue us. We have to grow to survive or we will be crushed or corrupted if we remain small and isolated. We know what we, as a club, have to do. The players today, though, weren't helping. The game was shite.

Today's game was the 91st-plus-one-day anniversary of the truce between British, French and German soldiers in the trenches in 1914. We all know that peace was called over Christmas between rank and file soldiers from each side and that a game of football ensued. That would have been a better game to watch than the big bag of biz we were witnessing today. The pitches of both the games might have had the same levels of grass on them but that is where the similarities cease as the 1914 steel toe cap boot wearing soldiers were more technical on the ball than any FC United of Manchester players were being here. We drew 1-1 and were lucky to get that. Flixton were mugged out of three points. I won't dignify the game itself with any more written coverage.

Besides to say that we saw a pissed up Faz at the game. UWS's leading seller had decided, after months of deliberation, hair loss and alcohol, to wrap up at Old Trafford. I lied about the hair loss as he only has three. And one of them is a wig. And another is drawn on. Blacky had now lost five match day UWS sellers to FC United of Manchester the poor sod. Although we all wished he had kept Faz as he is not quiet. Amongst Faz's latest boomings he did happen to tell us something of some interest, which is unusual for Faz, as Mrs Faz will no doubt tell you. Faz told us that his mate lives on the same street as Rory Patterson, FC United of Manchester's forward, and that he knows for a fact he was on the ale Christmas Day. Patterson came on as sub for Torpey and played well. What we can deduce about the effect beer has on a player's performance at this level is unclear.

Where's me buccaneers? Over there...

There were a lot of Yemen flags at the game. This is because the Board at FC United of Manchester have made big efforts in that country to increase the club's profile in what is potentially a very lucrative market for television rights and shirt sales. Either that or the red, white and black Yemen flag sells for £4.99 on ebay. There is a vast array of flags at our games and the majority have tried to get away from the 'Nameyourtedioustown Reds' flags that have lazily worked their way into football. These 'tedioustown' people have no knowledge of the importance of the part played by the countless 'Who's farted?' flags that used to bedeck Wembley every year on FA Cup final day before all seating came in. FC United of Manchester's photographers try to capture the more interesting flags and plonk them on the post match gallery on the web. I don't have the internet so I can't check but others tell me they are very good and worth a nosey.

Who put the fun in the FC fundamentalist?...

However, our photographers blotched their photocopy books when they missed an event at Flixton. There was a banner that went up for only a few brief but shimmering seconds whilst the game was on. Unless you are very, very young the simple slogan on it was very symbolic. The banner struggled to be raised at first. There was a reason. The banner was fumbled up behind the net so you could see it high above the line of the cross bar in front of it. Several Reds who were stood on some sort of large, brick electrical box held it across their chests. When it was finally raised up and unfurled properly for an all too short a time it said, quite clearly, 'Wonderfuel Gas'. During the summer we had discussed getting a banner that just had that on it. We were slow, as usual, and now we had been beaten to it. For a few seconds the Stretford End had transported itself a few miles up the road to Flixton. And then it fell apart. There was a reason. It looked as if it had ripped. It had. It was made of paper. Wallpaper.

Let him dye...

The makers of the banner had given blood for this club as they suffered severe paper cuts. Nick Dydna, a dark-coated member of the 'Take That' section of our support who insist on standing on their own at our away games, had gone to B&Q. He'd bought a roll of full blown vinyl wallpaper for £2.99. With other volunteers - no doubt in no way encouraged by the fact his Mam, who is reportedly fit as fuck, was there - went to his house, drew the outline in pencil and then sprayed it in. They laid it on plastic sheeting on flags outside and let it dry, as Nick's fit Mam made pizza for them all. They ran out of spray and had to go back to B&Q for another. It still hadn't dried and was giving off fumes as they took it in at night. Nick put it in his bedroom and slept on the settee. To give up your feather is giving enough on any day of the year but this day was Christmas Eve. The sacrifices Reds are making for this club. They made another wallpaper one that said 'On the 5,475th day God created freedom' but we'll ignore that.

Because somewhere in my youth or childhood, I must have done something good...

We are leaving 2005 making an FC United of Manchester house in stronger material than the wallpaper banner. It was a wonderfuel banner but it has to get better. We all know that. No shimmering, glorious seconds of unphotographed existence for us. I saw a Red give a granny stranger his gloves to wear during the game as she was standing at the side of him looking perished. I'm an atheist but little acts of goodness like that get you into heaven if there is one. If there isn't one then it builds you a club. It's doing the titchy little things that make the broader, better, bigger things arrive. The pedestrian access from the diddy to the not so diddy is a causeway with altruistic causes spliced with self-protection against evil. We left the 'hot pipes' of the Flixton marshlands behind and retired to The Garrick's Head for tea and a choux bun.

The next day I was on the settee watching Spartacus on the telly as I had had one choux bun for the road too many the night before. Spartacus and The Sound of Music are my two favourite films. Spartacus was Marx's favourite historical figure and The Sound of Music has Fascists being foiled, singing nuns, some of whom have sex, clothes made of curtains and all this whilst answering the longstanding question for vegetarians of how do you hold a mung bean in your hand.

I always cry at the powerlessness of the situation when Varinia and Spartacus first fall in love in the Gladiator camp. They touch hands but can't caress. I cry again when they meet up free in the forest and again when they make their pledge to always love each other and never let each other go. I'm sure I also saw Spartacus take the top off a pear and eat it downwards. He definitely said that anyone can learn to fight but to say things and have people believe them and be moved by them is special. We might never make it home but we fought and perhaps our children will go on to tell people about us. We just knew we had to fight. Perhaps we'll always have to. The absolute minority who are against us are like your ears before they pop at altitude. They can hear everything but hear nothing. They are aeroplane ear'd.

Hope hospital...

The monumental majority realise we are a firm, firm Red pair. One soul fighting; two lungs breathing. FC United of Manchester's part in the resistance has made us a small, mass party. We felt powerless mid-2005. We leave it with, and in, hope. In Hope Hospital you always deem that ailments, malfunctions and diseases can be mended. That is not always the case though. However, recovery is always aided by the self-belief of the patient. Our self-belief, though riven through with humility, has got its crisp, clean cotton pyjamas on. It's not slouching in bed, drip-fed, drugged and confused. It's welcoming to visitors, its conversation sharp and well versed. Its health is rising above the circumstances it finds itself in. Its suitcase is at the side of the bed, packed and ready to be used. The clothes in it are folded, unsoiled and rakishly, effortlessly timeless. It's just not sure what it's going to be wearing at present when it leaves.

CHAPTER FOURTEEN

ARDOYNE BREATHING...

Nelson FC versus FC United of Manchester. Sunday the 15th of January 2006. Kick off 2pm. Played at Accrington Stanley's ground. Accrington's a place where the majority of the residents are known to suffer greatly from toilet paper crumb'ing of their arse crack. The women also go: "Oh, look, I've got a bit of hard grit in my biz wax, no wonder me pot towel holder's chapped. I'll crack the grit with my thumbnail and see if it makes a nit noise" and " I only washed me clout Monday, it'll do, we're not having a late one."

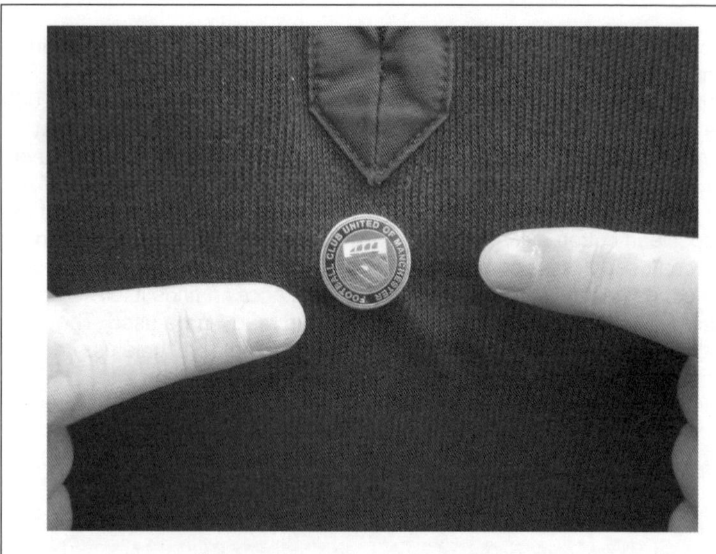

But for me they shine within your eyes...

Nelson is a town where disputes are still frequently settled with a crossbow. You always remember where you were, when your shoulders first flagged, as you found your first, single ginger hair growing in your sids. The argument with yourself that is was more auburn'y meant very little. You'll always remember your first visit to Nelson. Your shoulders will flag the same. If you've not been then you'll have to wait as Nelson FC moved their game with FC United of Manchester to Accrington Stanley's ground in Accrington. Nelson, as a town, never seems to get mentioned without people saying: "And Colne" after it. It might be the same 'doubling up of places' people who can't say "Trinidad" without saying: "And Tobago." We'd played Colne at Accrington Stanley's ground a month or two back in a NWCL cup game, so footballingly we've twinned Nelson and Colne again. Trinidad and Tobago would have been nicer. Nelson and Colne will do.

United had played the backwards in the derby the day before. I'd managed to abuse one backward on the morning of the game before 9.15 in the morning. I was going past the site of the old Johnson's Wireworks by the new big Asda in Clayton. The dickhead came past in his city shirt, none of my blue Mancunian mates would wear a city shirt. This dick was never going to get a game for city so there was no reason for him to be wearing one. He's a bloke. Children wear football kits. I wouldn't usually abuse blues in shirts but it was derby day, he was bigger than me and he was in our Red area trying to use his shirt as a way of showing off that he was part of the great loyalty that is city. Conveniently forgetting its crowd of 3,007 against Mansfield in 1996 of course. I was going past and I told him to fuck off out of our area, the fucking mill town josskin.

Councillor Street's oldest occupant…

They've built that cancerous stadium near us. You wouldn't like it near you. When there are thousands of them infesting it on match days it is very depressing. So, early in the morning a bell end thinking that he can walk around without a hard time on derby day is a much mistaken bell end. He can Baddiel and Skinner himself as much as he wants when he's with his pie-head mates espousing loudly that our city, that he visits from his white bread and Blue Band margarine village, is a blue one. Abuse at 9.15 in the morning might not fit in with his Soccer AM, we're all right rightly right blues brothers in Manchester when we visit. Only that special city BO that they all formulate saves them from a crack as no one wants to touch wet lepers. He'll still be telling you Manchester is full of blues when he visits your town. Ask him how an out of towner like him knows and he'll eventually crumble and admit that Skinner and Baddiel told him after Gazza was good in the World Cup.

To know a veil…

When our Ben was a baby we decided to try an experiment on him. None of the Bradys like coffee creams. This means that when we have a box of chocolates there are always coffee creams left. It's upsetting to leave chocolate, even if they are coffee creams. As Ben grew up we all went 'mmm' as we pretended to eat coffee creams. We encouraged him to eat them as if we all liked them so much, then he'd be missing out. This would mean that he could handily Hoover up the left over coffee creams as we selflessly acquainted ourselves with the strawberries, oranges and nut whirls. Hours and hours of Oscar performances were passed willing him to adore coffee creams. He wouldn't have it. He'd sussed the veil we were trying to avail ourselves with. Our mate, Noel, had managed to mug his child that the chimes of the ice cream van was the bogie man. The tight get. Mind you, his dog, which he had got off his child's best mate, is called Shammy. That sounds alright until you learn that the dog was actually called Sammy when they inherited it off his child's best mate. His child's best mate has a speech impediment. So they call it Shammy. Perhaps we needed a crueller streak, like Noel, to get Ben to like coffee creams.

Oh aye nosey Parkering…

No matter how other Reds try to tempt me, I don't like travelling with other Reds in confined quarters if I don't know them. Other friend Reds can tell me that it is great but I won't be coffee creamed. If I am travelling with other Reds who are unknown to me, I have to 'Oh aye nosey.' This involves saying very little but internally going 'Oh aye' in whatever intonation that is relevant to the 'Oh aye.' If a stranger Red says something divvy I can 'Oh aye nosey' internally with a tone going 'Oh aye – goon, compartmentalised you. Next.' This sounds as if I'm being a right twat but it has its nice side. If the stranger Red says something nice then I can go 'Oh aye – he seems alright. I'll remember that.' Classifying friendship, potential friendship and acquaintances is an organic process. Not everyone can be your mate. You don't mean any harm. Graded grains make finer flour. We all have our own Red friendship cake to bake so let's use the best ingredients. We can't make each other love coffee creams. Some might already like them. Good. Enjoy them. I'll try to respect your taste but it is not mine.

Scott, my FC United of Manchester'ing neighbour from our flats, had told me of this van that was going from town to the Nelson FC game in Accrington. Scott's possibly the friendliest man that's ever been invented. I mean that in a nice way, as he can recognise a not right with the best of us, but he gives people so many chances to redeem any flaws they may have. He'll talk to anyone without compunction, giving them all an early, equal respect. Actually, we're the same. It's just by going in and talking to strangers he is doing his 'Oh aye noseying' in a different way. Whereas I am wallpaper, he is windrush. He'll have no qualms about going straight up to someone if it will benefit the Red cause. I, however, will be in the background un-noticed. Knowing me, know-ticing you, oh aye. Until you, by being you, win me across. Someone I love once said something about me that touched so close and that I am beyond proud about. I hope and long for it to be true. If it is so, then it's a treasured honour that is my continued privilege to always try to make true. It would make you a life changer. That bestowed title - that can only be given by those who love you and whose life you have changed - means your life was worthwhile. There's no greater perspiration aspiration. The person I love once said: "When Robert Brady loves you, you know about it." When the people you love, love you back, then there is nowhere to go as you are already there.

Transgressive taste for the forbidden...

Unfortunately, we did have somewhere to go on Sunday the 15th of January 2006. Accrington. Scott's friendliness had got him to know of this van. I decided that I should start to travel to FC United of Manchester away games out of the confines of my usual mate surrounded way. I'd go in this van with Red strangers. Scott would be there, though, as a nicorette. You can't just give up a lifetime's habit. It started off well. Pebble, the only Norwegian I know of, who had totally come across to following just FC United of Manchester, was there. Many Norwegians support the idea of a resisting breakaway fans' club but Pebble was the only one I know of so far, who couldn't give a penny to Glazer. He is a fan of both United's but a supporter of only one. There was a Norwegian woman called Rox something or other on the internet site, but I'm not on the internet so I don't know. I've been informed that I've met her at the July the 5th 2005 birth of our club but I can't remember. I'm sure there's others but Pebble is my only, confirmed by travelling with, one. He'd flown in from Norway to watch a North West Counties League division two game. You have to pace a yard or two back sometimes just to see what is happening in front of you. Norway. North West Counties League division two. Come to see.

If it all comes out in the Wash then that stretch of water by Norwich has got to be very crowded...

One of the most unusual gangs I ever saw sang shang-a-lang as they ran with the gang, singing shoe-wop-be-dooby-do-hey. They apparently were all in the news with their blue suede shoes as they danced the night away. The human contents of this gang who picked us up in their van in town to take us to Accrington were unusualler than that. I only got in it because on the side of the van, by the petrol cap, it had written in small letters 'To open pull flap'. As I was mid-giggle Scott had pushed me in the front seat, slammed the door behind us and told the failed visa applicant for 'Fraggle Rock, the even tittier years' driving the van to drive off. I don't know everyone or everything about United. No one can. Those that say they do, know nothing. For example, I don't know who threw that knife from the Stretford End that went into the 18-yard box that got the Stretford End closed down for several games in the 1970s. What I do know, was that I didn't know any of these in this cuckoo flying over a nest of a van. If I wanted to find out who threw that knife into the 18-yard box all those years ago then I'm sure I could, by the simple means of someone I know, will know someone who knew. Apparently chance has no memory. It has. There is not a fucking chance ever that I would have travelled to an away game to see United with these bin liners.

This one is different because it's us...

What made the 2005/2006 season different from all those other seasons was that I knew at least two things about the 'end of roll' oddments in this van. They had made and maintained two choices. When Palestinian civilians are murdered by the Security Forces in the Gaza Strip or the West Bank, only approximate figures are given of the numbers involved. It might be two it might be three, it might be nine, it might be ten; it's about that. If an American dies, it is personalised. You get to see a picture on the telly of them, their grieving family, the homecoming in a coffin, comments from friends from the town they were from, the life the poor victim had lived. The conclusion we are meant to draw, after being brought so close to the victim, is that those involved in that person's death, are scheming, uncivilised barbarians who deserve to die in numbers. Unequal lives. Unequal deaths. Until you look and know more. In a billion times a billion, billion, billion or more smaller way at United, I had depersonalised Toby jugs such as these in this van. At United we couldn't really have time for them as they were unknown to me or my friends. Therefore, we could discount them until they could eventually be 'Oh aye nosey Parkered.' Now on every FC United of Manchester trip you know at least two things about your travelling companions. It makes it very homely and welcoming. It's for United bigots like me to accept it. They can still be annoying tits. But they're our annoying tits. They chose to be Red. They chose later to take on Glazer in a way they thought that would be most effective. They've done something that you know about, that you can defend to any outside aggressive body who might want to belittle them.

If I knew you were coming, I'd have spaced a cake, spaced a cake...

The van pulled up outside The Crown near Accrington Stanley's ground. It was early McSquirly so the pub was empty. It got rammed very quickly. It got noisy very quickly. I met a few old Reds in there from previous adventuring decades. One pint with these boisterous Reds we didn't know made us consider that we had served our time. We had to leave and find a quieter pub. We'd not done bad. I'd travelled with them. I was getting better, but there is only so much you can learn in one day. We left as a mob and walked up the road. We found a Sam Smith's pub called The Greyhound. As we walked through the door it was like a United away game of old. Same-minded old Reds had shied away from the giddiness. Different Reds with opinions knocked together over hard gained Red experience had found the type of pre-match pub they had always done without any real organisation. A natural match going orientation.

Anodyne extra...

As if a greater force was rewarding us for our suss the cask beer was only £1.33 a pint. We sat down and savoured its delicious warmth of taste by an open coal fire. With a middin lid sized chip muffin served from behind the bar for £1.50. It was in this relieved comfort that we discussed the flexibility that must be found in all the sides that had walked away from United. We accept you, you accept us. Just because we don't want to boing doesn't make us people who would pooper a party. We have taken representatives of all aspects of United away with us. Our aspect is one of measured nosey Parkering that might be wrongly perceived by others as moodiness. We like our measured assessments of our clothes, our football, our music, our city. We bring friends into the realms of this ancient match going friendship by way of invite. An 'Oh aye nosey Parker' recognises another 'Oh aye nosey Parker'. Therefore dear boingers, drop your bigotry against us if you've got any, we've all got to give. We all know something about each other now. We're all Reds. We always were. Now we are Reds who made a second choice.

Playing the 'red' devil's advocaat...

We had received an assuring sign by way of a cheap beer and smart atmosphere in The Greyhound pub. When we entered the ground we noticed the boingers had received theirs. Adie Orr, our titanium toothed forward, had dyed his hair red. It got worse when Torpey did a cartwheel when he scored. I'm absolutely convinced that every single Red in The Greyhound pub that we had just left would abhor such gooniness. If the whole crowd were of the mind of the Reds that had just left The Greyhound pub then a player, supposedly out on the pitch representing us, our city and the political points we were making, would not have felt he could get away with such dickhead Nationwide'ness. The giddiness of the boingers had encouraged such acts of plastic Premiership'ness. If you want to know how divvy footballers are, watch your lower league goals round up on telly with the sound off. The embarrassment, as these less than gifted galloots try to impress with pre-arranged dance routines, is amplified by the silence. These vacuous souls are lucky to have our love. For our children's sake we have to win out over this one. If you're going to celebrate a goal, celebrate it like Joz Mitten. Or even a rare Robert Nugent one. It is no coincidence that they are both sussed Reds who know the Jack Palance.

Something of the knight about him...

Even though we played some lovely football in that first half, taking a 3-0 lead into the break, I had temporarily lost interest. Whether it was because of Adie Orr's blatant, red haired disregard for the fans or the fact that we had just taken our Christmas decorations down only nine days before I'm not sure. That first fortnight of any new year is always the glummest. It was then I realised it was the 15th. The first fortnight was over. Let the glimmer shimmer. I could see that there was a women's game going on just outside the ground. The choice was to watch Nelson FC's number 14 with his submariner's beard or go and see 22 women sweating. My caring side came out as I reckoned that most of the young women playing football would follow fashion. The fashion with young women now was to show their midriff. This was resulting in kidney infections. I was needed at the side of that pitch in case anyone of them needed their midriff rubbing to take away the pain. I'm a knight. A Sir Vix.

You feminine hygiene product...

A women's team wearing maroon shirts and shorts with mustard socks were playing a women's team wearing white shirts with blue shorts and socks. I was watching the game from the top of the little United away end. I was getting a stiff neck turning between the two games. For investigative journalist purposes only I decided to leave the ground and go and watch the women's football for a bit. The women in maroon turned out to be Accrington's women team. The women in the white shirts were Mosley Hill from Merseyside. It was the first half and Accrington were winning 7-0. The little United end, if they knew, would have been very pleased to know that the Minnie's were suffering. Accrington's number 20 dinked it over the Mosley Hill keeper to make it 8-0. She walked straight back to the circle. Women are more intelligent than men and have obviously seen the dickheads attempting to do 'mad cap' men dances when they score. Women don't need to turn the volume off on the local, lower league goals round up to know that men are bad dancing buffoons with too high an opinion of themselves. Men footballers' insulting dance means they don't think much of you the supporter. They think you're only good enough for their 'heat and serve' pre-packaged goal celebrations not their honest emotion. This 'Earnshaw' idiocy on the part of footballers has to stop. The beginning of this halt should really be started by a club like ours.

19 out of the 22 women players had ponytails. Ponytails must be very practical for football. Accrington's number 18, however, had pigtails. This made her stand out as a minx in the making. There were two magic wands on the pitch. Both were mousey muffs pretending to be blonde but somehow this wasn't as insulting as Adie's red haired nonsense. All three would have had to go to the shops, hummed and arghed over the colour to use, said: "What do you think?" to mates, put their heads in a sink, got dye runs down their face and towelled it dry afterwards. Thinking of Adie doing that is our revenge for his disrespect in the first place. The ref and both line runners were blokes. Very smiley officials. They must know there is never going to be a vacancy for a back scrubber with the girls but the smiles persisted. It only has to happen once though to make it all worthwhile. The carrot and the dick. You couldn't see any of the women's visible Panini sticker line through their shorts which always leads you to believe they might not be wearing any. What you would give then to be that double stitchng on the inside of those short gussets? That double stitching would work its way up between the two serrated edges of womanliness as the game went on. You'd want every game to have extra time. You'd certainly want to be the double stitching inside the shorts of a midfield 'box to box' female player who really grafted and not a gifted, but bone eye-gull, forward who waited for the ball to be played to her feet.

Rajastan, Uzbekistan, Canestan...

What is the knickers protocol at women's football? If you go to the game in clean Alan W's then do you put them back on after the game and risk other team mates knowing that you're a re-usable knickers woman? Or do you just go in a pair that will finish up being washed even though you have only had them on an hour? Do your team mates then think that your 'O' ringed, wiggly worm is a proper fish that John West would reject if you're sardine'ing them in 60 minutes? If you are only going to be wearing them for an hour on the way to the changing room, do you bring your not so posh ones as you don't want to wear your knewies out by keep washing them after so little wear? Then your team mates might think your knicker draw is Ethel Austin. If I was a woman I think I'd wear the ones I had on to go out in the night before. I'd risk other team mates going "Oh I see you're ovulating" if they caught a glimpse of the gusset. Or "Your fanny must face north as that smudge in your knickers is proper grass stain green. The crust on it would take some cracking." I'd bring a clean pair with me to put on after a post match shower. It's no wonder that women aren't as good at football as men. There is too much mither with your mather. There is also a reason why the crowds for women's football are smaller. No one wants a lob on throughout a game. This is presuming most men can maintain a 90-minute erection like myself. Girls, I am single if you want to get in touch at www.propermakeitupmeloads.co.uk

Alfurr Rowmayo...

The Lancastrian voiced announcer brought my attention back to FC United of Manchester's game. I wish he hadn't. We had a very poor second half. Nelson FC got one back from a penalty and the game finished 3-1 to us. We were in the empty bit of terracing behind the goal where their penalty was taken. Because we were so close to the Nelson penalty taker we thought that we could put him off. We shouted: "You look like one of those people who paint the word 'Gouranga' over motorway bridges" and "You'd need that little torch that they use in CSI to find your dick" and "Do you say bumper cars or dodgems?" We also arsed around behind the net, walking funny and giving each other piggybacks to do donkey races. It didn't work. They scored. What had worked, though, was that the refreshing chirrupyness of our boingers had rubbed off on us. You cannot be moody looking whilst moonwalking and donkey fighting at the same time. You cannot also be taken serious when singing, to the first single by Shane Ward, the following:

> We're not here to say we're sorry,
> We're not here to say Man U,
> We're here to say we're ready,
> And we've finally followed through.
> You can fuck off Malcolm Glazer,
> Stick your franchise up your hole,
> We're Man United's heart and soul,
> That's FC's goal.

We retired, songily shamefaced, to The Greyhound. We cut a small piece of wallpaper from the wall in the vault to use as a nicotine patch.

Discussed how Rio had gone into 'Rags to bitches' a shop on Tib Street in town and spent £3,000 that last week and that it wasn't coincidence that a big animal feed place called 'Eureka' was opposite the Holland's pie factory that is in Baxendale on the approaches to Accrington. Apparently, in Exodus 35.2, it says that those who work on the Sabbath should be put to death. It's a good job we're young and lazy, as lazy as can be and sail with Captain Farrell..

Pissotieres really take the piss...

The day ended for me with my first ever piss into a pissotiere that had been placed around Piccadilly Gardens in town to alleviate the conscience of the wall pissers. Getting your knob out legally in public. They couldn't put a pissotiere at the side of a pitch if women were playing for obv lob onny reasons. Ferreting to get your firefighter out in public is now acceptable in Manchester town centre. Chiselling one out has a lot of public relations hurgles to overcome. We have a dream. I also got a phone call from Margy the Manager thanking the lads for trying to put the Nelson FC lad off his penalty kick. We'd made that twelfth shirt our own. It felt good to be recognised as the twelfth man on the pitch getting our three points. It was appropriate as there were three other points to the day: We recognise the boingers, the boingers recognise us and together we get to those three points. The day against Nelson FC might have ended for me all allegorically but this chapter ends for you with a treat. A coffee cream treat if you like them, an orange, strawberry or nut whirl one if you don't. I've learnt the value of both.

I mentioned at the beginning of this chapter that FC United of Manchester had footballingly twinned Nelson and Colne by playing them both at Accrington Stanley's ground this season. As a treat I'll give you Mike Duff's account of that day we played Colne in the NWCL Cup on Remembrance Sunday, 2005. Mike Duff is Manchester's Vladimir Ilyich Linen, our little cup of Bisto made with Evian or poteen. The cheeky bells you hear across Manchester are because of such scampanologists. Caressing the face of a lover with the outside of the hand is supposedly more sensuous than with the inside of the hand. I'm not sure if I agree with that. It will vary. The same 'Is it or isn't it?' complexity applies to feet with a ball. A delicate pass with the inside of the foot or a magnificent, but still hit with force, outside of the boot curver. If you read Duff's book 'Lowlife' then you will observe the swerve but recognise the intensity of the belt that launched it. A gentle literary touch of the face, with both the inside and the outside of the hand, accompanied by an unforeseen emptier that puts you down. Just help yourself by going and getting a copy. This next bit will have to do until you do...

Colne versus FC United of Manchester. Played Sunday the 13th of November, 2005. Kick off 2pm. Played at Accrington Stanley's ground. Our first ever visit. It was in the League Challenge Cup...

I get a call from Mark on Friday night.
-You goin to Colne Saturday?
-Naw, I say.
-Why the fuck not yer part timer? he sez.
-Cos it's Sunday an at Accrington, I say, yeah am gonna put me foot down an sneak out.
-No kids, he sez, just adults this one.
Me an Mark an his brother Rigga have bin takin a posse of kids to the home games, an even though we still manage ter consume a yard or two of ale, it's a bit of a ball ache runnin after em. An of course rememberin em all when we go pub ter pub.
So Sunday morning arrives an a get up an have a full English breakfast "two cans of Stella an a very mild weed". An the phone goes an it's me eldest Liam
-Dad you goin FC? he sez.
-Yeah, I say knowin the next line.
-Can me an Korky come?"
Korky's me third eldest who I only see at the matches.
-Yeah meet yer at Rigga's on Monsall, I say an go back to me Stella.
So a ring a taxi an a head down to Monsall to meet up with the gang. The taxi driver is old school United an we chat football. Anyway we get to Rigga's an there's music blarin out, the party has started.
Let me tell yer about Rigga, his house is a shrine to Manchester United past an present, he is a hoarder of memorabilia, an taste has nothing ter do wid it, the tackier the better. So I get in an say "hello" to everyone (including Stan the parrot). An Rigga's woman Serena is rollin a weed on the couch. An Rigga's holdin a can.
-Give us a can, I say
An Rigga sez
-help yerself in the cupboard.
An there's only three left so a grab one.
Then the door goes an in walks two of me kids, so a gives them a can each an immediately claim "after you" rights from Serena wid the weed.
Two minutes later
-bangerty-bang, on the door
An it's John "fingers", former barman in the City on Oldham Street. No guessin how he earned his sobriquet.
-Give us a can? he sez.
-None left, a say.
An that's when Mark arrives with a bag of cans.

-Fuck me, he sez, we say no kids an a get here an there's kids an no cans. Some fucker wants ter sort their priorities out.
An out of nowhere Stan the parrot sqwaks
-Fuck off the lot of yer.
So we share Marks cans an head for the Oldham Road an a bus to town. Town's lively an we need an offy, so we hit the Spar on London Road, an a get six Stella's, a mean we is gonna be on the bus an hour, Rigga, Mark, Fingers an Serena follow suit an get canned up. An me kids get a butty apiece an liam borrows a couple a things. Now a don't normally condone me kids shopliftin (not unless it's for me) but this is special it's F.C.'s first cup match.
After much ado we board the 41x bus ter Accrington, the driver seems oblivious that seven of us board an yet only four pay, an we take our place upstairs at the back, There's only two other fella travellers followed us upstairs, though a suspect they're standin up down below to avoid us. Then the fun starts, we hit the cans an Serena rolls a weed. An Fingers starts telling us a story about Rigga at St Etienne an how he woke from a slumber, grabbed the first bottle he seen an downed it in one, only ter find it was a bottle a piss.
The craic is getting up a steam an the Stella an weed hypin us inter the drunken frenzy we need ter be in ter function fully on the singin an dancin front. The noise level's are high an a suspect the driver below is wishin for the terminus.
All of a sudden me youngest lad Korky wants a piss, which means they all want a piss.
-Piss in a can, sez Fingers laughin.
Me lad goes ter get an empty can for said purpose
-No fucker pisses in a can, a say, we aint animals.
So they all split up on the top deck, an they're all windin me up that they're pissin, an me nerves are well fuckin shot. A don't usually make a fool of meself till am much drunker than this.
Liam sez
-Can a ask the driver ter stop while we get off for one then Dad?
I'm just about ter say
-don't be stupid, until
-Good idea, sez Rigga an we all troop down the stairs.
The driver pulls up by a church yard wid a four foot wall, an everybody trudges off for a piss apart from me an Serena. The downstairs is near full an everybody watches as they stand behind the wall an piss, it's remembrance Sunday an the Church yard is half full. I stand on the bus, can in me hand, tuttin. The driver looks like he thinks he's on "Beadle's about" or that he's landed the Rampton run.
-Bin drivin long? a ask him. An he looks the other way.
We disembark, leavin the upstairs like an Algerian abotoir, an we're right next ter a pub called the Crown, by now a can feel the combination of the

drink an weed, an the juke box in me head is comin on. The Crown is hammered an as we enter all yer can hear is "I don't care about Rio", an its music to me ears, football is about makin friends not millionaire's. An we fight to the bar, leavin Serena outside wid the remains of the cans, an a make a mental note ter safeguard me investment, before Rigga an Fingers cash em in. We get our drinks an stand outside, the Sun aint shinin but it's okay, a mean it is fuckin Accrington.
A got a pint an a weed, an two of me kids wid me, so a start singin "Collyhurst Road", Fingers joins in an even Serena comes in on the chorus, we have another an head down to the ground. It's a proper third round of the F.A. Cup style atmosphere, but back when the cup mattered, not like it is now.
As we get there the FC coach is unloadin, an we go over an the kids are gettin autograph's, an they get George the kitman's autograph, an he's real shy about givin it, but we're Monsall an he's our kitman an as important to us as the manager.
We get in the social club, an a say ter Liam
-This club where we're playin is one of the original twelve members of the league
an Liam sez
-A know dad yer've told me six times already.
By now am in a catatonic trance so a go wid "Collyhurst Road", by about the sixth rendition even strangers are singin the chorus.
A look around the only one's left sober are the kids an one of them is stoned.
We make our way ter the payin in an I go ter concessions wid me kids, they pay junior an I pay pensioner.
-This is concessions, she sez in a broad Lancashire ascent that matches her shoulders.
-Yep that's me, a say putting down me three quid, am sixty-six.
-You don't look it, she sez all dubious (but not dubious enough for my likin).
-Born durin the blitz, a say an shove in.
The atmosphere is electric, you'd think it was forty thousand an not four. All around us everybody's singin, an we all get split up, a got two cans one of cider an one of some dubious lager. I'm wid Mark an Korky. Fingers is sat next to the FC bench, Liam is moochin about an John an Serena are fuck knows where.
The game gets underway. An ter be honest wid yer a can't remember a lot. Half time Serena passes me a spliff an it sends me over the edge. Mark sez
-Let's have a mooch round, an we decide ter tour the ground.
By now we're staggerin inter each other, we stop behind the goal where the FC are mainly congragated an we give it em

-When I was young an lazy
as lazy as can be
a said goodbye to the mother-in-law
an off a went ter see
a sailed wid Captain Skipper
aboard the Mary Ann
an we all set sail down the Collyhurst Road
in a black maria van
Collyhurst Road I have forsaken
It's not that me poor heart is achin
It's the whisky an the rum that I have taken
For that darling little girl from Collyhurst Road

They is under impressed, so we give it em again an again. Mark pulls me away an we carry on wid our conga. Right round the ground, an it's buzzin, every fucker seems as pissed as we are. An it's song after song, we finish up behind the other goal singin to the Colne fans, an next thing a know is me kids are there draggin me away, an the Colne fans are booin me kids. They know a good singer when they hear one.

The second half was a blurr but wid about twenty minutes ter go, I'm stood wid Rigga an Mark near the dug-out an a "UNITED" chant goes up an we try ter keep it goin till the final whistle. Somewhere in there Colne take a lead, an the atmosphere steps up a gear. Then FC equalise, a free kick by Torpey, an I'm on the floor wid Rigga on top of me an a know how poor Serena must feel every Saturday night. No sooner are we back up on our feet than Colne make it 2-1. They're in injury time an three sides of the ground are willin an screamin fc on. The seconds tick away, the level a noise don't drop, all around reachin new levels.

All of a sudden in front of us there's a player pile up an tempers boil over an somewhere in there Fingers gets ejected for an altercation wid a steward. The whistle goes an it's over. We're out of the cup.
We're stood there dumbstruck. We wander outside an find Fingers an we're stood outside the main entrance, Rigga an the rest drift in ter get their programme's signed an have a natter wid the players, Serena gives me a spliff, an a stand there on me own pissed an stoned, happy yet gutted. An a just got nowt better ter do than sing.

Then it gets all bleary a sorta remember an off license an then we're all in the back of some fucker's Tranny, an it's pitch black an a feel an elbow in me back, at least a hope it was an elbow.

-Hey Dad is this a bush tucker trial or wot? asks Korky.

Then we're out of the Tranny an at some bus stop, an the 41x pulls up, an guess wot? Yep, you're right the same driver. We all walk on, mutterin that we "got returns"; the drivers face is a picture. A bet he spend his dinner break clearin up from the first trip.

We go upstairs an commandeer the back seats, two young lads come an join us. An we start rollin wid em, the upstairs starts ter fill an there's maybe twenty five or thirty people there. All of a sudden a kid in the middle starts singin

-We're the middle of the bus we're louder than you.
An it erupts "We're the back the bus an we're louder than you"
An "We're the front of the bus we're louder than you", as Cliff's crew at the front decide ter down cider an take up the cudgel.
An a singin competition ensues that takes us all the way ter Manchester. Back an forth the banter, an me kids are lovin it. Grass Roots the kid that started the singin decides a look like Sid Little an gets a good "Sid Little give us a song goin". Me lads are fallin about laughin. I reply wid the classic

"When I was young an lazy"
an the entire Monsall posse is behind me. An the bus is rockin, an the two kids sat at the back, when they got on they were like the "silence of the lambs" but they take over, an give it the middle an the front in true Salford style. An any fucker getting off the bus gets "We can see you sneakin off" sang at em.

An then we're in Piccadilly an they all is headin for Monsall an me for the Blackley Hills. An me last memory of the day is stood outside Malik's off-license singin

-"A can't stop lovin you" ter a winda full a drink.
An the next mornin a wake up an the first thing a think of is Rigga's face when Torpey's free kick went in an a laugh an a laugh an a fuckin well laugh.

Still crazy after all these beers.

CHAPTER FIFTEEN

THE DEAD DAD DIET...

Manchester Royal Infirmary versus Francis Brady. Thursday the 9th of February 2006. Kick off 1st of December 1925. This exceptional 80- year encounter finishing in a breath taking, lovely passing move between 9.30pm and 9.45pm. Also Daisy Hill versus FC United of Manchester. Saturday the 11th of February 2006. Kick Off 3pm. Played at Chorley FC's Victory Park ground in Chorley. A town where getting nine rashers of bacon in an eight rasher packet means you're a witch and they burn you.

He's gone wherever good ponies go...

Before we start this chapter: I couldn't imagine the place where good ponies go being all that good. As a consequence I wouldn't want to go to the place where bad ponies go, as that must be really shite. Anyway, back to less horsey matters. Don't be a porky pants blobbing about all the time. Your mates don't invite you round to their house anymore as the last time you put a dint in their settee. Even your freakishly over sized FC United of

Manchester shirt looks Italian national side, sprayed on. What you should do is get yourself a Dad. Love him, hold him and love him again for all his life. Then be with him for his last ever fortnight when you know he's going to lose. When he dies watch the weight fly off your body. I lost over half a stone in four days with the Dead Dad Diet. My Mam lost eleven pounds. Our Christine lost an eighth of an ounce but she is on HRT so not putting on half a stone in four days is quite good. The amount of money you invest in Closer magazine for weight loss recipes would be better invested on the life of your Dad, as you'll lose all the weight you want in the end. This diet also translates to Mams but I have no intention of going on that diet for a hundred years or more. Possibly a million years as they're going to invent something soon as no one should go through such crushing heartbreak of loss. There's definitely room in the market for major drug companies to invent something that stops your Mam or Dad ever dying.

When I've got it you can have it. When I haven't you can't...

We lost Frank Brady on the 9th of February 2006. He was Doris Brady's husband. He was Christine Brady's Dad. He was my Dad. He was our everything the lot. He was our everything the lot but with a cake or a trifle 'with a surprise in every mouthful' for afters after it. And a pint after that in the bestestist of company that you would never want to leave, that you'd always want one more with. With laughter so thumped that you were squeezed breathless, lifted gasping, but always re-oxygenated in readiness for the next squeeze. The night before my Dad died, the doctor, as she reeled off what was wrong with him, concluded with the sentence: “His blood is well oxygenated, though.” All doctors, after all his tests, always said that. We knew what he was doing. Copped you Dad. He was generating an excess of oxygen in himself so that he had a surplus to give out to everyone he loved so that they could breathe. If you're lucky then everyone gets to love their Mam and Dad. Everyone considers their Mam and Dad to be the ones. It should be no other way. That's lovely that.

I've lost one out of my two. My Dad, being one out of my two 'The ones', did so countless much in his life. Of all the episodes he started and went through, one was that he used to take me to Old Trafford when I was a young wage packet thinner. Our family theory is that when you're younger than five or six you're being taken to the game so that your Mam or Dad can show off how United mad they are by taking you so young. Admit it. If you are brave enough to admit it to yourself then you can patently see that the child gets bored. The Mam or Dad should, after one or two showings of the child at the game, stop taking you. Take advantage of these younger years where you're not being mithered. From five or six onwards they still get bored but they can look around and nosey more and even make Red mates. So take them regularly from then. You're doing well, though, if you get to half time without a fairly bulky sized moan from them. By the time they are reaching ten or 11 they are zealots and cannot understand why you are not in the ground as they open the curtains.

My first recollections of Old Trafford watching United are from about five or six. Apparently you never forget your first game. I forgot to learn that. If my Dad took me earlier to show off how United mad he was then I've forgotten. I'm almost certain he wouldn't have done. I can't even say "I wish he was alive so that I could ask him" as he wouldn't have remembered anyway. He would have much preferred to take advantage of my younger years and stayed in The Vic on Grey Mare Lane with his mates, before getting the 53 to the game. Knowing that the days were coming when he would have to be lumbered with me for seasons to come.

Proud of him for knowing the importance of beer and mates to the game. No children in pubs in those days. So those of you now showing off your half hour old baby at the game remember it is only for you. If you bring your child up right they will, in later years, think you were a knob for staying out of the pub just to draw attention to yourself and using them as a vehicle to do it. Very city. The first season at FC United of Manchester has had touches of perceived 1950's innocence about it. Though there have been far too many children at the front of all the matches for us 'Kids in cupboard' advocators.

Wooden seats, iron arms...

Me and my Dad always went early to the Stretford End seats so that we could get on the back row so that I could stand. I needed to stand because invariably the fella in front would be fella sized. I can't remember which game it was but very early in my United career - after establishing the Labradorial pattern in me that we went to the Stretford End seats and stood - the pattern was broken as the Stretford End seats were full. We finished up in the actual Stretford End. I'm only a five or six year old. We were in the middle, lengthwise walkway that separated the lower bit from the upper bit. The walkway you came onto if you entered the Stretford End via the tunnel. The Stretford End lower was packed in front of the tunnel. I was just about arse height. The wall of blokes in front of you as you walked down the tunnel out onto the terraces meant no view for me.

In my first few minutes on the Stretford End I cried. So many tears have watered various United sand, cement and stone steps since. Tears encouraging goodness to grow with everything we owned. But I always remember my first. That was my opening United heartbreak and I hold it close - more than any grieving for the loss of memory of not knowing my first game. Being in the Stretford End for the first time had me wanting to see United, not thousands of Wrangler or Levi jean pockets. That must have been a mither for my Dad. In a presumably lock out game he had still managed to get me in. That was important.

I never in all my 'Going to the match with my Dad' career suffered a lock out and the mess of turning around and going home. A couple of times when I was older, but never with my Dad. In acts of Unitedness that would go on forever I was found a space. Red youth, who occupied the higher bit of step and fencing that separated the lower bit of the Stretford End from the upper, squeezed up and let this child in. You might be one of those Reds reading this who did that. Thank you. You helped me and my family and I'll never forget it. You'll never know you did it. Unknowing oxygenators.

I could now see the full pitch and, even from this distance, gladly risked getting a chest infection from 90-minute exposure to the damp from the saviours' soil. I presume Denis was playing. I don't know if he was but that's the importance. Players go. United remain. Denis would understand. Every coat I have ever bought since I could buy clothes myself has been bought in deference, with sleeves that I can Denis. As my Denis was your Georgie. Having Denis length sleeves can sometimes make you look a bugger but not to those who know. So forgetting whether Denis was playing has been easily remunerated for by my big coat, big sleeve wearing throughout less 'big coat' friendly years.

Young boys burn...

My Dad was lower down in front of me across the passageway throughout the game. He had a conventional shite view trying to look over and around all the heads in front of him. They liked it that way. I encouraged him in a "Dad, Dad, Dad" way to come up and stand with me on this raised walkway step and fencing. As a bloke now, I understand why he didn't. As a boy I wanted my Dad to be at my side showing him what a great view it was and sharing it. He, however, knew it was a gift he had given me. The infant boy who thought Old Trafford belonged to him. All he surveyed. Raised high the scarlet standard. Given to him by his Dad. Facilitated by the Red community around us both. My Manchester United Football Club. Our Manchester United Football Club.

The Manchester United Football Club, Mancunian embrace with the temperate, giving smile that says here it is, it's yours. You came and found it and now it can no longer leave you. You were brought near by others' love, but for your own love you had to go on your own shaping walk. Those who love you knew that. They knew it because they had done it before. You didn't have to come back with anything. No one has ever asked you to. You saw. You didn't have to see. Nothing would be ill of you if you hadn't seen. But you did. Nothing is ever going to change that. I have Francis Brady in me. I love because he loved. I am able to give because he was able to give. Our family bloodline as always, Red laced with the football bloodline going back, on that unpaid for train, to those railway workers from 1878.

Nil - nil by mouth...

And here he was now. That young man who had given me that gift was now 80 and in Manchester Royal Infirmary. The bleeder had been taken into hospital in the early teatime before FC United of Manchester's friendly game against Glossop North End on the 8th of February 2006. The pest had cost me a Harold Melvin as I wouldn't be going to the game and using my ticket. A Harold Melvin is a Harold Melvin. If a pint at Accrington was £1.33, as we've established, then a Harold could still get you three and a half pints with 35 pence left for a packet of crisps. A good, good friend who had my spare ticket gave his ticket to the turnstile operator at the game that night. He then gave him mine and said: "That's just a donation to appreciate Glossop North End's footballing time."

Little our land...

In the summer months of 2005, between the hostile take over and the formation of FC United of Manchester on July the 5th, I had taken my Dad around Delamere Park in Openshaw. He was in a wheelchair. Amongst his vast array of 'Hospital Saturday' ailments was one where his lungs had gone bandit on him so any attempts to move around left him pooped doggy dog. Just getting up from the settee knackered him out. The shuffle from the living room to the front porch to piss in his bottle totally wheezed him over. He should have just pissed his pants. With the cancer in his bladder, he sometimes did. With the seven inches of bowel he had removed he sometimes did something else out of the other exit. Our house was like Belle Vue Elephant House at times. The poor, poor sod, he couldn't help it. He tried so hard to keep his dignity. And in always trying he did.

We'd go through the hardship of getting him dolled up to go out in his wheelchair, which would knock him up even further. One of his strokes had robbed him of his eyesight on his left hand side but a comedy bi-product was that you'd go around and his polo shirt would be on back to front. You'd think it was impossible to have a meaningful conversation with another human sat there with their shirt on back to front but you can do it. You almost got to miss it on the days when by 50-50 chance it was on the right way. I've just turned mine around whilst I'm writing this. It's not that bad. It's quite liberating. Preparing yourself for when it happens to you in later life.

Anyway we had plonked him on the wheelchair and off we scooted to Delamere Park. Everything in that summer of 2005 was upside down and speeding. I'd sort of let matters go on as no one involved on the Steering Committee really knew where we were going. We thought we did at times. I'd reasoned that there was no gain of confusing my Mam and Dad by telling them about events, when events were changing that quickly daft. After a few weeks, though, we got clearer as a Steering Committee. Now was the time to tell my direct derivation what his son was up to. Just the opening sentence would be the hardest to say. I wound his wheelchair up Vine Street, crossed Abbey Hey Lane and buffeted him up the last edging into the park. We nosey'd at events going on in there. Youngsters in United shirts playing, dogs turning out a mix, crisp bags blowing, forms peeling. It was a sunshiny day and I wheeled him to the shade of a tree and sat down on one of those peeling forms. I wanted to talk to him to his face not to the back of his head as I pushed him.

Do you want the short version or the long version? It makes no difference, as they're both the same...

It all came out. His son was involved in the breakaway fans' club that had been getting a tidgey bit of press coverage in the landslide media spill of the Glazer take over. There was nothing but intense interest in his face. His son rambled as his son does, trying to fit five hundred minutes worth of information into five minutes worth of conversation. Take your time son; I'm going nowhere but by your side. We'll do what we do because that is what we do well. In the elucidating to my Dad I was explicating to myself. Circuitously withdrawing the 'ex' out of explain to just leave the plain. Obvious to me now. Obvious to my Dad, then.

Every reason I wheeled in, every corner I came in at, every gone-back-to the comfy chair of history I had sat on so that I could look up, every hardship day that had past into excruciating weeks, every grind of emotion that had been wrought through, every face of others, every slump of shoulder, every lonely bed sigh, every uninhabited tin-cold place, every unlit deep dark room, every alone, every well, every bracing breath, every gritted, measured, arduous arising, every will not to go back to helpless, every using of feet and back and hands together to unwrangle, every early moment shone in on, every holding of faith, every 'We can do it, the power is ours, we can, we can, we can, it's ours, we can', every 'Fuck them and fuck their family, they're not having it', every 'Every' I had ever been taught without ever going to Every Street School on the Beswick/Ancoats border. My Dad just knew. And from then on so did I.

Every Street a Beswick Street...

If I have a place at this football club at the side of you, then it is because my Dad did. And does. He knew it was a gift he had given me on that childhood Stretford End. He was letting me rediscover. In that east central Manchester park on that sunshiny day I was part returning that unpayable debt. The only debt that any club should have. The debt of being immersed in love. The infant boy who thought Old Trafford belonged to him was here. He'd brought the scarlet standard. No longer alone. About to raise high. It was given to him by his Dad. Facilitated by the Red community around us both. My Manchester United Football Club. Our Manchester United Football Club.

The Manchester United Football Club, Mancunian embrace with the temperate, giving smile was asking how we were. Saying here it is, it's yours, you couldn't have forgotten. You came and found it; it never had any intention of leaving you. Or of letting others that would hurt it, take it away. You were brought near by others' love, but for your own love you had to go on your own shaping walk. You've just walked again. Around and around. And around again just to get on your own nerves. Those who love you knew that. They knew you'd do it. They knew it because they had done it before. This time we did it together. We didn't have to come back with anything. No one has ever asked us to. We saw. We didn't have to see. Nothing would be ill of us if we hadn't seen. But we did. Nothing is ever going to change that. I felt our family bloodline, as always Red laced with the football bloodline, getting back on that unpaid for train. Those railway workers from 1878 would be waiting. We owe it to them to get there. We'll get there by protecting the resistance that is FC United of Manchester.

Four degrees and rising...

And here was my Dad going away from me and my family. He really was going to die on Grafton Street. I decided to walk to the hospital from town on the 9th of February 2006. My Dad had survived the night of the 8th. It was Auntie Mal's 81st birthday on the 8th of February. He was never going to be so ignorant as to ruin it for her. I walked past the Poly and the University. A younger Manchester. My Dad believed that from our knowledge grew the capability to take back what was ours, from those that would steal it from us. He meant the means of production or your football club not someone having your video away. I had under my arm a posh pair of cotton pyjamas for him that had just cost me £22. I like the number 22, it was the reason I chose them. Two little ducks together. Quack, quack. He'll look nice and feel comfortable. However, my mate at work had been to see his Mam who had been in this same hospital. She'd had a few quid stolen from her purse while she was in. For a second I thought that if we can't get the pyjamas on him then they might get stolen, as they were still in the bag.

The ruling ideas of the time are the ideas of the ruling class. The loving man I was on my way to visit, who was going to die, had taught me that. I was Daily Mail'ing myself for no reason. If someone had indeed had those £22 pyjamas away then my Dad would have been the first to say, good. If someone is so without self-worth that they have to nick nightwear to get a few bob then they are desperate. Something traumatic has robbed them of that worth. They wouldn't have chosen to have that trauma beset them. If they are so distressed that they have to whip away others' small goods, then let the enjoyment of wearing a posh pair of pyjamas go some way to alleviate that fraught life. If I've got it, you can have it. If I haven't, you can't.

He was not being a turn the other hippy cheek, he just knew that we'll deal with our own lumpen proletariat in our own time. Not at the behest of private school educated criminals who run industry, own the media, have taken a seat in Sandhurst, who set the law and hold the key to your cell. The petty crime that might be pyjama stealing bears not the minutest resemblance to the billions stolen in unpaid tax by the rich. To the under funding of such Manchester hospitals, as the one my Dad was now in, betraying all the fought for ideals of those that had survived the '30s, come back from the war in 1945 and built the NHS.

I try to be a good man. My Dad didn't have to try. It was natural in him. As I walked on to see him at the hospital I had benefited again from my Dad's innate care. We'll put these £22 pyjamas down and we'll see what happens to them. I walked and balmed in the lovely day that it was. It was my Dad's favourite sort of day. A four degrees and rising day. We'd just had a cold, frosty, cloudless, winter night but the cold sun has come up in the morning to raise the temperature. Ideal brick setting weather. If the weather is below four degrees then brick are not meant to be set. On cold but sunny clear winter days like this, the crispness reinvigorates your enthusiastic sparkle. The 'one on top of two', one on top of two down, and walls get built. Cities rise.

As I passed all the students around the Oxford Road University corridor, I thought that one day some of these youngsters might be architects. They might help this city rise. Or they might be in medicine and eventually help to save me down at the same hospital on Grafton Street where my Dad now was. It is a university hospital. Then a snotty voiced get went passed me and that inverted working class snob came out in me again. And my pleasantness for students evaporated. Some students are alright, some want chasing with a big twig that has had the end dipped in dog shit.

At that very same moment I saw a young student face I recognised. I couldn't place her. She looked at me. She couldn't place me. I wasn't going to let on as a bloke going out of his way to let onto an 18-year-old is a bit pervy. As she passed I got who it was. It was wimberry charlotte woman. She was the young girl behind the counter in the cake shop in Openshaw. The cake shop near to the park where me and my Dad had discussed the formation of the new club. Our favourite cake shop. The young girl in the Openshaw cake shop was educating herself whilst giving out cakey goodies to the people of east central Manchester. I put away any negative thoughts of playing shit on a stick with students because shit on a stick is a game to be played for enjoyment, not in retribution.

On the clear night after a four-degree and rising day you look up and there is nothing but stars...

Cakes, education, youth, a re-inventing city, four degrees and rising day with all the possibilities to build again and building well, the importance of health care, the ability to place in context the minor criminality of our class against the vastness of their class - it was all coming together just as my Dad was going away. The Dead Dad Diet till the day you die. Not a short burst, weight loss tactic but ingredients that should always stay with you. Keep your poise, your founded equilibrium. They're yours, don't lose them. You couldn't have forgotten. See what the less scrupled and their henchmen are trying to hide from you. Watch how they scapegoat and manipulate, poison and condemn. They do it for a reason. They're scared. We really are the many. And those that control our lives know it.

From Sao Paulo to the CIS building, to that fly over going nowhere near the BBC on Oxford Road to the long road, maybe the wrong road. From Florrie North with her zipped furry boots who used to walk aimlessly up and down Grey Mare Lane to Nanook of the north. We all have something. Put it together. We are the many. We all seek asylum, an inviolable place of refuge. If we're all in that place then there is no need for anyone to be extradited. Those cruel callers for extradition will extradite themselves into a place where only they will be. They'll be there, inconsequential and isolated. They will be easily recognisable for the backward, divisive ruling class rhubarb that they espouse. They will be the ones that are not welcome here in our superpower of asylum. We serve neither King nor Kaiser, but our land. This land was made for you and me. My Dad never got to wear those £22 pyjamas. They stayed in the bag, unstolen by any Mancunian. I'll keep them always as final, farewell reminders to maintain a balanced view for all my life.

Red of team, red of politics, red of nose...

After fifty-seven-and-a-half years of marriage my Mam lost her husband in the half-light of the Examination Room in the Medical Assessment Unit. At half five in the evening, after a traumatic putting of a tube down his nose and into his stomach, we presume he was given a sedative. He went into the restful sleep that he had been craving. In the last few years, because of the mixture of drugs he was on, he was having bad dreams. Always bad dreams where he was helpless: He was on a scaffold and he couldn't set brick because he needed his walking stick or that there was an oxygen restriction imposed nationwide and he didn't have enough to breathe or he was in hospital and, after visiting the toilet, he couldn't find his bed. He'd always tell you about them. The one that made us all smile, though, was the one where he dreamt he was in Liverpool's Lime Street train station. He was stuck there, alone, out of breath and with no money to get home. He said that even in his dream he couldn't ask any passing scousers for help, as they would suss he was a Mancunian and they'd fill him in.

There was none of that restlessness as he slept in his last four hours. My Mam, our Christine, me and our Ben were all around his bed for those hours that could never be stretched long enough. We told him everything we had in us. We also arsed about. I hid my Dad's false teeth in our Christine's handbag. We discovered that my Mam can't whisper. That the only thing open in hospitals after seven o'clock was my Dad's bowels. That my Dad had a rare blood group. He had donated all his life but had probably got it all back because he was such a crank. I reminded my Mam, as I had done throughout my life, that our Christine had once thrown a teaspoon at me when I was a child and it had hit me in the eye resulting in a hospital visit. Didn't she Mam? Didn't she Dad? That we had nearly lost my Dad so many times that we reckoned we had lost a dozen Dads. That we might have come so close to losing him a dozen times but a dozen times we had got him back. That we'd never hear the squeak of the hospital wheelbarrow bringing his mountain of medical notes again. We lost him. With no ill ease or gurgled writhe he simply went off for a pint with his two best mates, Kenny and Tom, without us knowing it as those he loved, and who loved him, parroted around him.

You can only know everything you need to know after you've wiped your arse on a cement bag son ...

The apparent blanket protest that had been going on at my Mam and Dad's house in east central Manchester for the last few years was now over. Francis Brady was never coming back. He'd had his final shite. Filled his piss bottle in the lobby for the last time. Dropped his last cakey crumb on the floor to be squashed into the carpet by his trod-down-back slippers. His last rice pudding had been spilt down his front. His last counsel had been called. His knobbly knees and sparrow legs, that had battered back rickets when he was five, were about to be left behind by us in that hospital room. I hugged him and told him he couldn't get away as I'd got him. I took a clean tissue from the side and gently wiped a moistened tear from his eye. His last ever tear. It was a tear of a lifetime of pride as he'd gone with his family giggling at nonsense by his side.

On his first date with my Mam at the Metropole picture house in Beswick he had mortified her. He had laughed so loud at the Tom and Jerry clips before the main film that the seats on their row were rocking. My Mam was so embarrassed. Mind you, she knew what was coming. The first time she ever saw my Dad he was running past her in the lobby of The Welly pub in Beswick to be sick in the toilets. Valuable. So she was well warned before their first date at The Met. Those tears of laughter from my Dad as Tom 'Fred Quimby'ly ' got a frying pan in the face off Jerry or had his tail plugged into the electricity have to be his first tears in my Mam's company. The tear I had just carefully dabbed was his definite last. I took that tissue and put it in a little placcy bag without anyone knowing. I'll give that tissue to our Christine soon. I need it near me for a bit. I'll leave it till our Christine reads this sentence and then it will rightfully be passed onto her, as she is the eldest. And I love her so. The great thing is that she will be receiving something so precious, the result of the last ever laugh. However, what makes it that little bit greater is that she will always know that the little placcy bag I put it in, and that she will be receiving it in, had previously contained his false teeth. Shit shovel comedy.

Player's medium...

As my Dad died on the Thursday, FC United of Manchester were playing Daisy Hill at Chorley FC's ground on the Saturday. My Dad loved Chorley cakes. Everybody does, though, so we won't dwell on the symbolism and say that the 'FC' in 'Chorley FC' stood for Frank's Cakes. I've never done a full season at Manchester United Football Club where I've seen every game home and away. I could have done but chose not to. I know many, many good Reds who have but it's just something I never wanted to do. I must have been exposed to a div early on and have let it somehow subconsciously warp me. It must have been one of those whose life is only one of following a football club and nothing else. That bit is totally alright. It's when they have to tell you about it that sort of gets you worried about their motives. 'Look at me' is never appealing in a person. As I've said I know many, many Reds who have done the full season of not missing one single game and do it and just get on with it. They do it because that is what they do. No need to announce. Just be a good Mancunian. Being around such good Reds made it hard at times but I had come to a previous decision.

I ventured early in my United career that missing two games a season kept you sane. Tempered the addiction. Once the 'Can't miss' gets you, you're fucked. And skint. We've all seen it. I love beer too much to become an alcoholic. I think I applied the same to United. I proved to myself that I could do it. Obviously periods of being brassic helped as everyone in their lives goes through periods of poverty. If you're in a loving relationship and there is only a finite amount of finance to go around till the next payday then it was never a competition. Never let your football club make you selfish and change you into something you're not. It never asked you to. It wouldn't want you to. There are too many pint pots to pick up. Too many women to 'End scene of Benny Hill' after. Of course, you can do that whilst following United but variety is always needed. I always purposely missed two games a season so I never became one of those football characters who say: "I never miss, me." I'd have missed too much over the years to make the privilege of being able to say that sentence worthwhile.

Now, though, I was faced with the problem of missing two FC United of Manchester games in a season. If I didn't, I could become the man I had never wanted to become. Francis Brady turning up his toes solved that one. Missing the Chorley game enabled me to get my footballing consistency back. FC United of Manchester beat Daisy Hill 3-0. They've got twice as good or we've got twice as bad as we'd beaten them 6-0 at home earlier in the season. A player called Simon Band made his debut for us. Call me Elastic. Or Bonzo Dog Doo-Dah. Daz Lyons, our substitute forward and player coach, came on and apparently scored a 25-yarder. He went to school with my Dad so that was nice of him. It turned out that Margy had hidden Mr Lyons' angina tablets and wouldn't give them back to him till he scored, so it was more of a medical necessity goal than a memorial goal for my Dad. Margy put Daz's catheter back in for him after the game so there were no grudges to fester in the dressing room.

The attendance was quite a lowly one of 1,682. It would have been one more with me there. Mind you with the make it up, 'One for me, one for the taxman' crowds going on and the big Blackpool away game the following week, a lower turn out of 'only' taking 2,000 fans to an away game is not that bad. All my mates commented on the friendliness of the locals and their pubs so it was a shame to miss it, but my Dad had only just gone. He was still warm. Granted you'd struggle to heat up a pie to an acceptable temperature with him but he was not that cold that you could keep your lollies from running. I suppose we'd better get him cremated as his smell by date was approaching.

So then comrades come rally and the last fight let us face. The Internationale unites the human race...

He had a Humanist funeral at Manchester crematorium at 3.35pm on Friday the 17th of February 2006. We were supposed to carry the coffin in to 'Bridle hanging on the wall' but the CD never arrived from America in time. Why he always sang a song about a dead horse we will never know. The closest thing he had come to a horse was living near, and retching at the smell, of Dean and Woods where they boiled them down to glue. We finished up carrying him in to the instrumental 'Roisin Dubh' played by The Dubliners. There are mandolins and all sorts on the track. All the instruments he would have loved his children to play but we never did. The crematorium holds 120 apparently. It was over full, as there was standing at the back. There always has to be a standing section. The Order of Service that we had put together ourselves in an 'MDF/make your own football club/ get glue and nails and get going' sort of way was given to those there. As well as having the words to the Internationale written in it, the Order of Service also had the following on its back page:

Frank Brady...

> He took his first Bolshevik breath at home in east central Manchester on the 1st of December 1925. He took his peaceful last on the 9th of February 2006. On both occasions he was in his family's arms.

We all laughed that he was born so poor that he didn't even get a middle name. If we could have chosen one then it would have been Frank 'Everything' Brady, or Frank 'Ours' Brady, or Frank 'Hospital Saturday just-how-many-ailments-have-you-got Dad?' Brady.

Big coat building...

A thousand brick a day craftsman bricklayer all his life; he built homes for others to live in. In ours he built a life long marriage with Doris, the woman he loved, his adoring and adored family, a forty gallon drums' worth of chirrupy friends, and his socialist politics for a kinder, caring, more equal world. He did all this whilst abhorring 'forty pocketness' and always getting a beer in. And, eating cakey.

One of the last conversations he heard as he rested, was his two thicky children and our Ben discussing why woodpeckers are called woodpeckers. He heard Christine say "I thought it was because they sharpen their beaks on wood", then Robert say, "I thought it was because they ate trees" - Ben just shook his head in disbelief at us. Sorry Dad, we didn't mean not to know.

What we do know is that the world we will win will be immersed in the love he gave. He didn't melt. Neither will we. xxxx

Left for love...

My Mam was stood in the front row inside the Crematorium. I managed to gently touch the back of her hair as I passed her whilst carrying the coffin. This was no easy task as I was carrying the coffin with five dwarves and I had all my Dad's cakey weight. The five fellow carriers commented afterwards on how light he was. There's a reason you found him light to carry and the reason was my left shoulder. If you five had only taken the time to grow a bit more you would have found out. I thought he was wearing chain mail overalls. And an anvil hat. And lying on a mercury filled waterbed with fluffed up, cement bag pillows.

Our Shirley, who is a Humanist Officiator, introduced the ceremony going on about all things in my Dad's life including Manchester United Football Club and FC United of Manchester. Then I got up and spoke. I can't think of anything harder that I have done. I can't think of anything easier. I had spent all my life telling the world how great my Dad was. This captive audience, who couldn't leave out of politeness, were going to get it for the one last time. I rambled at first. Our Shirley the Officiator had told us that with so much emotion it is vital that you have a script.

I had prepared a script but I ignored the advice to stick to it in the initial moments. When I got up to the podium, or whatever it is at the front, I talked off script about how I had carried my Dad in on my left shoulder so that he was closest to my heart. Left for love. I have this OCD thing where if I am, say, doing a meal for someone I love I always put their plate on the left hand side as I'm dishing. Left for love. Closest to your heart. This can apply to other things, say; such as topping up wine glasses in the kitchen. You pick up the empty wine glass of the one you love with your left hand, you put it down on the left hand side of your glass on the kitchen worktop, you fill it and then you take it back. All done with left for loveness. This can also have a practical as well as loving side if the scabby mare'ess has got a cold sore. There's a reason you have a script though. Going off it, as I had just done, only made you break. I couldn't break; I had to do this for my family. Having a script means you can edit the things that are really going to get you, that you know will finish you up as a blubbery bugger, all snot and whinge. I got back to reading. It would have been too much if I hadn't. It went:

> My Dad used to always say to us all 'Put me in a bin bag when I turn up me toes.' I do not know why I did that voice then as he talked nothing like that. He'd also say, and I'll take the F swear word out 'No man in a ffrock is burying me.' He meant no insult to the Transexual community.
>
> Sorry Dad but the local authorities are not that keen on bin bags - with bodies in - being left on buses - so we failed on that one. What we didn't fail on - was the fact he said nothing about a woman in a frock seeing him off - so I'd like to thank our Shirley and all her family for that.
>
> On the front of the Order of Service it talks about a continent coming for all our lives. A continent is a big fat, enormity - but it's

not an omnipotent, singular force. It's a powerful influence - but it interacts with other continents, recognising other continents for their strength and intensity.

They're constantly shifting with each other but constantly there. That's what my Dad was and is. Our family's continents are, and can never stop being - my Nana who I lost when I was sixteen - my precious, precious Mam and my chuckling, entertaining, wise Dad.

When I first went as a bricklaying apprentice into my Dad's working world and on to a building site - I was always Frank Brady's lad. Never once as a dissenting teenager did I rebel against that label. Being defined as Frank Brady's lad was an honour - an acceptance as you entered a blokey's world - benefiting from someonelse's greatness - that had been bestowed upon you - It was like being Eric's son but a billion times better.

It's the closest thing our class could get to an heriditary peer, I was related to working class royalty. I was the son of Frank Brady.

I could see then the regard he was held in by everyone around him. My friends - at the back there - had always loved my Dad. My family had always loved my Dad - but being a young adult then for me it completed it - all his friends loved my Dad. If you knew him, then you loved him. You couldn't help it. He'd haul you in with his infectious friendliness. His gentle tone of kindness.

Mine and Christine's Dad was a very loving man. When I was only three I got knocked down by a motor car on Wellington Street. Wellington Street housing the pub where my Mam and Dad first met. I finished up in Ancoats Hospital with a fractured skull. After losing the twins - Paula and Steven - my Mam and Dad must have been beyond comforting. When I woke up with my daft fractured head I was asked by them what I wanted.

I said - "I want a big red bus Dad."

What an awkward get. I could have just gone for something simple to find like Lego or Scalextric but no. My Dad searched everywhere for a big red bus traipsing and traipsing until he found it - and bringing it back to me. When you hear that story you think - aww that's lovely Dad - but why didn't you just go to Toys R Us?

I found myself in Toys R us on Great Ancoats Street on Wednesday. I was looking for a big red bus to put in his coffin. There was nothing too much trouble for my Dad to do for his children. There was nothing too much trouble - for his children - to do for their Dad.

I searched everywhere in town before going to Toys R us. I couldn't find a big red bus anywhere. As I stood there distraught and defeated on the Toys R us shop floor - surrounded by blipping and whirring things - my Dad brought me back.

For aswell as being a loving man my Dad also knew the importance of when to fight for the class he belonged to. My Dad never learned to drive. He believed in a properly run, public transport system. I've never learned to drive. I believe in a properly run, public transport system. And lifts from our Christine.

I could hear my Dad's calm, class analysis saying - the reason there are no big red buses in Toys r us - is because of the tory deregulation of buses. They ruined the transport system for greed and private profit. Why should children want a big red bus when they don't get on a big red bus?

And this was the well educated and erudite side of my Dad. The self taught, working class intellectual. - Who deregulated the buses? Who privatised the trains? Who decimated the industry in east central Manchester? Who closed the pits? Who first brought trusts into the NHS where his daughter now works as a nurse? - margaret thatcher.

My Dad was a loving, caring, gregarious, charming, humorous, witty, hilarious human being. - But he hated that bastard thatcher with a passion.

The loving man we have been going about would, at length, talk about what he was going to do to her.

He was going to put matchsticks under her fingernails - Dad you don't smoke anymore.

He was going to hang her by the tongue - how do you do that Dad - it wouldn't work?

He was going to pull her teeth out - without anaesthetic.

Everyone of us can dislike someone - for example he couldn't stand Mavis from Coronation Street, and had to go in the kitchen to turn the tap on when her - 'euuhh Rita' voice came on.

But the symbol of my Dad's recognition - of the unequal world we live in, was, for me - his unquenchable desire to see thatcher suffer for her crimes against us.

We won't forget Dad - and when the vicious, unfeeling ruling class warrior that she is, expires, we will have a day off on the beer to celebrate. If I can, I'll try to go and piss on her grave as you wanted to - as she's pissed so often on ours.

I hope you'll forgive me and hope I've not gone on too long about that - it is just my Dad was so honour bound - in his intolerance of injustice.

He was also great at nosey parkering. He was always at it. He could have worked at GCHQ. The Frank Brady listening device.

You'd think he would have got better at it but I suppose that time when a red faced bloke went past us, and my Dad said - very loudly and pointing - "Now that's what I call blood pressure" and we're going "Dad shut up, he's only there" - that was sort of final proof - that he would never get a job with the diplomatic service.

His nosey parkering also got him to notice loving things that happened around his family. When all Ben's mates went past our window in Openshaw - he noticed that Daz was always last to go past - and always with a ball at his feet.

Daz - or to give him his full title here - Daz Roper - Browning. The only double barrelled name in Gorton - was to forever become - in our family - 'Daz at the back with the ball.' - My Dad knew the importance of that red thread of friendship - that we are lucky enough to be surrounded by.

Never allow it to falter. Cherish it. He knew it always comes back. He taught us that. Philosophers have only interpreted the world. The point is to change it. My Dad changed ours.

When my Dad was in his forties he went and told the relevant people that he would be an organ donor. When he went last week he'd had five heart attacks - so no one would want his heart. He had a pulmonary odema that meant his lungs were goosed. He'd had cancer in his bladder. His liver had enjoyed a life time of ale so we can only presume that they weren't exactly - still in the wrapper - pristine. This only left his kidneys. His kidneys went on him last week.

In so much pain - and for so long - he still couldn't stop amusing us. As we left the side room in the MRI - that he had been stuck on a trolley in for more than nine hours - we turned around to see him with the portable piss pot on his head - wearing it as a hat. Just for his and his kids pleasure.

He gave us his cheeky thumbs up as the door closed on him and the doctor took us outside. She told us that this was it - she was amazed that a man that had suffered so much could still be here. Still laughing.

She was undoubtedly a good doctor - but seven years at medical college cannot teach you the importance of Doris Brady. My Dad got ten or more extra years on his life because of the love of my Mam. We got ten or more extra years with him because of the love of my Mam - and the incredible love and nursing she gave him.

There's my Mam - take a look at her she belongs to us.

I gave my Dad his last shave in bed at home in a proper 'Auntie Mal buffeting him about way. Our Christine - amongst many, many other things - took him for his last Xray. As she took him for it - devastated as any daughter would be - Frank said " Have I shittem?" Glorious man.

Of all the thousands of doctors my Dad saw, the last one - a man called Scott Levison - gave him the last few hours of restful sleep he had been desperate for.

We were lucky to spend the last four hours of his great, great life - at his side hugging, laughing, crying, tickling. We know not everyone gets that - but after so many years of suffering the last things he would have heard - was all his family around him, telling him things they had always told him.

He'd always taught us to free think and express. We free thought and expressed our love everyday. He nodded for my Mam when she asked him to nod if he could hear us. Made of east central Manchester iron my Dad - forged in devotion. Made of love my Mam.

Music is played at funerals because it can be moving. Other families though seem to get lovely romantic songs where they can say 'aww that always reminds me of my Dad. ' - We get bleeding 'Bridle hanging on the wall.' It's a song - about a bloke - missing his horse.

It's not even an old Irish rural tune where you could say - well at least that's where his family was from . It's about a cowboy. He hated cowboys. Every time he saw John Wayne - on the telly obviously - as John Wayne rarely ventured past pin mill brow - my Dad would say 'He wants kicking up the arse.'

But oh no, hating cowboys or not, after a few latchlifters in the pub - the shirt would be out of his pants - the fingers of his left hand would be playing the table like a piano - looking upwards - his right arm would be in the air and he'd be singing - 'There's a bridle hanging on the wall.'

And he sung it really serious and solemn as if we were going to go - 'You know it's a great song that Dad, it's really meaningful.'

We didn't. It's a shit song Dad. No wonder we all used to threaten to hit him on the head with something heavy.

That's why it would be lovely to see you all later on Oldham Street, at the Castle pub if you can make it. He ran off to Oldham Street on a Monday afternoon. He didn't like Monday afternoons working. I'm very proud to say that I didn't work a Monday in 2005.

In the Castle we've organised it so we can eat tater hash, with a pie crust, and with a couple of my Dad's favourite cakes - wimbery charlottes and potted trifles - he didn't have a favourite cake as he liked anything with processed sugar. We can also drink beer.

The Castle pub has not changed since I first went in there in 1976. And it was hanging then. My Dad will have sat in the same seats as we will be sitting in later. - It was his Oldham Street. - His Manchester.

You know what my Dad did? - He did alright. That's classic, under emphasised, Mancunian modesty at its most Mancunian. That was Francis Brady and I loved him - and love him so.

There were so many, many uncountable things I had to say today but I'll have to leave you with this - Our Christine threw a spoon and it hit me in the eye - didn't she Mam? Didn't she Dad?

xxxx

I went and sat back down again. Our Shirley finished proceedings up, only leaving me to come back to the front and introduce the singing. There would be no religious hymns at this funeral, as they meant nothing to my Dad. They only reminded him of good hidings from Father Fitzgerald from St Brigid's School in Beswick, received after he missed Sunday mass. I wrapped up by saying:

My Dad would want us to sing the Internationale. It's a song recognised as the song for all the working people of the world.

Many of you know it - Christine, Gailly, Shirley, Arthur Brady's family, Vic, Mr Madden, Basher, Blacky and others - it's your class duty to sing as loud - and as out of tune as possible.

My Dad - contrary to only his opinion when larroped - was a terrible singer, he didn't care. Neither should we.

The rest of you just hum along as noisy as you can and join in where possible. It's your song, sing it...

Arise ye starvelings from your slumbers,
Arise ye prisoners of want,
For reason in revolt now thunders,
And at last ends the age of cant.

So away with all your superstitions,
Servile masses arise, arise,
We'll change forthwith the old conditions,
And spurn the dust to win the prize.

So then comrades come rally,

And the last fight let us face,
The Internationale,
Unites the human race.

So then comrades come rally,
And the last fight let us face,
The Internationale,
Unites the human race.

Maggie, maggie maggie, out, out, out.
Maggie, out,
Maggie, out,
Maggie, maggie, maggie, out, out, out.

xxxx

We left the Crematorium to the Dubliners singing 'A pub with no beer' and headed off to one that did. We all went back to The Castle in town. In the bar there our Nicholas, a respected steward at United, told Diane, a home and away Red, a story about him and our John waiting for a young George Best when they were only children. The pair of them would wait at the exit where they knew Georgie would come out from at United. Georgie got to know them. After a few weeks he always brought them fruit pastilles. Diane went into floods. Her fella, Scouse Lee, was always told by his Mam and Dad when he was young, that when he couldn't go to the game with them, that the fruit pastilles they brought back for him were from Georgie Best. Such a little thing.

We got out of The Castle around one in the morning. A load went back to ours for more proceedings. We had an absolutely unsurpassable night of singing, reminiscing and future planning. It came as a surprise to find out afterwards that no one actually lost their life through drowning in beer. Tens of Reds came early to the Castle and then got off for the train to Blackpool. FC United of Manchester were going to be playing Blackpool Mechanics the next day and the game had been designated as the first Euro away. Other Reds stayed who were either going to Blackpool in the morning or off to Anfield, as United were playing Liverpool in the FA Cup.

It was the community and more that had been together at the Arsenal FA Cup final in 2005. The long year, still in progress, that will be unforgettable. One of the last conversations my Dad had with us was asking how United were going on. Not the United's. FC United of Manchester were such a fans' part of Manchester United Football Club that there was no separation to be had. You ask about United in general and you get a reply about

United in general. If you ask "How are United doing?" you will get a general, none separated, conversation about Bolton charging United fans £39, we might possibly win the league at the Norton United game to be played at Port Vale's ground, IMUSA are organising a fans' George Best's 60th birthday celebration at Samuel Platt's, and that what is the point of having the power of a fans AGM if then not to use that hard fought for power to ban players from celebrating their goals divvily?

If we had a label in the back of our shirts, giving care instructions on how to look after this precious garment we are now in possession of, it would say 'Don't wash or talk about separately'. You ask a more specific question about United and you'll get a more specific answer. A conversation going: "There is nothing he cannot do" and you'll know it's Rooney - or "What crowds are we getting?" and you'll know it's little United. You now instinctively know. It's taken some many months. Some still don't. Francis Brady got it from the very first moments in Delamere Park on that east central Manchester sunny day, when I first told him of our intentions to form an ongoing fans' resistance.

You ask me why the teardrops fall?...

Life is beautiful. Let the future generations cleanse it of all evil, oppression and violence, and enjoy it to the full...

We gave my Dad a hard time over his singing of 'Bridle hanging on the wall' because it was such a poor song. We were wrong. It's an uplifter. We can now only sing it with him in our dreams, it's the best we can do. Luckily we sound a lot better in there than real life. We missed the opportunity with him to tell him how much we now see it. He'll know. It was a gift he left for us to find out. We were brought near by others' love, but for our own love we had to go on our own shaping walk. Those who love you know that. The song is an analogy about love, goodness and loss. It's disguising its meaning using atrocious lyrics and a rhubarb tune to do so. Truly atrocious lyrics and a truly rhubarb tune.

It might take you many times to understand it. But you must. Always appreciate the goodness in what you have. Always appreciate the goodness in what you've had. I'll write it in biro on the back of my hand - the bricklayers' filofax. Don't just throw the blankets back off the bed in a big pile. Pull back the blanket layers one at a time. Untuck them separately to value their togetherness, so that when you can finally see the sheets, you have seen everything on the way to getting there. Freshly unmade and made bed day. My Uncle Jim lived next door to us. He used to maintain those big gasometers at Bradford gasworks in east central Manchester. He retired before my Dad. Years of getting up early meant that he could never sleep in. He used to hear the front door closing next door as my Dad was going out in all weathers to set brick. Uncle Jim would knock on the window and wave at him. With only an inadequately insulated single glazed window, my Dad's reply of "Bastard" was always audible. My Dad has gone to wherever good ponies go.

CHAPTER SIXTEEN

DONKEY'S EAR TICKLING...

Blackpool Mechanics FC V FC United of Manchester. Saturday the 18th of February 2006. Kick off 3pm. Played at Bloomfield Road the home of Blackpool FC. We left every light on. It really is like Blackpool illuminations in here...

Then he breaks down and he tells her, that the pub's got no beer...

I got up the morning after the funeral to find a collection of Bradys strewn around my home at various angles of odd discomfort. Except John Brady who had somehow managed to get a double bed to himself and spread out like Lady Cadocca all night, unmithered. The beer and the Jack Daniels brought back from The Castle and the 24-hour Spar would no longer have to worry about going past their sell by date. Our Shiv had told us that in the night she had slept walked out onto the communal corridor of the flats. She'd then opened the fire exit door to the emergency stairwell. As she walked out onto the emergency exit stairwell the door had closed behind her. There is no way back in as there is no furniture on that side of the door to allow you to do so. Then she woke up. Bugger.

She had shouted for help for two hours but no one came to her rescue. She broke the fire alarm and eventually the fire service came. A load of gum booted firefighters gallooting about our house and not a peep out of us, as we didn't hear them. Any burglars reading this then please take note: All you have to do is follow the Bradys out on a session. When we get back home, leave it a tickle until we're all playing noddy. Then you can break in whilst driving a tractor with the Grimethorpe Colliery Band walking behind you playing 'Just one Cornetto: The air horn years'. They can help you shift my possessions away inside their tubas and other, bigger der ders. Our Francis, pissed up May Queen'd on the settee, is a firefighter. He could have just got up and done a firefighter foreigner and saved his brothers and sisters of the FBU a trip out. If he wasn't so shellac'd. Our Shiv is a very attractive girl and even in her distressed state, with panda mascara eyes and her hair wild woman of wongo'ing, she looked beautiful. She has got that inner, unruffled serenity as well as the outer in a lovely combination. Our Phil is a lucky, if somewhat curly haired, fella and we're proud to have her in our family.

The Brady's were huggily left behind, as I had to get to Chorlton Street to meet the coaches that were going to Liverpool, as United were there this early afternoon in the FA Cup. Our Michael, at 15, would soon be going on his first meander across Stanley Park. I wanted to see the lads on the coach who were going to Anfield and tell them to look after my bloodline. Their bloodline. Our Michael won't need it soon as he is already past six foot. Earlier in the pre-season, when he was 14, I had contacted him about FC United of Manchester's first ever friendly at Leigh RMI. As a Family Stand season ticket holder at United since being a child, he had no concept of what 'pay on the gate' was for that match. A shy boy met the lads on the train from Victoria to the RMI game. By the friendly at Stalybridge a couple of weeks later he was shy no longer - ringing me up to see where I was, as he was in the ground already, so what was I doing in the pub? He then ignored me in the ground because he was with his mates in the United end singing "Under the Boardwalk" when it got its first ever popularist outing. That's the way it should be for youngsters: You go to the game with your mates and you arse and learn your history and your independence.

The coaches arrived just as I got to Chorlton Street and I missed Michael. 200- plus, dark-clothed characters on a street at half nine looks a moody prospect. I was wracked and knocked. The delicacy of my buffeted outside was backed by chasms of deep, hurting unknowns inside. I'd just buried my Dad the day before and yet here was more pain. I wanted to go and see my Manchester United Football Club play in the city next door. Yesterday had been a family and friend all giving, unashamed, 'He did alright' festival of love and past imperfect and perfect. It was an obvious continuation that I should go to Anfield. I can see my Dad there now, all those fading years ago, by that bad brown twist nylon settee that we had in Bosworth Street in Beswick. It had turquoise cushion covers. Brown twist nylon settee with turquoise cushion covers – it's no wonder I wasn't scared of going to Liverpool away, as I was scared every day when I went into the living room and got used to being shocked. Turn the light on to that bastard when you got up early or got in late and you'd know about it. My Dad had five heart attacks – there could be a correlation between that settee and my Dad's health.

I'm a young, young boy and my Dad's telling me that I couldn't go to Liverpool as it was too rough, especially for such a small child. I let it drop. He knew his facts and was obviously only concerned for his lad. Later in the week I told them I was going boxing training with Ian Nixon in Moston that Saturday. Consequently, getting back from Moston would mean me being late. The reality was that as small children our little group of Beswick Reds would, with the protection of the thousands of other Reds, be witnessing first-hand the Stanley Park tea party. Bring your own knife and fork. Forks being optional. Liverpudlians were shown Mancunian hospitality around the streets of Old Trafford when they came to ours. They showed the same levels of hospitality when we went to theirs. Except they had more grass and gravestones to accompany it with. My Mam and Dad never found out that I had been to Liverpool for the first time. Fuck. My Dad now never will.

The look after of love...

Blacky tried to bungle me on the coach. Jesus and Chrissy Bolton, who had been in The Castle pub with the Brady's last night to the death at around half one in the morning, were in no fit state to bungle. I told them that when they found our Michael to look after him. Waiting in his Ted Taxis 20 yards away was Ted. He'd dropped their Patrick and David off at the coaches. He'd come to ask Blacky and the lads to look after his bloodline. Me and Ted would be going to the 'Bernie' Clifton Hotel on the front at Blackpool. This time my Dad had told me not to go to Liverpool and I had taken notice. The week before I had been handing over the details of the 30 of us who were staying at the Bernie in Blackpool to Scott and Jane my lovely neighbours in the flats. I had no intentions of going after my Dad had jossed it. As I handed over the hotel booking details to Scott I saw that the hotel had been booked on the first of December 2005. My Dad's last birthday.

That loving date told me to go to Blackpool with FC United of Manchester. No matter how much the damage inside me or how much I was bungled to get on the coach by Reds who wanted to mend that damage, I knew where I was going. Me and Ted then drove off, solemnly waving and leaving the coaches of Chorlton Street behind and onto Gorton to pick up Basher. All these years later, and the same nucleus of three who had gone to Anfield as diddy'uns, were now going to Blackpool. The same nucleus had also gone to Blackpool as diddy'uns in the '70s when we had played Blackpool. Now we were off too play their A.E.U. mechanical wing. This time, though, we had to pick up Kennybobbles in Hattersley.

All over Hattersley, some hope and some despair, woohoh, woohoh, you're the one for me fatty...

We're not saying that Kenny had put on weight since the Arsenal Cup final. Actually we are. He can walk across grids with abandon, as he's not going to fall down them. He might bend them though. Kenny used to work in a scrap yard in Beswick but it was cleansed for the stadium cancer that came nearby. He now works on demolition around the country with all the 'Blokeys living away, fried breakfasts, chippy and late beers' that that comes with. We circled the roundabout twice at Hattersley waving at him to get on his nerves. He had a suitcase. I had a toothbrush. This was our European away. Suitcases were only taken if you were bringing back cigs to sell to fund your trip. Unless he had his 'Leon Mike Slim Slow' cartons and his electrical 'Slendertone' toning pads in there. Or he had a frock packed and was going to go off to the Winter Gardens for a waltz later. You never know with Hattersley. Someone said that of all the thousands who live on the estate there are only three surnames. And one of those is Mr Parveen from the papershop.

We're equal but different, we're equal but different. It's obvious...

We rang the lads in Blackpool. They told us that they didn't get in till five'ish and so consequently they were lounging around in their hotel rooms watching women's curling. Women curling what? We could only presume they had copped and were watching a lady doing something Amsterdam'ish. We hoped that there was enough toilet paper to cope. We found out later that apparently it's an Olympic event. If that can get in then why can't 'Cig burning a T shirt' be in? This is the event where all the contestants wear white T shirts. They then use one of their fingers to rub the back of the T shirt in their ringpiece. The biggest 'cig burn' on the white T shirt is the winner. We had arrived too late to see the mass match on the sands. I'm not sure whether we would have gone anyway. There is enough myth around the one from 1974 so why repeat it in 2006? Fat blokes shouting "Wahey" and pushing each other about is a bit too DH Lawrence 'Women in love' men wrestling for that time in the morning. Miserable gets us but FC United of Manchester is, as we are always telling each other, an 'Equator's width who's put on weight' worth of dissimilarities. We are founded on a cheery but event hardened unity. We've also got a disparity and divergence that would make some powdery chalk and some high fat, mature cheddar walk up the aisle together in unholycaschmoley matrimony. As the powder and the lump took their vows they would celebrate their lack of differentiation when compared to FC United of Manchester fans.

I would have this argument later with two good female Reds inside the ground. They're not knobs so I had to take seriously their thoughts and reassess myself. They were calling me a snob because I said I didn't fancy The Old Bridge pub later as a post match venue. The Old Bridge was designated as the pub to meet in by the FC United of Manchester electrical message board. I understand the need for a football friendly pub so that those who want to can huddle together and have a hoot. Frank 'Kev' the Manc, the Collyhurst caretaker from our flats, would do such a thing and we were made up for him. Fortunately for me and my mates, there are already 30 or more of us so going into a crowded, ten-deep at the bar, pub would only heighten the wait for a beer for those who wanted the necessary huddling and hooting.

When the split came in May 2005 we all respected each others' decisions. All our ongoing decisions can be treated with the same respect. Unless they're totally twatty. Ours are that we have a load of mates already. Of course you always want more mates, except when you don't, but if you want them, they will come naturally. They won't come for me by being told where to go and possibly having the night ruined by someone who has had too much ale or beak. Something ruined by one of your own is never a good thing. And so, in the main, we stay away from our FC United of Manchester own, just in case. Our potentially uncontrollable own. However, when it comes to the chosen for company friends, we are controlling. When one of our lot has too much intake of hallucinogens we have a rigorous self-policing of our own. It is FC United of Manchester calligraphied small. It's called 'Stop it you dick, you're getting on our nerves. Shape up'. And because they are mates for a reason – that is – you don't get to be a mate by being a div, then our mates that are being over giddy will usually reduce their giddiness. It couldn't be simpler. We're aiming to be a community club. My friends and yours are that Diaspora of community. Your mates might get on my nerves; my mates might get on yours. Sometimes it's each to their controlling own. We'll get there though.

B of the boil…

In the spirit of 'splitters' we all left the Bernie Clifton and went to the Yates's across the road. It's not great but it was designated as handy. That can happen. We could all get in and watch United on the big screen. In an act that our more boisterous fans would be proud of Two Mowers put his 'Openshaw solid' red, white and black South Yemen flag under the telly. He wouldn't have done anything so outrageous at United. The only time we've had anything to do with a flag was the Direct Works' dust sheet from Manchester Corporation that had 'Get Kinkladze to wash the pots' sprayed on it. Dave the Hair - whose Mam at the time ran the Strawberry Duck pub in Clayton where United's firm met up at the last derby – climbed up an advertising hoarding on the Old Trafford forecourt and hung it up. There was also a rumour of another Manchester Corporation dust sheet with 'Merryn Myatt's midweek knickers' hung out at Villa once. Actually, I helped put the 'J Stand – we do alright' flag up at Dynamo Bucharest away. I'm a proper bell end when you look back on it. The 'Openshaw solid' flag got coats put in front of it and it finished up 'Openshaw lid'. You could work with that.

Billy and Caroline Brayshaw came in. Caroline's arse, which we have graciously volunteered to monitor for her over the season, was looking fine. You could use it as a campfire and warm your hands near it. Peter 'Good shape you loads' Crouch came on the telly. He had a boil on his big daft neck about the same size as Caroline's arse. He wants to get that lanced. Billy was saying something about doing his best lancing Caroline's but he's bobbing on now. What he needs are some helpers to give him a lift. That's the community spirit again coming to the fore at FC United of Manchester. We just give, give, give. When Wes Brown nutted Crouch later on in the game, and Crouch bled, we all looked at Billy and thought: 'Oh, Billy don't do it till it bleeds, that's a bit Strangeways'. We'll leave Caroline's arse alone for a while now. So should you Billy. Get some Sudocreme.

My Dad had once worked at Booth Hall Children's Hospital bricklaying an extension. He had told us that he had once seen a poor child with his feet on back to front to his body. Alan Smith did the same 'I don't know whether I am coming or going' impression as he was carried off the pitch at Anfield. There was much furore in the press about Liverpool fans mocking Smith's injury. It would be hypocritical of many to call them. It's a tough game at times and a fair sized majority like to see players from the other side injured. Without comment I have to admit that we sprayed 'Colin Bell's leg' on Ashton New Road, approximately opposite where years later they would build the cancerous new stadium. We've sung, to the tune of 'Go west', the song 'Paul Lake limps like Colin Bell'.

We cut out and kept from the back page of the Daily Mirror the picture of Beglin's bendy leg injury. The three Reds sharing the house at the time put it on the back of the front door as it used to cheer us up on our way out to work. All not very nice when analysed away from football but all still part of football. Someone cleverer than me should analyse why that can be acceptable in a large section of football fandom when not outside. They probably already have and I've just not read it. Smith won't melt. Bell didn't melt. Lake didn't melt. Beglin didn't melt. Where that leaves Reds, singing to the tune of 'Oh, Andy Cole he put the scousers on the dole' the song 'Oh, Tommy Caton's England caps' or blues at one of the closest pubs to their stadium at the last derby in January 2006 playing a recording of the Munich air disaster, on loop, to the blue clientele I have no real - not depressing - answers.

No more executions of Private Slovik...

Blacky's Dad had died three days before my Dad had died on the Thursday. It was very fitting that his Dad, who had been one of the first members of the Manchester United Junior Athletic Club, should die on February the 6th. Sorry Blacky. After his Dad's funeral last week we convened in a pub for post- funeral chirruping. I had recounted to the characters there an incident I had once gone through whilst bricklaying for Salford Corporation. It was a Monday morning and I was fedster, as everybody is. I was building a load of backyard walls on these terrace houses. I had to toothe some brickwork out of an adjoining, retaining backyard wall so that I could tie in the new brickwork I was about to set. There was this one piece of annoying wall by the bottom that was odd. Somehow it was mixed in with the concrete path and it just wouldn't toothe out. I was pissed off as it was Monday morning but this awkward get of a bit of wall was making it worse. I did that bad thing when you get angry that you should never do: I started talking to an inanimate object. Actually, in secondary school parlance, I started offering it out. I was pointing at it going: "Right, you bastard, think you're clever do you? What you going to do about this then you little fucker, hey? See this? You're going to get it." What I was threatening the bit of awkward wall with was a 14-pound sledgehammer.

The niceties of the lump hammer and chisel had been dispensed with. This cheeky bastard of a wall was going to get a good hiding off a sledgehammer. It had driven me to it. I'm normally a balanced lad who would only ever treat bricks with respect. I'd tip and tap until the old mortar was off and a clean arris had been gained for the new mortar and brick to bond with. Not this morning. This was Monday morning war. It wasn't going to be pretty. You wouldn't get your craft certificate for such a ropey act of tradesmanship. Nothing was going to stop me from exacting revenge by battering the awkward get to pieces. I picked up the sledgehammer whilst all the while being in constant communication with the bit of wall. I grabbed the handle, I picked it up, I swung it over the back of my head and with all the brutality I could summon I swung the sledgehammer at the awkward bit of wall. On the way down, as the sledgehammer had gone over my head and was, with bitter venom, on the way to its intended titty target, it hit the unseen washing line that was going across the backyard. The sledgehammer hit the washing line and bounced back. Straight into my kite.

Sparkled. It could have been worse as it could have taken all my Newtons out or smashed my nose. It hit me over the top of the eye. The thing is, with such swelling and bruising people think you've been having it with West Ham. It always had to be revealed how I had done it. Self-injury that people laughed at you for. You laughed with them, obviously. Self-injury brought on by a rash action, a dash to daftness when other, well used ways, were appropriate. Reason would have outed. Self-harming can never be considered rational.

When a couple of Reds with me watching the game in the pub said: "Look at all these home and away Reds here watching this on telly when they should be there. They deserve to be there. They've done so much, felt so much, lost so much, been through so much." You couldn't disagree. This morning, when me and Ted had left the coaches going to Anfield on Chorlton Street, it would be foolish to deny that there was not an element of self-harming in there. There was the coach; there was the fine set of mates. Just get on the coach and go. We didn't. Neither had this packed pub of Reds in Blackpool with their equally fine set of mateyness. There is a difference with accidentally hitting yourself on the head with something heavy and intentionally hitting yourself on the head with something heavy.

FC United of Manchester had seen the washing line across the backyard this time. We might have hurt, and be hurting ourselves, but we know why. This time the self-harming was rational. No one has had all their Newtons smashed out with little United. Internally, if people could see the bruises, it looked as if we had been having it with West Ham, but if we weren't hurting then what would that make us? This wasn't a rash action on our part, brought on by a dash to daftness. We felt other, well-used ways, were now no longer appropriate. We just knew. Look underneath the Openshaw lid and there is a wholesome stew of Red tenderness. Stir in the goodness. Taste a little bit on your wooden spoon. It's warm and inspiring. Break some fresh crusty bread and sit down with it. Burp if you want. Pat your full belly afterwards.

Cranked up really high. A jubilationing...

Constant reassessing, that's what FC United of Manchester fans do. Every time we are faced with a dilemma – this time being: 'Why are we watching United on the telly?' – we address it. We undress it, dress it, address it and then do it all again until we remember why we are here. In Yates's in Blackpool we all had done it in our own sometimes private, sometimes public, ways. We could get on now and enjoy the rampage that was FC United of Manchester's Euro away. The SMS had been born the night before. The Slaughter and Mither Squad. There could be no separation between slaughter and mither. They were intrinsically linked. The slaughter and mither squadists had their own tune: Cliff Richard's 'Congratulations'. The mime was that, as you were singing the 'Congratulations' bit, you were miming punching someone in the ribs. By the 'and jubilations' bit you were kneeing the imaginary foe in the face.

They were going to get 1980 calling cards with a selection of the following written on them: Congratulations and jubilations. You've been slaughtered and mithered by the SMS: SMS - no slaughter or mither too small: The MRI has been informed that you're on your way. We hope you enjoyed your SMS'ing: There's slaughter and there's mither. Put them together and there's slaughter and mither: SMS. No copper is going to take the laces out of my Major Domos: SMS gives a bigger choice, yes. That last one has to be sung to the tune of the old advert 'ELS gives a bigger choice, yes. Der de de der, yes, yes'. This advert tune robbing can also be applied to the old 'BOC, better people to buy from' advert when they sang: "SMS, better people to cry from."

A turd in the hand is worth two in the bush...

Others Reds could not get their minds off the birds back at the hotel. Some had experienced problems with pigeons cooing all night. At first they had thought that the windows to their rooms were frosted because they had such a bad view. The reality was that the pigeons were so dominant that they had requested the hotel management to frost the windows, as they were tired of the hanging view looking in. Management, scared of the pigeons as they were mixing up their Hitchcock films, capitulated to the pigeons' request. This only encouraged the cockiness of the pigeons. So much so, that if you opened your window they stood there in SMS T-shirts giving the visiting Reds a hard time. Obviously, the 'Slaughter and mither' bit on their T-shirts was written in pigeon English so it just looked like feathers to the non-SMS speaking eye but we recognise a jubilationing when it is being offered. Others, regardless of the pigeon problem, couldn't get to sleep as they had inadvertently seen the Ginger Princess in her purple, flowery shower cap, vest and brush cotton Primark pyjama bottoms. A sight that would frighten a Black Mariah. Take that view to Stanley Park before any United and Liverpool game and there would be an immediate cessation of hostilities as the "Aww, hey, no"s would ring out. A truly frikening, slumber stealing sight. Except to Two Mowers the erectioneer.

No doorknockers. Actually on reflection…

Doctor Adam Brown, an FC United of Manchester board member, is a clever lad. You don't get to be a doctor without being a swot. He was sharing his room with a Red electrician from Crumpsall Hospital. Doctor Adam would go on and on, perfectly analysing the state of where FC United of Manchester were after these short eight months. He could break down the different groups of fans that were following the new team, how our support had got to where it is, where it had come from, what it might want or do next. When he puts it in such simple, clear terms even the most buffoonish of Reds can follow it. He's one of those gifted people who say something and you think: That's great that. I wish I had said it. His grasp of the part little United can play in the Manchester community is truly motivational. He whacks down everything to the Reddist essentials and then puts it back together in a form that is instantly recognisable.

He's a Tefal head. But our Tefal head. The smart thing about Tefal heads, though, is that they don't realise the low saturation point us normal thickies reach when faced with inf after inf. After a night sharing a room with Doctor B our Red electrician has hit that saturation point. He's had to go through the experience of seeing the doctor go to bed in an 'Einstein a go-go' T-shirt, and counting his collection of brass rubbings to get to sleep. Our Red electrician is going down for breakfast with Doctor B. The long, tight corridors of the Bernie are a Warren 'Mary' Barton of doors that all look the same. As the cerebrally unmatched couple leave their hotel room the doctor is going on about how he couldn't understand why people get puzzled when he pronounces the telly programme ER as "Here you are." The Red electrician can put that nodding 'I know, good point' face on no more. In the middle of the hotel corridor landing he reaches across the doctor and wraps fuck out of a stranger's door. And runs off. The doctor is stood there perplexed. Why have you knocked on a total stranger's door? Why have you just disappeared out onto the stairs? The power of postman's knock is a revengeful force in the universe when used with dexterity. However, female Reds, if Doctor Adam Brown comes near you with a stethoscope, then knock him out as he is not one of those sorts of doctors. He just wants a tit nudge. He's not that daft as to not try to use his doctorology as a knicker removing device.

This could be Rotterdam or anywhere, Blackpool or Rome…

We left Yates's and walked down to Bloomfield Road. United had gone out of the FA Cup 1-0. We also can't sing the song that uses the 'Ring of fire' tune anymore as Liverpool have popularised a version. They've Athenry'd it. I had a Yorkshire fishcake on the way down to the ground. Don't. A layer of potato, a layer of fish, another layer of potato and then all cooked in batter. Don't let it sound nice to you. Especially if the fish is off. Which it will be as no one is going to have one of them regularly enough to keep it fresh. The Yorkshire fishcake got binned by the side of the ground. The two-sided Bloomfield Road had changed some from my memory. Which is not surprising as it is a new build. It's gone up in price accordingly as I'm sure it wasn't the seven pound we'd just forked. Alright, so with 30 years of inflation it might be around the same price. We should have hired Stuart Pearson for the day to wave at the United end in his trenchcoat as he had done all those years ago. We'd just signed him from Hull and I don't think he was eligible yet. Or he was injured. It was decades ago; I can't be precise.

The game against the AEU today saw us win a four-four-two, four-two friller. I thought they might have played in oily overalls and said: "Flamin' heck, Sally" a lot but they didn't. The cheeky gets took a 1-0 lead into the half time break. The reason the Blackpool Mechs had not taken to the field in oily overalls became clear when Phil Power, our assistant player manager, came on at the start of the second half. Phil had sneaked into their dressing room and used the oil off their overalls to rub in his 60-year-old joints. His oiled addition in the second half revitalised the team, if not his scalp. We went 2-1 up. They got back to 2-2. Then Will Ahern, whose Great Grandad hadn't been born when Phil Power got his National Insurance Number and who certainly isn't as shiny-headed, put in a third for us. Another penalty from Mrs Patterson made it 4-2.

In the previous weeks to the Blackpool game a dozen or so Reds in the Main Stand had tried to get a song going to a bad tune. The tune was bad but the words were coming very close to being the perfect FC United of Manchester song. The tune was 'Spirit in the sky'. Don't give up on it, though, just because it has had such a bad start. The words go:

> Won't pay Glazer or work for Sky,
> Still sing city are going to die,

Two Uniteds but the soul is one,
And the Busby Babes carry on.

From August 2005 we had put the 'J Stand – we do alright' flag at the front of the Main Stand at our home games. The Manchester Road End was all-dominant then, with its noise and colour. We wanted the Main Stand to perform the role that J Stand used to do against K Stand. We knew it would come and it did when the Manchester Road End was locked and full against someone. I've forgot what team it was. I could ring someone and find out but I can't be arsed. The drunks who came late went into the Main Stand and history was born. Since then the noisy bastards have been bang at it. Knowingly or unknowingly stood behind the J Stand banner. The only place in the ground where you could hear our half time music and PA'ing effectively vanished, as the Main Stand started singing through the half time break. So it was with J Stand affection that I like the 'And the Busby babes carry on' song.

At Bloomfield Road, the J Stand corner positioned mob of 20-odd or so wouldn't let it go until everyone was singing. And everyone did. Across the two full stands. The Arthur of the song is a bloke called Gaz. We can only hope for his sake that his second name is not Topp. Unless he is the Gaz Topp. The emphasis on the 'thee' sounding 'the' in that last sentence should not be over emphasised as talking about animals on telly whilst having a lisp is not that celebrity worthy. Blackpool Mechanics have a Val Singleton as a committee member so they're always going to win any fame claim. You can't compete with a woman who reputedly, as she often demonstrated on telly, is fond of stroking her own and others' pussy. Gaz is from Macclesfield but chooses to live in Stoke. I'll just say that again – he chooses to live in Stoke. You're not going to believe it was him now who made up the song, as anyone who chooses to live in Stoke has got to be a bit tapped.

Gaz was going to the pub and assures us that the words just fell into place. The first line of the song outlines the honourable stance of many FC United of Manchester fans. The original song had the word 'sky' in the first line. This probably explains why the tune was chosen despite its shitness. The second line nods to our rivalry. The third line explains our two team, two lungs breathing, one heart beating, position, and the final line ties us all together to the bloodline. Outside of threading us to our east central Manchester bloodline of 1878, the song is a class one. Except for the shite tune. But that's how far our standards have risen. If we can get away from that Piranhas tune we will. And do.

As the song ripped across the ground we knew from previous experience that someone somewhere must be very proud at the moment. That someone was Gaz. Him being Topp or not. He, fittingly, as well as inventing the song on the way to the pub, was also at the bar underneath Bloomfield Road when it first got quietly going. He returned from the bar to find the two stands singing. That song meant a lot to me on the day as the 'Busby babes carry on' part obviously resonated around my Dad and our 15-year-old Michael at Anfield for the first time that day. Michael is also a season ticket holder at FC United of Manchester. Mind you, at only £32 for under 18s for a full season, what Mam and Dad are tight enough not to buy one for their youngsters? And what youth can't afford that from wherever they get their money from?

Email the FC United of Manchester General Enquiry line at: info@fc-utd.co.uk for further details. There's probably a separate season ticket line but it will do you no harm to find out other general bobs and bits about us if you want. Anyway the 'Busby babes carry on' song had got going, without my knowledge because I wasn't there, at the final whistle at Chorley the week before. Gaz should really move back north. If you know him, tell him. I've only ever spoken to him on the phone. They have phones in Stoke. Ring Pickfords.

They are clearly a most primitive people ah ah ah...

There was a load of drunken mayhem in the United end behind the net. You can feel a pitch invasion coming. There is always something crackling when one goes. We've improved a lot over the months. I'll be surprised if there is not a pitch invasion near the end of the season if we win the league away. The board will officially have to discourage it, of course. We understand that. The authorities, however, have been inspector'ing us all season in the hope that we'd fail. They can all fuck off. We will have survived a season of monitoring in a league where children are regularly invited onto the pitch to grow an affinity, and where prizes of beer are given out and drunk on the terraces. We have been forced to be all prim and Premier League proper. The first few invaders on the pitch were rightly boo'ed. Good. We've come afar since the Leigh RMI days of July 2005 where pitch invasions, with gratuitous nudity whilst you were doing it, prevailed.

When Brian and Antnee chased the Dane...

The drip, drip, drip of invasions, though, sort of reached a crescendo after the final whistle. Some Reds just couldn't contain themselves. I saw Rigga

– minus his parrot – run on the pitch and hug a player. The Monsall you wot?s weren't far behind him. Margy himself, whilst at first trying to discourage any more invaders, was always courteous with those that came up to him. None of that Scheimichel at Villa nonsense from the cup game a few years ago when we came from 2-0 down to win 3-2. Schmeichell, his wages from our labour still warm in his pocket, started dishing out cracks. He had no Eric concept of how to be a hero which thoroughly explains his time with the backwards at maine road. Margy himself, whilst at first trying to stop Reds running on the pitch, then finally accepted this harmless post-match act of glee, and threw himself into the front of the crowd, hugging his brothers Anthony and Brian.

We left the pub walking past the crowded Old Bridge pub and onto a quiet pub called The Ardwick. It was painted green. The cask bitter was £1.10 until seven o'clock. We stayed in the Ardwick through that post-match lull that always comes between five and seven. The football breaking your beer session always has you thinking that you might spew it during that lull but you always come through. The Ardwick is on a rundown depressing back street of Blackpool. These back streets only seem to have tanning parlours on them. Tanarife won our vote for the best named one. Although, with the amount of Scots that go to Blackpool, one called 'Tandabbydozy' would rake it in. Actually do Scots tan? That's probably why there's not a 'Tandabbydozy'. One opened, but reflecting Scottish people broke all the tubes and all the workers got pieced up.

A stitch in mime saves nine…

We finished up in Scruffy Murphy's till last orders. That's not as bad as it sounds as we all managed to get a full back room where around 30 of us just sang the "And the Busby babes carry on" song, and the "Go on home Malcolm Glazer, go on home, have you got no fucking home of your own" song. The "Take a trip down Ancoats, Little Italy's so grand, take a trip down Rochdale road and you're in Ireland, China and Japan are Upper Brook street, Africa's in Moss Side so they say, and if you want to go further still, snide Lacoste in Cheetham Hill" song. The bouncer trying to keep us quiet – which we did when the turn was on as we're not ignorant – looked like Aled Jones. This was never going to help his bouncery cause. If you heard gangs of men and women roaming the streets of Blackpool that night singing high pitchedly: "We're walking in the air" then you will know why. When the turn was on we mimed the words to the songs we wanted to sing. Miming 'Save all your soap on a rope' was difficult but not undoable. Everyone, it seems, had learnt valuable lessons from the great Mimers Strike of 1984/5. The SMS were in the corner plotting their jubilationary itinerary for the coming games. For the first time in nine days I did not cry.

We all thought that at lasties we would all traipse off home, as the clubs are that bad and full of kiddies fighting in Blackpool that it might ruin the day. We got a call from Soya Milk Mark and Donna that they had found a club on the front called 'Soul Suite'. It was two quid in and it played soul. It was pointed out it was 'obvious' soul around the Four Tops and all that but it would do. The clientele were in their 30s so the youngsters would have to suffer. Good. We all got in and formed an orderly gang up one wall. Outside of the three oljebols of me, Ted and Scott everyone was dancing. In that relaxed state you get to when you have had an all dayer - but an all dayer where you have paced the beer as it is a marathon not a snicker – I looked along the line of happy FC United of Manchester faces. In Blackpool with its tacky lights, bad pubs and brash atmosphere we had all managed to stay together from the very first beer to the very last. A soulful day finishing in the full of soul soulful Soul Suite.

We had officially taken 4,300 fans to a league away game. Few premiership clubs take that. There were hints of that bad taxman maths going on again. This will probably deny us our 5,000 crowd for a while but over 4,000 to an away game, whilst United were also playing, in a league where crowds of a dozen paying in happens, was a feat for the feet. In the Soul Suite the blissed FC United of Manchester fans danced their tasteful footwear off. It was dancing of a North West Counties League standard. With some pub team standard. Some danced as if they were putting out a fire. Some could have got a grant from that land mine charity. The FC United of Manchester women danced as dancing should be, with heat and sweat and balance and sexual rhythm. The blokes were just blokes.

Cancel house...

The soul music played captured a '60's and'70's sound. The soundtrack was reliving the times of the soul suite. The brown twist nylon settee with the turquoise cushion covers soul suite. The soul suite that my Dad had stood at the side of and told me as a child not to go to Liverpool. The soul suite that he had sat on and told his children of the way the world is. That he had sat on and raged at the television when ruling class lies about our class were being heaved out and being presented as presentable. That he had come home gassed and flagged out on after a Monday afternoon session. That he had eaten his tea on, including anything that was out of date or had dropped on the floor and my Mam had said: "Oh, it'll be alright, give it your Dad. He won't mind, he'll enjoy it." And he didn't, and he did.

I wouldn't be in this late night Blackpool soul club if we hadn't booked the trip on the first of December. My Dad's last birthday. I'd organised and booked it for everyone and then was going to back out after he died. He'd brought me here because living is meant for those who are alive. Get your gollies on it's going off son. Leave your coat on the coat table only for a short while as there is so much to cuddle, countless things to count, hurgles to hurgle, Brick Eklands to brick, Alstations to station, benches to call forms, afacings to be stood afacing to. If you're going to breathe, breathe deeply. On this ninth day after his death the tears stayed where they were. I knew that the people I love, love me back and that is worth getting up for. Worth going to sleep for. Worth getting up again for. You know I nearly danced but Ted would have thrown me out of the blokey brotherhood. He's my oljebol moral guardian and even in moments of extreme glee one must always maintain an oljebol decorum. It's Beswick law. Almost certainly.

The feather works was calling. I could have slept on Tinker from Lovejoy's shoelace tie I was that tired. Little Bobby had had a busy day. The next morning I got to tickle behind a donkey's ear on the front. I was devode, though; as I'd forgotten my bottled water as I had been told that they were always thirsty so take them water not a carrot. We also got to discuss with Kenybobbles the ongoing problem of sharing a room with Basher's bollocks. Basher comes home pixilated and falls asleep not in, but on, the bed with his bollocks stuck out of the back of his legs like a sack cloth bag of dablooms. We have organised it so that when, not if, he does it again we are all going to be prepared. We are all going to have brought a stick a piece with us. Preferably it should be a bamboo cane type one measuring over four or five foot in length. We will have also brought with us some disposable surgical gloves. We are then going to go to the room where Basher is asleep and poke his bollocks with sticks until he puts them away. Or we push them back in. Firm but unfair.

CHAPTER SEVENTEEN

YOUR THEIR TO ...

Great Harwood Town V FC United of Manchester. Sunday the 29th of January 2006. Kick off 2pm. Also Great Harwood Town V FC United of Manchester. Monday the 27th of February. Kick off 7.45. The 'Two visits but only one game' game was played on both occasions at Accrington Stanley's ground. When aren't they?

Because we all have a problem, we all have fears but there's always got to be a way...

Four visits to Accrington Stanley's ground but only three times were they in when we called. The Sunday the 29th of January game was postponed. We found out at one o'clock. The game was due at two. This made no difference to us, as we were in The Greyhound near Accrington Stanley's ground, the pub that we had found at the Nelson FC game a fortnight earlier. I know I've said it before, but Sam Smith's cask bitter £1.33 a pint. You'd marry it if it was allowed. It probably already has been married-to, but to one of those attention seekers with homemade blonde streaks in his hair that have just turned out clumpy because his sister did them. They'd attempt anything to be the last item on the local telly news, even using the sham wedding to our £1.33 ale to get there. We'll just treat our £1.33 pint as a lover we visit secretly. We might not be there for Christmas and New Year for them but we love her when we can.

To help our liaisons The Greyhound pub, on a day so cold that they cancelled the game, came up with a couple of coal fires. Outside of rubbing congealed animal fat over the light bulbs to mellow the lighting and throwing down a faux bear skin rug, the pub could not have aided our love-in anymore. The phone call to Andy Walsh, our soon to be elected General Manager, to confirm the game's cancellation was met with no real devastation as ten pints for £13.30 was now the challenge. If we had spent £13.30 it would have meant that next morning we would not have known whether the game had gone ahead or not. There would be no flicking through the back of the Daily Mirror to check, as there would be if you overdid it at a big United game. Get cachoozelled at little United and you only have your mates to confirm anything. And they will take advantage of your unfit state and lie, saying something about frayed pantyhose, winter green with chunks in and a borrow of Kendo Nagasaki's mush mask.

However, there were some bailers in our midst. They wanted to get back to Manchester. There was a reason besides the obvious risk of saying: "By rack of th'eye" if we stayed too long in these odd speaking parts. Today big United were playing Wolves at Molineux in the FA Cup. A good allocation of 5,500 and the fact it was on the BBC assured a quality turn out from the fans unwatered by executive'isms. The bailers wanted to watch it surrounded by people that had the requisite amount of digits per hand. We knew exactly what we were missing in not going to Wolves. It was grim. Our part consolation was that a percentage of the ticket price would go to the Glazers and that was never going to stay down with some if they had to swallow that. The pub and surrounding area, including a police horse's arse, were decorated with 'Love United Hate Glazer' stickers before we left.

The journey home took 23 minutes to get back to the Blackley turn off on the M60 in the Ginger Princess' car. Away games in the NWCL are handy. Before Michael, the Ginger Princess' brother, finished telling us about his farting Boxer dog and the progression that The Alliance pub in Harpurhey was making in keeping fights under double figures on weekend nights - fight as much as you want midweek – we were dropping him off. We dropped him at The Ben Brierley in Moston. It was rammed with Reds having a beery day by the box. Who in there was not at Molineux due to not wanting to pay the Glazers' debt? Who in there would usually go but missed this one? Who in there wanted to go but couldn't due to United's constant, constant, unlike any other club in the world, constant sell out of tickets? Who in there had stopped going due to being priced out or alienated by the aliens who can swamp Old Trafford due to the snot friendly policies of the board? Who was just disillusioned? We'll never know. It was just a good Red pub with a large, unscareable mob inside it.

You'd put that pub against any derby day mob and it wouldn't get a second prize.

Time will pass you by. Tobi Legend...

Before you could say: "It's lucky for those Goths in Exchange Square that they all have naturally black hair", it was Monday the 27th of February 2006. We were playing the rearranged game against Great Harwood Town that had been postponed the month before. Big United had played Wigan the day before. They'd beat them 4-0 in the League Cup final at Cardiff. Some Reds who were there had enquired of the whereabouts of the 'Under The Boardwalk' bridge. I gave directions but I'm not sure from their poor camera phone pictures whether they found the right one. I didn't like saying, as placebo comfort from a bridge can be just as effective in these turbulent times as a real bridge. Everyone knows that.

Playing on a Monday night was, unfortunately, very traditional big United. It was FC United of Manchester's first and almost certainly last, Monday night kick off of the season. All our visits to Accrington Stanley's ground had not been on a 'When FC United come out to play, it'll be three o'clock on Saturday'. Accrington Stanley, at this time, look shertainties to go into the Football League. A conspiratorial cynic could say that they have had us playing at two o'clock on a Sunday and 7.45 on a Monday because they are going into the televised world of the full time league. They were going to make us suffer disturbed kick off times as a way of cuddling up to those in the top flight who were against our presence. The reality was that on the days we needed to play our games at Accrington's ground, that Accrington were already at home on the Saturday. Almost certainly. Although Great Harwood Town play their home games at Accrington's ground now, so if they were due to be at home then why wasn't it on a Saturday? Bulgarian tipped umbrellas.

I'm on my way. Dean Parrish...

The '23 minutes' option by car had been dispensed with. I was going on the train from Victoria. Lads on the train at the postponed game had informed me that the journey from town to Accrington took "One hour and one minute." That was such a precise description of the time involved that you could do nothing but believe it. It took an hour and 15 minutes. Why lie about the one hour and one minute? Some people just can't help it. Proud of them. There was absolutely no need to lie. Shaving 14 minutes off the actual time of the journey served no purpose. They just felt the need to give misinformation when at a game. The same atmosphere of distrust from previous exposure to illogical, unnecessary fibbing had resulted in everyone disbelieving their various informers when they were told the game was off on our last visit to Accrington.

That's the class, though, in quality making it up. If you lever in a truth every so often then the pawing, no matter how much you want to dismiss it, will paw the scrapings off the inside of the rounded bone protecting your brain. The inquisitive scrapings, with repeated question marks in their chemical compound, will fall and sprinkle the possibility inside your box that the blatant fib might just somehow be true, as it had been before. I'm getting better but I am the invariable victim of 'Uncle Bobby abuse', where those less trustworthy around me know that I am gullible and they will take advantage. Old fashioned or not, I prefer to believe people when they tell you things. Actually, I think I'm getting better but the more prosaic explanation is probably that I am just too easy and not worth having over, as it is just bullying if there is no opposition. I suppose it is a tradition and the reason Euro away rumours are always with us.

I had decided to get the train on my own hoping to discover some miniscule soul journey. To Accrington? The train was full of scriking kids and smelt like shiny trousers packed in thick, amber curdled Tupperware. Thankfully, I had to change trains at Blackburn to get the Colne train to Accrington. I held out little prospect for the Blackburn to Colne train smelling any less tenanty but supposedly your gills are always less greener on the other side. Oh, hello, that's why the journey might take more than one hour and one minute, as I have to change and they might have got a direct one. No. They were just lying. Stop being a victim, Bobby.

Blackburn station is as anomalous as the residents of the town. The station states it has four platforms. It doesn't. Platforms one, two and four are platforms in the way we regard a platform as a platform. A platform does not really have to work that hard to be a platform. It stands there. You stand on it. Then you get off it. Blackburn station has no platform three. It pretends it has. Blackburn must think size is important numerically. Somewhere in some council chamber the dignitaries of the town have gone on about how it's great to be a town with four station platforms. Some hillbillies only have three. Or some even have two, the josskins. However, Blackburn's platform three is just a long hole. You could store some ladders on their back in it or lay out some long rope to stop it getting knotted, but that's about it. I'm sure others might push for a 'Poorly lamppost hospital' to be put in there but I'd have to disagree.

I was going to go on more about Blackburn's platform three but my train came. The reminders I was making in my notebook, reminding me to call platform three, made me look as if I was train spotting. I was being mistakenly patronised by the people on the train. People – who were going to Colne - were feeling sorry for me. Inverted world, indeed. There was little I could do besides accept their sympathy, as to state loudly that I was not trainspotting would only have served to confirm to them that I was. I was a man, with a notebook and a pen, on a platform looking interestingly at stationy stuff. My coat even had a hood. It was one of my FC United of Manchester big coats but to an uninformed prosecutor it could have been a blouson. The sort that cheats wind. With big inside pockets for papershop porn.

I got off at Accrington. I tried, desperately, not to look at the insignia of a train parked across the Accrington platform but I just couldn't help it. The more I knew I shouldn't the more I had to. The viewing crowd had expected me to perform and, depressingly, I had done. It was only a quick glance but it was still a look. I had in a short journey, apparently, become the man they thought I was. The passengers I had just left on the train looked at me looking at the other train and they knew all they needed to know. They were wrong. Only by close contact in my company over a sustained period could they begin to determine me. Morally, you need all the facts to rightfully and successfully convict. If you don't have them in your possession then it is a wallaby court.

As a new football club we'd been wallaby'd enough from others outside the club, to start letting Colne residents affect me as an individual. If we get promoted perhaps we will be playing Colne next season as they are in the division above us, at present. I might see the Colne train passengers again and state our full case. Telling them that just because something at first looks like something that someone else has spoken adversely about doesn't mean to say it is. They might have had intravenous-fed misconceptions filling them up for so long, that they were no longer able to make independent conclusions that weren't washed with the negativity of others. Look at me, though, defending the rights of trainspotters by default. I, also, regularly convict small towners for their small town'isms. Actually, I'll stick to that last one the lurcher dog stroking, suit trousers with the white-inside-waistband-turned- piss-coloured wearing bumpkin bastards.

Long after tonight is all over. Jimmy Radcliffe…

This self-discovering train journey was turning out to be the gollocks I'd suspected. I know just over an hour to Accrington is hardly trans-Siberian but I could have got at least a splosh. It was just a train journey that was leaving me sploshed, as I was getting pissed wet through in the drizzle as I got off the train. Accrington in spring sunshine is not going to induce the young lovers of the world to come to its four-panelled, on a steep incline, door. Accrington's precinct in its town centre in February would, if it could, carry a placard with 'Behead young lovers' written on it. Or was that just intravenous-fed years of misconceptions about small towns warping my independent views? I was going to give Accrington town centre the care it deserved.

'Jack Fulton – famous for frozen value' the shop said. If you've got anything of value and you want it freezing, go to Jack's. A cryogenic shop on a small precinct. If you're feeling a bit peeky then just whip your head off and take it to Jack's. He'll defrost you when they've invented head cheering up gear. That is a very good start. Then there was also a Poundland. The Poundland in Piccadilly, Manchester has closed down. The rumour is that it was forced out of existence by Pound Empire across Piccadilly Gardens. Everybody used to like Poundland, though, as its slogan outside was: 'Poundland – where everything is pound'. Not: 'Where everything is a pound' but 'Where everything is pound'. A cute 'English is not my first language' typo, we all thought. Not so. In Accrington it had: 'Poundland – where everything's pound'. There is only a slight change from an 'is' to an apostrophe 's' but there is still no 'a'. We can conclude from this, that even though we are upset that the Poundland store in Piccadilly was not as individual as we had thought, it was also positive proof that the chainstores are coming to Accrington, which is a sign of increasing prosperity for any town.

It also had an Iceland. This shop might suffer for using 'land' in its title as after you've already seen something end in the word 'land', then seeing it again just makes you think they're land mad. No one likes to see such a crude expression of greed. I didn't want to concentrate on this downer, though, as I spotted the YMCA charity shop. It was fun to stay in there. It really was. Donna Summer's 'I feel love' played out on the shop's stereo. There was only me there to witness it. The Icon sport shop opposite had a female section that sold 'San Smiths'. As I turned out of the town a gang of young lads were stood outside a replica gun store. They asked me if I would go in and buy pellets for them. That's very nice that lads so young should be concerned at the damage slugs can do to the allotments of the elderly. On the tail-end of the town 'La Dolce Vita' had a solitary, hand-written piece of paper sellotaped in the window that said: 'Hot soup and bun or wrap - £1.70'. There's a heroin problem, apparently, in Accrington. I do not know why.

Muffin the kagoul...

It was a straight walk to the ground, up a single undulating road. I spotted 'York Street chippy' which was conveniently placed on York Street. It announced it was award winning. Award winning is a good enough excuse to get me in a chippy. When I got in there, the only awards I could see were hygiene awards stuck on the wall. I left with a chip muffin. There was a hair in it. Only one, though, so the award winning status remains intact. The muffin lasted me to the ground. The Oaklea and Crown pubs were empty. Empty as in, not just not full, but empty as in not one single person was in them. This was in ridiculous contrast to our last games there, when they were packed. I went down the metal steps to the ground. This ground has got Football League grading and yet those metal steps are treacherous. Metal ices when icey. Is slippy when it lags. They cannot surely survive if Accrington Stanley go up next season. Everyone goes up or down them as if they've shit'em. This is not a fire escape; this is an entrance and exit to a football ground. Get some concrete on it.

Stanley Street Club...

Having negotiated the metal steps of death, I saw the sign on the wall of the ground. 'Parking for visiting Directors'. I never got back to check if any of our board had had the cheek to park there. One must be always vigilant though. Any signs of mini Edwards'ing will be stamped upon. Even though it is logical that our board, out of courtesy, have to meet the board of other clubs, parking in a privileged spot is a bit too Politburo for us. We know the one, or possibly two, who might. We're watching. Far, far superior Reds have shifted to the right when leaving the gut-raucous politics of the shop-floor. When a workplace representative represents their workforce, they have to suffer the same conditions as their fellow workers. If a Shop Steward becomes a full-time union official, his or her working conditions change when compared with the workers he/she is representing. They now wear a tie and their job is to go and spend their day negotiating with management. Management now brew up for them. It is then you have to watch them. Any good representative would be proud to be watched and admonished for any discrepancies. It's not that people are naturally shithouses and always sell out when they rise. It is just that their working environment changes and fighting against it or not, they become divorced from the normal working persons working day. Our board need us to tell them. If they don't listen then they are subject to our immediate recall. Well, yearly. Or a crack. Following protracted negotiation with them, of course.

In the main car park of Accrington Stanley's ground sat a sports car. It had 'A5FCX' as a registration plate. It belonged to their chief executive, Rob Hayes. Our vigilance is warranted. They can keep that car, whilst we keep that white 17-seater van with 'FC United of Manchester' written down both sides, and the club badge on its front bonnet. A fiver to all games. Youngsters go free. It would soon park in The Crown pub's car park, only one hundred yards away from the sports car. One hundred yards; but a billion miles.

I met a Mick Schultz, Accrington Stanley's full time Safety Officer and Lottery Manager, in the club car park. He politely told me that the clubhouse wasn't open till 6.10, as all the volunteer staff were still working at their other jobs. He was a very nice man, Mick. However, he got worried quite easily. I suspect this is prevalent in Safety Officers. His main concern of the night was that he hoped that FC United of Manchester fans would not bring beach balls.

Considering that FC United of Manchester fans have a bit of a reputation for knocking back the ale, with the resulting inconveniences that sometimes causes, a beach ball concern was not too bad a concern amongst concernable concerns to be concerned about. Our fans, at the last game, had pulled down the curtains of the clubhouse, as it was so cold against Nelson in January that many had gone inside it. You could see the pitch from the clubhouse through glass so it was a bit executive box, but when your ears are bleeding from hail stone inhalation some girlier Reds could be excused. It was a bit divvy of them to pull down the curtains but if CCTV footage did exist, then my money would be on a drunk falling over and grabbing the curtains, pulling them down by mistake. We have come too far and have done too much to let any gratuitous act of goonyness go unself-policed.

Not nice at all for the clubhouse to have its curtains rearranged, but the wedge they must have made at the bar to get the drunks so drunk in the first place would far, far and far again outweigh the cost of mending the curtains. A cynic might say there was always the option of closing the bar, but the coin was too much. Beachballs and 'Oops, sorry' curtains, although not acceptable, were also not that forbidding for a visit by a few thousand alcoholics. Of course you want perfection but the day we get it has already passed, on the 26th of May 1999, so it's not going to come twice. If, in a closed boardroom, the people who were going to earn from our visit had the option of beachballs and curtain abuse set against us not coming at all, then we know the answer. Although Mick, their Safety Officer, said that there were four holes punched in the ceiling of the clubhouse from excessive chanting. The goon putting his hand through a ceiling tile knew that they had done it the first time. Unless we have four separate Reds doing it once, drunkenly and accidentally, then we have a goon in our midst. Hunt him down Reds. However, the same closed boardroom would still be, even with balls, curtains and holes, slavering over the till we put in their hands. We are glad to hand out that till. That's what football can be about. Invest it wisely.

Huh Huh, you said wood, huh huh...

What makes Great Harwood great? Great Ancoats Street in town is a nice street, but it's not that great as to warrant putting a 'Great' in front of it. Harwood probably just had a 'Blackburn's platform three' moment and stuck a 'Great' in there to make it appear better than it actually was. Unless there is a Harwood and a Great Harwood. If you had to choose between the two where would you live? Would you live in Harwood? That could just be considered not as great as Great Harwood, as the title of where you lived told you that. Or was Harwood just modest? A quiet, dignified: "Listen, we're Harwood, we don't need to platform three you. If you want to find us, you know where we are. We've got pots of tea." Just because it doesn't tell you its great, doesn't mean to say that it isn't. Don't let your intravenous-fed misconceptions fester in you. Be brave enough to mooch outwards.

Or would you live in Great Harwood? Just for the problems it has caused the dyslexic Greta Harwood it deserves to have no occupants. Great Harwood would have a personalised number plate that had to use a number as a letter or a blackened rivet to, say, change a 'c' into an 'e'. It would put its enormous Thompson or Pacific flat screen TV in the bay window so that the only thing that the passing world could see was the ugliness of the back of the telly. Harwood would put fresh, own-garden grown daffodils in a vase in its bay window. It would also have a bright van with windows down both sides, probably with a cut-off, comfy, deep-piled carpet in the back that was Hoovered regularly. The van would always be willing to give lifts - be that human to the pub or to visit, dog to vet, or to the tip with boxes. If there's not a Harwood then there should be.

There is a spectator haunting Europe…

We had to beat Great Harwood for its crimes against Harwood. There was a grudge match growing. FC United of Manchester fans will always try not to tolerate injustice. They want their team to reflect that crusade. It was this smouldering cause that just about managed to get our arses up, and for us to leave the warmth of The Greyhound pub and go out into the freezing, raining night and into the ground. The manager, Marginson, had his Adidas Samba on, so there's every chance he was up for it. His Mamba or Bamba nights are never quite as successful. The weather was atrocious. We had never-ending driving rain with intermittent breaks of hail or snow to lighten the mood. The Great Harwood team, with the blood of Harwood on their hands, had the hard face cheek to play well. None of this: "Sorry for our heinous, historical crimes." There was just denial. Denial that revealed itself in fluid passing movements and a gritty determination to win.

Our midfielder, Chris Simms, played as if he had been down to Cardiff the day before to see United play Wigan – cough, Ahern - and had spent the day on the piss. We might also incur a fine from the football authorities as I think Leon Mike broke the halfway line whilst warming up as sub. It wasn't going well. Great Harwood were pushing us aside as they had done all those years ago to the innocent van and flower owning residents of Harwood. The majority of the FC United of Manchester fans were down the sides under cover, in either the seating side or the bus stop stand across the way. A hundred or so braved the uncovered end getting absolutely drowndeded, but these were probably Catholics with all the guilt to cleanse out of them with Lent coming up. Two blokes were stood on their own at the other end. I knew who they were despite their black, hooded raingear.

Take both sides…

This four-side'ism to our support always weakens it. At home games we are packed into two sides of the ground with a third never really used. This adds to the stereo of noise. We have visited some four-sided, smaller grounds, such as Raddy B or Holker, and I think it diffuses the support. A thinned-out perimeter of four sides is cosier in one way as you can see Reds totally surrounding the 11 red items they crave on the pitch. These 11 items are encircled by their supporters, with no hole for any mischievousness to nip through and hurt them. So I can see the liking that some have for smaller ground, four-side'ism. However, even in small grounds an away following of two or three thousand can still be lost when spread sparingly. I know FC United of Manchester fans aren't all as divvy as me, and understand the necessity to pack together to create that crowd blast that can help the players and other fans. They understand the necessity for uproar because they are the creators of that uproar. The reason we have got so many youngsters wanting to re-return to our matches is because others are creating a beat that bangs and bangs.

Two thousand or more travelling FC United of Manchester fans cannot be compared to other crowds in the lower Football League getting two thousand. There is no: 'We are here to be entertained, entertain me'. FC United of Manchester fans know we are all together. Club, players, fans. The unbeatable, indivisible treble. Every real fan of every club knows that treble importance. FC United of Manchester have been described by outsiders as probably the most political of football fans in Britain. There is a certain truth to that but if politics is realising that we all play a part, and our participation is a prerequisite to our presence, then we are political. Every fan of every club wants to have a good atmosphere. There is an ache sometimes after a great atmosphere of that it should always be that way. It should. Almost all fans of almost all clubs know that, but somehow a two or three thousand crowd at lower league clubs matches will in the main, and despite the valiants trying, be quiet.

FC United of Manchester fans have grasped the necessity of noise because they have lost so much. But gained so much. Because many of us are experienced home and away followers of Manchester United Football Club we already know. Away games with Manchester United Football Club kept the singing and obsessive passion alive through so many corporate years. It is nothing but understandable, therefore, that the days of taking three thousand away fans with Manchester United Football Club, with all the rawness and willingness to not accept the unacceptable that it established, would be replicated with two or three thousand FC United of Manchester fans. Obviously, many were the same Reds. However, it is always confirmed by lower league, FC-friendly fans when they come to our games. Their visits never pass without comment of the unbridled bawling and bodger and badgering that makes a small cauldron.

Poor four. Two...

When you have no other choice than to be in two sides because the other two sides aren't open, then the tendency to string out is taken away from you. Blackpool packed into two stands was Blackpool packed into two stands as the finest example of two-side'ism. Tonight's atmosphere at the Great Harwood game, though muted'ish, was still good. Still boisterous and loud from loud enough lumps of Reds spread about. Reds still willing to shout a funny, still unshy to make oral the anxieties or the pleasures, and all in an atmosphere where no one is going shout at you to sit down or call a steward. It's all good but just not as good me thinks and I blame it on four-side'ism. We're not big enough, as yet, to fill four sides to the adequate levels of bubble. It's with cheeky chop Charlie'ness that I comment on this subject as I rarely sing. Actually, I had a few minutes singing; "Two Uniteds but the soul is one, and the Busby Babes carry on" but it gets me out of puff, like 'When ever they're playing in your town, get yourself to that football ground' does. I just have no Sinatra timing to my lungs.

Our significant other...

It was a lashing down, bitter cold Monday, though, so no one was that up for anything smart as it's work tomorrow. I spilt pie, peas and gravy on my mobile screen. I'm not sure how but when in Accrington... Pitta Patterson put us 1-0 up with a penalty. They equalised. The ref was ridiculously tall and skinny. He'd be alright for peeping Tom'ing over large walls. Before the game we had told him that if he gave us an undeserved penalty, then we'd try to get him buried at platform three at Blackburn station due to his perfect shape for it. His fear was that members of his family would embalm him, have his head not unduly but noticeably sharpened, and use him as the family snooker cue at Christmas dos. He might have given us a penalty, but it was deserved. He never gave us an undeserved one. Therefore, we are going to wait till he dies and his family have embalmed him - with all the stiffening that incurs. Then we are going to break off a leg to use to poke Basher in the ball bags with on our next Euro away.

We drew 1-1. No one ever said football was going to be good to you or was going to love you back. We had tried to beat the Great Harwood unfair foe but had failed. Not all stories end well. Homage to Catalonia is not renowned for its funny finale. Over one hundred of the crowd died of frostbite that night. The Murdoch-controlled press publications never reported it. He has never forgiven those Reds responsible for his twatting in 1999. Vas Wackrill, FC United of Manchester's Safety Officer, who has been on courses with Accrington Stanley's Mick Schultz at Goodison Park, stated that if we'd had a load of beachballs nearby we could have let all the hot air out of them slowly, warming the victims up and saving their lives. Vas has experience in not letting intravenous-fed misconceptions cumulus nimbus his opinions. Everyone hates beachballs for the danger they are and the threat they pose. He saw through that bigotry and now there is a beachball in every First Aid box on FC United of Manchester away games between November and February. It's been blown up by Margy so the air is very hot inside it.

I've also since had contact with Stuart from Blackburn. He's from Blackburn. He tells me there is not a stand-alone Harwood. There's a Little Harwood that's actually part of Blackburn. This means it comes with the same platform three brush that has previously been used for tarring. Calling yourself Little Harwood can also be construed as being self-effacing. 'Oh look at me, I'm little'. Only a Harwood can be a Harwood. It doesn't have to apologise or boast with littleness or greatness. Although we have been known to call ourselves little United so there might be some excuse to be softer on Little Harwood if we play ever them.

But it remains imperative that until we have built our own Harwood in every town that FC United of Manchester visit, the fight goes on.

CHAPTER EIGHTEEN

ENTITY TIL I DIE ...

Oldham Town versus Football Club United of Manchester, Wednesday the 22nd of March 2006. Kick Off - whenever we found a referee and a few line runners - 8pm'ish. Played at Oldham Athletic's Boundary Park ground in Oldham. A town where they still say "Gubbins." And "Jam rag."

You give your hand to me and then you say goodbye...

The night before we played Oldham Town, FC United of Manchester had presented its first General Meeting to its Industrial and Provident Society members. I know we've gone through what an Industrial and Provident Society is in preev chapters but it's worth going through again because it has got touches of the 'off side' confusion about it. An Industrial and Provident Society is a hows-your-father that we had to set up, that sort of thingummybobbed us into an whojar kind of a thing that we can oh-aye about. It's worth clarifying that as the General Meeting, which only contained Industrial and Provident Society members, had to re-go through it all. It was a re-saying of vows that we had said on July the 5th 2005.

To quote Margy the manager's favourite word "basically" then basically an IPS is a legal, transparent, fair, democratic way of us all owning our 'one member, one vote' club. You want to own your own football club, wanting to just be following football at a lovely level with a proper ration of supporter control. Wanting to belong, wanting to be a treasured part, wanting to be in the dinghy with your football destiny and having a say on who gets to steer the steery stick at the back and how far we stay away, or go into, any deeper, more treacherous waters.

Dictatorship of the goalatariate...

That can sound idealistic, utopian even in this period of wampant commercialism and 'watch it in an executive box behind glass on expenses' world. Forming a fan-owned club in the mush of this mess was daunting. So many outsiders were scoffaloffagusses saying that it wasn't possible. Whatever the ins and outs of a cat's arse of legal speak of Industrial and Provident Society'ism, we got our goal because of its existence. Even the name 'Industrial and Provident Society' reminds me of older, perhaps more honourable times. You just don't hear the word 'industrial' anymore, as there is no industry. And, despite thatcher's famous proclamations, we believe that there is society.

I was reading something the other day about architecture - as I have no friends - and I noticed the bloke who had written the article quoting a bloke called Ernst Bloch. I haven't a knickknackyknoo who Ernst Bloch is but the bloke writing the article quoted Ernst saying: "The island utopia rises out of the sea of the possible." Now Ernstykins might be in Margy's squad as it's that big and interchanging that no one knows who is in it. A fair proportion of those 'Missing persons' that find themselves in the paper or on your milk cartons can be found training with us on a Tuesday and Thursday. There's at least two Japanese infantrymen from the Second World War who think the war isn't over who play for us.

But even if Ernst Bloch isn't in the squad, he should still get a game for summing up some of our feelings about where we are now with that quote. We might be doing a dire doggie paddle in that sea of possibilities but at least we're in. We've got water wing armbands on helping us but it is undeniable that we blew them up with our own lungs. We're also wearing good shorts, not the sort that clingily stick right onto your genitals when you get out of the water so that you have to fluff them out to avoid showing everyone your sea-gained semi. We've also, possibly, got one of those nose things on that stop water getting up it, but, over- cautiously dressed or not, at least we're making a splosh. We're splashing around the shore of the rising island, weighing up suitable sites for the building of substantial sea defences but at the same time as fortification, we're also recognising suitably safe, sheltered, deep water harbours to welcome all future visitors. We should get the FC United of Manchester re:boot boys to hunt Ernst Bloch down on the internet and offer him a game. A beer mat of equality rising out of, and floating on top of, the cask-conditioned froth of the resistance.

The long bawl game...

The two pound payers...

The General Meeting, held in the Central Hall on Oldham Street in town, was the same venue as in the first time of FC United of Manchester's official birth on July the 5th 2006. It was full top and bottom, as last time. We heard about, or debated or voted on, why we have a membership fee for the IPS and why we have to renew it every year; if we should change our inaugural shirt this year; the state of the club's finances; the club's work in the community and its development. Although disgracefully this part of the discussion was beaten by time and had to be painfully curtailed. Never again. It should be at the fckn beginning not knit-one-pearl-one'd on the end. We're a community club that needs development; the manager did a question and answer bit on the progress of the team; that 28% of match go'ers are under 18; that the love already shown for the club's badge was an indication that future kit design would be voted on; that the strip should never be blemished with any sponsorship. We realise we work in an environment where a few bob is necessary but we are also very sensitive to the piss take profiteering that we have walked away from. Having no shirt sponsorship, despite knowing that clubs smaller than ourselves receive a wedge to sponsor theirs, was a political stance that the majority of the club's membership was very, very proud of.

Hanging on the shirt tales of others...

Personally, on the shirt changing issue I think we should change the home kit every two years. I know there is an argument that in the old days if you started changing the kit all the time then Directors got an Harpurhey email through their window. For those not knowing the area in Manchester called Harpurhey or its colloquial forms of communication, then the email aforementioned is in fact a brick. If the throwers were feeling polite then they'd attach a note, sometimes written in the Director's kidnapped child's blood, telling them to fuck off and die and to leave the kit alone.

You know the scene it's very humdrum, my favourite song's entitled boardroom...

I hope that if you have got to chapter eighteen of this book with me then you know I am a keen admirer of the sentence 'You are worse than a boss, you're a bosses' man' when it comes to class collaborators within our own. Outside of our own, a management job has never been one that I have felt alright with. I don't want to order people around whilst others above me are ordering me to do so. I'm not that shy at saying when shit is shite but I'm also not stuck. Seeing how things change and being flexible doesn't make you a class collaborator. What made things enlightening during Britain's period of Enlightenment in the 17th and 18th century doesn't mean to say they are enlightening now. Pantaloons being the most obvious example.

Of course, polyester football tops were as relevant to the bourgeois free thinkers of the Enlightenment as Combined Studies degrees are to us now. Time passes. Unlike FC United of Manchester's Rory Patterson. Football shirts have become political. Children like to have a new kit to knock about in. I'm flexible to change and accept that. Perhaps one of the reasons I'm not that keen on Billy Bragg the singer, was that once he had a song that went: 'I was a miner, I was a docker, I was a railwayman between the wars'. I'm sure he was trying to get some sort of valid statement across but all I was left thinking was that he should just have stopped being so flighty in his vocation. Especially as it was in such a harsh period of economic instability. FC United of Manchester are not being flighty in any kit changing proposals. Especially as we're in such a harsh period of economic instability. We could not exist at any time. There is a reasonable time period for changing kits. I'm in favour of changing the home kit every two years. Change the away kit every two years in the alternate years. That's not outrageously exploitative.

Only fear change when the tea machine won't accept your five pence pieces...

Except in a real minority of cases, the argument that a family would be skint giving all the kids kits is a spurious one. All our kits are below 28 brick a shirt. Smaller sizes are cheaper. The wear youngsters get out of a kit is phenomenal. It's all they want to wear. For bed or for school the kit is wanted for wearing. That makes life easier for the Mam and Dad. No decisions to make about what they are going to wear for the week, no arguments as the shirts get put on, no ironing to do, no stain removal. Just sling it in the washer and get it out later. The initial, larger monetary outlay is easily recouped over the coming two years as polyester has been abandoned here by badly dressed aliens and never wears out.

That polyester, environmentally unfriendly, ungreen side of the kit will always be a non-wearing out, FC United of Manchester time capsule. Its ungreen side is part outweighed by the electricity not wasted in ironing and the lack of other clothes worn by the youngster needing to be washed. It keeps your fat kid slimmer as well, as they sweat like a ginger scaffolder in August in them. I'm sure, though, if a paper biodegradable kit is invented FC United of Manchester's progressive fans would be at the front of the call. Sod the fat kids' waistline. A paper kit would also encourage the much-missed re-emergence of Origami. If the game is boring just fold your recycled paper shirt into a xylophone or into a corunal ridge with warts shape. Also, if you have a child, and it fails to grow over the two-year period of the life of the shirt, then the Mam and Dad urgently need to review the dietary intake of that child. Unless you are the neighbours of our less-than-petite goalie Phil Melville. Then all you need to do is install several five lock lever mortises on your doors and nail your windows shut at your child's teatime. You might want to draw the blinds as well, as Phil's slaver is notoriously difficult to get off the windows.

Some is rich and some is poor and that's the way the world is...

The media, always looking for ways to feed the anti-Manchester United section of society, unjustly picked on United. On less lazy journalistic inspection, United's kit changing policy was easily equalled by many of the 92 clubs. I suppose never being a shirt buyer it never really affected me. In the past you hoped that the money made off shirt sales would find itself in the new players acquired for the team. In reality most were left with the feeling that it went into shareholders' dividends. With FC United of Manchester now, every one pence spent on the kit will go back into your club. Simple maths.

Maths for the first time ever becomes easy to understand. On the one side of the equation we have pleasing your children by getting them a not too expensive kit, saving the planet by not ironing them and reducing the nation's child obesity problems by making the fat gets sweat. When juggled, this side of the equation comes out with the result that the politics of the frequency of shirt changing, changes into the politics of shirts without a sponsor. The joy of the first part of the equation means that joy now sponsors the shirt meaning that we can turn down the £40,000 or whatever we are offered for strip sponsorship. The more we express ourselves by buying the kit with no sponsor means that the kit will remain without a sponsor as our joy compensates any loss both financially and aesthetically. It's a shelf full filling shircle. It's probably even simpler than that. That is your team, carrying your hopes and your heart out onto that not-as-grassy-as-it-should-be grass. It's not a de-humanised human advertising hoarding. For just the once we can escape the slip on shoe'd, overwhelmingly over deodorised armpit of the advertisers. No matter how many mints they try to quickly suck just before meeting us we can still smell their decaying plaque. The outside revealing their inside.

Hugh Holdem...

The General Meeting was hot. Oldham is its polar opposite, with the emphasis on the polar bit. I'm just not having this 'Ice Station Zebra' Joe Royle shite. No zebra would ever go to Oldham. I think any deeper investigation into if there has ever been any zebras in Oldham will prove me correct. If they find any pictorial evidence then the zebra will have a coat on. And a hotty strapped to the underside of its belly with a Lemsip in its hoof. Or it will be a picture of the back of the zebra's arse as it's running away, with a little speech bubble above its head saying: "Fuck off sheep teeth, I'm perished." To prove the theory that Oldham is two coats colder, I wore two coats. It was a practical solution in two ways as a) I could get a coat I wanted back to ours from my Mam's and b) the weather was worthy of wearing two coats.

Me and Two Mowers got picked up in Openshaw by the Ginger Princess and her Dad, Alan. It was obvious Alan didn't have his hearing aid in as he was singing along to Motorhead's 'The eight of spades, the eight of spades'. He should really live in Hoylake. Two Mowers obviously caught something off him as he got a phone call saying that Reds were in a pub called 'The Plate and Arms'. We couldn't find it. It turned out it was the Clayton Arms. Before we knew this we decided that seen as how it was pre-Enlightenment, pantaloon-wearing Oldham, it must be called 'The Plate and Musket' or 'The Plate in your head and Tuberculosis' or 'The Plate and Sunday dinner between two plates'. If you built a Wacky

Warehouse in one of the mainly Asian areas in Oldham you could call it The Timmy Malik. Pubs with smart names, though, are smart. Where the daft Printworks is now in Manchester town centre there was once a pub called 'The Swan with two necks'. We used to call it 'The Duck with two dicks'. Now, technically it wasn't called 'The Duck with two dicks' but it wouldn't have been pulled down if it was. Just as we were parking we finished on the unanswered question of why the Labour movement has never had a pub called 'The Len Inn'?

Being the first person born with only a tonsil...

Outside the ground Andy Walsh, our General Manager, told us laughingly that you can never get used to the NWCL division two - we had no referee or line runners. It was 20 minutes before kick off. The match officials thought the match was off and hadn't bothered turning up. We thought it was the officials who called a game off? One of the eventual match officials was in the queue to the game when he was rang and asked to officiate. That is not far off biased Dads running the line at inter-primary school games. I'm glad something odd had happened, though, as I wasn't looking forward to Oldham. Three out of our last five games have been re-arranged to be held there. This was our first. It's miles from the train, awkward by bus and the ground is too big for us for a Wednesday night. It would thin out the crowd and weaken the atmosphere. It didn't in the End of the ground, as that was very noisy, but it definitely did in the Main Stand where we were.

I'm going to put a crease in my jeans...

The game had the air of an Oxford Road bus timetable. You know it exists and has some sort of pattern but it is just too hard to see in all the rush. In the midst of this maelstrom was the calm of musing. A first half that ended 0-0 gave you plenty of time to muse. Musing has its place at football. So muse we must. Women's slippers are better than men's. Timeshare caravan salesmen. There is no reason why armpit hair stops growing. T'Mobile is from Yorkshire. Women change their bed sheets after they've been on, whether they've dribbled in them or not. If we allow 'Fishes' to be a word then people will stop bringing it up. Cunnilingus is more prevalent in Catholic households on a Friday. Drive across cattle grids a lot and practice for Parkinson's. People seem to sneeze and tinkle at the same time but coming and following through at the same time is less common. Some people are good at putting quilt covers on and some aren't. Clumpy, heavy-footed people who are described as 'Fairy Elephants' have probably been to FE College.

You thumb ring...

Trombones are a much-liked instrument as they can knock your hat off mid-tune. You'd apologise to the musician for getting your hat in the way but really he was having you over. Toilet brushes gone brown. Going to a memory boosting class the day before the lesson. And the day after. The working classes keep their scissors in the cutlery draw. And keep soap between the two kitchen taps. Pillow slips or pillow cases? Never sleep in a room with a fridge as it will keep you awake. Don't blow your nose in your black boxers and put them in the wash basket or else it will look like spunk to visitors. Shout "Veron" if you win at Bingo. Minimallist - an American who likes corner shops. The man who shot Liberty X's valance. There is no door shinier than 10 Downing Street's. People carrying food shopping bags walk faster. Women get pissy knicker pissed.

Varley Street Wet The Bed Clinic...

It would be a funnier world if your eyes squeaked. Wimbledon tennis games would be a proper, noisy affair and put everyone off their strawberries and condensed milk. Builders secretly blimping women's arses as they went past would get copped. They'd pretend they weren't blimping but as she turned back to cop them, she'd hear a quick squeak as they looked elsewhere and it would give them away. Glue sniffers would change to spraying WD40 in their eyes along with people who missed the old non-eye-squeaking days of sneaking up behind you and saying "boo." There would have been no squeaky noises from the Main Stand in the second half if eyes did squeak as we pressed them back in their half for most of it. Their number eight, Taylor, who had been a good natured but still psychopathic psychopath at the home game earlier in the season was relatively quiet. They had sort of bullied us in the first game. This is no surprise as they had a player within their team who is from a, what's the words here to stop me getting a bout of being shot, oh, that's it - notorious family.

The - cough - notorious family member on the Oldham Town side was playing again tonight. They backed this up with another member of this - cough - notorious family being at the side of the pitch. Chrissy Bolton pointed him out to me going: "Him there at the side of the pitch. I've seen him on a video, bare knuckle fighting on a caravan park in Collyhurst. The - cough - notorious family member playing against us tonight was the camera man urging him on." You don't get this at Premier League level. We have within FC United of Manchester's squad some, shall we say, connections, but in the interests of liking living I shall leave it there. It seems it is needed sometimes at this level. It is not mard down here. Buy any beans necessary.

Wheel tapas and shunters club...

Margy was telling us at the side of the stage, before he went up on the night before in the Central Hall General Meeting, that Rory Patterson had been illegally tapped up by a league club. They should have approached him but they didn't. This club shall remain nameless; only suffice to say the club has made a very brave decision to name their ground so camply. The tapping shunts. United played them a few years ago in a pre-season friendly. It's only about an hour and a quarter away. I thought it was miles and miles away. Rory has been playing to a lovely standard all season. He is a talent and I can see us losing him.

That's an unusual feeling for a Manchester United Football Club fan, as it's not really happened since Mark Hughes going to Barcelona. Now if we pick up players who have had a good footballing foundation - for example, quite a few of our squad were in United's youth team - then they may well rediscover that earlier potential. Players drop out for all sorts of reasons. With a noisy FC United of Manchester crowd behind them they can re-invent themselves and become targets of lower league clubs. We would be sorry to lose good players but it is something we'll have to get used to. Get them on contract and put a few bob in the Development Fund to ease the loss by keeping the youth season tickets cheap. If we help players re-find their ambition of playing professional football then that has got to be a good reason for us to exist as well. If I was a manager of a lower league side looking for bargains, I think I would come to us as we are schooling them well and giving them the experience of playing in front of crowds. Karl 'Dario Gradi' Marginson.

Hands Blix and bumpsydaisy...

Just as I was having the Karl 'Dario Gradi' Marginson thoughts the United End requested Margy to give them a wave. He doesn't wave. He puts his arms up as if he is going to wave. Most Reds will be mugged by this, thinking he is going to give a traditional wave. Then he goes off and does an odd thing with his hands. It looks as if he has got a 'Lamb chops' sock glove puppet on them. The sort of motion he makes with his hand is the one you do when accompanying it with the sentence: "You're coming in here, giving it all that." Not as if I'm being pernickety or anything, the odd-handed bastard. He's a good lad but also at the General Meeting the night before, he had said that Barrie George, our 19-year-old goalkeeper was staying on the bench for the next few games. Barrie had done so well but he would learn from watching Phil Melville command his box. "What? His fucking butty box ?" As someone said at the side of me. He is a good player Phil, though. His experience does shine through. Or is that the shine from the silver plate with all the butties on he's got stuffed up his goalie shirt?

Awwnofollowjists...

Dave Chadwick mustered some sort of GM cropped scissor kick and gave us the winning 0-1 goal. The attendance was announced as 1,767. That Wednesday night can affect you. Still, that's not a bad away following for most of the 92 clubs. If we do ever get to a level where there are home fans in numbers equalling ours, then we'll be known as crowd doublers rather than just the crowd. Meeting another club that gets 2,000 crowds whilst we bring 2,000, will also cure some of the problems of four-side'ism, as discussed earlier, as we'll only have half the ground. The atmosphere and inter-club banter will increase accordingly. It is smart enough now but it is self-amusement most of the time. Wanking is good but you need intercourse eventually. But for now we'll put up with and enjoy self-pleasurement. Part way through the second half the false bird of prey stuck up in the Main Stand roof was noticed and picked on. The songs went as follows:

> "We've got Kezzy, Kezzy, Kezzy, Kezzy kestrel on the wing, on the wing."
>
> "If the Reds should play underneath a bird of prey we'll be there, we'll be there."
>
> "Kestrels come, I don't know why, coz after the match he's gonna fly."
>
> "And the budgie babes carry on."

By far and away the worst, though, was the bloke who sang:

> "Kezzy kestrel king of all kestrels."

I had to tell him to get out. The songs seemed to die off when some voice chirped up that it was a chaffinch. The fact that no one is going to know whether that was bollocks or not sort of shut the songs up. It was agreed that the false birds that were in the roof at maine road went to far more games and were far loyaler and far louder and flew miles better than Kezzy kestrel. Except for cup games when they got flu.

Octopuses Hoegaarden ...

Joz 'It's the thought that counts' Mitten and Simon Carden came on as subs by the 'Tim'll fix it' advertising hoarding. I'm devode that Joz is not getting more games but Margy has to mix it to find it. As Joz, and indeed Margy at the General Meeting said, he will get more goals as we go higher and leave the less talented/technical behind. That is not being disrespectful to the less talented or technical as the vast majority count ourselves within that category. It was enjoyable to see Simon Carden back after injury though. His song, to the obvious 'Octopuses garden' tune that goes: "I like to be, watching FC, with a goal from Simon Carden if he plays" is now getting on my nerves. It's a good song and that but I've let it get on my own nerves. You see Jane and Scott live in our flats. It's very handy having FC United of Manchester fans upstairs.

Scott, the poor sod, is sort of proof reading this book due to the fact that he was handy and you can get him mashed and he volunteers for anything. That and the hypnotism I took up without telling him, to be able to get him to do it. He sees a Timex and there's no getting him back till you click your fingers. We took him to El Rincon, the Spanish bar off Deansgate in town, where they do that clicky fingers Flamenco dancing. Show him the watch, off he nods, hears the Flamenco finger clicking, up goes his head awake, show him the watch, hear the click, show him the watch, hear the click. He was off work for a week with a stiff neck and he still doesn't know why. Now I can get him to volunteer for anything except showing his mates his fit wife's underwear draw. Tight bastard. Although, as a bi-product of going around to show him each chapter I get to see her flowery matching bra and knickers sets on the clothes maiden. Scott thinks I'm really conscientious but really it's just a Jane's grubbie blimping exercise. If my eyes squeaked I'd be fucked.

This thing of ours...

Anyway, the Simon Carden tune before we go on more about Jane's thongs. as I don't want to discard my chance on the Jane list. You see I've told Scott that when he dies, that obviously we'll all be upset and that, but with his good train driver's pension, left behind Jane will need looking after. So we have to get on Jane's good list. As Scott is naïve about the conscientious book visits, so he is naïve about all his mates trying to make sure he takes up smoking untipped Park Drive. That he goes white water rafting in a bucket, high wiring with Side Show Bob's shoes on or abseiling with cotton. When he bends down in the kitchen to pick something up that he's dropped, I open the wall cupboard door above him so that when he gets back up he bangs his head on it. He also never fathoms why his gas stove is always left on unlit after I've gone.

Will you lot stop going on about Jane's linen trousers wafting across her crotch with the freedom of the sails in the opening titles of the Onedin Line. And her big bouncing table polishers. Perverts. Anyway, the Simon Carden 'Octopuses garden' tune. I go up to Scott and Jane's and, as in people have their own ring tones when they ring you, so I have my own knock on their door so they don't think it's the clubman coming around for money. My knock is the Simon Carden tune. Now it might appear a straightforward tune but it isn't. Your head is humming the tune as you knock but the result to the outsider's ear is just an annoyingly long knock.

Of all the times I have tried it, I have only ever really succeeded in getting it right once. It was absolutely perfect. I was made up with myself. I felt I had arrived as a musician to be taken seriously within the industry. The man who could Simon Carden tune. The postman always rings 11 times if you're just doing the 'With a goal from Simon Carden if he plays' end bit. The bastards weren't in. I'd spoken to another Red the night before at the Woodley friendly game about how Simon Carden'ing letter boxes was smart. About how it was hard but worthwhile if you put the practice in. Reds should try it in honour of their goal scoring midfielder. However, I had to text her to say I had just been robbed of having witnesses to my peak performance of Simon Carden letterboxing. I knew loneliness. If a tree falls in a forest can anybody hear it if it falls on your foot? Seeing Simon Carden coming onto the pitch against Oldham Town, to play for the first time since that day when Scott and Jane weren't in for my highest musical moment, brought the devastation all back.

Frizzell me fizzle...

We left the ground past the Frizzell bar and the sign saying that a full match report would be in the Oldham Chronicle the next day. Can't wait. We went back in 'The Plate and arms' for one. Discussed that there is nothing sexual about seeing a woman in a bubble bath. You just know it is giving her thrush so your first instinct is not a sexual one but one of health and safety to get her out: That no players, according to George the kit man, had tiger striped their shorts this season. The closest they had come to it was when he had got in the shower with them after the Great Harwood game. We left the car park at the side of the ground. When you're told you can't park there you just have to say you co-own the club and you get on. We're not lying, we do. Surely on the next two visits the car park stewards will cotton on. It is Oldham though. They're too busy lying about zebras. And not stopping fights where men are knocking about women because they always finish up with the women saying: "Gerroff him I love him" if you intervened.

CHAPTER NINETEEN

YOUR NOSE IS TOO NEAR YOUR ARSE...

New Mills AFC versus FC United of Manchester. Saturday the 25th of March 2006. Kick off 3pm. Played at Hyde United's Ewen Fields ground. We've got a ticket to hide but you couldn't as they were cardboard, bright yellow and as big as your head. There are smaller flags at the game than them.

And time leaves sparkle remains...

There was a woman who used to work at Manchester Council before retiring a few years ago called Marrie Mee. Apparently she never did. Whether that was through choice or not I'll never know as I didn't know her, but it doesn't stop everyone going "Aww" whenever they hear that little story. I hope she was happy. She might very well have been a totally satisfied, independent woman who rejected the bizarre belief that love has to have paper attached to it. In my old house we used to have a piece of paper on the wall that told you all the different items like silver, gold and ruby that represented your years together. I think paper meant only one year. So the need to have paper involved in love has hardly been recognised in the anniversary celebrations. It's lovely for the loved-up people who get the piece of paper and it's lovely for the people who don't feel they need it.

There was a friend of my Mam's also called Marrie. She also never got married. Marrie was a bit of a Janet Molby. You'd never want to get behind her in the queue for the shower. You'd be waiting ages as there was loads of her to wash. You couldn't bend down to pick up your dropped fork if you were having your tea with her at the same table. She'd nick your roasties, put them on your buttered bread, dipped it in your gravy and have swallowed them all before you sat back up with your retrieved fork. If you drop your fork in Marrie's company then it is staying there and you are eating your tea with a knife and your hand or suffering the Marrie tax. Unfortunately, however nice a woman she was and however much she liked her food, however much good company she was, that smiled and laughed, underneath the whale bone corset and American-tan, surgical stockings she wasn't a happy tubby. Whenever the girls from the pub went away to Benidorm, under the disguise of ladies' darts international peace accords, Marrie would fall into the role she didn't like.

The girls would go out on the piss, all in rounds and suitably alcy flushed up. Marrie was involved with all the raucous giggling, shouting and drinking that came about. What would happen later, though, would be that the girls would be pissed up May Queen'ed and want to go dancing. They'd go to a place where they could dance and they'd get up and dance. Marrie would mind the bags. The next day the girls would go sunbathing. They'd get up for a swim. Marrie would stay in the shade and mind the bags. If they were doing a bit of sight seeing that involved a bit of walking then Marrie would find some shade near to where they were sight seeing. And mind the bags. Her friends always encouraged her to come and do everything they did. She felt she couldn't. She'd imposed a restriction on herself. And in self-imposing that restriction she'd then stopped herself from discovering. She played an enchanting role within the group of girls, being so kind to mind the bags, but it came with another high banded, Marrie tax. She was a self-taxer. In a quiet moment, in the midst of a lovely holiday, Marrie told my cousin: "No one means me any harm when they leave their bags with me. They're my great friends. It makes sense. But for whatever reason I have done this to myself, don't you. Don't become like me, don't become 'Marrie mind the bags'."

I would walk 500 yards and I would walk 500 more...

All players for New Mills AFC live within two miles of their Church Lane, New Mills ground apparently. That's either a fantastic fact or very disturbing. Or a pre-fabricated fib. There are arguments for all three.

However, New Mills AFC had chosen to travel and see the world. Albeit a Tameside'ish one. They gave Hyde United a rumoured three and a half thousand quid and for that they got to hire their ground for the day. New Mills AFC in a hired Hyde United costume. It was a shame really as we'd looked forward to packing their nice little ground in the High Peak with its capacity of 1,650. Some Reds had argued that you can always safely get a few hundred more in at this level and if the tax man doesn't know then grass roots football gets a straight cash injection. We were never going to be taking more than 2,000 Reds. We could have done though. So, yes, they were right to move to get everyone safely in. Shame though. We're just popular gets. You can get the train straight to New Mills from town and it's not a bad little beery place. I'd heard it described as a mixture of the half a million pound house and the £10 bag of brown. Posh enough not to be rundown and beaten. Knowledgable enough that you'd get a crack if you played up. It has got something about it, though, as it has a Swizzels factory there where you can buy Swizzels. And Lovehearts. The Plain English Campaign is based in New Mills. The talk of the day, though, was that if New Mills AFC were brave enough to come further than two miles out of New Mills then we were brave enough to go to Leipzig in East Germany. A city with a 'z' in its name. Very continental.

Pontinental...

The Ronald Rumour had been at it since the preev Wednesday's game against Oldham Town. FC United of Manchester were to play their first Euro away in history. There's no disrespect meant to Blackpool there as Blackpool was our first Euro away, but then again so was Leigh as Blackpool and Leigh are both in Europe. It's the pavement cafés. Or the people lying on them. I think I'll possibly applaud myself here for not saying "Cuntinental" as I was really tempted. The old, whispering friend of Euro away travel "We got a flight for a tanner plus tax" entered our 'ten leagues down' vocabulary for the first time since that last Euro against AC Milan in March 2005. Many clubs in Europe had offered us a game. However, Leipzig were very generously going to pay our expenses. A trip to fly and house all the players could cost the club three to five thousand. It's not a light decision. Leipzig, a club that had fallen on harder times since the fall of the Berlin Wall, made the decision easier. We could use it to recruit other players to replace ones we might lose. If you were a player in the lower leagues playing in front of only a few souls and FC United of Manchester came in for you offering you the chance to play attractive football in front of four or five thousand and throwing in trips to Germany you would be tempted.

No price on the pain of loss...

Flights from east Midlands to Berlin were one pence there and a Harold Melvin back before the preev game against Oldham Town. They'd now gone up due to FC United of Manchester demand. We finished up booking Liverpool to Berlin. It unfortunately cost us £96. We thought the airline was having some sort of sick joke asking Mancunians to pay that to fly from Liverpool, but that's what the price was when we booked it. We're not into that Hillsborough shite that some fans can't rise above. I nearly didn't mention the price but thought fuck it; we've nothing to be guilty of. We know it could have been us in that semi-final. Just as it was us in Munich in 1958. I still maintain, though, due to my experiences of Bolton Wanderers' games, that if you find a credit card in Bolton then you have a more than modest chance of its four- digit chip and pin being 'one, nine, five, eight'. If it is then ransack it silly. If it isn't then give it back. That Bolton chip and pin number theory depends on whether credit cards have been invented in Bolton. You can't be presumptuous.

Hyde and chic...

Hyde United have a lovely little ground. The pitch is in nice nick as well. It wouldn't cost too much to build such a little cutey. Mind wondering over the possibilities... No wonder United reserves play there. Does this make Hyde United Glazer collaborators? They are allowing Glazer to make a profit if the youngsters come through. Or are Hyde United taking money off him, therefore making his tight budget even tighter? I'm not sure where to go on that one. The debate couldn't go on as our attention was diverted as several fans fainted and had to be stretchered out of the ground to the nearest pub as Joz Mitten scored. And it was a belter. I'll say that again. Joz Mitten scored. And it was a belter. I was made up for the lad. He ran into the front of the crowd and got a bit mobbed. He wasn't booked for it. Oh, the inconsistency of refereeing at this level. Mind you the ref will have noticed that his alopecia scar on the side of his head is getting bigger. If he books him he might potentially increase the stress that supposedly causes it. That or he didn't want to get any alopecia flakes on him.

Magenta Divine. In Salford...

Our attention was also diverted to the 'Salford FCUM, Spirit of the babes' flag that had appeared. The top half of the flag was white. Traditional enough as that's one of our three colours. The bottom half, though, was pink. Pinky and Perky pink. Not a red that has gone runny but a definite one million percent pink. Now that's very brave of them to use such a

Canal Street colour at a football match. FC United of Manchester fans again confronting bigotry. Almost certainly. The flag owners will, of course, tell you vociferously that it is not pink but magenta. It is the same magenta that Salford Council insist is not pink as they use it on the road signs to welcome you into the borders of the city. I remember the debate raging in the Salford Advertiser about how dare the council use such a fey colour. I'm not up to date with opinion there now but if the Salford FCUM flag is anything to judge from then it is certainly on its way to being accepted as a Salford colour. They could paint the outside of the Ashley Brook in Seedley, magenta. Actually, don't. My Dad was the bricklayer on that so it would be a crime to paint over good craftsmanship.

PP'ing...

It was also noticed by several of the more immature Reds within our company that our Assistant Manager, Phil Power, has his initials PP on his tracksuit. I'm sure if our Assistant Manager was Val Doonican then we'd have more of an obvious problem. That would be smart having Val Doonican as Assistant Manager. We could go to away games in Rafferty's motorcar. If we ever got a new ground of our own we could install Val inspired, rocking chair seating. Let's see the callers for safer standing resist the temptation to watch a game without being coaxed in. The sentence 'The crowd was rocking' would be an actual statement and not a euphemism. I'm sure the quiet sight of a total stand moving in the peripheral vision of our players would be a mood enhancer. We could rock really quickly at moments of high tension. Combine that with singing and we're on an atmospheric high. We'd have to oil the seats regularly, though, as if we didn't and squeaky eyes came into fashion at the same time – it is the future, they both could happen - then it would be proper, squeakily annoying. I suppose we could self-police and bring our own oil in just in case it had been a really damp week and a seat the week before that didn't squeak, now did.

I could bring my wooden rocking chair to the game like people bring their own metal pewter pint pot into the pub. My Nana smoked herself to death to get that rocking chair for me on the Embassy coupons. The wooden rocking chair - with the arm that wouldn't fix on right, as it was a flat pack rocking chair - is there in my bedroom as a smoking gun/lighter reminder of her life. She didn't start to smoke until she was in her 50s. The doctor told her to take it up for her nerves. Outside of suggesting she gets an asbestos rocking chair to smoke in, he did well there. The same doctor prescribed thalidomide to my Mam when she was pregnant with me. Good care loads in Beswick from the health service professionals in the '60s. And we're getting bothered over whether Omega 3 is good for you or not.

If you're worried, save your Omega 3 capsules to oil the rocking chair terracing that will be brought in.

Unfortunately, Val Doonican is not our Assistant Manager. There's time, though, as I don't think he is dead. We must have vision as a club. If you're a board member of FC United of Manchester and you first proposed Val, then your place would be assured on the board forever. Imagine the time in the future when the telly might be there for a post match appraisal interview and they get Val Doonican's Gaelic smile and cheery, lilted demeanour instead of Margy's Ancoats' ragpicker drawl. No one could dislike us. Margy's job would be safe, as even if we were being relegated all over the place, all he'd have to do would be to put Val on the loudspeaker to talk to the disgruntled crowd and everything would be alright. And afterwards in the pubs near the ground he'd come in. And instead of putting Val Doonican on the jukebox, the actual Val Doonican would sing. It would be an honour if he sat in my Nana's rocking chair. Her premature, high tar death would then mean something.

He'd be cheap to keep as he's earned a few bob being a middle of the road, easy listening superstar so he wouldn't want a wage. He'd do it out of his own goodness. We could buy him jumpers for Christmas. He'd like that. It's settled then. Val Doonican has to be asked to be our new Assistant Manager. It all makes sense now why Phil Power has 'PP' on his tracksuit. The more immature Reds within our company, on this day against New Mills AFC, say: "I've been PP'ing" when they mean they have been out having sexual intercourse with women. This is because 'PP'ing' is short hand, in their world, for 'Pussy Pumping'. That's why Phil Power, our present Assistant Manager, has got 'PP' on his tracksuit. He has got an insider tip over the hiring of Val Doonican. He is trying to fight back by getting down with all the youth so he can keep him out. "Look at me, I'm 'PP' and I 'PP' " he's saying. It won't work Baldylocks. You might have played with Zola and Hughes but Val has played with Mary Hopkins. One winner.

Leaning on a tramp post…

In a portentous moment of easy listening things to come, the half time DJ played George Formby. Andy Walsh, our General Manager, turned round to us and said that we're never that good on the PA at Gigg Lane. Oh, how he had to take that back. It is not our fault the PA at Gigg Lane couldn't waken a cheese cracker supper'ing light sleeper with a urinary tract infection. We had indeed played George Formby at Gigg Lane. Two Mowers had actually got his DJ brother to do a George Formby mix. It was played at half time back in our home game against Winsford on the 2nd of

January 2006. We know how to 'Night Nurse' an audience. It's just you can't hear us. The DJ then went on to play 'Agadoo'. He wins.

Harangue the DJ...

Their DJ also told two children to get off the safety barrier at the front. Twice. The third time he said fractiously: "As I've said, I'm trying to be nice about this." We waited for his fourth plea knowing that it would begin with: "Right you twats, I've told you three times, I'm going to knock fuck out of you now." It finished up: "Listen, move now or I'll have you ejected." Quality Percy Sugden grumpiness from the Tannoy. Me, Simon Go and Peanut can only dream of having the ability to pick people out of the crowd to abuse. Perhaps that's why they won't make smart the Tannoy for us at Gigg Lane. You'd all get it. Bastards. I suppose the first home game against Padiham when, during the game, Peanut got on the mic and went: "How skenny are you?" at a poor goal attempt by a Padiham player might have given the people who might invest in us a reason not to. At the same home game when the crowd were singing 'The man with no name' he also went: "He's called Rory Patterson." When the crowd continued singing it he said: "I've told you once, he's called Rory Patterson." That might also be another reason for them not to invest in our audibility.

Cough Ahern...

FC United of Manchester's Will Ahern was having his usual good game. He's only 18. I was standing at the side of Chris O'Neill who has known him a long time. Will had just finished a load of plastering for Chris at his house. He assures me Will is one of the nicest, gentlest lads you could meet. When he's not had a drink. When he's had two pints he turns into the biggest pest who wants to fight everyone. Will had just been for a trial that week with Grimsby. If ever a town is going to drive you to having one or two too many blood thinners then it could possibly be Grimsby. The clue to the town is in its name. If I was on the Grimsby Tourist Information Board I'd extol the town's cultural assets of 'Chippy, pub, fight' as loads of people seem to be attracted by that. I hope Will wasn't tapped by the Tourist Board as a sort of 'We took this gentle Mancunian and see what we turned him into' sort of marketing ploy to get stag nights visiting. Will is an excellent midfielder with so much potential. As in, perhaps losing Rory Patterson, so we might lose Will. Bugger. No wonder one of the first things the characters from AFC Wimbledon said to us was not to get too used to liking players. Unsurprisingly it's turning out to be true. We might be safe, though, with the 'Two fat laddies, 88' that is Leon Mike and Phil Melville. Two - cough Ahern - larger than life characters as we have said before.

Stamp duty…

We were never going to lose the game as Margy had his Adidas Samba on. The tongue on Adidas Samba always falls to the side of your instep. They're shit shoes. I love them. None of this sticking them in the wash to freshen them up with Samba. You've got them till the sole goes yellow. Whilst on the subject of tongues and washing machines: I was stood with Sue and Sarah, two Independent Manchester United Supporters Association stalwarts. In fact the pair of them were at the first meeting of a dozen or so Red activists in the Gorse Hill at the very founding of IMUSA. It was the tail end of the 94/95 season. I say 'stalwarts' in a general 'very good at licking envelopes and stamps' way. The male activists had heard so many Reds say Sarah was good with her tongue that she was invited along. Sarah's second name is Hotpoint. This is very applicable as she is a single lady and she likes electrical appliances that vibrate. Sue's second name is Bowers, which sounds like bowels but not quite. It would have been an applicable second name if it was Bowels because once, Sarah was on telly for ages at the Liverpool Cup Final in 1996. The Cup Final cameras panned around and stayed on her for ages. Sue, however, had gone for a shit and just her seat was there. Sue disguises the fact she was having a Hajduk Split by making us call her "Wee'ing Sue." She thinks this somehow makes her more of a lady, the pissy arsed get. Two days before any FC United of Manchester game Sue takes Dio-calm and only eats boiled eggs on white bread so she can at least see part of the game without going to turn out a mix. In those two days she cannot go past a 'Carpet Right' shop because the rhyming slang makes her follow through.

Now it's no longer Cup Finals against Liverpool but league games against New Mills AFC when we stand at the side of each other. We still get to see great footballing moments though. Darren Lyons, our player coach, had come to take a corner near where we were standing. He's been taking advantage of people discarding their Omega 3 oil capsules and rubbing them on his two hip replacements so they don't squeak. FC United of Manchester are plagued by squeaks at present. Squeak this, squeak that. Enough with the squeaks already. Anyway the squeakily clean, well-oiled-hipped Darren Lyons came up to take a corner near where we were standing. As he ran to the corner a bloke's coat on the front fencing fell off onto the floor. He couldn't reach it when he was bending over the fence. Darren Lyons was running towards the corner flag to take the corner. Without stopping or even looking up, he just instinctively ran to the coat, picked it up, put it back on the fence, turned around and took the corner in one movement. Those who were there and witnessed that won't forget it. It's such a normally polite thing to do but not on a football pitch. Sue shit herself with joy. Sarah will wash Sue's pants in her vibrating washing machine. Football's the winner.

Whatever you do, wherever you go, whatever you say – say nothing...

We finished up 2-0 winners with the second goal coming from Mrs Patterson before he was sent off. Again. For a team that plays a passing game we lose some balls over the low roofs. There were so many balls hoofed out of the ground that we finished up playing with a yellow ball. The attendance was 1952, which is about right for the dress sense of Hyde. Hyde is one of those places where if you ask someone: "What day is it?" and say for example it is a Wednesday, they'll say: "Wednesday." Now that would at first appear to be polite in that they have replied. Unfortunately, Hyde is one of those places where they just have to say, after telling you what day it is, they just can't help it, they have to say: "All day" after it. Genetic. It's the 'Not three bad' syndrome in reverse after you have asked after their well-being. These annoyances can have a scientific side though. The science to see if someone loves you. The scientific test for love is as follows: Your partner is going out somewhere. They get their key, they tell you where they are going, they give you a kiss and then they shut the door and go. Seconds later they return as they have forgotten something. At this point you become the scientist. You say to your partner: "You were quick." If they laugh then they love you as love is blind to: 'That was quick/ all day/ not three bad'isms. Don't try it with 'It takes one to know one' or 'He who smelt it, dealt it' and expect a laugh as that's too much for any love to get through.

Dandelion and Murdoch...

A crowd of 1,952 was respectable, as the authorities wouldn't let us have pay-on-the-day as they had been frightened by adverse paper reports in the press from our visit to Blackpool. There were some arrests and that diddy pitch invasion at Blackpool, but it's Blackpool. The place is wiredly violent with alcohol binged stag nights Wild West'ing about. It's like one long 'Will Ahern in a Blob shop on his third all-in with sugar and lemon' theme night. Someone had said the negativity was most prevalent in the Murdoch owned press. Apparently there have been no positive reports on FC United of Manchester in the Murdoch press. I don't know whether that is true or not but it wouldn't surprise me as the beating he took from IMUSA is something he is not going to forget. We offer flowers to our enemy and he tries to lop off the pretty bloom that means no harm. The bloom that is only trying to give pleasure. We'd put the dandelion under his neck to see if he likes butter but it comes out reading, he likes being bitter. He couldn't buy Old Trafford and he couldn't buy me. Actually, it's buttercups you use to see if you like butter. For no apparent reason my

Nana used to call dandelions "Piss-the-beds." There's no science to discover why that was so.

Glow surrender to the IPA...

We went back to The Sportsman pub near the ground after the game. We meant to stay for one but it was lashing down and we finished up having a glue pot. It is a very nice real ale pub and we had a selection of Phoenix Brewery beers at £1.60 a pint. We finished up red of alcohol faced on IPA which is a pale ale, Pale ale is very 1952. When in Hyde... The beer drinking, sexual deviants in the local population are known as sado-mackesonists. I'm not sure if IPA is Phoenix Brewery or not but it was nice. I like real ale. None of that chemical nonsense. It's the closest thing you can get to a clean cannabis grass, giggly high. Real ale is live in the barrel so it's a pro-biotic. A good bacteria that is good for your digestion. The pub was singing. Mostly due to the fact that their stomachs were so healthy from all the good bacteria they were putting into it. Later when it began to thin out, the Landlord, conscious of the fact his half seven/eight o'clock clientele does not want to meet the all daying drunken crowd, turned the jukebox on to drown the singing out. Landlord, put your own music on next time. If you let Reds have the jukebox they will just put records on that they can sing along to. We did. At first the locals were a bit wary, as you would imagine. Eventually they all sang along with us. It's usually a quiet pub. They had a great night and I'm sure they'll miss us next week. I'm not saying that happens every week wherever we visit, as that would be a bit hippyish. Actually I am as it has happened all season.

Love United, ate Glazer...

Amidst the jollifications and bags of Quaver eating was intense United debate. Soya Milk Mark, perhaps in beer, has got the glums. He thinks that we will never be able to win United back. Peanut was definite that we would. The worrying thing, though, was the timescale. Early in the season I don't think anyone would have uttered anything other than two or three seasons. Peanut was now saying: "In my lifetime we will go back." He is 24. They finished up saying that before 41 years were up, before he got to retirement age, Peanut would be going onto the pitch at Old Trafford and putting a MUFCUM flag in the centre circle. The 'Will we win' debate might have ended in the 'Ticket to Hyde' tune of:

> Think I'm gonna get pissed, I think it's today, yeah,
> We're in a pub in Hyde drinking IPA, yeah.

We've got a ticket to Hyde,
And it's outsized.

But behind the singing there was, as always, a great sadness. 41 years? That's ten more than the backwards since they last won a trophy. Some sieges take longer than others. Keep your grubbies pulled up and your vest tucked in, it's going to be a grueller. There was no other way though. If it's going to be a long one then we need everyone. Don't become the person you never wanted to be by self-imposing restrictions on yourself. If you haven't been to an FC United of Manchester game then get yourself to that football ground. There's another season next year. You can choose to get married to it or to not get married to it. Hopefully Marrie Mee had that choice of whether or not to marry. She was given that name that meant so much to all around her.

We were given the same name of Manchester United Football Club and Football Club United of Manchester that means so much to all around us. It's up to us what we do with the name we were named with. If the unity offensive between the two sets of fans continues and grows we can all be there when Peanut puts that MUFCUM flag in the centre circle of Old Trafford. With all four sides of complete four-side'ism cheering. Hopefully some of us could be sitting in a rocking chair seat. Val Doonican would want that unity. Don't over indulge on the wasted calories of misinformation that can make you bloated and unhappy. We want to have the choice of whether we get married or not. We don't want to never have the choice because of something we had done to ourselves as 'Marrie mind the bags' did.

A heart needs ventricles…

United fans can have a good life without those who chose to not give Glazer any money. Little United can have a good life on their own without United fans who said they couldn't just leave United. If that situation of separation continues, then Glazer wins. No one wants that as no one wants to be knobbed by a gnome, unless you're odd. We can have our two teams but we need a continuing unity offensive between ourselves. 'Marrie mind the bags' had a good life. A life enlivened by the presence of her mates being with her. It would have been a better life if she had not damaged herself so much. If she hadn't self-inflicted harm on herself her mates could have all minded their own bags and let her dance. Or left the bags there and all just danced together. Despite the two Marries that I have known of never getting married, after a lifetime of their name telling them to, you can still marry for love. Don't ruin a lovely peace accord holiday with crippling reflection at what you could and really should have done. Don't impose something on yourself that doesn't need to be there. Go out and discover. Go out and find Tommy Tate's old soul classic 'If you've got to love somebody, why not take a chance on me?' Don't become 'Marrie mind the bags'. She told you not to. You only had to listen to hear her. 'Marrie mind the bags' died alone in her flat. No one found her for days. She deserved so much better. So do we. And the Busby Babes Marrie on.

CHAPTER TWENTY

ALL THINGS ARE COMPARATIVE BESIDES THOSE BEYOND COMPARE...

Norton United FC versus FC United of Manchester. Played on Sunday the 9th of April 2006. Kick off 2pm. Played at Port Vale's ground. All men in Stoke really should wear sheepskin nose-bands as they're all the size of Hos's horse. The women are all three peggers. That is it takes three pegs to hang their knickers on the line.

Oh my heart it stumbles forward, as the light declines,
I remember Man United in the rare old times.

Raised on songs and stories, heroes of renown,
The passing tales and glories that was my football ground,
Duncan Edwards passed to Bill Foulkes, Law passed to Cantona,
Then went in rounds with Norman, Robson and Paul McGrath.

But farewell my home Old Trafford, I can no longer stay,
And watch the corporate changes, all in Malcolm Glazer's pay,
My mind's too full of memories, too old to hear new chimes,
I'm a part of Red Manchester from the rare old times

Oh my heart it stumbles forward, as the light declines,
I remember Man United in the rare old times...

We weren't playing Norton United at a good time. It wasn't a good time because of the football, as we were still six or seven thousand points clear at the top of the table. The only reason we have not been declared champions is because, mathematically, teams that have eight or nine games in hand on us could catch us. These games in hand are a constant feature of football at this level as there is no undersoil heating at the clubs we play at. Indeed many consider themselves fortunate to have soil. Consequently abandoned games happen with gay abandon. Very few people in Stoke can be accused of under oil eating.

This wasn't a good time for us as this was the time Gene Pitney died. Obviously it might be a slightly worse time for Gene Pitney. Gene Pitney's music meant absolutely nothing to me but I didn't resent him. What I did resent was the proliferation of Gene Pitney jokes that barraged my phone from Reds who really should know better. Once you have heard 'It will take three weeks to make Gene Pitney's coffin out of oak but only 24 hours from balsa' more than a dozen times, it really does wear. If Gene had sung, which he didn't, the 'Witchita Lineman' then we could have taken the text senders to Witchita, at great cost to ourselves, but no matter as it would be worth it, as we could have hung them from the line. I am sure, from your own experience, that you know what weekend FC United of Manchester played Norton United FC, as you yourself must have suffered.

If you work with a blue, put a pen in their fruit...

The day before we had all met in Sinclair's in Shambles Square in town for Donna's birthday. Her and Soya Milk Mark are in the process of splitting up. We are all devode for them but they're sorting themselves out. Everyone wishes them nothing but well. When we got in Sinclair's we were with the residue of Reds who had been Ladbroke'ing that afternoon. It was Grand National day, the bookies busiest time of the year. Ladbrokes is a sponsor of Glazer. Sixty or seventy Reds had been dark-clothedly going round the Ladbrokes in town, storming into the shop and re-arranging them. A man, hopefully named Bill, would sticker the shop with the 'Love United, Hate Glazer' stickers and then they would get off on the toe train. But they'd be off also knowing that the shops had previously been leafleted. A very convincing, snide Ladbokes' leaflet had been given out, with doddery Grannies especially targeted, offering a free £1 bet to celebrate 120 years of Ladbrokes on Grand National day. I know it's gnat fly annoying tactics but the thought of customers wanting a free bet and producing our leaflet and thereby clogging up the queues on such a queue'y day was alright. Go to another bookies would be those Reds' advice. The unfortunate blue who happened to be coming out of Kendall's as these lads were going past got stickered from his Adidas-one-stripe-too-many's to his main-road-fin haircutted haircut. He just stood there and took it.

Mrs Scratchit…

The beer in Sinclair's is Sam Smith's like the beloved Greyhound in Accrington. Except here we were paying town prices. In Accrington they charge £1.33, as we know. In Sinclair's, right in the Selfridges' circle/Shambles Square two sided triangle, they take you around the corner and latch another one pence on. As you're paying your £1.34 you know you're being ripped off. It might be cask- conditioned ale, medically good for you and taste delicious but that one pence is taking libbos. It was mentioned that there had been a Budget since we were last in Accrington and that beer went up one penny, so I might forgive them. Donna's hair was stuck up for bother but you couldn't tell her as a) it was her birthday and b) she was on the organic ale as her thrush was playing up and she wanted to keep her scratching down to a birthday minimum, so we had to be supportive over that. We went in Sinclair's for one at five o'clock. We got slung out at lasties. They all sloped off to The Brickhouse and I managed to backdoor to fetherlite. One of our party finished up copping for an ex-wife of a famous United player. We were undecided as to whether we could do it or not. As you're getting a touch on would the thought of the ex-player put you off? It's not even as if you could say: "He's a really ugly bloke, so that would make it even worse" as that would mean, by implication, that you would find some blokes more sexually attractive than others in an ex-wife decorating-of-cake situation. Many find the thinking of other men whilst you're at it is one to avoid but it must be hard not to with an ex-wife of a player you've watched all over the country. Now you're watching all over the cuntry. It sounds the same but is very different

Size is important…

I woke up the Sunday morning of the Norton United game still proud of my healthy habit of the last three or four times I'd gone out. That of having a donner burger from Taste Masters on Oldham Street. Despite the clear culinary guidelines of not having a food that's been shaven there is no amount of potato peeled meat you cannot eat after a session. The more they pile it in the naan bread, if you're having a kebab, the more you can down it. With a donner burger there is just the right amount stuffed in the muffin. It's a half-the-fat, diet donner as well as it is half the size, therefore it must be 50% reduced fat. I decided to build on my new healthy lifestyle by going for a speedy breakfast at the Metro Café on High Street for my

Sunday, pre-coach at half ten to Norton from Chorlton Street, breakfast. Their 'Manchester breakfast' is a lot bigger, so again, only having a fried Harry Gregg, two pieces of bacon, one sausage, beans, tomatoes and two toasts must be a reduced fat diet as the 'Manchester breakfast' has loads more. The place had a couple of tables of still-pissed Irish men in it. I knew they were over here for the United versus Arsenal game as they had that gaggled, dishevelled, just-one-too-many look that we have when following United on a Euro away.

The place also had a table of about a dozen of what I thought were Italians, who were all dolled up in United gear. The make up of the United fans in here meant that this was not the right time for my survey. My survey to see if there was a divide in Manchester between the unified north and east against the west and south over how they say "Advertisement." Is it "Adver-ties-ment" or "Adver-tiz-ment?" I went up to the 'Italians' and found out they were actually Greeks. As we started talking about United they asked where I was going today, as I began to say we are part of a breakaway club, they immediately interjected that they knew all about FC United of Manchester. A lad who badly wrote his name down in my little notebook for me, I think it's Grigoroudis Asterios, stated that all the Greek lads here were against Glazer. It's just that for them coming to see the team that has meant so much to them on telly was a fantastic treat. I wished them well and again told them to give United 39 years of my love. The irony was not lost though, as again, some Mancunians were leaving Manchester as others came in from far off shores. A couple of fried breakfast burps later and I was at Chorlton Street boarding the coach to the glamour that is Stoke.

For England knows, and England fears, the famous northern gales...

Water is nature's natural moisturiser from inside. If you drink loads and loads it will keep your skin young looking. You get used to drinking eight glasses of water a day apparently and the need to keep pissing all the time fades. Or you've got used to it because you're a diabetic, as thirst is a bi-product of diabetes. I had got on the bus without any water. I was going to be an old looking, diabetic before I got off. You could have sanded down your sideboard with my tongue bringing out the natural grain of the wood. The Ginger Princess reminded me that the other week on that BBC 'Planet' programme narrated by David Attenborough, that they had followed a load of camels around the Gobi desert. They can drink up to 200 litres of water a day. No one has ever commented on camels having lovely looking skin the humpty-backed but nice footed bastards.

Our minds were abroad on sunnier things as we were going down Princess Parkway to get to whatever 'M' that would take us to Stoke-on-Trent. It was that 'The-day-they-crucified-Jesus' weather again as it lashed down. It was appropriate on this occasion, as we passed 30 or 40 Catholics walking down the road behind a lead Catholic bloke in a red and white frock. They were all carrying crosses and big plants. It turns out that the big plants weren't some part of a scheme to freshen up a Catholic office space or anything. The big plants were palms as it was Palm Sunday. We had an on coach Sunday school lesson from Peanut. Palm Sunday was the day Jesus went back on a donkey to Nazareth and they put down palms for him as he came in. It might have been Bethlehem as I was only half listening. I was thinking it would have been nice if he had come in on a camel. They'd have nicked all Jesus' water, though, and he would have to turn the other cheek, as he couldn't be seen to be picking on camels in front of an audience. Him and his Dad eventually getting their own back by turning them into coats and cigs and taking away their freshness of face. The donkeys get the dicks for their good deeds. The attempts to make camels look cunts, though, backfired as everyone likes them for their Tony 'They're just one size above a hoof' Howard sized feet.

I'm against indoctrination. What even for mumps, measles and rubella?...

The less religious of us pointed out the harshness of the sitch. On Sunday they're ripping up plants from the Nazareth/Bethlehem botanical gardens to put under Jesus' bottom ends and the next Friday they've been to B&Q for a bag of nails, a mallet and some half sawn. Peanut then insisted he was crucified at three o'clock. Jesus, not Peanut. Jesus had a three o'clock kick off? It was obvious they had no telly in them days as Murdoch would have got it moved until all the swaddling clothe manufacturing and reed basket making armchair'ers had got home from work and had broken bread for tea. Then he could have saturated them with adver –ties-ments for anti-locust lotion, frog resistant hats and 'grow back your hand ointment' if you've had it cut off for nicking. We argued that they didn't have watches in those days. The bus was devoid of Catholics to see if Peanut's three o'clock kick off protestation was right or whether he was such an evangelical convert to FC United of Manchester'ism that he had developed a speech impediment whereby it was impossible for him to complete a sentence without saying the words "three o'clock" in it. His new religion would attempt to steal tradition off the previous religions as Christians had stolen Christmas off the Pagans. He'd stolen the custom of three o'clock, a mythical time that only older members of the Manchester United Football Club order can remember. Peanut had read about this 'three o'clock' in old parchment chronicles somewhere and it had captivated him.

No customers, no Prophet...

The coach was either devoid of Catholics or absolutely full of Catholics, who were in so much guilt over not knowing what time Jesus got wall mounted, that they had to deny him three times. FC United of Manchester should start giving priests free season tickets as United used to do to recruit. And Imams. And Jehovah's Witnesses but that's only so Alison Watt, FC United of Manchester's 'Give blood' NHS zealot, can mither them to become blood donors. I think she'd win as she could talk Gerald Sinstadt back into a picture-house during a fire. If I were a Jehovah's Witness I'd get a hit man on her as she could ruin your religion. You'd be giving blood before you could say: "Oh, watch me collapsed vein." Scott, my next-door neighbour, is a railway worker. I always like that a United season ticket holder, who gave it up in the 'No customers, no profit' protest, should be a railway worker. And a Soul DJ. It is proper, appropriate FC United of Manchester bloodline back to 1878. Scott knew that England didn't have standardised times till the Victorian era. It was the railways that standardised them, as Manchester time in those days was 20 minutes in front of London. Of course, the cockneys will tell you that they were 20 minutes in front of us.

For those guilty religious types amongst you who don't know what time Jesus got aerated, we found out over the day, that apparently, there was an earthquake three hours into Jesus' crucifixion. That's why there is always a mass at three o'clock on Good Friday. Earthquakes at the time of something momentous happening? Mythical religious tripe presented as fact. Unfortunately it's a possibility. There were earthquakes in Manchester when they were building that stadium on the bones of Johnson Wireworks. The epicentre was east central Manchester. They moved bodies buried in Phillips Park cemetery to accommodate the infrastructure around it. My brother and sister are buried in Phillips Park cemetery. It was the earth of east central Manchester fighting back against the contamination that was being put on top of it. Mother Earth knew the shame that was being inflicted on her and she tried to warn us. Dick Leese, the Huddersfield-blue leader of Manchester council at the time, ignored her and carried on. He comes from a town where the locals sing "Hudders, Hudders, Hudders" at the game.

Ear-ly to bed, ear-ly to rise, keeps the ears out of your eyes...

Gorton earless...

When we arrived in Stoke none of us could be sure whether time had been standardised here. We knew, though, that an earthquake might tidy it up a bit. In Gorton our Ben had a mate whose ear was bitten off in a tussle. His nickname was 'Lobey-one-kanoby' He has got another mate, also from Gorton, called 'Eighteen months'. He had also lost part of an ear in a fight. He was called 'Eighteen months' because it is an ear and a half. An old Red mate of ours from Clayton lost part of his ear in a fight outside The Vic on Grey Mare Lane. Next day when he woke up, he deduced that the biter would not have swallowed his ear. So he went to look for it on the car park of The Vic. He found it. He went into the pub and asked the Landlord for some tomato sauce as he was going to eat it on a muffin. From the evidence presented here it looks as if statistically, you are more likely to lose part of an ear in east central Manchester than most places. On the evidence presented before us today in Stoke, ears are too precious as they are the treasured recipients of many a gold looped earring. That's about as girly as they get, though, as every single one of them are fucking enormous.

Portly Vale...

We got a text from a mate saying 'Is Stoke in England?' When first read that might read as if it was a little Englander saying that Stoke are so backward that they can't possibly be in England. Not so. That text was just recognition that every over sized person in Stoke wears something with an England motif on it. On hats, coats, shirts, badges, flags, tattoos and pub signs. A woman went past wearing an England shirt without a coat. It was snowing. That was bad enough but she had a Rottweiler with her. It also had an England shirt on. We never got close enough to inspect whether it had a tattoo of a bulldog on its hind leg. We had been assured that The Jolly Carter pub we went in was the friendliest around. When we got in Tim from J Stand was in there with all his mates. Tim is another home and away auldy like us. He's not seen a United game this season. This is from a lad who never missed. He had also been told it was the best pub around.

Either the pubs around here are shite or The Jolly Carter has a really good public relations department selling it to us all. It was nice to be together, though, to witness it all, and have it all confirmed. The toilets told you everything you need to know. The women's had 'Ladies' written on it and the blokes just had 'Mens'. As with all things in Stoke, time went very slowly. It was almost a pleasure to get out in the driving wet and snow to get to the game. Usually a game can get in the way of a good session. Not in Stoke. We had arranged with everyone on the coach for it to comeback to The Jolly Carter after the game to watch United versus Arsenal. Oops.

Espesh nesh...

This was the first time since the summer of 2005 that I had come to the match without a jumper on. It was snowing. Sunderland versus Fulham had been called off the day before but that happens in August up there. We'd come further down south for a warm and were getting freeze-dried. Without the dry bit. There's a poor song that calls the wind Mariah. Around here the wind was calling us. It was calling us 'Puff'. Phil Melville was in net. They should call Burslem, where Port Vale are from, Melville as Phil could be the town dwarf. Phil was stood there in the driving snow. Everything was white. The area we were in struck me as an area that liked it like that. If a pitch invader had run on the pitch he would almost certainly have stuck two pieces of coal for his eyes and a carrot for his nose on Phil, and got a laugh instead of a boo for pitch invading. No they shouldn't call it Melville, they should call it Neshville, Elevenessee. I know it was just a one off day where it was just pretending to be Barra but it was still bad.

I hate Pink Floyd...

The side Stand had 'PVFC' written out in seats. It would have been more pleasing for the local STI clinic for it to have 'HPVFC' on them. There's a warts and all joke in there if you look for it. It was fitting that the '100 Club' that the Sex Pistols had played so early in their career, should have a Sex Pistols' song being sung as we joined the 100 club getting our 100th goal of the season. To the tune of 'Anarchy in the UK' it went:

> I am an FC fan, I am a Mancunian,
> I know what I want and I know where to get it,
> I want to destroy, Glazer and Sky,
> Coz I want to be, at FC.

When you are young you laughed at your Mam and Dad singing old songs sincerely and thought that the songs you were buying now would not have such a fate. Me and Karen Rafter sneaked up and put The Pistols 'God save the Queen' on at the street party on Bosworth Street at the time of the Queen's Silver Jubilee in 1977. Our songs were there to cause lumber, not to translate to later times. Yet here we were now at the back of the stand at half time. All the old folk were reliving their youth and singing the new song to the 'Anarchy in the UK' tune. The majority were kalide and had that real 'We mean this' face on that you used to see on your Mam and Dad. I swear as they danced about I saw one or two pogo. Oh dear. Most of the FC United of Manchester youth looked on embarrassed at the drunken antics of the elderly. Circles. Round in.

The 100th competitive goal was scored by Josh Howard. Phil Melville, distracted by the snow reminding him of Christmas dinners, let the ball go underneath him for a Norton equaliser. But an own goal and one from Torpey saw us win the game 1-3. The attendance of 1,284 was no more than passable. We discussed why things had gone a bit quiet over the last month: We discussed that a mix of postponed matches combined with today's atrocious weather, knowing we were going to win the league, the knowledge that you could pick and choose at the last minute to go which is usually fantastic for the last minute-bring-a-mate sitch but can go against you, the two o'clock enforced kick off when United were playing Arsenal at four on the telly, those who had wanted to come for a nosey had mostly been for a nosey now, those that had come in big groups, say for the games at Stockport County and Blackpool, were probably saving the next visit for our next big one, which is our last home game when we hopefully should be presented with the trophy, all added to the lower crowd.

There's a figure that's saying more than 20,000 different people have been to see FC United of Manchester this season. A fair chunk of those are going to comeback occasionally and happily. Also having said that there was, as always, more than that there and the atmosphere was described by one Red as the best he had been at all season, especially in the second half. And that statement has some competition. Margy calls it the "90-90-90" crowd when 90% of the Reds sing for 90% of the 90 minutes. But look at me. I'll have to step back as I did when observing our Norwegian visitor, Pebble, when I said he came over to see a NWCL Division Two game. All these Reds had travelled to see a NWCL Division Two game. I should be celebrating not moaning. I should know that as Pebble was there again singing his Stoke sized Norwegian head off. I said right back at the third away game at Victoria Stadium against Ashton Town that we will have to get used to crowds fluctuating. If this is fluctuation then we are doing alright. What we can't get used to is the roughness of the pubs in Burslem.

The fucking hell shaped room…

Lay the blanket in the ground…

We left a few minutes before the end. There was a woman in front of me who had wrapped herself in a tartan blanket. I had to go as I was very close to asking her if I could have a borrow. Or a lend. I always get mixed up which it is. It's the same with 'affect' and 'effect,' 'The Detroit Emeralds' and 'The Detroit Spinners' 'Top Yates's' and 'Bottom Yates's' 'Newton Street' and 'Lever Street' and 'I dream of Genie' and 'Bewitched'.
We shut the door after we had left to keep the George Raft off the crowds who had remained. I can't remember seeing that at a ground. Usually you just have a walkway you go through. Port Vale have closing doors at the back of the stand that close and keep the heat in the concourse to keep you warm at half time. The warmth, though, only encourages older folk to dance about singing so perhaps if we ever comeback here we should keep them open. We made our way back to The Jolly Carter sucking lemons to keep the smiles off our faces as we were so happy at the prospect of going in there.

If it was possible The Jolly Carter had got rougher over the two hours we had been away. They had brought a roulette wheel into the corner and these bears, pretending they were human, were playing. There was not a fucking chance I was getting my notebook out as they would think I was C.I.D. The pub had a fixation with John Wayne pictures. If just one of these bears had taken a turn against us it would have to be like the Wild West. If we'd sellotaped about four or five of our lot together it would have only made one of them. Talkative Chris, one of our lot, had gone to the bar. To order a lemonade. We've seen these films where a stranger walks in and they order sarsparilla in those cowboy saloons. Pianos stopping, people leaving by those half doors, Landlords taking mirrors down from behind the bar. Talkative Chris was also sporting a black eye from a second prize he had received in an altercation on the Friday night. It involved a uni-cycle. We thought it was a knocking bet that as soon as he ordered his lemonade – he was driving – then the Landlord would ring his bell and announce to the pub: " We've got a right Mary Helen here ordering a woofter's drink. He's also got make up on one of his eyes like that Phil Oakeykadokily from the Human League. Gerrim."

It was at this point I considered it an option that we should make an orderly exit. Simonella then informs us that one of the pubs nearby, that he had just been in, had a large swastika engraved in the wall as a sort of pub feature. The pub we were in was the best pub. Talkative Chris lived and got his lemonade. In fact all the bears around us kept calling each other, and us, "duck." They were friendlier than they looked. They were just that big you had to step back to get them in focus. There was a mutually assured destruction issue going on between them all so they might never fight. We clumped together at the back of the pub near the beer garden and relaxed. The beer garden was just a backyard with a couple of broken Magners bottles littering it.

Beer and birds wahey…

And a model hawk on an extractor fan outlet. We discussed: "What did we feel?" watching United versus Arsenal on the telly. A number of feelings were expressed. Whether my attention had been elsewhere concentrating on the prospects of living for the last ten minutes I don't know, but my only way of telling how I felt was that I'd never really been a telly watcher of United so I had no real experience of it. If I was forced to make a statement today then it would have to be that, if before I was a floodlight, and a proper stand alone high one, stuck in a corner as part of a set of four and not one of those European-football-night-friendly, roof mounted ones, then today I was only a 22 Watt bulb in a table lamp. It's on a table. There's no lampshade. It can still have radiance in a darkened room. It would just be mellower. And clarity would be lost where the corners of the carpet met the skirting boards because it was further away from the reducing, but refusing to die, light. Objects that were once easier to see were now getting harder to ascertain in the dusky twilight.

A 'roar-titty-roar' coal fire has to start with a single Swan Vesta. A pilot light is still a pilot light that can flicker up and burn to greater extents when called upon. We'd come second behind Liverpool in 1987/88 and I don't remember it being a cause for extensive celebrations. The Champions League has warped our perspectives. Look at Managers now described as 'genius' for getting their team to come fourth. Look at the old league tables. You come fourth and you got fuck all. Fittingly so. Coming second is not coming first. It's better than coming third but all things are comparative. Besides those that aren't. Tim from J Stand and the rest of the lads we had met when we first came in the pub, went wild as Rooney's goal went in and wilder when JS Park nudged in the second. I was made up for them. They're good lads. I was freezing, in a bad pub and watching United in circumstances I'm not used to. My opinion of what I felt had been distorted, so consequently it did not feel valid. I was more worried that we had been phoned by Billy and Caroline Brayshaw to meet them and we'd missed each other. We only have two games till the end of season to do our assessment of Caroline's arse. And to see the dinghy again.

Happy slopping...

The coach journey back to town saw us dropped off outside the Crown and Kettle on Great Ancoats Street. On the journey I had enjoyed my first piss backwards on a coach. When you go in the toilets on a coach they always tell men to sit down and lag. Not with all that piss-on-seat you're not. However, if you turn around and lean your back on the sticky-out wall above the toilet you can piss below you into the bowl. It was very comfortable and far sturdier to stop you getting rolled about by the movement of the coach. I shall do it again. You might all do it. No one is to know. The male world is secretively divided into blokes who aim their piss to knock off dried shit on the side of the bowl and those that don't. What it is hopefully not divided into is the new habit that I was informed of before going into The Crown and Kettle. Young lads are going into a toilet and chiselling one out into their hand. Then they are 'Happy Slapping'ly' filming it as they slap it on someone's head. It's called 'Sea gulling'. That's not good.

When we went in the pub we all piled into the back little snug. There was a couple there who had been to see United. We could tell because they had their programmes on the table. Friendly as friendly is, we started chatting. They were fucking despicable snots. She was an Arsenal fan and he was a rich bastard who, in his words: " Came down from London to see Man U once or twice a season for the last few years." He had slip-on biker boots. And car keys. There is a telly advert for a company called 'Picture Loans' where the fat faced get of an actor says: " Those people at Picture Loans are great.It's really easy to talk to those people at Picture. You can actually have an adult conversation." And his wife, who he is talking to says: "About football?" He then proceeds, as he has done once or twice before in the advert, to thrust the ball he is carrying right into the lens of the video camera she is filming him with. We are somehow meant to have an advertising affinity with that horrible act of pretend aggression. Not only that, he has just agreed a £25.000 loan with 'Picture Loans' over the phone without really knowing how much they wanted to borrow as a couple, as he had to confirm it with his wife mid conversation with the loan company. He agrees the pay back rates without discussing it with her as: "Yes, we have a mortgage." If I could describe the two despicable snots who were in The Crown and Kettle as we arrived, then they would be the type of unknowing fools who think adverts like that are acceptable. Throwing a ball into the face of someone you love is meant to be tolerable, almost funny, within an affair. Not in our fucking home it isn't.

The 22 Watt light bulb made a dignified exit. The floodlight raged on. This was not television, neither an advert or a televised match that required an un-valid comment. I'll defend my United from destroyers like these. They knew absolutely fuck all about Glazer and the gentrification within football and just didn't give a fuck. And were cocky about not giving a fuck. Manchester United Football Club was there to entertain his Arsenal girlfriend. Compare this to the child innocence and spilling out bliss within the faces of the Greek lads I had met in The Metro Café only ten hours earlier. They loved the pleasure of the visit but they also had the love of football to hate the Glazers for what they had done, turning us from a club with no debt into the most debt laden 'franchise' in the world. This time last year the arguments would have rose to crack the plaster in the ceiling with these two snot galloots. They were candidates for a happy slopping if anyone could be bothered to waste their jizz on them. This year, I balance it with feeling it is my duty to defend the honour of FC United of Manchester for our roll within the resistance, and at the same time hoping/knowing that the Reds who stayed can fight these buffoons. We can give puss like this the hard time they deserve. Reds who stayed can put these fuckers back to where they came from. They'll die with their supposedly London fashion slip-on biker boots on.

Disco Texts and the Textelettes...

I got a text next the morning after the game. It told me to pass it on. If you eventually got a Chinese whispered text passed down to you and it said: 'He should pin the intrigue on Saint Pens' day. Gas a swan' then it was meant to say: 'We could win the league this Wednesday. Pass it on.'

CHAPTER TWENTY ONE

ANAT, ANAPPLE AND ANAMMER...

Chadderton FC versus FC United of Manchester. Played on Wednesday the 19th of April 2006. Kick off 7.45pm. Played at Boundary Park, Oldham Athletic's ground. Again. They're getting 'Accrington Stanley'ish' in their frequency in our lives. In Oldham they drink Mantunna tea leaf tea, with four sugars, in a white pint pot mug that has dark blue hoops on it. I've also included bits of the Chadderton home game just before this one, and the last home game against Great Harwood that came just after it. It's near the end of the book now. I'm just going wild.

With this ring I promise I'll always love you, always love you...

Chadderton FC do exist. The home game with them had been postponed more times than blood has been mopped from the walls of The Amber Club on Oldham Road. The away game had also been postponed from Saturday March the 5th 2006. Now we've played them twice in a week. The Chinese-whispered-text- message after the Norton United game, saying that we could win the league the following Wednesday, proved incorrect. When we played Chadderton FC at home the week before, we had only gained promotion. We were not playing a league match on the Saturday between these two Chadderton games. We had now become winners by virtue of other sides dropping points whilst we weren't playing. So that's it. We're winners of the NWCL division two 2005/2006 season. The bottom step of the pyramid that we were trying to knock the ball off the top of, so it would fall our way, had been surmounted. It's still a fucking long way if you look up, but you'd definitely graze your knees if you fell down from where we were now. We could celebrate in a 'Take drugs-have sex-wear-a-bath-towel, debauched late-nighter at Dwight's house, probably with a '70's porn track funking away in the background', way.

Fallowfieldaraki...

In the last ten minutes of the Chadderton home game I had left the PA box and gone and stood amidst strangers in the Main Stand. With rushing around before and during the game, it all wasn't going in. For those last ten minutes I sang "And the Busby babes carry on" with the rest of the Main Stand. Some Reds wish that they could go forward to the day when fanny whistles have been invented, as they are not as impractical as they first sound, Some Reds wish that they could go back to The Club Tropicana, as the drinks were so competitively priced. I wish that I could go back in The Mancunian pub in Hulme, a few bus stops down from Old Trafford, on those past Friday afternoons. There was an old bloke who was in there every Friday. He used to go up to the jukebox every week and put on the same song that went 'Does my ring hurt your finger?' Get it eased. Not too much, though, as you don't want it coming off, so that you get that funny look off the triage nurse in Accident and Emergency as you attempt to get it extracted. Outside of the fanny whistles option, those other two things might never happen as The Mancunian has called last orders and the 'All that's missing is the sea' issue with The Club Tropicana finally got too problematic, as we all knew it would. There appears to many that there is no way of going back. Fast, fast, fast, forward, forward, forward, forward, fast, forward then.

The night against Chadderton at home, when we had achieved promotion, was in the middle of going back and going forward. So, so much to peer back on, so, so much to giraffe neck to. The Lovetones' 'Until I repossess the key to my happiness, I'll go on' was the beating rhythm in my box, explaining the rows within 'Should I stay or should I go now?'ism. The night was special. It wasn't '26 year wait' wild. It wasn't Barcelona 'Kill me now' knocky. No one could ever want it to be any other way. Though it was definitely as exciting as when you got a balloon on a stick from the Rag and Bone man. You knew you shouldn't have it as you were sure that there had been some breach of the 'A fair exchange is no robbery' rule, as you knew that your Mam and Dad's new radiogram you had just swapped it for, was probably not a fair trade. You'd get your crack later when they came back and found out, but for now that balloon didn't half waggle on the top of the stick.

The balloon on the stick was still being waggled at the Chadderton away game tonight. We all met in The Clayton Arms by the side of Boundary Park. We knew we'd meet those we hadn't met in the pub, under the Kezzy kestrel in the Main Stand. Only two games at Boundary Park and already we were institutionalised. I know the last away of this season against Padiham was to also be played at Boundary Park. I'm almost certain we'll do the same. You can only have so much newness in a season. Within all that newness it is excusable to find a tidgey pattern. We can hargly be accused of stultifying within our FC United of Manchester first season.

United's Utilities...

We stultifyingly met under Kezzy kestrel. Adam Brown insisted it was a sparrow hawk, proving clever people aren't that clever. If he was really clever, and knew it was a sparrow hawk, then he would have said nothing, as he would have been clever enough to see the lack of admiration that was going to come his way for knowing that it was a sparrow hawk. You hardly see any sparrows anymore for sparrow hawks to hawk. The last flock of sparrows I saw was road-working down the side of Ted's toilet the morning after we'd passed a night, whilst drinking too much beer, admiring the honesty in the carpet in Bookbinders night club. The word 'Bookbinders' is woven into the pattern of the nightclub's carpet just to keep reminding you that you are there and that are you sure you want to be? Apparently, outside of Ted's toilet facilities, sparrows are becoming extinct. They're becoming extinct because they won't travel far from where they were born. As their environment changes they would rather sit there wormless and starve rather than move. Do not go to them; let them come to you, just like I do, just like I do. I like that level of laziness. Tonight Kezzy looked like a surveillance camera, the sparrow murdering get, as it kept gently spinning around looking at us. We could see the television screens in the police place across the ground. Kezzy was a midnight mass, the grassing, birdy bastard. We didn't sing him any songs.

Gassius clay...

We were probably too disturbed to sing as we were seeing our centre forward, Joz Mitten, at centre half. He had played there in a friendly against Jimmy Clitheroe FC last Saturday. I'm unsure of its positional wiseness. It's frustrating, as Reds don't want him to become some Chris-Sutton-dressed-as-lamb, back-to-front, front-to-back, utility player. We'll C. Said the blind texter. Young Mike O'Neill also got a game, he's another lad who came through the Open Trials we held on the park for players in Fallowfield in July 2005. He scored as well. It was odd to see a young child you'd seen around United games at Old Trafford who smelt of Napisan tablets, grow into a young bloke who you were now watching on a pitch. We didn't know whether to cheer him or buy him a fort with lead soldiers to play with. We went from the youngest, Farley's Rusk'er on the pitch, to the antiquarian undead, as Daz Lyons passed to Phil Power. The combined age in that 'embalming' fluid move was worthy of Grade One Listed Status. Unfortunately for those two, it was a night of mixed emotions. The bandages they had unravelled themselves from, and left at the crypt at Manchester Museum where they both live, had been stolen. That bloke who you see on telly from Manchester University, who reconstructs faces out of clay on the skeletal skulls of the long dead, usually watches their bandages for them whilst they're playing. He was busy on a surprise for those two, though, as the two clay heads he had constructed for them, and they had been playing in all season, were wearing out. He was making them two new ones as a promotion present.

The match finished 2-3 to us. It was the first mass outing of the 'Sit down for the champions' song when everyone sits down. Then stands up again. I thought that very tired song could not be made funny. I was proven wrong yet again. Inventing the refreshing; re-inventing those in need of refreshing. Very FC United of Manchester. Swarms of youngsters run behind the net when we score, free of stewarding, free to arse. Grown men going: "She doesn't frighten me when I've had a drink" are staying out for just one more livener. We had something to drink about. We were winners of the NWCL division two. We weren't champions of the league as that would have to wait until, or if, we ever win the NWCL division one. Then we'd be proper champions. That might appear to be pedantic. It's not. Consider the 'laughing at' that city and Newcastle received for their self-back-patting immodesty as they came up from the lower leagues with their champions' flags. Not so pedantic now.

This beautiful creature must Sky…

Scarily, we're not the 'Granny-in-a-home-whose-a-hundred-and-can-remember-powdered-egg' story that fills in the news when there is no other news, but then gets dropped if a penguin falls over and can't get up. We can last all day now within the news items as a worthy piece both on local and on Sky Sports news. Simon Mullock, The Sunday Mirror journalist who first broke the breakaway club story, had just done a very positive piece again within the Sunday Mirror the weekend before the Chadderton away game. Henry Winter and many others in the broadsheets have been consistently supportive. Jim White, one of the Telegraph's leading sportswriters and a longstanding UWS contributor, was never going to be anything but understanding. Stuart Brennan from the Manchester Evening News has been exemplary. Buy him a beer if you see him in The Waterloo. Fuck it, buy him two, he was there when we needed him and continues to be so. We can get an aura of 'Very FC United of Manchester' about us. It will only last, though, if we become little Margy's. When Chadderton had a player unjustly sent off against us at Boundary Park, hardly anyone noticed Margy's response. The lad, Ricky Wilde, was playing in possibly his biggest game and now had to leave it. As he went past FC United of Manchester's bench, he was greeted with a handshake and a pat on the back from Margy. An understated winner, who gets it right. Naturally where possible, working at it where not, to make it possible.

Charlie sez "I wish, I wish, I wish I didn't keep losing me birds." Actually that was 'Meet-Mike-he–swims-like-a-fish'. No it wasn't, it was his jealous mate who couldn't swim...

As the 2,350-plus Reds, of the 2,352 in attendance, left the ground I bumped into Charlie Mitten, Joz Mitten's Dad. You don't have to be a genius to realise that Charlie is called Charlie after his Uncle who played so skilfully for United in the 1940s and '50s. I asked him what he thought about Joz's switch to defence. He liked it. He told me that Margy had approached Joz and asked him to consider it. Charlie thought it was a great idea. He told me outside the ground, with fatherly pride, that Joz has got a great touch and when he gets the ball he distributes it so well. He reckoned that not all of the present squad could make it at a higher level but it will become easier for Joz. By Joz reverting to the back four, Charlie said: "It would add ten years to his career. He wouldn't have to work his two danglers off chasing the two or three chances that come along in a game like Van Nistlerooy does." He then finished off by saying "I don't know if you've noticed but our Joz is not the fastest lad in the world." I feigned shock as if I, or every single other FC United of Manchester fan with eyes, and even those without, hadn't noticed. He's a dedicated Dad.

Linda Bellingham's biff in 'Confessions of a taxi driver' was an untrimmed Smithfield shelf like the clematis growing up the side of the concrete wall on Piccadilly approach...

Reading the programme after the game in The Clayton Arms pub we found out that David Platt and Mark Owen from Take That had played for Chadderton. That reads wrong. David Platt has never been in Take That. We also found out that a chiropodist called P.E.Hartley, advertises with the slogan 'Put defeet in my hands' and that Chadderton have 46 members. 'Members' is a dual meaning word. Two pound well spent again. We supped up and left but not before seeing Steve Torpey, our forward with the haircut belonging to the lead singing bloke from that band who sang 'Ballroom blitz', getting in a car with the registration 'S7ORPY'. We must be ever vigilant. I got home and did as I always do after a midweek game that's involved a pint. We need some constants in this season of change. Knowing to meet under Kezzy kestrel signifies that. I got home and I tried to count the amount of little lumps on Kirsty Wark's left cheek. It's not a detriment to her fitness. On the contrary, her little flaws make her more accessible to us Joeys. Most Reds think she has four little lumps but they are mistaken. It is not their fault as it is midweek, they have been concentrating on the new players at FC United of Manchester and they have had a pint. Also the lighting in the BBC studio tries to soft focus her, making it very difficult to count, clouding her face as if you are viewing it through Charles Clarke's sticky out red ears.

I believe Kirsty has five little lumps on her left cheek. Two are very close together, thereby mugging you that there are four. If you dot-to-dotted them it makes the shape of a sparrow wearing a 'Hasta la siempre victoria' T-shirt. She has the whitest legs and greasiest hair on telly and yet still finds time for an automatic unity with the oppressed. Pay no regard to the comment that "You just know she's got an 'Empty Rancheros bag full of Swarfega' for a mather." Mousey coloured muff or not, you'd love to put your finger on her ladies' large papercut. In a Linda and Kirsty appreciative mood, I wafted off to sleep for the first time as a vicarious winner of a NWCL division two trophy. Submarines send out echograms to the bottom of the uncharted oceans not knowing what is going to comeback. The sent out echoes return back to them, telling of the depths they have fallen to, the depths they could safely fall to, what outcropping side bursters they mustn't bump into and the safest flow to follow. Slowly, the uncharted all finishes up charted. We're surfacing with a torn off, corner piece of an oceanographic map. The deepest depth was the May of 2005. I could now smell fish. We score shoals galore, we score shoals. That means that somewhere above us, but within our little proximity, was life giving sunlight and the shallowing of the crushing weight that had been on us for 11 long months. There was no lack of profundity in our depth.

Buck up for Benidorm...

I once got invited to a 'nibbles' party in Chorlton. Don't think ill of me. Go on then. Outside the house someone had painted graffiti on the garden wall. It read 'I love books'. They want a wetting in epoxy resin and gluing to the outside of the Beetham Tower. Not on the top floor, but on the bottom, so that passers-by can irritate the 'I love bookers' bare wrists by brushing them with loft insulation or by pushing prams into their legs or making them put the tips of their fingers on both hands together, and to keep pressing, until it feels like there is a piece of glass between them. It's always rewarding to at first go "Oh it feels like there is a piece of glass between my fingertips" but if we make them keep doing it for hours the reward will soon wear and really get on their nerves. The word 'love', in the 'I love books' graffiti, had been replaced with a heart shape. You see we are not being so cruel after all. Expressing your love of books has got to be a nice thing to do. Expressing your love of something by painting it on a wall shows that you care. Unfortunately, combining the two and expressing your love of books in such a wally-painty wall way deserves death by insertion of a lorry load of liver up your shitter. This would be achieved by using the bottom end of a cut glass decanter to knock all the liver in down the funnel. The death sentence would be administered after they've been unglued from the side of the building, obviously. You can express your love for your football club on a wall or a banner and not meet a grizzly livered end but not books. As that's just a bit too twatty.

The Tannoy tea party...

You can also express your love for the Redness within us by having a party. So, those involved with the FC United of Manchester Tannoy over the season, did. We chose the final home game against Great Harwood to party in the face of the visiting imperialists. Not a nibbles eating party of course. You can bring a multitude of painted banners. If you'd painted something on a wall and wanted to cut it out and bring that, then you could. No one did. We brought tater hash from Westwell's bakery from the east. And vanillas from Slattery's just up the road from Gigg Lane. And der ders. And something to drink. And red, white and black balloons, except there were no black ones as they were very hard to find in celebratory balloon packs, as black mustn't be considered a jolly colour. We got three songs for half time that would give the Tannoy tea party's answer to the 'Is FC United of Manchester a soul or a punk club?' question. We had 'Let me down easy' by Betty Lavette, 'That's when the tears start' by The Velvelettes and 'Good bye cruel love' by Linda Griner to soul your soul away for the summer. A brass band ruined all that, though, as they 'oomparparred' a medley of approximate terrace tunes. Someone said:

"You can't beat a bit of brass." We also refused to let a Margy texted joke about 'Chelsea, viagra and not getting past a semi' get in the way of our celebrations. If it was possible to drink Dubonet whilst viewing a football match, then we would have drunk Dubonet.

Our reception desk. All tables polished...

All season the team has been brought out to the words "Sisters, brothers, Red, White and Black, open your soulful souls and welcome onto the pitch FC United of Manchester." For the last game of the season, when apparently for the first time the crowd could hear me, the NWCL division two winners were brought on with "Oh, here they are" after they had mugged me into two false announcements of their arrival. The crowd of 6,023 wished we had boarded the tunnel up as they played terrible and were beaten 0-1. It didn't matter really. It would have been nice to score a few goals, as the goon token we were spending today surely would have resulted in extensive conga'ing and large-cardboard-packing-boxes-full of japery pokery. We're all allowed at least one goon token to spend in a season. And we were spending. Margy's Auntie Pam was there. She had taken Margy to his first game at Old Trafford. It was the 1978 game where Buchan scored that 30 yarder against Everton. Margy missed the goal as Pam had taken him out early and he was by White City waiting for a bus when it went in. The football today would have made her want to leave early again. The spectacle and emotion would make her want to stay. Coincidentally, that Everton game was also Phil Power's first game at United.

Your face has been taken out of the start of the day for me...

There was a short open top bus ride to The Swan and Cemetery pub. Amongst all the fine flags that were draped over the side of the bus there was a big, scruffy, red, white and black flag with ripped edges. It went from the top of the bus to the bottom. Even though it was tied at the top with plenty falling onto the bus's seats, it still dragged on the floor. The bus could not start until the bottom part of it was removed from underneath the wheels. It wasn't symmetrical shaped like all the others. It was imperfect. It knew it was. Its absolute was near. It had 'Caring' written on it. The bus eventually pushed its way through the Red filled roads and arrived at the pub. All the flags were stripped off and given back to their owners. The big scruffy flag remained up there till the end. I heard someone from the crowd below go "Look at the state of that, leave it there." They didn't know. The big, scruffy red, white and black, mis-shaped flag held itself, looking down patiently. Its spirit and gentleness represented. It will wait and wait and never tire. We may. It won't. Its place was assured. It contains within in it an envoy heralding the droplet-wet eyelashes that have closed together, touched and then released those many splashes. Its heard the lost passages passing through the holed insides of those present. Known or unknowing. Too upset to set. As yet unrecognised by some. Recognised and adored by others. Follows mercy tied. It was gathered up by those who loved it, and it went for a drink with them as it had done before.

I see your toecaps shining and the razors in your crombie lining...

Margy was in the pub. He was asked to sing. He got a hush and then broke into "I sell asparagus." Pebble, the Norwegian, had an enormous Cuban cigar to give him. I told him I would go up to Margy with him, as a Scandinavian giving someone something so phallic shaped to suck on needed authentication that it was harmless and had not been previously used in a sexual act, or it would be binned. You know what Scandinavians are like. Apparently Voxra, the Scandinavian female I had met but couldn't remember from our July the 5th 2005 birth date, wears a long leather coat. And fuck all else underneath. Rumour or not I'm keeping that one. We're a community club and that is definitely good for the community. They call him the kit man George got Lucinda and Joanna, Russ Delaney's daughters, onto a pub table to speak, They managed "This means so much" before crying and getting back down. Thanks girls for being there. Russell's Mam and brother Pat were also there along with Susan, the Mam of Russ' daughters. The bendy 135 Ch'Hill buses passed and tooted their horns and "For one two seven years, we've fought you and your peers" singily floated its way back to Old Trafford. Where, weirdly, Chelsea and Liverpool were playing a semi-final. Glazer had a stroke the next day.

There was a little downside to the day though. A fine Red mate went to the players' reception do afterwards. He reported: "That knob from the board who has been consistently unsussed all season, got pissed and threw a glass at a bouncer." Remember your one member, one vote if you want to save the aura of 'Very FC United of Manchester' about us. It will only last if we become little Margys. We remain vigilant to protect our FC United of Manchester own against such behaviour from board or fans. We are not innocent hippies, who can be had over. We know the disingenuous. Let me assure you that knobs will be isolated. Fan ownership, combined with the unshiftable footballing belief that beauty will always remain to see its hopes cleared, will make sure it remains so.

And all the times I closed the door to keep my love within…

All wars are meant to be over by Christmas. They never are. Ours will carry on. If there are any FC United of Manchester druids they are bound to have said it will all be over by the summer solstice. We've got our war economy working. We've got our hat that used to be nailed on but now just provides voluntary protection from the weather. We've got our apple for all the goodness of the footballing fruit and veg Margy has served up for us and we have got our hammer. It's a claw hammer that we've used the claw part to pinch off our nailed on hats. The other part of the hammer we've more traditionally used for nailing the hats of those who would nail ours. We can do it together. At one time we didn't know if we could. Now we almost certainly do. When female friends are driving me around they unfortunately do the same thing. There is absolute goodness in their generosity to drive me around. However, they consistently go over hump-backed bridges too fast for males. When males are driven over hump-backed bridges too fast their tripes drop. It's been a loving-but-sometimes-forgetful-female-driving-you-over-a-humped-back-bridge-too-fast season. Accelerations and survivable discomforts, all palletised and strapped on a solid casing that wants to do nothing but look after you and stop your feet getting cold and damp.

Sea section…

In Jason and the Argonauts, Jason gets the golden fleece. As he is scooting off back to the ship he is confronted by the king of the island he is nicking the fleece from. The king stands in front of Jason and his two mates and says: "There is no escape from The Children of the Hydra's Teeth." For a second Jason and us, the captive TV audience, are frightened to fuck of what 'The Children of Hydra's Teeth' are. The wait and the, as yet uncloaked tension, was scarier than the events. 'The Children of the Hydra's Teeth' are just a load of boney skellingtons. Their 'no escape' reputation was built on otter-bollocks-fear induced by not knowing what the unknown was. There was an escape from 'The Children of the Hydra's Teeth' because they were taken on by those brave enough to go on an epic search. We might have been forced into existence, as we were involuntarily cut across our womb by a violator, but a Mancunian infant came out. It's been a cocky little get at times. We were partly unafraid on our FC United of Manchester journey because spookyspookster ghosts might exist, but no one yet has ever heard of one haunting a caravan.

Since the first pre-season, the first away game and the first home game against Padiham, in the July and August of 2005, we have seen our ringered motorised home taken at speed down the sometimes fat, sometimes thin, sometimes humpy-bumpy road. It is about to nerner its hooter at the last away game against Padiham in the April of 2006. Time has whipped by. That bloke who sang: "I think I'm turning Japanese, I think I'm turning Japanese, I really think so" is probably Japanese now. Shaun Ryder now sings: " Son, you're 30." It has been a voyage in search of something healing. Jason's golden fleece had the power to heal. That's nice if you've a whitlow or if you've slept on your ear funny and it feels swollen. Its finest treasure, though, was its ability to reclaim life. We've only got slung-up-and-down-hump-backed-bridged bollocks to mend. The power of what we have stolen from those that would try to keep it from us is still much unused. It's not really been touched on. Everyone wants a touch on.

CHAPTER TWENTY TWO

TWO LITTLE DUCKS, 22, QUACK, QUACK xxxx …

Padiham FC versus FC United of Manchester. Saturday the 29th of April 2006. Kick off 3pm. Played at Oldham Athletic's Boundary Park. As it always is. Same as it ever was. Where music and passion were always in fashion. Almost certainly.

Every road I walk along, I've walked along with you, no wonder I am lonely…

It's an established fact that bus drivers and hospital porters have the most heavily tattooed forearms of all the working population. It's also regarded as true that if you walk into a strange pub where you feel the temptation to go: "Landlord, I've got a hairdryer with me here if you want to dry your Alsatian off" or "You've got it really nice in here Landlord, all it's missing is the flypaper" or if you find yourself saying:" No, that's alright thanks, mate, I prefer my ears without anyone else's teeth in them" then this might mean it is possibly a ropey establishment. If you're not too sure about it, then the 'Postie' test will help you decide if it is alright for a glug. The 'Postie' test means that if there is a postal worker in there, in their uniform, then it will be a good pub to have a beer in. The scientific reasoning behind this is that the Postie will have finished work and considers this a good enough place to relax in without getting mithered. It's also meant to be a fact that winters eventually get fed up of working at being cold, go all 'Prestbury A-level student' and have a gap year and let spring have a turn. The winter of 2005/2006 was definitely a poly student from Crumpsall who couldn't afford to stop working. Whose only two academic achievements were to discover that 'refectory' meant canteen and that you could befuddle posher studies by trying to get them to spell 'Crumpsall'. And watching them fail.

While they were down he'd get them to spell 'Blackley'. As they went weak legged and woozy, calling for the ref to stop the bout, he'd finish them off with 'Droylsden'. Do not feel sorry for the victims of this posh student abuse, as their life has been soft. They had been to such posh schools that the school bully was called 'The Admonisher'. They came from such posh homes that their pots were dry-cleaned. They'll bully us when they're higher management, dictating our wage and working patterns. They'll also be the ones laughing over-loudly at certain preordained moments in a Shakespearian production to emphasise that they're accomplished enough to get the joke. Even though they must have read the line many, many times. No comedian is that funny to make you keep re-laughing at the same story. It's falseness for effect. To summarise – the winter of 2005/2006 could never have been given the first name of 'Burny' as it was freezing and went on for pure time. We were considering getting yellow jaundice just to get a bit of colour in our cheeks as it was just refusing to get warmer at games. Until now. One morning on the 29th of April 2006 there appeared a yellowy round thing in the sky. We vaguely remembered seeing pictures of it. The FC United of Manchester circular email informed Reds that they need not be scared. We could come off the Linoleum we were taking for our nerves.

We could all stop hunching and walking the chicken quickstep in a poor attempt at keeping the cold winter off us. We've spent the league winning months doing the 'unattended crumpet scuttle' all around all the diddy grounds of the north west. Crumpets spend a fortnight under the grill and don't change colour. Until they cinder within a second. Even though you know they are going to cinder, you get so fed up of watching them not change colour that you leave them there, and go off and put your Mintolas and Fry's Five Centre in the fridge before going off and seeing if you know anyone who knew how many Kumar Brothers there were. Sigourney Weaver in 'Aliens' was lost in space for 57 years before she was found. She had the same knickers on for all that time. Impressive. Sigourney's 57-year damp to crispy knickers makes you remember the unattended crumpets.

Walk this way…

The scuttle back to the grill from the room you've wandered off to ensues. The layout of furniture impedes any real build up of momentum to get to the unaccompanied crumpets. This doesn't stop you adopting the comedy quick-leg so that you can comedy quick-leg around corners that have to be turned or around LPs that have been left in the way. And all this whilst knowing that at the end of your short, quick-legging journey you have to avoid building up too much pace so that you don't crash into the stove. We have spent the majority of the last season moving at 'Unattended crumpet scuttle' speed. We've been comedy quick-legging from coach to pub, pub to car, car to pub, pub to train due to this cold winter. It's also been very wet and very windy. Actually the wet and windy bit might just have been the fanny farts from some of our female fans, as they're a bit rough. Today was sunny.

Hymen to that…

If you go on the overhead monorail at Rhyl Sun Centre you acquire the posture of Saxe Coburg Royalty as you go around. You can't help it, you just do. Going to Oldham gives Mancunians the same subconscious feeling of superiority. Mancunian males have even got so cocky that when out in Oldham they politely keep josskin women away by having T-shirts on that say 'Please don't ask for a poke as a refusal often offends'. They would rather snap their banjo string chiselling one out than get flangella fever up there. The diet for the Hattie Jacques Oldham girls is to get bigger handbags as a slimming aid as it's all about perspective. Even though carrying a small, portable boating lake with them might work better as they look like Platt Fields in their flowery frocks. If it's puppy fat it's 12 to a litter. Although, there is always something to be said for bra fat at the back of the bra in a lusty woman. Most Mancunians get the impression that most Oldham girls are 'front wipers'. This means that when they have a chod they wipe from the back of the two pence piece towards the vagina, leaving the perineum with residue from the cracked crust from the top of the turd smeared across it.

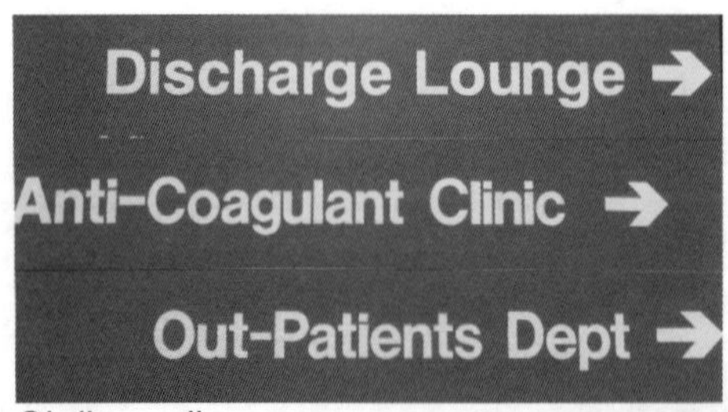

Girdle curdle…

Most Mancunian women get paranoid about discharge when they find their knickers after you have secretly wiped your early morning eye goz in the gusset. Oldham girls pick it off and eat it. It's a pizza topping in some districts. No amount of back stock at Floors-2-Go could rebuild their pelvic flooring. In a survey done by Reds, Oldham has the highest proportion of women who stand on their doorstep in their nighties in the daytime, for a prolonged period of time, than anywhere else in Europe. This announces to the world that they have not washed it since at least yesterday.

Slinging from the same him and her sheet…

Oldham men aspire to be one of those refuse workers who glovelessly throw bin bags in the back of the bin wagon with one hand whilst having a roll up in the other. As a visiting Theology student might say: "Just what the good Jesus am I doing here?" Sartorially they are city Burberry. Oldham Coliseum was rumoured to be the only theatre to put on Reg Varney and Jack Smethurst's critically acclaimed 'Othello'. In Oldham it is accepted as territory-marking when in August you get up in the morning after a clammy hot night in bed, sit on the side of the bed, and then as you get up, put your weight on your arse cheeks, letting them spread and letting the fitted bed sheet wipe the over night biz wax from your sticky, sweaty, clumped-up arse. In the same hot weather they do that disconcerting thing where they publicly drink a pint of room temperature milk out of the bottle as a supposed thirst slaker with their dinner, leaving their teeth off-milky-cheesy. They know all the words to 'Tie a yellow ribbon round the old oak tree'. It's not a coincidence. If a Mancunian saw yellow ribbons tied around a tree in Oldham they would have to query what the returnee did to serve those three long years? It will almost certainly involve being required to have your name on a register and involvement from Social Services. They still put army coats on their bed in winter to keep warm. They have blood crows. In a survey done by Reds, Oldham has the highest proportion of men who comb their hair in a reflecting shop window, putting the comb back in their back pocket before entering the pub door, than anywhere else in Europe.

We're off, we're off, we're off in a motorcar, 60 coppers are after us and we don't know where we are. We fell, we fell, we fell in a dirty well, 60 coppers are after us and they fell in as well...

Why does Manchester pick on Oldham? It doesn't necessarily just pick on Oldham. It can be any mill town or any non-mill town surrounding it, as FC United of Manchester fans have proved on their visits all season. All big cities do it to those that would surround it. They do it back to us. When Hanging Paul from Newton Heath went to live in Glossop they called him, and still call him, '061' in the The Norfolk vault. An intended insult that is not an insult. It would be unexplainable to them. We are Florence. Except we have an elliptical fountain with chewing gum measles on it and an in built Mancunian sense never to trust anyone who says "git' instead of "get." We can't deny our city's cheekychopcharlie'ness. We are Florentines with a black line on our gums where it meets our capped fillings. We are Florentines who just happen to know the tune of the Football Pink sellers on the Old Trafford forecourt when they used to songily proclaim: "Half time scores, racing results" just as the game finished. We are Florentines who can appreciate the sentiments when they see written upstairs, on the back of a seat of a deserted 192, "Sshh quick, have a wank." We are Florentines with an irritable vowel. Who know the importance of taking down your Christmas decorations on January the 6th. Of not putting shoes on a table. Of shellac. Of preparing yourself for the knowledge of realising that the elation of finding a tenner in your jeans, that you didn't know you had, will be followed by that the low of "Aww, why couldn't it have been a twenty?" That if Kitty Lester had married Conway Twitty, then she would have been called Kitty Twitty. That, unless you're Deidre Barlow, women don't make passes at men with half pint glasses. That we're the 86th best supported club when we need to be 69th. That the 'Veron debate' divided more than anything we are witnessing now. We've just got unresolved fraternal conflict that we're in the process of resolving. And after stating that we are Florentines I wish to state that we are not. We're Mancunians, and Florentines should really want to be us if they had any Florentinian taste.

We don't always get it right. We're obviously not always a unified mob. For example some Red music lovers have been disappointed by Tony Wilson's ridiculous outbursts that United should charge £60 to get in. He's a maverick galloot, ignore him. He's good for some stuff but not for others. His stance on Edwards was always pots for rags, so few expected any better with the more recent developments. He got The Sex Pistols their 'So it goes' telly slot but at the same time he was in The Ranch on Dale Street wearing flares. He'd leave the boxing to straight-leg-jean-wearing lads from Beswick, Moston and Wythenshawe when we had to go outside and face the Oxford bagged beegees on Piccadilly. And that's all after a knackering night avoiding Big 'always looking' Alf, the enormous - and some suspected not adverse to forced under age sex - doorman. He can quote Latin – Wilson not Big 'always looking' Alf - and make up sage statements from historical figures with lots of 'Qs and 'Vs in their second name but he is exposed on his knowledge of United. Leave him to his "Filo Radio will make it" memories. He's harmless. Today it was the turn of Padiham to receive Manchester's ribbing. They just happened to be playing at Oldham.

I like Nicky Butt and I cannot lie...

We got the '£2.55 return' train to Oldham Mumps from Victoria. I had seen 'Mumps' written on the front of loads of buses and had always wanted to go. I had hoped that the locals would wear bandages over their heads and around their faces as in the style of cartoons when the cartoon character is portrayed as having a toothache. Disappointingly they didn't. We resisted the Labradorial instinct to get a Joe to The Clayton Arms by the ground. We went in a little pub called Pickwick's by the station and watched United lose 3-0 to Chelsea. The pub was crowded but that was not difficult as Pickwick's is crumb sized. Nick and Baz, our portly people from Yorkshire, were already in. They might not be able to volunteer their less than washboardy stomachs for their women folk to do some hand washing on but you can't dislike an away pub they're in. They're like a football 'Postie' test. If they're in it, it must be alright to relax in. We are used to having decade upon decade of usual Red faces when we go to away pubs. Nick and Baz's faces were always there. They're still there now. They've given up so much, more than many, and faced some hard times but nothing has deterred them from their first honourable stance of telling Glazer to go and fold his wank sock, the OCD bastard. As a bonus you can get them to say "Oil of Ulay from Boot's by ring road" or "Two point two Dewsbury shoes" in their Yorkshire accent for pure amusement.

They had a woman with them called Kathryn with a 'Y' who was also from Yorkshire. She was in Yorkshire denial, though; as she had a rocket, vine tomato, cracked black pepper and feta ciabatta with her. You could tell she had been at home, pacing up and down her lobby, practising saying the butty's contents out loud as she was desperate to just call it 'snap'. Unfortunately, she'd just had new wall lights fitted either side of her chimney-breast and with that came certain cultural attaché duties for her county. It turned out that she part owns that Yorkshire Branch flag that I'd abused in the Barra chapter. It's a small world. But you wouldn't want to mop it. It got smaller when she revealed to Doctor Adam Brown that he had taught her in 1999 when she had done a dissertation on the European Cup final. We all deliberated around what the word 'taught' could have meant. Stay away from his sticky-up stethoscope, Kathryn. Listen to him humming 'So here's to you Mister Robinson' to know he's up to his usual licentious, doctorate endorsed, student sniffing. That's why he was a drummer in the band 'Ratfink' who played at Rotterdam at our Cup Winners' Cup victory over Barcelona. The other band members wouldn't let him at the front, near any lady Reds. He had to sit behind a drum kit at the back to hide his burgeoning investment.

Excuse me while I don't disappear...

We had too much beer, too early. I tried not to. Listen very carefully Doctor Adam Brown - the only real G.P. around here is the Ginger Princess. Me and the G.P. had thrown £40 each into the Jack 'The Hat' McVitie. A kitty knows no law of economics; they never seem to run out of money. My plan to keep sober by going in rounds with the Princess, her being a girl and all, failed as she is not shy at getting them down her head and torso connector. Her opinion that seen as how it was hot, then it would be more cost effective to drink fast to avoid evaporation, won me over. It beerily transpired that if she wins the roll over lottery she wants to buy a panda. They're not cheap apparently. She argued that they never try to shag your leg due to their low sex drive and that they're dead easy to keep as all they eat is bamboo shoots. With the Hing Fat and the Dragon City just around the corner on Rochdale Road it would never starve. I'm sure the panda would get used to the free prawn crackers they throw in for regular customers. She was even aware of the Hing Fat shutting on a Sunday dinner and the Dragon City being closed all Tuesday. The Hing Fat was the only chippy she knew that did three ladles of peas per pea portion over your chips and gravy. It's attention to the small details such as these that separate the good panda owners from the disreputable. We highlighted the fact that the International Panda'ing Commision might not like her keeping a panda in a back bedroom in Harpurhey. Her sworn promise that she would always keep it warm, as she fiddles the leccy and consequently has a load of fan heaters, made her certain she could sway the IPC. If that failed she promised to buy it a cute pair of one-tens as pandas, she assured us, would look even cuter in a pair of John Waynies. It's rumoured she had a wee behind one of the chairs in the pub before we got off to the game but of course this is totally unfounded.

We can fly higher than Chris Eagles...

Some even got the train straight back to town to go on a session, missing the match. I was pissed off with them at first but then totally changed my mind, as it was just a reminder of the beauty of where we are now and of the old days. You'd be in a pub and blokes who would have no intention of going to the game as Football Focus came on in the pub, would finish up going as we could all get in. To accept that side, we have to accept the other side of blokes just deciding that football would interrupt the beer. As it so often does. We'd walked the league, there was nothing to play for. We arranged to meet them later in town. The beer had an effect on our group. Some thought the game finished Stuart 'one' Hall. Some thought it was Bridgewater 'two' Hall. Goals from Carden and Torpey saw us actually win 1-2. The crowd was 1,905. Disappointing in Vinny Someways, but good in others as it gives us a chance of arguing for clubs to stay at their own ground next season instead of bleeding Oldham all the time. As the game ended an Oldham groundsman came onto the pitch at one end with a Jack Russell. Our players were taking the fans' plaudits at the other end. The Oldham groundsman was throwing a Frisbee for the dog. 'Under the boardwalk' was sung like an old friend by the United supporters. The song was celebrating its first birthday 22 days early with the backdrop of a twisting dog enjoying itself on a football league pitch. We've come so far and we've reached so high.

You're twistin' my melanin man...

My Nana used to have a song about being stood up on a date. If she ever saw a man hanging around, say outside a picture house, looking as if he was waiting for someone, she would sing it. I can't tell you the tune; you'll have to ask me to sing it for you if we meet. The song went: "She never came, how unkind, a pound to a penny to a piece of shit, she changed her mind." It's an infectious melody and an infectious observational skill that most of our family has acquired. We can spot someone waiting for someone or something that will let them down. Sometimes. We all have some sort of insight into seeing when someone has let you down or is about to let you down. Sometimes let downs can surprise you from nowhere, sometimes they come with a klaxon fixed to the top of a lorry, that has been fixed on to the top of a liner that is on dry land but being rolled along on thousands of giant logs, worked by tens of thousands of ancient Egyptians declaring 'I'm going to let you down'. How you reason with that loss, quantifying, qualifying and evaluating its centrality to the 206 bones within you, determines the essence of your time and how you're going to keep all that marrow synchronised and plodding. The last match of the NWCL season against Padiham was never important. If my poor punctuation has taught me something in this book, then it is that I now realise that the Padiham game was not a full stop, but a semi-colon to the next series of situations that we will face. It would have been nice to work a semi-colon in the text somewhere there but I'm not that good. Have one anyway;

Bandit the Bundesliga dog…

When metal lids were still on milk bottles there was a dog called 'Bandit' in Beswick. It was the Fox's dog from Aldridge Walk. It was a nice enough dog to us all, except to Ted. It used to go all non-panda'ery when it saw Ted and always used to start dry powdering his leg. Ted just couldn't shake it off. He almost got used to being beasted, walking along like Dick Emery with this dog-shin-pad on. We called it 'Bandit the bum dog'. It would come really quick and splash all over Ted's docs. After it had come it would cast him aside. Used. Ted is frightened of fuck all besides men in frocks with beards but that dog has scarred him. Oh, and he's also petrified of that dream he has where he has been reincarnated as an alarm clock so that he starts everyday being hit on the head. That dream is part understandable as that might just be his marriage. The one where he dreams he is a steak pudding on top of a three-curries-and-rice-for-£3.50 at Hunter's off Shude Hill in town is more of a delver.

It was with trepidation, then, that Ted learnt that our first European away would be in East Germany against Lokomotiv Leipzig. It stood a good chance of being our very last game of the 2005/2006 season. You never know at this level, though, but as far as the majority of Reds were concerned this was the last. It was to be played exactly one year to the day since Glazer took over. It also celebrated the 50th year since Matt first took us into Europe. The week before going to 'Bandit the Bundesliga' country we would play AFC Telford in a benefit match for Jamie Turner, a Red who is going through an unfortunate period in his life. He needs Red help and hopefully we can continue to give it. Lokomotiv Leipzig had gone down seven divisions in the German league and was now fan- owned. Ted didn't give a shite. Until he saw that their mascot wasn't Bandit the Bundesliga dog he couldn't rest. He certainly wasn't wearing suede shoes.

Don't cross on the stairs or we will never get married…

'Inofficious', I've found out, means contrary to moral obligation ie it's an inofficious will if a child is disinherited. It's an inofficious sitch that we have lost our Manchester United Football Club. To the well used 'disenfranchised and disaffected' we can now add 'disinherited'. Contrary to moral obligation, that club is owned by the undeserving. It should be ours, we've all put so much in, we've all spent so much time with her, we have all loved her for so long, we all thought that somewhere it had our name written through it. It's not though. The Manchester United Supporters' Trust, the organisation that came out of Shareholders United, has recently stated that it might take a hundred years to get her back to the way we want her. If we can sing “For one two seven years, we’ve fought you and your peers” then I can do nothing but admire the graft they will put in to achieve that. If they are successful then it will mean that the fight from within, that we heard so much about in May 2005, would have been a fight worth fighting.

It is understandable that many can’t wait that possible hundred years. The instincts of those who chose to go down ten divisions to continue the resistance, feel they can hear tens of thousands of Egyptians shouting something down a klaxon. They don’t feel let down by the Reds involved with the fight from within, as that was always their fight, to pace at their own pace. The resistance that went down ten divisions would of course want that fight of our sisters and brothers to be far more widespread, far more threatening. So would the activists from within fighting now, but we all made choices over the last season of 2005/2006. The FC United of Manchester choosers cannot substitute themselves for a mass movement that, at the present, isn’t there within those that remained behind. It has to come. We can only encourage.

We can encourage because we have the resources to give out encouragement. What was by far the worst potential situation in May 2005 has turned into the easier decision. It never should have been. To chose to leave your football club behind, with all that meant, should have left us weak and devastated. It didn’t, as our date turned up. A pound to a penny to a piece of shit the girl didn’t change her mind. She’s not used us as Bandit the bum dog used Ted’s leg and docs. The girl might very well turn into a beautiful woman. Or in a few years she might not age well and turn into a right grot. The section of the resistance who chose to go down ten divisions can now luxuriate in 2006/2007 that they have only gone down nine divisions. By far the most important issue, though, is that they can also choose the nature of their relationship with FC United of Manchester in open, free discussion with her. All love should be based on passion and equality. Your tears are my tears. When I look down your beautiful throat as you cutely yawn I can see that beauty is not only skin deep.

She considers it lovely that she can’t do anything without us; she wouldn’t want to. We consider it lovely that we can’t do anything without her; we wouldn’t want to. The spirit, the valuing of defiance, in knowing that you are free to love or free to go of your own free will is intoxication served in a Bayern Munich beer keller stein. When the waitress can carry six of them at once. No. It’s far, far bigger. It’s intoxication served swishing around as ballast in the hull of that liner being very kindly pulled along by those tens of thousands of Egyptians. You’ll have to keep me and Peanut off the klaxon, though, as you won’t be able to understand a fucking word we say.

And you would want to hear us, as we would be saying: "No one is going to be letting anyone down. We've all got the pound and the penny and the piece of shit. The power is ours." On the Leipzig trip I looked around me and saw all my many friends who had made the same decision as me. There were many more left back in Manchester. The friends who stayed behind to fight from within were also back home in Manchester. In our wide company of friends the FC United of Manchester builders were the lucky ones. As we all sat around the tables in Berlin the night before the Leipzig game, laughing, ribbing, knowing, someone in our company said something. It was true of our Red friends. It might not be true for all Reds but for our specific wide group of Red friends it was. Someone said: "We've taken it with us." And he was right.

You want your arse sole and heeling ...

Nothing, however, is going to make me leave the Red friends who chose to stay. Manchester United Football Club. Football Club United of Manchester. We're two second hand shoes tied together with string on a back market. The string goes through the lace hole of one shoe and through the lace hole of the other. The bow they are tied in is a double bow. Secure. An innocent child could have tied it. A wise old fool could have tied it. It's voluntarily avoiding being a knot. A knot implies forcing. A double bow whispers lowly that we're here, because here is great. Untie the simple bow and we could be elsewhere of our own Mancunian choosing. We chose here. The two, second hand shoes, tied together with string on a back market, know that on their own they're useless. Even one-legged blokes have two shoes now, with pirate'y ahh ahh'ing wooden legs being replaced by Delorean'y, leaf-light metal that could enable you to sneak up unnoticed, across that rice mat with David Carridine, and surprise that old Chinese bloke with the white mincers.

Two shoes tied...

Even together some might deem our two shoes not so clever, but together is the only place where they make sense. They can be functional; they can fill what roles they were meant to, people passing can see the importance of them being inseparable. They might not fancy them themselves but they can see how others might. They might want a different pair, at a different price, from a different shop, but after it all, we all need something to help cover us and not hinder our journey with unnecessary foot pain. That string tying our soul sole full shoes together is a dried out umbilical cord. It was still a life giving cord in the past. Now it's courser and roughly hewn but it still has all its history in it. Moisten it and it will not be so dry. It binds tight. It binds loose. The two, second hand shoes that are us can role around within the great big pile of other second hand shoes, indistinguishable from the rest, our connecting string hidden in the morass. Until you pull one, then the other comes out with it. Pull them out, put them at the side of each other. Look at them as they should be looked at. It can be no other way.

The Manchester Guardian...

As a club FC United of Manchester will be dovetailing with other sport development within our surrounding areas. Sport development will eventually find talent that is in the self-interest of the club. It'll also get our fatties fitter. Community development of our club is something different and means using the club, either through its name, its personnel or its facilities to form partnerships with organisations that are experts at community development. It means facing issues that are non-football related such as health, crime reduction and education and accessing already existing social inclusion agendas. If we run coaching sessions it wouldn't be too difficult to integrate a message. Margy and his five portions walks that without you even noticing.

Last season a load of east Manchester youngsters kept making their way up to our home games. They were causing murders on the back row of the Manchester Road End breaking seats and annoying everyone. Football League ground policy would be to get the stewards to launch them out. Ours was to invite them inside the ground, show them what we are doing, explain how they are wanted by us, that they are part of it, they could even become part of our ladder of sport development if they wanted to, that it was theirs to have if they wanted it. Under the stands, in amiable conversation with our club's two full timers and also Margy and Adie Orr, those lads stated that they loved being at FC United of Manchester, as they had been witness to nothing like it before. They explained they were just being giddy in their new-found freedom and that they meant no harm. They left being made up that they had been treated like adults but within our club's self-policed boundaries of arse-about free expression to be as daft as they wanted.

Of course they will get on our nerves again. But at least they will be there to get on our nerves, watching live, affordable football and perhaps they might adapt because of it. And all in an environment that beats in the basic

Where the hilarious always beat the nerarious…

'Hey, shape up you dick' with the prosaic 'Why rob from your own or harm your own, it doesn't make sense?' to the more progressive-but-smart-if-done-right 'We understand why you're doing it, as we've done it and this is why you shouldn't be doing it and perhaps this might be how you might be able to stop it'. Not wishing to get too Wenger'y but having engagement with the most at risk young people requires youth work skills as much as football development skills. I've not got them; as I've said I'm a proper 'kids in cupboards' philosopher when it comes to the annoying gets. However, we know that 'community' is not something that can be left with the community officer or department. Like we're big enough to have a department. It has to be horizontal and vertical throughout the club from our ticket prices, dealing with local business rather than large suppliers or our initiatives throughout the local community. I don't really get it all, as the subtleties of it are very complex. However, the bigness of it all is simple - we're here to build as best we can. We value each other because we are all, somewhere, worth valuing. Besides the ones that aren't of course.

Sluch fund…

If FC United of Manchester have done nothing on their little journey this season then they have at least cured people of calling Joz Mitten 'Josh'. We also know that Malcom Glazer still hasn't been to Old Trafford. That Castleton Gabriels pulled themselves out of the minus points club and got one point for the season. They still came bottom so things are consistent. They won't get relegated, as that's not really possible as there is no lower level of football. FC United of Manchester came in at the lowest level we could have without being a pub team. Although being a pub team would have been highly appropriate. We could have gone in higher, with one club actually romancing us for amalgamation with them so we could go straight into the Conference North. The consistency in Cassy Gabs' NWCL bottom was echoed in the consistency of Caroline Brayshaw's bottom over the season. She maintained a healthy plumpability throughout that has to be congratulated.

We lost the consistency of the Dinghy, though, as it never reappeared after the Barra game. It's fitting that it should remain a distant early to mid season memory as we've all found something and we've all lost something. We've had Sepp Blatter do a two-page article in one of our programmes. I'm not sure if that is a good thing or not, or whether he's more or less important that Brian Spittles of Leek, but it shows some sort of influence and standing that we can take something from if we needed to. I never managed to persuade enough Reds that our nickname should be 'The Ferals' coming as it did after the Greater Manchester Police's outburst in the press about our inner city youth. Over 28% of our FC United of Manchester crowds being under 18 adds to this call. Actually, nicknames can only come about naturally, they cannot be forced on. For proof of that - outside of our Ben wanting to be called 'Oidy', no one, including our Ben, is sure why - you only have to ask yourself whether you have called Old Trafford 'The theatre of dreams'. Rumoured to be Bobby Charlton's idea. He'd want the rumour to be true. And so would we. Both for different reasons.

Our FC United of Manchester electronic message boarders, who introduce themselves in real life by the name they use on the message board, should really sit on some Cillit Bang and become better for it. We should be the first club that insists upon its players that they wear black boots. In the coming years we should play a pre-season competition between us, AFC Wimbledon, Telford and Enfield. That's not that unusual. What is, though, is that we should hire a full ferry for the fans and take us all to the Isle of Man. There is enough accommodation there for us. We could call it The Love Boat. We could take our own birches. Or we could play Rhyl FC and hire the whole of Sunnyvale Caravan Park. FC United of Manchester should make their own breadbins as you can always tell a nice person by the niceness of their breadbin. I've, personally, learnt that 'aswell' is two words when I was convinced it was one. I never managed to say 'rambunctious' in any FC United of Manchester conversation as I intended to do.

Monday's child is fair of face...Tuesday's child is full of grace...Wednesday's child is full of woe...Thursday's child has far to go...Friday's child is loving and giving...Saturday's child works hard for a living...But the child that is born on the beer'ath day...Likes beer and women... Wahey...

FC United of Manchester are considered by many to have been born on a Tuesday, on the 5th of July 2005. This would make us full of grace. I was born on a Thursday. This would mean that I have far to go. I feel as if I have been issued on two days. I have so far to go but I have graceful Tuesday-born Reds plodding it with me. I have no idea what day that east central Manchester bloodlined team of railway workers came into existence. It possibly remains an historical hole for someone to take the time to find out. If it was possible to find out, then I know Reds, and know of Reds, who would be able to find out for me. That's the sort of family we live in. We've all lost a lot of family over the previous years. We don't need to anymore. The Red armoury for our city now has all aspects of footballing apparel apparelled. We have a Manchester United first team with all its extended reserves and youths, and we have a second team formed by fans of Manchester United Football Club operating as FC United of Manchester. Rosa Parks was a seamstress in Alabama, in 1955, when she wouldn't stand up on that bus. We are obviously not a billion billionth of a Rosa Parks.

However, we stand in the sunlight brought about by her defiance. Our defiance saw 30,000 to 40,000 of us stood up at games in 2005 saying "No" to Glazer. We won't sit, as she wouldn't stand. That 30,000 to 40,000 weren't just personalising Glazer. They were getting out of their reduced width seats to put rivulets of red, white and black cotton to defend themselves from that corrosively attired, polluted breaker of commercialism that's poisoning our game of choice. Those rivulets of red, white and black cotton were protecting their family. Our family. It doesn't appear sometimes that we are strong, but separate blankets tied together can get you down any wall, and out of any prison that had you put aside for a life term. What we can be is one of the seams that Rosa used to sew. Any flaw in the seam between the two Uniteds will be used by those that would do us harm.

Manchester isn't always sausage shaped...

At the last home game of FC United of Manchester we saw that big, scruffy, red, white and black flag draped over the side of the open top bus. We could see it wasn't symmetrical shaped, as all the others were, it was imperfect. It lacked. There was loose red, white and black cotton everywhere from its edges. Red, white and black cotton that had been used in the rivulets of resistance. It had 'Caring' written on the side. Only a few Reds present that day knew what that flag was. It had brought something with it. We were all at Old Trafford a few seasons ago when the players, after winning the league, had chipped in and bought an enormous flag in the shape of a shirt to present to the fans. It was huge. It swung its way around the ground, crossing K Stand, covering all their ugly faces, which was a welcome relief. It eventually found itself billowing into J. Characters from east central Manchester at the back of J Stand grabbed it and started pulling. I huffed and grumped and told them to stop it the young gets. They ignored me, as usual, and finished up having one of the sleeves off. Potty hole here ended up being lumbered with it as we all went back to town for a beer, as I could put it in ours. And there it has remained since. A big, fat, red, white and black short sleeve as big as a living room. The 'l' that was between the 'r' and 'i' in 'Caring' has been sprayed over in black to take out the sponsor's name.

My own, every dream I have known, has been built of but one desire, just to call you my own...

Somewhere within Old Trafford, our Old Trafford, there is an enormous shirt with only one sleeve. FC United of Manchester has the Cinderella slipper that will fit perfectly when slipped back into place to complete its absolute. Except it's a shirt sleeve not a slipper obv. We will not change its shape to make it symmetrical, it is the only shape it can be. It was paid for by the players the last time we won the league playing 4-4-2. The other part of the shirt has got to be somewhere, waiting to keep its bargain to be re-united in whatever way the fans regard as re-united. The seamstress resistance of Rosa Parks in us all will sew the seam back together. Until that time we'll wait with Peterloo spirit, patience and gentleness as befitting our city. However, we won't wait sat on our fat arses. Commercialism might keep trying to take the bulb out of our flame-effect fire, keep trying to shit on our living room rug, keep trying to rub our noses in it and keep trying to throw us outside, but they misunderstand our city as dim fuckers do. The big, scruffy red, white and black flag with the ripped edges that FC United of Manchester is, has found a pulsing, unlicensed signal. It won't keep quiet. A scream idyllic. It washes that in with a calm, unruffled composition that knows the honest beauty of its reason and why that is so. The two combine. Matrimony. It asks for some energy from the stored resources of the environmentally friendly solar panels around the CIS, and it is given it.

It takes it and goes and puts a tune on at Corbieres; it will never come on but at least it tried. It tuts at the prices of the food in Thomas' Chophouse, appropriates something from Kendall's, before making public the sordid lives of the judges at the courts and their lack of worth to stand in judgement of us. It crackles up the mastic around the PVCu windows of Thorn Court, then goes skimming down to sail over the roof of The Paddock, perhaps popping in to buy a couple of ham shanks to put in a pea soup later, before tootling past The Brass Handles' 'Live entertainment on Sundays' sign. It ambles around Salford docks in the sunshine, showing deference to Manchester's twin city seafront and putting some discarded crisp bags in the bins. It gets up and tips its way over to the Seven Sisters, giving them balconies if they haven't got one and then lollops up Ayres Road giving the people adequate parking spaces, whilst at the same time giving them the improved driving skills to appreciate it. It whips off to Dougy's to pick up a goat curry. And perhaps a soup at Kim By The Sea. It emanates over the croft that was the Reno and washes the windows, doing all the corners, of Saint Mary's where so many Mancunians are born.

It remarks that Victoria Baths looks like Bagpuss before improving the timetable at Hyde Road bus depot in Ardwick. It rubbers up and swims underneath Gorton reservoirs cleaning out the polystyrene and the dolls' heads as it goes, before getting out and tickling behind the ears of the donkey's at the sanctuary nearby. It goes in 'The Winchester' that is Gorton WMC, the glue pot that is near Abbey Hey's ground and FC United of Manchester's reserves games. It gets in there and interrupts Basher mithering all his women who cook him Sunday dinner. It crosses Ashton Old Road at the lights near The Grove and goes down Burman Street.

East central Manchester's bloodline…

It finds Westwell's Bakery at the end of it and stocks up on a number of items before taking in a couple of turns on stage at Openshaw WMC, slurping a £1.87 pint of Guinness as a livener. It bangs its head on the 'big six' corrugated roofing covering the stalls of Grey Mare Lane back market then shimmies over the foundation bones of The United pub at 391 Ashton New Road where so many of my family have met. Where pre-First World War Reds would have talked over the virtues of the 0-0-10 attacking system employed at the time by Manchester United, having a quick last lag, then getting off to Bank Street.

It cuts into Phillip's Park and sees where the Medlock was red tiled as it went through it, making it go quicker, and it was given its name of 'The Red river'. It says a greeting to those who were born and then they lived and then they died in the park cemetery, takes one last sniff of Dean and Wood's knackers' yard, then on to Conran Street market so that a comparison of the two markets' 1930's electrical wiring can be done, to see which arcs the arcy'ist. There is no winner, as it's the taking part in the shitting up of the shoppers that counts. It checks that the lidded flats of Monsall still has a small fleck of brick from the old Collyhurst flats placed up there looking down on the new village. It scoots around Nobby's St Pat's, whizzes back up to Moston cemetery, telling anyone who'll listen, that our insider sources say that there is only about seven or eight years to get in there before it is full, so hurry up.

It takes the last remaining leg from the remains of the last cockroach from Harpurhey baths, dumps it in the soil to replenish the rose bushes of Queens Park, washes its hands in the blokes' toilets in The Milan, after getting a spanner to ease the taps into working, as it's the first ever time they've been used, and then off it trots down Queens Road. It turns right at the old 53 terminus to go further into Cheetham Hill and gets something nice wrapped in a chapatti before turning back and getting a bagel on Leicester Road for later. It returns to town where a freshener is taken in The Smithfield, The Burton and Fringe, karaoke is achieved in Gulliver's and the Bottom Kings, before taking a relaxative real ale in The Castle, the real juke box of Manchester.

Come rest awhile…

It phones its mates who it left in Corbieres, and they tell it that its song still hasn't come on, so wait in The Castle for them as they're on their way. It asks them to pick up a custard from Ho's bakery for it and then it'll be done. In no instance on its journey was it not singing 'Take a trip down Ancoats'. It's drinking on Oldham Street, the gateway to all Manchester, and that unlicensed signal from the ripped edged, red, white and black flag is pounding out peace, withstanding and building across our boundary walls. This is our Manchester to build in, our imperfect ripped sleeve of a flag, our ossifying bones of a club, our respected rules, our big kagouls. It's bathed in everything we are. It was gathered up by those who loved it, and it went for a drink with them as it had done before.

And still I live in hopes to see, the holy ground once more…

Watching FC United of Manchester in the early season, used to have the feeling of standing on a self-made, poorly knocked up, rickety viewing platform to look over the wall to observe the pleasantries of breast washing day at the nunnery. There was something in its daring, cheeky, unconventionality that told you that this was right, that this was not right, that this was right, very exciting, but not right. We have changed to revel in seeing the remarkable clothes that suit her. We have changed so that we can giggle and chuckle as we put up complicated deckchairs with her. We can fall about and not get the deckchairs up right away but we know that we can. And it's the knowing that has changed us. We have changed to hold her hand and thereby create the greatest of all human construction. Two hands holding. There is nothing as romantic. When did it change? When did 'M/c' turn into 'Mcr'? No one really knows it just all sort of did. Now it feels as if we are inside the nunnery walls giving the girls the Knights Castille and perhaps helping them dry their mellodians after they've finished. Helpful and kind, dancing with sexual and passionate and then all going for a worthwhile walk with daring.

High cranes look out over your city. Unless you really look they are not there. They're higher than any of our early season rickety nun observation platforms. Outside of the slight embarrassment they feel at Christmas time when companies put lights on them, they are a dignified presence. They do so much, and as they witness your every flummox, your incurable-by-cold-key-administering hiccuppy eggcups, your amassing of joy, your storage of wants, they carry on. They afford the change as we have changed. They build voraciously. They change your city's nature; they carry on its nature. FC United of Manchester has to build hard and build separately. If we don't then we could dissolve in defeat, which would be to the detriment of football, with only big business benefiting. A respected, honourable and deeply admired Red changed my perceptions of FC United of Manchester at the Cassy Gabs game back in September 2005. He told of movements within the city that could facilitate our return to east central Manchester. Our own ground. We're going home. We have to get our caravan in Manchester, if we don't then we become a permanent caravan, and as lovely as caravans are, that's a trailer park. Flying about homeless is just rendition.

That early season optimism has been dashed. And re-dashed. It was always going to be. We will have to fight for every beer-mat-thickness worth of ground we progress over. A community club can only progress with its community. Our bigger Red community appears divided in two at the present. It's not. Cranes build separately during the day. They must to get it right. It appears as if they graft apart. It doesn't take much to see that they build in unison to complete the entirety of the construction site. Cranes are left unlocked at night. To lock them would be to put them in unnecessary conflict with the weather. They don't need to pretend that they can take on all of existence. They need a flexibility to maintain their height and ability to build so well, to oversee so much. At night, when Manchester is looking even less, the cranes move. When silence patters down, swallowing the busyness of the busy, our ease eases in. We are as we always were. The alignment natural. All cranes wake up facing the same direction in the morning. We start every day with our unity offensive undeterred, knowing that there is no automatic unity of the oppressed, that it has to be grafted for. Everyday this graft will happen until we defeat those who would hurt us. What they forgot to kill went on to organise.

The poverty of philosophy, what is to be done, and Awky Duck walking...

It's twenty two minutes to two. I'm in Chetham's Library to finish this last bit of the book off. I wanted to write it by hand. I was going to do this anyway but this morning, in a heavy hint to remember, my coal-fired computer got fed up and collapsed. I had been in Chetham's before whilst on a noseying session around the city but I never went into the library. All Mancunians should go in there. It's the oldest surviving public library in Britain. Engels used to sit in the only alcove. I'm sat in it now. Smart. I can't fart as someone else is in but the hardwood seats are made for squeakers. I've been in the Baronial Hall in the room next door once before. It was empty. I'd got on the front stage and sang: "The saints smile shyly down on you, they couldn't get over your nine leaf clover." Today I had got on the empty stage again. This time I sang: "Oh my heart it stumbles forward, as the light declines, I remember Man United in the rare old times" right the way through, getting more emotional as the song went on. It reflected our first season together.

No one heard as no one was there besides those who I love and who are inside me. I wanted them to be there, so I brought them into my daft head. I opened the lid of the on-stage piano and played two notes with my left hand. I waggled my Francis Brady right arm in the air to carry on the beery-singing sacredity. The next time I go back, I'll get on the stage again. I'll sing: "From a team of railway workers, to the team we love today, our hearts are Man United's, it could be no other way. Our blood is red, our shirts are red, and as the great Matt Busby said, go and thank your Mam and Dad that you're Mancunian, go and thank your Mam and Dad that you're Mancunian." I left and came and sat down in this alcove. It's now two o'clock.

My Mam used to write notes to my Dad. That sounds romantic. My Dad used to meet Kenny Fowler and Tommy the carrier at exactly two minutes to twelve outside The Vic on Grey Mare Lane. It was in the days when they were only opened 12 - 2pm. If earlier that morning his face was covered in little scraps of newspaper, where he was mopping up his shaving blood, then my Mam knew he was going to be late. She wrote a note to Kenny and Tom asking them to excuse Frank's lateness and that he promised not to do it again. The only other time my Mam wrote notes, outside of Grand National day, was to attach the medical condition of 'Bilious' to it when her children needed a sick note for school. This time there is no need for excuses. No need for notes. We have done what we have done. In an old episode of 'Crackerjack' Peter Glaze told Leslie Crowther that nothing was impossible. Leslie Crowther replied by saying: "Try striking a match on a piece of wet tripe." We were told it was impossible to form a football club that would represent the feelings of Manchester United Football Club fans. You can only represent the feelings of all the fans if all of them are listened to, and then those feelings are then acted upon. We all talk enough tripe for it to never be in short supply. The repeat strike and repeat strike of our Red matches will keep on trying and trying and trying to ignite. Every match we play we're all watching United, we're all United game'ing, they're all United games. We'll do an Awky Duck walk whilst we're doing it. No one in my family knows who Awky Duck is, or even how to spell it, we just know it was a duck that limped. That's alright, as all we really know on our walk, is that the last year of 2005/2006 has played its Red Mancunian part in our 127 year history. It's twenty two seconds, past twenty two minutes, past two. No one has gone away. No one ever could. We won't melt. We'll do alright…